Date Due

197		
7		

RIOTS, REVOLTS
AND INSURRECTIONS

RIOTS, REVOLTS
AND INSURRECTIONS

By

RAYMOND M. MOMBOISSE

Riot Advisory Committee, President's Commission on Law Enforcement
Advisory Committee, California Peace Officers' Association
Deputy Attorney General, State of California

CHARLES C THOMAS · PUBLISHER
Springfield · Illinois · U.S.A.

Published and Distributed Throughout the World by
CHARLES C THOMAS · PUBLISHER
BANNERSTONE HOUSE
301-327 East Lawrence Avenue, Springfield, Illinois, U.S.A.
NATCHEZ PLANTATION HOUSE
735 North Atlantic Boulevard, Fort Lauderdale, Florida, U.S.A.

© 1967, by CHARLES C THOMAS · PUBLISHER
Library of Congress Catalog Card Number: 67-21772

With THOMAS BOOKS *careful attention is given to all details of
manufacturing and design. It is the Publisher's desire to present books
that are satisfactory as to their physical qualities and artistic possibilities
and appropriate for their particular use.* THOMAS BOOKS *will be true
to those laws of quality that assure a good name and good will.*

Printed in the United States of America
H-2

To

Grandpere	Pop Pop
and	and
Grandmere	Naoni

With all my thanks for their love and understanding.

ACKNOWLEDGMENTS

IT WOULD BE IMPOSSIBLE to acknowledge herein all of those who have aided in the preparation of this book. Over the last few years I have had the pleasure of working with literally hundreds of peace officers and members of the National Guard and Armed Forces, both in actual field operations during demonstrations and the Watts and San Francisco riots, and in the theoretical study of the problems herein considered. As a result of that close association I have developed the utmost admiration for these men who, irrespective of the personal danger and sacrifice and forgetting their own injuries, pain and fatigue, have day in and day out gone forth to perform their duties in spite of the jeers, ridicule and false charges of thousands whose rights they are protecting.

First and foremost, I owe a special debt of gratitude to my wife, Mary Jane, and my three sons, Michael, Steven and Mark, for their patience and understanding during the long months of work on this book. Next, my secretary, Pearl Mitchell, who is not only a great secretary, but a loyal and close friend, deserves my very special thanks.

I wish to acknowledge the assistance received from the other members of the Riot Advisory Committee, President's Commission on Law Enforcement, with whom I had the honor of working in preparing the Federal Riot Manual, namely, Colonel Gordon D. Rowe, Harold K. Light, Federal Bureau of Investigation; John T. Kelly, Chicago Police Department; George E. Causey, Washington, D.C., Metropolitan Police Department; John Nichols, Detroit Police Department; Peter Hagen, Los Angeles Police Department; Charles E. McCarthy, New York City Police Department; Daniel Sharpe, Rochester Police Department; Adolph Jacobsmeyer, St. Louis Police Department; Edward Epting, San Francisco Police Department; and James Herron, Philadelphia Police Department.

There are others that must also be thanked. They are: Paul Hannigan of the Sacramento Police Department for his advice and constructive criticism, which was always tempered with encouragement;

Justice Stanley Mosk of the California Supreme Court and Brad Crittenden, former Commissioner of the California Highway Patrol, who set my feet on this path by pointing out the need for research and training material in this field; Colonel Chester Reed, Military Aide to Governor Reagan, who was always present to give me encouragement and advice; Gene Mulheisen and George Puddy, who have always stressed the importance of education and the professionalism of police and have done so much to make this a reality in California and now throughout the nation; California Attorney General Thomas C. Lynch and Chief Tom Reddin of Los Angeles, who during the Watts riot epitomized all that is desirable in leadership; Chief Thomas Cahill of San Francisco, who is a leader in law enforcement; Wayne Kranig and Bud Coster of the California Disaster Office, who have shown the importance of organizing a statewi de program for meeting the problems; and last, but far from least, Arthur Desmangles, Art Aurich, Duane Webber and William Bennett, who have always been there to help when I needed them.

RAYMOND M. MOMBOISSE

CONTENTS

SECTION II

ORGANIZATION AND GENERAL PROCEDURES

SECTION III

FORMATIONS AND WEAPONS

SECTION IV
CONTROL PROCEDURE

RIOTS, REVOLTS
AND INSURRECTIONS

SECTION I
THE PROBLEMS

Chapter 1

CROWDS

INTRODUCTION

A CROWD IS NOT A MOB, but it can become one! Each crowd constitutes a police problem, and each, even the most casual, has latent potential for widespread civil disturbance.

Each person in the crowd is an individual with a background of family training or lack of it, and with primary group influences that have been good in some and imperfect in others. Each individual's behavior simply reflects that early background. Although the crowd situation may offer an occasion for getting by with some liberties that the person would not ordinarily take, the general pattern of behavior is little different from that expected of the individual.

Definition

A crowd is a large unorganized group of people without leadership collected into a close body whose members are acting and thinking as individuals, not in unison. A crowd may be defined as a congregate group of individuals who have temporarily identified themselves with common values and who are experiencing similar emotions.

Characteristics of a Crowd

An outstanding characteristic of a crowd is its awareness of the law and willingness to respect the principles of law and order, resulting from the individual member's ingrained respect for the law. It is unorganized, without leadership, hesitant and ruled by reason. The police have a clear choice in this type of situation. They can provide their own leadership and exercise authority without creating mass antagonism, or by inaction may permit control and leadership to pass to a member of the crowd who takes over as an incipient leader.

TYPES OF CROWDS

There are many ways of classifying crowds. For example, they could be grouped according to size, sex, race, religion, political beliefs, or in many other ways, but these would not be useful classifications for our purpose. The factors of greatest interest to law enforcement are the behavior and motivation of the people. In other words, we are most concerned with what they are doing and why. For our purpose, then, crowds are best classified by their mode of behavior. The important types are casual, conventional, expressive and aggressive. It must be emphasized that there is no logical sequence of development of a crowd from one stage to another. A crowd may be aggressive when it is initially formed or it may be casual and become aggressive without passing through the conventional and expressive stages.

Casual or Physical Crowd

The crowd in its simplest form is called a *casual* or *physical* crowd. It has no psychological unity. A casual or physical crowd is a casual or temporary collection of people who happen to be present at a given place but who are not unified or organized. Chance alone determines who will be drawn into it. It may be anyone who happens to be in that particular spot at that particular time. Certainly there is nothing premeditated about it.

The members of this crowd show no cohesive group behavior but merely denseness of contact. Such a crowd has a common interest for a few moments, such as a group that gathers in front of a store window to watch a demonstration. But, the people in a casual crowd are bent on their individual ways. It has little organization, no unity of purpose, and its members come and go. Traffic control will usually handle this crowd. Such a group responds easily and directly to a "move-on" or "keep moving" order.

Conventional or Cohesive Crowd

The conventional crowd is one that is assembled for a specific purpose, such as witnessing a ball game, parade, play or fire. The members of this type crowd have similar common interests and gather because of and are held together by this interest. Their attention is directed toward some common focus, but for the most part they behave and think as individuals.

The members of this type of crowd have no dependence on each other. Each can satisfy his individual needs without the active participation of the other persons present. The person sitting beside you at a football game is incidental to your enjoyment of the game, and he comes to your specific attention only if he conducts himself in such a manner as to draw your attention.

Such crowds vary from the quiet, passive group to groups surcharged with emotions and capable of turbulent reaction.

All conventional crowds of any size should be policed, and those which are especially threatening should be well policed. The restraining influence of the mere conspicuous presence of the police uniform has proven its worth on such occasions. Where they can be properly trained and inspired in the importance of law and order, ushers, teachers, student leaders and other responsible citizenry augment a police force in preventing disorder at conventional crowds. However, in any disturbances which may develop, primary responsibility and effectiveness rests with the police. When the disturbance starts, the professional police officer who knows how to act is less likely to provoke tension by his actions, or to display the obvious lack of confidence in his authority which characterizes the well-intentioned but inexperienced and untrained recruit.

The Expressive Crowd or Revelous Crowd

An expressive crowd is so named because its members are involved in some kind of expressive behavior such as dancing, singing, or other channels of release. Such groups are expressing their feelings and sentiments, releasing their energies through the actions of their movement. Such a crowd is not aggressive, nor is its energy directed toward a damaging objective. Such activity type of escape behavior provides those involved with a temporary release from the humdrum routine of normal life.

Like recreational types of behavior, revelous behavior is complete in itself; and the satisfactions which are derived from it are immediate and direct. In most instances, therefore, revelry functions as a means of discharging the psychological tensions which accumulate over a period of time. Thus, revelry *per se* is not to be condemned, since it serves the function of discharging the psychological tensions of the individual and of returning him to his usual pattern of life, content for a while to follow its course.

Unfortunately this type of crowd is often mistakenly confused with the aggressive crowd and is treated as though it were dangerous. It is important for police officers to avoid this mistake, for it is far wiser to permit such activity to continue and to permit the group to so express itself if there is no serious breach of the peace. Indeed, interrupting the release of energies in an expressive manner may divert the latent energies of such a crowd into aggressive and destructive channels. Nevertheless, it is essential that the police keep its members under very close surveillance, as the feelings of this crowd are very volatile and subject to sudden change.

Hostile or Aggressive Crowd

A hostile or aggressive crowd is an unorganized throng willing to be led into lawlessness, but it is hesitant because it lacks organization, courage and unity of purpose. It is composed of a few determined leaders, active participants and a number of spectators. So long as it is controlled, it remains a crowd, but if control is lost, it will evolve into a mob.

The aggressive crowd is, at the same time, expressive and cohesive. Thus we can see that the above classification provides a progression in which the police problems increase as each step is reached.

Chapter 2

MOBS

INTRODUCTION

Wʜᴀᴛ ɪs ᴛʜᴇ ᴅɪsᴛɪɴᴄᴛɪᴏɴ between a crowd and a mob? The essential difference between crowd and mobs is this: the crowd is law abiding; the mob takes the law into its own hands. The difference in many cases is borderline.

Certainly, mob behavior is not an inherent characteristic of any race, any type of person, any geographical section of the world. Mob behavior is not something which occurs only in certain sections of the country involving only certain types of people. It may occur anywhere and for a great variety of reasons. Mobs arise as "solutions" for particular circumstances and can only be prevented when such circumstances are not allowed to arise.

The word *mob* has been given various definitions. It is said that a mob is a crowd whose members, under the stimulus of intense excitement or agitation, lose their sense of reason and respect for law and follow leaders to lawless acts. Another source tells us a mob is an assemblage of many people, acting in a violent and disorderly manner, defying the law, committing or threatening to commit property destruction or personal violence. A mob is an unlawful assembly of persons who are gathered together to commit, or attempt to commit, an unlawful act. A mob is a congregate group of individuals who feel strongly that certain of their values are threatened and whose attitudes direct their overt behavior toward a common goal. Whatever definition is used is of little consequence, for once seen, a mob is readily recognized.

All mobs are said to have certain general characteristics. These are the following:

1. Organization.
2. Leadership.

3. Common motive for action.
4. Ruled by emotion.

Mobs are characteristically emotional and frequently irrational.

TYPES OF MOBS

Mobs, according to their intent, actions and behavior, can generally be classified by type, i.e., expressive, escape, acquisitive, aggressive. These classifications are not necessarily intended to be mutually exclusive or all inclusive. There may be combinations of these behavior patterns or others observed in many mob situations.

An aggressive mob attacks, riots and terrorizes, as in the case of assassination mobs, race riots, lynchings, political riots and prison riots. The action is all one-sided. The mob's aim is the destruction of persons or property. Similar aggressive behavior may be seen in juvenile "rumbles." The objective of the violence differs, of course, with the situation. Often the objective of the violence is some person or group of persons, while at other times it may be property. In some cases it is both.

An escape mob is one whose members are in a state of panic. They attempt to secure safety from some real or imagined threat by flight. Panic creates and motivates the escape mob. Because of their tenor, members of the escape mob have lost their power of reasoning and may go so far as to destroy each other unless controlled. Escape mobs tend to overrun anything in their paths creating great damage and loss of life.

An acquisitive mob is motivated by a desire to acquire something. The mobs in food riots and looting are acquisitive mobs. Law enforcement officials have observed that what starts out in some cases as a riot soon changes into a wild and uncontrolled looting spree. Other examples of acquisitive behavior would be a run on a bank and hunger riots.

An expressive mob is a mob expressing fervor or revelry. The occasion, be it religious activity, a political convention, a New Year's Eve celebration, or a sporting event, provides a release for pent-up emotions and an escape from the dull routine of the workaday world. Religious revivals, carnivals, county fairs, jazz festivals, parades, wild parties and orgies all may contain elements of expressive behavior.

With the exception of the religious revival in which the main police problem is one of traffic control, all of these may provide situations which are difficult to control. Those who witnessed the wild celebrations on V-J Day are well aware of the potential danger of such a crowd and the tremendous challenge it presents the police.

Of these four types of mob, three have external objects or goals: aggression seeks a target; escape seeks an exit or means of removal; acquisition seeks some economic good. Behavior in an expressive mob has no such clear external goal. The behavior itself seems to be the only end. Pantie raids and spring riots at colleges are usually revelrous as are celebrations of victory at war or in football.

PANIC MOB

Special consideration must be given to the panic mob, as it in many ways differs from other mobs. Panic is the child of fear and ignorance.

The word *panic* has never been used to designate orderly escape behavior. The term is reserved for cases when the social contract is thrown away and each man single-mindedly attempts to save his own life at whatever cost to others. Panic is an overpowering unreasonable terror with or without cause inspired by fright, creating highly emotional behavior, violent action, paralyzing immobility, or blind, unreasoning or frantic efforts to reach or secure safety by flight.

It is impossible to convey in mere words a true perception of what a panic is. Words cannot convey the horror of a wave of mankind breaking upon itself, shattering and crushing each other in a blind, wild scramble of self-preservation. Nevertheless, it is hoped that the pathetic examples that follow may present some indication of the problem.

On June 5, 1941, Japanese bombers raided Chungking, China, and sent 5,000 civilians into the city's biggest air raid shelter. The people started to come out when they thought the raid was over but fought their way back when the Japanese bombers returned. The guards slammed the entrance gates shut. Then panic swept the shelter. Fear spread through the people so that they lost control of themselves; they tore off their own and one another's clothing in a blind frenzy; and they struggled over one another's bodies toward the air inlets, thus blocking the ingress of air. Locked in the shelter for five hours, husbands, wives and children died together in the most horrible civilian episode of the Japanese-Chinese War. Four thousand persons died in this hideous catastrophe.

The Iroquois theater fire of 1903 is still cited as one of the great examples of the awesome effect of panic. The cry of "Fire" rang out in the theater and struck instant panic into the crowd, which began to surge toward the doors. All attempts to quiet the crowd by telling them that there was no danger were futile. There were thirty exits from the theater, but few of them were marked by lights and some had heavy portieres over the doors. Some of the doors were locked or fastened with levers which no one knew how to work. It has been said that some of the doors were either rusted or frozen. The fire escapes were hardly adequate to handle the mass surge of humanity and many fell or jumped to their death below. But it was inside the theater that the greatest loss of life occurred, especially on the stairways leading from the second balcony. Here most of the dead were trampled or smothered, although many jumped or fell from the balusters to the floor or foyer. In places on the stairways, particularly where a turn caused a jam, bodies were piled seven or eight feet deep. Heel prints on the dead faces testified to the cruel fact that human animals stricken by terror are as wild as stampeding cattle. Many of the bodies had the clothing torn from them and some of the flesh trodden from their bones. From the start of the fire until all in the auditorium either escaped or died or were mangled in the halls and stairways had taken only eight minutes. In that eight minutes, more than five hundred died, and the toll eventually reached over six hundred.

One of the more recent examples of the destructive force of a panic mob is the panic that occurred in Lima, Peru at the soccer match between Peru and Argentina. In the last half a tying goal was disallowed. This decision triggered a tremendous outcry of anger and frustration in the stands. Spectators threw hundreds of bottles and seat cushions onto the field.

A nine-foot-high steel-link fence surrounded the playing field, but a man climbed it and dashed for the referee. The police intercepted him and hustled him off. Another man broke onto the field and was also carried off. The referee called off the game, infuriating the spectators even more. Dozens of men and youths tried to climb the fence. The police beat away their hands with clubs. Then the fans sat down at the foot of the fence and, by pushing with their feet, in rhythm, incredibly tore three large holes in the steel links. Hordes of people raced onto the field, where they were met by police clubs and police dogs. In the stands, some men started bonfires, while others tore apart a retaining wall and began hurling bricks at the police. The police lobbed tear gas grenades at the fence to keep back the crowd. Then they hurled the grenades into the stands.

Thousands of people gagged and coughed, were temporarily blinded. They tried to grope their way to fresh air, but were blocked on all sides by a solid wall of humanity.

Then, in one flashing instant, panic ran like an electric current through the crowd, charging people with crazed energy. They had to get out!

They rushed for the exits and poured like coal down a chute into the tunnels, fourteen feet wide, narrowing to ten, that led under the stands and into the streets. Men, women and children fell and were trampled to death. Three policemen were murdered, one strangled with his own necktie, another thrown from the upper stands fifty feet to the concrete in the lower stands and the third deliberately stomped to death. A tall man tried to save two children by carrying them on his shoulders, but he lost his hold and they vanished in the crush.

Then came the ultimate horror. In the extremely crowded north section, the steel doors at the end of three tunnels leading to the street were closed. Attendants at two of these doors apparently had left them about ten minutes before the end of the game to watch the final minutes of play and had not been able to return. The third door was permanently closed and not in use.

The vanguard of the rushing mob tried to turn back, but their pleading screams were never heard. Even those who tried to keep calm were irresistibly swept along by the rush. Wave after wave of humanity piled up against the closed doors. Most of the victims died of suffocation or were trampled to death.

Causes

The origin of panic lies in the fear of being exposed to immediate or imminent danger, such as death, or ruination physically, financially or socially. To put it another way, panic is due to abnormal circumstances—such as fire in theater, ship sinking, earthquake—that are not anticipated, for which the people are unprepared, and which suddenly occur unexpectedly. But danger and fear alone are not enough to generate panic. There must be the possibility of escape, and also the possibility of entrapment.

Characteristics of a Panic Producing Situation

The characteristics of a panic producing situation are the following.

A PERCEIVED THREAT. The threat, real or imaginary, may be physical, psychological or a combination of both, and it is usually regarded as being so imminent that there is no solution except frantic efforts to escape and survive. The perceived threat may be a rumor, such as: a dike, levee, or dam has been blown up and a tidal wave is rapidly approaching the crowd or mob; or that the area is dangerous due to radioactivity, deadly gas, or germs.

The threat may also be an actual disaster, i.e., large fires, earthquake, explosions caused by rioters or natural causes.

PARTIAL ENTRAPMENT. There is only one, or at best an extremely limited number, escape route from a situation dominated by the perceived threat.

PARTIAL OR COMPLETE BREAKDOWN OF THE ESCAPE ROUTE. The escape route becomes blocked or jammed or it is overlooked.

FRONT TO REAR COMMUNICATIONS FAILURE. The false assumption that the exit is still open leads the people at the rear of the mass to exert strong physical or psychological pressure to advance toward it. It is this pressure from the rear that causes those at the front to be smothered, crushed, or trampled.

FORMATION OF A MOB

Mobs, other than escape mobs, do not suddenly spring into full bloom. They are the product of a process of evolution. Individuals who constitute a mob always have certain common interests and needs.

Their need may be of a physical variety, such as a need for food or shelter, or it may be of a psychological nature, such as the need for a recognition of status, a feeling of superiority, or a desire for vengeance.

The two basic characteristics of mob members are, then (1) common needs, either physical or psychological, which are intensely felt; and (2) a strong desire for some meaning or explanation of the difficulty they feel they are in. These individuals are preconditioned, for tension conditions do not as a rule arise abruptly. There may be a series of irritating events or a deluge of vicious rumors which create a climate of tension. Frustrations are built up.

The first step in the transformation of a preconditioned and responsive group of individuals into a mob is some climatic event. It may be an accident or an organized expression of sympathy or resentment. If the incident is one which directly affects the group, such as indiscriminate shooting into their midst, the transition from desperation to wrath is quick and involves little verbal interaction among the members of the group. When, as is more commonly the case, the incident does not directly affect any member of the group, the transition occurs through and during the verbal interaction which is based on that incident. This is the period when the mob "mutters."

It may be no more dramatic than many that have preceded it. By its nature the incident tends to attract attention and is usually of an exciting nature. It causes a crowd to gather at the scene. Its members mill about like a herd of cattle. The gathering of a crowd automatically causes more onlookers to accumulate.

These persons usually have little if any direct knowledge of the incident which gave rise to the mob. They are more often impelled by idle curiosity and are attracted by the sight of the crowd. Rumors are numerous and spread rapidly. People assembled in a crowd are characteristically timid, or even collectively cowardly. They hesitate to commit themselves to a course of unrestrained violence, though some of them might readily do so if they thought there was a chance to escape arrest. In an incident involving representatives of different racial groups, members of one group are usually inclined to line up with members of their group, regardless of the merits of the conflict.

As an incident proceeds to attract numbers of individuals, they are pressed together. They quite naturally begin to brush and contact one another. There may be half-accidental and half-intentional jostling and a good deal of name-calling. They initiate conversation with strangers. They move about in an aimless fashion, all the while communicating with each other the collective excitement of the situation. In the interval they "mill" about. The term *milling* was originally applied to the slow, circular, aimless movement of cattle. Some such movement often occurs in crowds before they become actively aggressive or expressive and some students of collective behavior have considered milling to be an essential prerequisite to mob action. What is it that milling accomplishes? It seems to be primarily a process of informal communication, a process by which members learn that they are of one mind, that they are individually eager to lynch, riot, or otherwise "let go." It is a process of acquainting one another with their preferences. Through the milling process, the crowd excites itself more and more. Individuals will break off to warn friends, enlist recruits, pass on rumors, not only in face-to-face conversation but by telephone, and generate hysterical excitement. More and more people appear on the scene. Some of these are mere bystanders and curiosity seekers while others will immediately join the activity. As the crowd grows, so do the rumors, and, through social facilitation, increasingly dangerous behavior is encouraged.

The members of the mob, particularly the more active ones, move around from one small group to another, often aimlessly. There will be an undercurrent of excitement, uncertainty and testing as they contact each other. Words can be used little or not at all, conduct alone may be a rapid, accurate and efficient means of communication. Soon they become vocal. By shouting they further excite one another. They are sure to be warmly sympathetic; they will cheer the smallest act of courage; they will also be profoundly sentimental.

The result is a spiral of stimulation. One excited individual stimulates excitement in another who in turn stimulates a third, who may in turn restimulate the first individual to an even higher pitch of excitement. Thus, by circular influences, stimulation and restimulation of each other, a high state of collective tension and excitement is built up like front and back logs in a fire. The heat of one log is reflected across to the other, which then fires up and sends more heat to the first. The heat is reflected back and forth, steadily increasing and consuming the material of the wood. So anger, resentment, hatred and revenge mount higher and enter into more and more of the personalities of the combatants, consuming all their energies, to the point of utter exhaustion or destruction.

As tension mounts, individuals become less and less responsive to stimulation arising outside the group and respond only to influences from within the crowd itself. This process creates among members of the crowd an internal rapport, a kind of collective hypnosis, in which the individual loses his self-control and responds only to the dictates of the crowd as a whole. The individual loses critical self-consciousness, his ability to act in terms of cool and rational consideration for mob anonymity absolves him of individual responsibility. Brutalized emotions rise and receive the sanction of the mob. Latent feeling-states are both intensified in the situation and given a path of discharge. Except possibly for the leader of the situation, the behavior which occurs in a mob is never motivated by ulterior considerations. It is entirely uncalculated.

Once a crowd is really formed, once the members of it have fallen under one another's mesmerism, the individual withers and the crowd is more and more. The individual is in fact absorbed for the time being into the crowd and merely contributes his life to the vitality of the collective body. The individual is under the domination of the mob mind, the domination of low-intelligence people, the domination of lower instincts and emotions.

As group wrath generates, symbolic behavior becomes incapable of providing a satisfactory outlet for the feeling-states of the individuals involved. Some form of overt, nonsymbolic behavior is imperative. Such overt behavior is, of course, always violent and destructive. Within certain limits, however, the specific direction which it takes will depend upon the leader or leaders who rise to the occasion. In any event, the behavior will be a collective expression of the wrath of the group, comparable to the wrathful action of the individual who slams the door, pulls off the telephone, or, as the case may be, bangs his head against the wall. The opinion of a crowd has no relation to the reasoned opinion of the majority of its members, but is a mere infectious passion which sweeps through the whole body like an electric current, and frequently is originated and propagated from a single brain.

The first persons who express their feelings and who take definitive action are likely to be the most impulsive, the most suggestible, the least self-controlled, the least inhibited. The most ignorant and the most excitable are the ones who are likely to trigger the violence.

The agitator temporarily converts the "muttering mob" into an audience and proceeds to convert that audience to the acceptance of a course of action. To accomplish this, he uses the standard dramatic formula, building up stereotypes which are appropriate for the group and for the ends he has in view. His technique is comparable to that of any conversional-audience leader. Building on the incident, he personifies the forces of opposition and casts his audience in the role of a collective hero, who by a designated course of action will rescue the heroine from the machinations of the villain. The heroine is all those things which the members of the group want but have been unable to secure by individual strivings. The villain can be almost any person or group of persons, preferably someone who is accessible. Assisted by audience interaction, the agitator may succeed in activating his audience to such an extent that they are ready for overt action.

Triggering mob action is a kind of leadership in the sense that the trigger does first what others do subsequently.

Leadership in a mob that violates conventional norms falls to those in whom the norms are weakest, to persons of low status. The leader is a person who, quickly sensing the difficulties of those around him, expresses their troubles. He can identify himself with each person and, in turn, each person identifies himself with the leader. The leader cements his position of leadership by providing his puzzled and frustrated followers with some simple, easily comprehensible and generally superficial explanation of their difficulties. If he is particularly clever, he coins or picks up slogans and symbols or appropriate cliches. His explanation includes, of course, some positive suggestion for action, the very thought of which begins to release the pent-up aggression of the mob members.

Potential participants in an aggressive or hostile outburst can never be as sure of what others will do. For this reason hostile and expressive outbursts usually must be triggered. Someone must initiate action so

that others can believe in the action-readiness of the mass. In a large
and unruly gathering, there will be many incidents of bristling and
jostling going on at the same time and any one of these can un-
predictably spread to involve many people.

When the frenzy reaches a fever pitch, all that is needed is a spark
to ignite the smoldering mass into a roaring conflagration. The
precipitating event is usually one of a series of similar incidents. It
may be more serious than any of the others, but it occurs at a time
when everything else is ready. It may be the influence of professional
or incipient agitators, a harangue by a fiery speaker, the appearance of
a hated political or industrial leader, or police action that antagonizes
and incites acts of violence. On the other hand, unjustified acts of
violence, arrogance or viciousness by the civil authorities or the military
may swing the sentiments of the participants and spectators against law
enforcement and still further build up mob tension to an explosive
pitch.

Apparent weakening in the strength or attitude of the forces of
law and order—indecisive or inefficient police action or lack of proper
authoritative police action encourages violence. A single successful
act of violence—breaking windows, or throwing missiles at police or
soldiers, or resistance—may arouse a hope of possible success for the
cause with which a crowd or mob is sympathetic. Being that which
the members of the crowd each unconsciously wished to do, it gains
general approval—"it is a blow for righteousness"—a "cause" appears.
Casually associated persons at once become a group, brought together
by their interest in vindicating the principles at stake. Standards are
judged to be good if they will help achieve the mob's goal and bad
if they impede such achievement. It seems as if some electric current
flows through the veins of all the citizens and leads them at once to
rejection of all law. The mob finds itself suddenly doing things which
its members had never really dreamed of doing.

An actual victory in an initial encounter with either civil or military
personnel may so whet and gratify the crowd's appetite that its
members will press forward more determinedly and dangerously. Once
action has begun, it usually spreads quickly, engulfing even the more
intelligent and self-controlled.

The immediate and psychological function of riot behavior is simple and evident. To the members of a rebellious group, violence of whatever order provides an outlet for their feelings. The action is analogous to the behavior of a man who wrathfully kicks a chair: the act expresses his feelings and provides him with at least the satisfaction of expressing those feelings.

Now that the violence has begun, the acts of the individual mob member are without logic, completely unreasoned, hysterical. The individual mob member tends to feel a loss of personal identity. He becomes merely an anonymous member of a large group. As he sees others engaged in the same kind of behavior and under the influence of the same excitement, there is a tendency to believe that everyone is involved. The psychological effect of this anonymity and universality is to absolve the individual of responsibility for the brutal acts he commits.

When the mob violence "gets into high gear" the objects against which the violence is directed become more generalized. Whereas the violence may originally have been directed solely against members of another race, against management, or against school authorities, the emotionally driven, nonlogical destruction spreads to include other persons or property which, no matter how remotely, represent to the mob members symbols of the conditions producing the initial frustration. They may see the policeman or other authorities as symbols for their hatred. The police station, churches, grocery stores, pawn shops, liquor stores and all sorts of establishments become "fair game" once the violence gets out of control. No rules apply; there is no fair play. The behavior is governed by mass hysteria, hatred and impulse.

In some instances the agitator, when he has his audience sufficiently activated, steps from the role of agitator to that of mob director, and crying "Follow me!" leads the mob to direct its attack on the villain which he has built up for them. More frequently, however, the agitator simply harangues the group until some member of the audience cries out "Let's go, boys!" at which point leadership shifts from the agitator to that member. The typical labor agitator, for example, seldom attempts to do more than convert disgruntled laborers to the idea that some particular employer, or employers in general, is responsible for their troubles. He provides them with inflammatory oratory in the hope that, from the group, there will arise someone who will lead the mob into action.

When the agitator does not follow through to direct mob action, it is always somewhat problematic whether the directive leadership which does arise will take the mob in the direction which the agitator desires. Many an agitator has succeeded in activating his audience to mob action, only to find that the directive leader which the mob has accepted is headed for the wrong object.

Even when the direction of action has been established, the mob tends to remain fickle. Like a pack of hounds, it is likely to follow the loudest voice. The agitator may, for example, have established the fact that the strikebearers are the villains who stand in the way of economic plenty; and the mob may have turned actively to the task of routing this enemy. Anyone who comes to hand, however, may then serve as a satisfactory enemy to be chased. Once the pattern of the chase is established, the mob may, in fact, shift attention from the original victim to the nearer, and equally satisfactory, directive leader. The leader becomes the hunted, and someone else takes his place of leadership. This characteristic irresponsibility of the coordinated mob makes directive leadership of such a mob a rather hazardous occupation, particularly during periods of intense and prolonged social stress.

PERSONALITY TYPES IN MOBS

Introduction

Even though the members of a mob have to a degree lost their individuality, they will retain certain basic characteristics which, when recognized, will assist in taking action to control the mob. Indeed, if the background of the individual is known (social and religious training, attitudes, etc.), his probable behavior in joining the mob can be generally predicted.

Leaders

Every mob realizes its own inefficiency and is ready to accept a leader as soon as one becomes visible to it. Thus, the mob leader is of great importance. He focuses the attention of the crowd on an incident or defines the situation to the crowd so that its members will take positive and possibly violent action. He guides and controls or incites the crowd to action. Indeed, mob action depends to a great extent on the ability of the mob leader to bring the emotions of individuals to a peak of intensity.

The leadership is sometimes spontaneous and sometimes calculated and organized. At times, persons who are not known previously as leaders will assume that mantle.

The leader of the mob usually has been a part of that mob. Although the mob leader may not be a local person, nor even of the same economic or social class as the group, he must be accepted before he can lead. He may be sent to the locale to promote a cause, to unionize unorganized workers, to propagandize for racial or social equality, or for other purposes. In small cities, towns or rural areas, the stranger is usually suspected. The alien leader is unlikely to gain sufficient prestige to become a leader in such areas, until he has been there long enough to have gained the confidence of the more trusted persons in the community and in many communities this is long in coming about.

In urban centers the situation is somewhat different. Many of the people have themselves migrated into the city from other areas. Individuals come and go. Leaders and potential leaders also may come and go. Some types of organizers are even trained in the practice of infiltrating existing groups and organizations. They also are skillful in cultivating association with key persons and in being identified with activities of organizations, knowing that they must be accepted before they can assume leadership functions when the time is opportune.

There are several types of natural leaders, each being effective in his own way.

1. The dominant leader is one whose main idea is to secure action in connection with immediate problems. He usually has a knowledge of the reason for the conflict but he is not a thinker. He does not concern himself with details. He is cold and aloof and will suppress conflicting ideas and acts with whatever means he may have at his disposal.

2. The persuasive leader is one that maintains a personal feeling with each member of the crowd. He is seemingly sincere, but he reshapes the thoughts of the people so as to get credit for any good that may happen.
3. The opportunist leader is one that feeds on the emotions and conflicts already underway. He may not even be concerned with the immediate problem, but sees an opportunity to gain recognition.

Professional Agitator

This individual is experienced in participating in and fomenting disturbances. He is not swept away by the mob spirit, rather he retains complete control of his facilities. His actions are deliberate and calculated, all directed toward the realization of his fixed goal. He attempts to build up emotional tension by defending the assumed or real cause of unrest. He will suggest lines of action to release emotional tension. He will use subordinate leaders or stooges to shout agreement. He will usually attempt to justify or make a pretense of justifying the suggested mob action.

Young Leaders

They are impulsive. They are the most excited and violent of the mob. They usually imitate the first impulsive violent act which will be emulated by the rank and file.

Activists

They are the "voices in the crowd" supporting the agitator, urging the action. They are a vocal minority spreading the virus of infection. They are impulsive persons whose mob behavior is not unlike the behavior they exhibit in their ordinary daily lives. These people are short-tempered and hotheaded, the kind that are always spoiling for a fight. They need only a fancied insult or a slight provocation to excite them to violence. They start the riot or incite others to violence.

Criminal Elements

The criminal element of a community may take advantage of riotous conditions to commit individual acts of lawlessness. In recent widespread disorders, these lawless elements have participated in rioting and cause great disorder and destruction.

Psychopathic Individuals

There are some individuals with a pathological personality structure who might be part of a mob. There are people who are angry at the world, because of frustrations or mental illness, who could use the riotous situation as a means of getting even with society.

Suggestible Persons

There are those who are easily influenced to follow the lead of the more violent. They get into the action early.

Cautious Individuals

Cautious individuals are those not impulsive enough to initiate violence, and who would like to get into the fracas but who wait for the cloak of anonymity to give them courage by hiding their identity.

Supporting Individuals

Supporting individuals are those who do not actively participate, but who enjoy the show and even shout encouragement, or who do not explicitly show disapproval of mob actions. Such idle observers are considered supports since, to a mob member, they seem to approve of the action; therefore, they enhance mob feeling of cohesion.

Bystanders

Bystanders are spectators who merely watch the mob. Those who are visible to the acting crowd give emotional support to the mob merely by their physical presence. Further, they must always be considered possible participants.

Resisters

Those whose values and standards of judgment are not swayed by the emotional frenzy of the mob, who maintain level heads, and who disagree with the actions of the majority are *resisters*. A mob is intolerant and meets resistance with violence.

PSYCHOLOGY OF THE MOB

Introduction

The specific conditions giving rise to mob behavior will vary enormously with the economic, political, racial and religious characteristics of particular cultures at different times and in different places. However, the psychological effects of these various conditions will be more uniform. The more the officer knows about these psychological factors, the better able he is to cope with the problem. Likewise, there are certain psychological influences that work in favor of the agitator. By recognizing and understanding them, the police can set in action forces designed to utilize these very factors to dispel the mob. Let us then look at man and the factors that affect his behavior.

Poor Nutrition and Poor Health

The existence of poor nutrition and poor physical health is a critical factor in the production of emotional disturbances. The individual who is deprived of a properly balanced diet or who is in poor physical health is in a receptive state to react to an impending danger with panic or some other behavioral disorder. He is beset by a certain degree of anxiety about his own health. He feels that he is below par in his capacity to take effective measures. He is unduly concerned and feels himself in a precarious state. He feels inadequate and therefore in a somewhat inferior position in regard to other members of the group.

Fatigue

Fatigue is an important contributory element in the causation of undue anxiety. With the development of fatigue there tends to be a loss of perspective. Minor happenings become intensified, threats lose their true significance, and actual anxiety attacks appear.

If weariness progresses to an undue degree, certain behavioral changes of a more serious nature appear. The individual may become more and more tense and may become anxious minded. In some people, depression sets in and this results in a still further reduction in the amount of work the individual is capable of doing. Others, when unduly fatigued, become suspicious and resentful. Irritability is another frequent consequence of undue fatigue. It is apparent than an individual in such condition is a prime candidate for a mob.

Homogeneity of Mental State

By homogeneity of mental state we mean that members of the mob share common attitudes and opinions, common dissatisfactions, frustrations and conflicts; all of which add to the makeup of the mob's "sameness." Their needs may be of a physical variety, such as the need for shelter, food, or clothing, or they may be of a phychological nature, such as the need for a recognition of status, a feeling of superiority, fear reactions, or a desire for vengeance. When a group is subjected to a common frustration, the cohesiveness of the group is increased, that is, common frustration draws the people closer together psychologically.

People who become members of mobs are further characterized by the fact that they are not aware of, or not convinced of, the really basic causes of the problems they are facing. Because mob members are filled with some grievance or other and because they are less likely to know what it is all about, they are in greater need than most people for some solution, some interpretation of their problems which they can understand.

Fear and Anger

Fear and anger are closely allied. They have the same purpose— to separate a person from a living creature, force or situation considered by the person to be painful, threatening or dangerous to his comfort, well-being, or his very existence. If that threat is wholly removed, the fear and anger also disappear. Thus, fear is itself a powerful incentive for an individual to participate in mob action, because the resulting riot gives him an opportunity to destroy the cause of his fear, which hitherto he dared not do. The emotional temper of a time of crisis is exaggeratedly marked by fear. This means that the impulses to hit out at someone are unusually strong.

Contagion

Man is variable, not constant. He reacts to the behavior of others just as they react to him. Such interaction is brought about by communication between individuals by all of the methods known to man, such as gestures, body contact, spoken or written words. The people become emotionally stimulated by the action of others even though they may not share the grievance from which the emotion originated. This sharing of emotion may start in the form of sympathy, but often develops into anger. People imagine themselves in the same difficulty as others and thus become enraged merely by thinking about the result or injury. The communication of ideas and influence from one member of the mob to another is quick and contagious.

Novelty

The new and the strange have a unique fascination to the average person. Indeed, an individual subconsciously welcomes a break from boring routine of daily life and may react enthusiastically to new circumstances. But, when an individual is confronted with new and strange circumstances, the habits which he has formed may not be fully operative. The specific stimuli which usually govern his actions will be absent, and the lessons of previous experiences, which were employed in solving customary problems, will be inapplicable.

Lacking any guides, the individual may resort to trial and error. More than likely, in the press of a crowd or mob situation, the individual will succumb to suggestion.

Suggestion

Suggestion takes place when one person induces an idea, belief, or act in another without the latter's use of logical reasoning. Obviously, most people are susceptible to suggestion. If, as a person walks along the street, he sees three or four individuals looking up toward the top of a building, he is almost irresistibly drawn to look up himself. In an audience, when one person begins to clap, others follow. The conduct of people in crowds seems to be contagious. One person takes his cue from another. Many people readily fall in line and follow a leader, taking his suggestions as to their conduct. In other words, they imitate the actions of the leader or of each other.

Many influences are likely to make people susceptible to suggestion. Feelings of insecurity and instability, ignorance, intense worries, lack of self-confidence or self-discipline—all make a person susceptible to suggestion.

In a novel situation, such as being in a mob, one is lacking in experience and thus more prone to accept the suggestions of one who apparently has knowledge and experience. Indeed, in such situations, the least intelligent mind tends to lower the intelligence of the whole to the lower levels due to increased suggestibility. Consequently, the individual is more susceptible to suggestive thought and action of the group.

Thus, a professional agitator, a dominant personality, or a "crackpot" will assume a position of prominence and suggest lines of action to the crowd or mob.

People normally will accept the ideas of a dominant personality. Ideas spread throughout a mob without a restraining or rational thought to the consequences or objection being raised in the minds of its members. There is no follow-through in the thinking process. Rather, the individuals in the crowd will go along with the ideas and shouting.

Imitation—Conformity

The primitive urge to conform, to do what others are doing, is always very strong. The individual is generally afraid to express views contrary to those of the majority.

The mob atmosphere increases the normal urge to conform. In an emotional crowd or mob, which is likely to turn its anger against a dissenter, this pressure for conformity is extremely strong. In a mob situation, people find it psychologically difficult to "buck the trend." Their expressed opinions, therefore, may not always represent the true intensity of their feelings. This means that many may not feel as strongly as their utterances would seem to indicate and, in the face of a strong stand by the police, they will soon "cool off" and back down.

Release of Repressed Desires

All human beings are subject to certain drives that are aroused by basic desires, instincts, or emotions, such as hunger, sex, gregariousness, self-preservation, anger and fear. Society demands that these

instincts be controlled and diverted to socially acceptable ends. The
savage in us is repressed, but these repressed impulses remain always
explosive, always ready to ignite at the first moment of weakening of
the forces of repression.

In a mob, the repressed and unsatisfied desires of an individual
are readily released. In effect, the mob is a mechanism of escape and
of compensation. In the mob, the primitive ego achieves its wish by
actually gaining the assent and support of a section of society. It is
as if all at once an unspoken agreement were entered into whereby
each member might let himself go, on condition that he approved the
same thing in all the rest.

Anonymity—Facelessness

The size of the mob is important psychologically in that it gives
the members of the mob a feeling of anonymity, power, righteousness
and universality. When an individual is within a mob, he tends to
lose self-consciousness because his identity merges with that of the
mob. He supposes himself to retain anonymity, generally with good
reason, because of the difficulty of identifying and apprehending
the lawbreakers whose activity results in mob action. This anonymity
results in a loss of sense of responsibility that prompts illegal and
unacceptable actions.

Sense of Power

The sheer force of numbers tends to dispel doubts and fears. The
size of a mob gives the individual a sense of invincible power which
encourages him in an unrestrained yielding to his instincts. He can
then exalt and exhibits himself to almost any extent without shame,
oblivious of the fact that the supremacy, power, praise and glory which
he claims for his crowd are really claimed for himself.

Universality

Universality refers to that impression of a member of a mob that
the mob encompasses all and that everyone approves of an unlawful action and that the action must therefore be right. "Everybody is doing it." This is the general impression easily gained by
mob members. This results as people have a tendency to believe

the attitudes and emotions which they are experiencing are being shared by everyone present. The mere fact that large numbers of people are present has a tendency to discourage behavior that is different from that being exhibited by other persons. Crowd members stimulate each other and, before long, the individual gets the impression that everyone feels as he does.

From this, it is an easy step to the supposition that the entire community approves, since supposedly if they were all there they would do the same things. Such a feature of the mob explains to a large extent the "righteousness" of many mob actions and riots.

Sense of Righteousness

The unity of purpose of the mob causes the individual to rationalize until he is convinced of the mob's righteousness. This rationalization is often orally expressed as follows: "How can we be wrong in our anger and our actions when everyone about us is also angry and is participating in the same actions?" These utterances by a number of those in the mob will only tend to convince the members of the mob that what they are thinking and doing is justifiable.

Irrationality

The behavior of a crowd of people is essentially irrational. Crowd behavior is governed not by intellect, but by passion; not by cool calculation, but by impulse. The fundamental reason is that, although no two individuals can ever think alike, any number can feel alike. Who needs a definition of love, of pride, of grief or joy? Everyone can unite without the smallest difficulty in such emotions, and moreover, such a union of feeling is a different kind of union from that which is described as an intellectual agreement. Union of feeling promotes, and flourishes in, a state of enthusiasm. It is like a mesmeric condition. It heightens one's sense of life; it carries one beyond the limitations of his intelligence; it takes him into another world—higher or lower as the case may be—but at any rate other than the world in which he normally exists.

Hence it is that a crowd has all the emotions and no intellect. It can feel, but it cannot think. It has in common a subtle sensibility to feeling. Passion sweeps through it. It can reason about nothing, for it has no reasoning apparatus in common. The nerves of all its members may be in connection with one another, but not their thoughts. They can applaud or "boo" in common, but they cannot criticize or differentiate. Acceptance or rejection is their only alternative; feeling can accomplish those operations with hardly any help from reason.

Because they are emotional, crowds and mobs are extremely sensitive to dejection and elation; they break up and disperse or swarm aggressively into the streets, as they fail or succeed initially. Being without discipline, they can neither be checked in the excesses that follow a partial victory, nor rallied from the discouragement of defeat.

There are two aspects of a mob's irrationality. The first is the distortion or narrowing perception. The panicked mob, in a theater fire, collectively perceives only one course of action and rushes for the exit. Since the exit they rush for may not be the only exit available, the mob increases the danger rather than alleviates it. The irrationality of the members of the mob consists not of their supposed stupidity, but rather of their narrow perception of what to do, namely, one course of action—rush for the exit. This applies in all cases of mob activity. The lynch mob doesn't consider and weigh various alternatives. It generally perceives only one alternative: hang the victim illegally. Similarly, the opposing mobs making up a riot do not consider alternative ways to resolve conflict or dissatisfactions concerning the other group (such as legal action or economic reprisals). Riot participants perceive, narrowly, only a few alternatives—destroying or injuring the body or property of the competing mob.

The second aspect of the mob's irrationality is its strikingly regressive character. The individual reacts to frustrations or dissatisfactions through immediate, unsophisticated, usually violent behavior that releases existing tension.

It is not necessary to dwell on the homicidal tendencies of the crowd. Every crowd is "against someone." Hence humanity's unhappy record of persecutions, wars, riots; hence the orgies of wanton killings which have stained the record of every revolution.

Chapter 3

INCITING A MOB

INTRODUCTION

ALTHOUGH MOST mobs result from a fortuitous chain of circumstances, at times there will be deliberate attempts to incite a crowd to riot. The organization of a mob can be divided into five stages: preconditioning; selecting proper revolutionary slogans; creating the crowd nucleus; on-the-scene agitation, and manufacturing martyrs.

PLANNING

Planning is normally centered around one central incident or circumstance which will be used as the basis for the disorder. Contingencies that might arise are carefully considered. Proposed locations, weather conditions, police strength and tactics, and the morale of the population are carefully studied.

Preparations also include the establishment of a chain of command and the designation of alternates to replace them. Plans must also be made to obtain and distribute necessary supplies, banners, flags, placards, armbands, scarfs, caps and leaflets. Transportation and communication must also be arranged.

In order to minimize police and other suppressive action, subversives and advocates of violence will often ally themselves openly with other groups with political power and thus seek to form a united front. At the same time they will continue mob agitation and incitation in a clandestine manner.

PRECONDITIONING

Careful study of a society to be pressured or influenced will normally reveal definite problems facing that society. For example, a deficiency which exists in the human needs of the people could be used by a pressure group as a basis for inciting riots. If no well-defined problems face the whole society, the conflicting aspirations of various segments of the population can be used to generate a problem. This problem is then accentuated to create unrest.

Another preconditioning approach is to create the image of the common "enemy," be it the capitalist exploiters, the imperalist, the *Yanqui,* the cleric, or the Jew. In addition to the "anticause" cry, the propaganda apparatus seeks to "precondition" a mental attitude that, in the crucial moment, can be whipped into a blazing fury of righteous, self-justifying violence. Their theory is that when the "hot" area of the brain is in a state of excitation, other areas become inhibited, as it is impossible to concentrate consciously and deliberately on two different lines of thought at the same time. Constant hammering on the chosen themes is intended to ensure that, at the crucial time, the "hot" area will inhibit normal social restraints and override everything except the obsessive compulsion to pommel the personalized enemy or vent the frustrations and aggressive passions.

METHODS OF INCITING MOB VIOLENCE

Oral and printed propaganda certainly is of importance and helps to crystallize the formless feelings of discontent. The propaganda barrage mentally preconditions the individual. He is thus more responsive to mob-creating stimuli. Included within this is the employment of all methods of communication such as newspapers, telephone, television, radio, leaflets, placards, posters, banners, whispering campaigns, rumor circulating, cartoons, provocative mass meetings and signs on buildings.

Issue

An issue of some sort will most easily bring an assemblage of people together. It need not necessarily be a matter of great importance, but it must be something which catches and challenges attention without great effort, which carries with it the element of conflict. The professional agitators may wait for some situation or issue to arise, or they may create one. This will vary from planned assassinations to the blowing up of monuments and buildings. The means is not important if the results are obtained.

The planned assassination of the popular figure, Dr. Jorge Gaitean, in Bogota, Colombia in April 1948, was used to set off destructive mob violence; it cost millions of dollars in damage. The popular Latin slang expression, *bogotazo* is now commonly used to describe a destructive, planned, mob action.

Slogans

Among the tools of the professional agitator are slogans and symbols. They not only rally and unify supporters and direct their actions toward precise targets and objectives, but they also terrify or discomfort opponents. Symbols, such as flags, insignia, or caricatures of the enemy, are further short cuts crowded with meaning. People seem to get worked up into a higher emotional pitch when they are reacting to symbols rather than to general programs or ideologies. Slogans and symbols are selected in accordance with circumstances, with the view to organizing and mobilizing the masses on the broadest possible scale.

Recently the cry of "police brutality" has been effectively, and professionally, used to precondition the mob. Proponents of violence have capitalized on this theme, and have effectively employed it as the "ignition" to spark riotous action, violence, looting and destruction. Likewise, during the past several years, minority groups have expounded this theme as a means to unify their groups to a common cause.

Organizers well understand the extra mileage they can get for their basic causes, no matter what they may appear to be, by including "police brutality" as a major ingredient in the overall formula. This theme apparently has an underlying appeal even to the person whose only contact with the police may have been an overtime parking ticket.

The Manufacture of Martyrs

In promoting any strike, demonstration or insurrection, agitators know that bloodshed is very effective in imparting proper impetus to the "cause" they happen to be promoting at the moment. The spilling of blood can turn the ordinary grievance into a *cause celebre*. The mob feels a "holy commission" not to "break faith with the dead martyrs."

CREATING THE MOB NUCLEUS

Forming the nucleus of a mob is often a simple task; it involves little more than mobilizing a specified number of people. This group inevitably attracts an equal number of the curious, the excitement seekers, and the chronic malcontents. Of course, the agitators always organize as many sympathizers and sincere citizens harboring legitimate grievances as possible.

The original nucleus can be assembled by calling on members of an organization or by using the standard ballyhoo methods of newspaper publicity, leaflets, radio announcements and offers of free transportation. Crowds may also be hired. In Brazil, an American mingled with demonstrators protesting the death of Redleaning Congolese politician Patrice Lumumba. "Who is this Lumumba?" he asked the people around him. Nobody knew. "Where is the Congo?" Nobody knew that either. "Why are you here?" The answer: "I was paid ten cruzeiros."

Sometimes a series of demonstrations will be conducted by the organizers before the scene is set for actual concerted mob action, or enough strength of numbers and confidence is developed to touch things off.

A classic example of a well-organized creation of a mob deserves study. In this case, prior to the riot, a number of rallys were held on the campuses of universities and colleges located in the metropolitan area. Feeling was built up against the congressional committee which was to conduct hearings in that area at a future date.

In order to assure that an adequate crowd would be present at the time of the hearing, pamphlets and handbills were circulated on all the campuses requesting the appearance of those who wished to protest against the committee. In addition, a systematic telephone recruiting campaign was launched. An individual would contact those on the list given him, would notify them to join the protestors, would find out whether or not they had transportation, and if so, if it would be possible for them to take others. If they did not have transportation, free transportation would be supplied. Likewise, baby sitting services were offered. The person contacted was asked in turn to contact as many persons as he possibly could and interest them in participating. Needless to say, in any such campaign the fact that a professor or student teacher would be present or would personally take part in the demonstrations was in and of itself persuasive and assured the turnout of a number of students interested in impressing that professor. The method worked. The mob nucleus appeared at the given time and place and were quickly whipped into a riotous mob.

AGITATE THE CROWD

Once the mob nucleus has been assembled, it must be emotionally built up to fever pitch. This is done by means of planned demonstrations designed to heighten emotions and cause incidents, with banners, signs, hand-outs, music, chants.

The use of music, chants, drums and clapping must be stressed. These motor impulses diffuse themselves with great facility, for they give rise to emotions which spread more rapidly than ideas or opinions.

However, the most effective method will be a forceful harangue of a fiery speaker, who pursues the following pattern:

1. Whips emotional tension to a peak of ferocity.
2. Suggests a course of action.
3. Justifies the suggested action.

He is able to raise the heat of passion in members of the crowd. He says with eloquence, power and enthusiasm that which the crowd about him dimly and vaguely feels. He is the voice of the crowd, and his utterance is really theirs. He in fact borrows his thunder from them and gives back to them what he himself received from them.

TRIGGERING THE MOB

When tension has been built up, when the frustration has existed long enough, and when rumor has done its damaging work, the conditions are ripe to start the riot. All that is needed is a spark to ignite the conflagration. It is essential to choose the proper moments and the appropriate issue to ignite the available sparks into a roaring flame of civil disorder.

The following are incidents which may incite the mob to riot:

1. Baiting of police, by verbal or physical abuse, into using excessive force on the theory that a martyr and violence will excite the mob to greater violence.
2. Violent outbursts against an investigating committee, while being interrogated by the committee.
3. A person conducting himself in a discourteous and offensive manner, so as to necessitate his removal in a way that receives the sympathy of the mob and incites its anger against the police for removing the malefactor.
4. The successful commission of an act of violence which convinces the mob of the weakness of the police and encourages further outbursts.
5. The appearance of a hated individual or a member of a hate class will often trigger a mob into violent action.
6. Attacks on small groups and vehicles. Many times a mob is incited to violence by a directed action against some small, specific group of individuals or their property. In this manner hatred can be aroused that may result in beatings, killings or burning. Racial minorities are often the object of such an attack.

ORGANIZATION

When a mob is organized by professional agitators, they will have established a chain of command to maintain and direct it. That organization will usually consist of the following:

External Command

This is composed of demonstration commanders well removed from the activity, stationed where the entire "battlefield" can be observed. In a moving demonstration, it remains apart from the mass. It consists of the professional agitators who are experienced in participating in and fomenting disturbances. They are not swept away by the mob spirit, rather they retain complete control of their faculties. Their actions are deliberate and calculated, all directed toward the realization of a fixed goal.

Internal Command

This is a cadre of professional agitators within the mass. They are responsible for directing the demonstration, under the external command's orders. These mob leaders are of great importance in inciting a crowd to mob action. Mob action depends to a great extent on their ability to bring the emotions of individuals to a peak of intensity and subsequent release. Mobs naturally tend to follow the leader's suggested courses of action; however, justification for a course of action may be necessary before a mob can be incited to violence. Once they have set the wheels in motion, whipped up the frenzy, they stand back and let the younger, more impulsive, persons do the actual fighting, for they are too valuable to be sacrificed, thus great importance is attached to protecting the leaders of this group. The internal commander, always closely guarded, often posts himself near a particularly conspicuous banner so that scouts and messengers can find him at all times.

Bravadoes

This group acts as a loose bodyguard surrounding the internal command, protecting the leader from police, and screening his escape if necessary. A line of these guards flank processions and protect banner carriers as well.

Messengers

They stay close to leaders, for whom they carry orders between internal and external commands.

Shock Guards

These individuals accompany mobs but march along the sidewalk where they are screened by spectators. They dash into the mainstream of mob action only as reinforcements. Their sudden and violent descent on the battle is designed to provide sufficient diversion to enable an orderly retreat of the main body of professional agitators who, upon signal from the external command, melt quickly into the ranks of spectators, leaving the milling bystanders and unwitting excitement seekers to the police.

Banner Carriers

The slogans used by this group and the cheering section are adapted to suit the prevailing mood. In such demonstrations key agitators will often be found close to certain conspicuous banners. In this way the command knows their location at all times and can dispatch messengers to them with instructions for stepping up the tempo, shifting slogans, or inciting violence.

Cheering Section

Specially briefed demonstrators are carefully rehearsed on the slogans they are to chant, and the order in which the cries are to be raised.

Police Baiters

Specially trained women scream hysterically, faint at policemen's feet or claw at their faces. Other pawns are instructed to roll marbles under the hoofs of policemen's horses, attack them with razor blades on the end of poles, or jab them with pins, causing them to rear and charge through the crowd and thus provide photographers with "proof" of "police brutality."

Chapter 4

THE MOB'S TACTICS AND VIOLENCE

TACTICS

THE TACTICS employed by the mob will indicate the caliber of its leaders. They will vary from maneuvers to embarrass the police to the application of the methods of guerrilla warfare.

Embarrass the Police

The mob leaders will try to embarrass the police and gain the sympathy of the public. To achieve this, mob leaders may place women and children or wounded war veterans in the front rank nearest the police to play on the sympathy of police and to discourage the commander from using force to disperse the mob. The rioters may carry American flags and sing the national anthem in order to discredit the police who are arrayed against them.

Weaken Police Line

The agitator will do everything possible to weaken the police line. One of the basic methods employed against police is the "baiting tactic." Realizing that any individual action on the part of a police officer dissipates the police force, the professional leader concentrates on police officers as individuals. The purpose of this tactic is to "bait" the officer into leaving the formation, to entice him into premature action or individual encounters so as to weaken the police unit and the respect of the mob for its discipline and efficiency. The purpose may be more sinister, that is, the officer is enticed up a side street, alley, or into the midst of the mass, where he is overcome by force, and often killed.

The well-organized and well-led mob may appear to disperse so as to cause the police to break or be drawn out of formation or to actually withdraw from the scene. Once that has been accomplished, the mob reforms and proceeds towards its objective.

[40]

The resourceful mob leader will utilize various diversionary tactics, such as disorders, destroying property, setting fire, feinting an attack on some other objective, in order to divert the attention of the police and, if possible, to divide or weaken the police force blocking the path to the actual objective.

The following constitutes some of the tactics that have been employed by the professional agitators or leaders to diminish police effectiveness:

1. Numerous false alarms directed to the fire department, causing the premature or incorrect deployment of fire fighting equipment and resources.

2. False calls of "officers in trouble," resulting in the deployment of police manpower to a certain area. This tactic can be used to divert police resources, or to cause police to converge on a certain area and attract a larger crowd for the agitator to incite.

3. Interfering with police officers in their line of duty, forcing them to take action against the agitator or at least turning them from their primary purpose. This tactic is invariably followed by cries of "police brutality" directed at the onlookers by the perpetrators.

4. Reliance on the emotional appeal to the mass, such as "Power Structure," "Police Brutality," "Black Nationalism."

5. Blocking police switch boards by calling and leaving the line open, or a flooding of the police switch boards with petty calls and excessive petty conversation.

6. Cases of the leader on the surface cooperating with the police, but actually he is not working for the police, but obtaining information or police plans and activity for the true leadership. This tactic may also be employed as a means of removing a key police commander from the scene by the leader requesting they accompany him to a certain location, such as city hall.

7. Use of walkie-talkies on citizen bands to control operations and maintain communication between leaders. Where police do not have a separate tactical net, this is used to confuse and jam police radio communications. Police should have a citizen' band monitor, but must be alert to detect information being fed to the police to detract them from the main effort.

Disrupt Police Supply Lines

Many times to damage tires large tacks are scattered in the streets along routes police vehicles will use to approach the mob. On occasion trucks, buses, and similar vehicles have been stalled, or accidents created that will block off streets and prevent police elements from entering areas or leaving their headquarters.

Disrupt Communications

Cutting off electric power and telephone facilities is one of the first moves to be expected in support of any organized mob action. The intentional jamming or overloading of telephone and telegraph communications to police and fire departments can also be expected. This is particularly effective in areas where such facilities are limited and there is a lack of radio communication. A number of individuals are assigned to place continuous calls to the police switchboard, reporting false incidents, fictitious fire alarms, bomb scares, and making groundless complaints. Wire tapping of police lines, faking police orders and communications, and other "decoy" type instructions are interjected into the communication channels whenever possible.

Looting

It is a standard tactic to organize or to encourage looting. In this manner, the uneducated, non-dedicated mob elements will be attracted. Promises of easily acquired wealth, either in the form of material goods or money, is always a sure way to attract mob members.

Liquor stores, hardware stores, banks, gun stores, jewelry stores and food stores are all prime targets. In conjunction with the general looting by the uninitiated, the professions will concentrate on police stations, newspaper offices, telephone, radio and television stations, government buildings and banks.

Outflank and Envelop

The basic tactic of such a mob is to outflank and envelop the police units, destroying their maneuverability and effectiveness.

Guerrilla Tactics

During the recent past, police have been confronted with a new mob technique. This is the "guerrilla" or "hit-and-run" mob. The conventional large mass of individuals confronting police in a rather confined, or defined, area is not encountered. Instead, roving bands hit and run, the classic military tactic employed to counter a superior military force. It thrives on deception, confusion, and the "divide and conquer" theory. It is not a happenstance occurrence; it is a carefully planned tactical maneuver. There is a very definite leadership, and a most devious and systematic organization. Quite simply stated, it is a new tactic adapted to counter the effective measures that have been employed by police and military forces to subdue the conventional mob techniques.

Like the conventional mob, the guerrilla mob has both external and internal command. The external command structure consists of the trained, professional agitators and planners. The internal command consists of the dedicated and violent element, normally youthful dissidents, gang leaders, and a criminal-prone element. These are the leaders of the "insurgents," a well-trained group of professionals. Their job includes inciting the crowd through emotional appeals and statements (such as starting the "police brutality" theme at the scene of a police arrest where a susceptive crowd has gathered). They will initiate the breaking of windows or starting of fires to incite the crowd to violence, and are the vanguard of this action if the destruction of property and looting is their goal. If the destruction of defense industry is the goal, these are the groups that would be assigned the mission by the external command.

After the incident has been initiated, selected members of this group will remain with the mass to direct their activities, consisting primarily of actions requiring the diversion of police or military manpower to their activities, thus creating a smoke screen for the insurgents who move on with their mission. The majority of this mass are probably unaware of their role in the overall plan. The professional "insurgent agitator" relies on basic mob psychology to accomplish his objective. The level of mob frenzy in various individuals participating in the rioting or looting is reinforced and augmented by seeing others who are equally excited and also rioting or looting. In this type of mob action, there are no banner carriers or cheering sections, shock guards are replaced with strategically placed snipers, and total reliance is placed upon total participation within the area following the theory of "In Rome do as the Romans do."

TYPES OF VIOLENCE

The activity engaged in by members of mobs are limited only by their ingenuity, the training of their leaders, the weapons, supplies, equipment and materials available to them. The degree of violence will depend upon a number of factors, such as composition of a mob, number of people involved, location, cause of the disturbance, weapons, climatic conditions, degree of skill and training of the mob leaders. As a matter of policy, the communists do not deplore bloodshed and violence. The concept is that martyrs and violence will excite the mob to even greater violence.

When the mob violence "gets into high gear" the objects against which the violence is directed become more generalized. Whereas the violence may originally have been directed solely against members of another race, against management, or against school authorities, to name a few, the emotionally driven, nonlogical destruction may now spread to include other persons or property which, no matter how remotely, represent to the mob members symbols of the conditions producing the initial frustration. They may see the policeman or other authorities as symbols for their hatred. The statehouse, police station, churches, grocery stores, pawn shops, liquor stores, and all sorts of establishments become "fair game" once the violence gets out of control. No rules apply; there is no fair play. The behavior is governed by mass hysteria, hatred and impulse. Any attempt at remonstrance or control is met with immediate retaliation.

Violence takes many forms, both verbal and physical. The state of emotion and the violence of the mob wlil depend upon a number of factors to include the composition of the mob, the number of persons involved, the cause of the disturbance, and the location of the disturbance. Some of the types of violence that may be encountered include the following.

Verbal Abuse

Police should anticipate verbal abuse in the form of obscene remarks, taunts, ridicule and jeers when encountering a mob. Sound trucks or hand-powered megaphones may be used not only to direct the mob, but also to heap abuse on the police units in an attempt to demoralize them. Confidence in their leaders and a sense of responsibility and discipline are vitally important to police officers in carrying out their orders in the face of verbal abuse.

Written Abuse

Printed material, posters, signs painted on walls and streets, leaflets and handbills, which attack the police may be used. Police should forbid the use of signs and posters mounted on wooden (or metal) sticks in demonstrations that are questionable in nature or purpose, as these sticks may be used as weapons against police in case violence erupts.

Noise

Noise is always to be expected. Shouting, chanting, singing and every imaginable means of making noise may be used. In addition to increasing the level of excitement and aggressiveness of the members of the mob, it tends to fatigue and demoralize the police as well as interfering with police command and control. Police must be prepared to control their forces when voice commands are ineffective, such as use of megaphones or a system of visual signals.

Attacks on Individual Policemen

Groups of rioters can be expected to give vent to their emotions upon individual or small groups of police officers. One method employed by the rioter is to spit upon the individual officer, many times directly into the officer's face. This is often a follow-up to an unsuccessful attempt to "break down" an officer with excessive verbal abuse. Other violence may include striking at the officer with fists, sticks, crow-bars, brass knuckles, chains, bottles, knotted rope. Attempts may also be made to disarm the officer of his riot baton, grab-

bing at his tie, badge or Sam Brown leather gear. Many departments
have directed that officers performing riot control duty remove the
leather cross-strap of the Sam Brown, ties and badges. This type of
violence by the rioter is directly related to the mob's baiting tactic.

Attacks on Police and Related Equipment

Vehicles may be overturned, windows broken, tires slashed with
knives or punctured with ice picks. Vehicles have been set on fire,
both by throwing Molotov cocktails at the vehicle, either moving or
parked, or by a deliberate action in conjunction with overturning
the vehicle. Logistics or command vehicles are often the object of
such action. The same type of violence may be directed against fire
equipment and other public utility vehicles. Fire hoses may be cut
or punctured with a knife or ice pick. Equipment should not be left
unattended; if the equipment is necessary to the operation, it must be
protected.

Thrown Objects

Almost anything may be thrown by the mob. It will include such
items as filth and trash or may be missiles or improvised bombs.
Some of the types of violence in this category encountered by police
include the following:

1. Throwing rotten fruits and vegetables.
2. Trash contents from garbage disposal units, such as empty
   cans, food refuse, bags of filth.
3. Empty bottles (not Molotov cocktails).
4. Rocks and bricks. These may be thrown by hand or propelled
   by various devices, such as slingshots. They may be thrown
   from within the mob or from various vantage points, such as
   roof tops. Within a tension area, rocks and bricks have been
   prepositioned on roof tops and in the rear of various residences.
   Police should be alert to detect such stocks; it is a good source
   of intelligence of impending trouble, and detection will permit the removal of these "weapons." In one department,
   police periodically survey probable trouble areas by helicopter,
   looking for stockpiles of bricks or similar missiles on roof tops.

5. Molotov cocktails, thrown at the individual or at the various types of equipment, such as police and emergency vehicles.
6. Acid, thrown in the face or on the clothing of the police officer. Many departments use the riot helmet with the protective face shield, which will protect the officer from thrown acid and other missiles. Wearing the gas mask also provides facial protection.
7. Scaling glass, which are pieces of plate glass that are "scaled" at police by individuals hiding behind buildings or in side streets. This is particularly effective against the lower extremities of the body. Boots and shin guards provide adequate protection for the individual.

Rolling Vehicles or Objects

When police are located at a lower level of an incline or slope, dangerous objects can be rolled toward the police force. Carts, barrels, large rocks, garbage cans, logs, liquids, vehicles and trolley cars are some of the objects that may be employed. On level ground, vehicles can be driven under their own power at high speed against the police or to overrun a barricade. The driver of the vehicle may remain in the vehicle and direct its forward movement, or he may jump out before the vehicle reaches the target. Where possible, such as near a stock yard, animals may be stampeded toward the police. A police counter-measure would be to use vehicles, preferably heavy trucks, in their formations to protect against this form of violence.

Destruction of Property and Looting

In addition to overturning, damaging and setting fire to police and related vehicles, similar violence may be directed to private vehicles, buses and street cars. Private residences and businesses will have windows broken and often burned. Business establishments will be looted of merchandise. Experience has shown that an initial target will be liquor stores, both for the consumption of merchandise, which will further incite the mob once consumed, and to use the empty bottles for the making of Molotov cocktails. Fire hydrants may be knocked over or tops broken off, causing the water to eject, adding to the confusion as well as rendering them useless. Lines may be broken, poles knocked down across the street to impede police progress, and power stations destroyed or damaged to deny electric power. Telephone lines may be cut throughout the area to deny a means of communication to the police and nonparticipants in the area.

Demolitions and Explosives

Rioters may employ natural gas, dynamite, or other explosives to create damage, demolish buildings, or block movement routes. An explosion can be timed to occur as police elements are in their most vulnerable position. Explosives may be employed in conjunction with the rolling objects type of violence, such as directing a burning vehicle, with explosives inside, toward the police force. Once stopped, and while police are attempting to extinguish the fire, the explosion will occur. Another method employed is to flood an area with a volatile solution, such as gas from a normal service station gas pump. When the police reach the area, the gasoline is ignited. Police must anticipate the employment of demolitions in numerous places. Good police intelligence, careful planning, and constant vigilance are required to prevent or cope successfully with these situations.

Weapons and Firearms

Weapons fire against police may take the form of selective sniping or massed fire. Weapons will include hand weapons and rifles, both homemade, such as the zip gun, and the commercial or military surplus variety. It may well include automatic weapons, or even the cannon-type weapon. In the recent past a weapon of this nature was used in a robbery; do not underestimate the imagination and resources of the professional riot leadership. Regrettably, there is a numerous variety of weapons available to the public, both as souvenirs and "collectors items." These weapons can be, and have been, employed by rioters. Mob leaders can employ weapons-fire against police elements to inspire more daring and violent action by rioters or cause police to employ more severe measures against the mob. The latter action would tend to foster antagonism toward the police force.

Just as the law enforcement command is concerned with the mob leadership, the mob leader is equally concerned with the police leadership. Sniper fire can be effectively employed to eliminate this leadership, as the commander can be easily identified by his white shirt or braid on his uniform or cap. Consideration should be given to dressing the police commanders in identical uniforms, with only the insignia of rank on the shoulder or arms to identify his command position. Snipers have also been effectively employed against officers manning road blocks or barricades, especially during the hours of darkness. The "white helmet" stands out in the dark, especially when silhouetted against a background of burning buildings or in the headlights of an approaching vehicle. The sniper, once encountered, *must* be eliminated. If he can be dislodged with a gas projectile, this should be employed. However, if this is not practical or effective, a counter-sniper marksman should be employed.

Other weapons available to the rioter include commercial guns or "pins" that emit tear gas, water pistols loaded with a liquid acid solution, and toy guns designed to shoot a cork or plastic ball, loaded instead with a harmful projectile designed to inflict bodily harm at close range. The relatively simple bow and arrow may be encountered, ranging from the dime store variety with the rubber suction tip removed and a lead head substituted, to the sporting variety, professionally constructed arrows.

Violence will take many forms, and will be limited only by the ingenuity of the mob leadership and emotional state of the group. The longer a riotous situation exists, the more disastrous the violence will become. One successful act of violence invariably leads to attempting a more serious act of violence. Riot, and mob violence, is like a cancer—the longer it is permitted to survive, the more serious and disastrous it becomes—and the further it spreads. When prevention fails, rapid, effective and positive control measures by police are the only successful anecdote.

Chapter 5

SIGNS OF TENSION

SPOTTING AND REPORTING TENSION

Before getting to the symptoms, however, we should note that they will be displayed more plainly in the behavior of certain kinds of people. If an officer wants to learn about the criminal activities of someone, say a jewel thief, he does not seek the information from schoolteachers or the clergy. Similarly, one does not look for the symptoms of a riot by observing the behavior of persons attending the weekly meeting of service clubs. The pulse of social circulation, like the heartbeat, must be taken at the pressure points. In this case, it is the temper of the most rabid of our people we must observe and give constant analytical attention. What they think and what they do with their time will probably be more important as a barometer than the feelings and actions of more stable individuals. Also, we must be constantly alert to the activities and exhortations of the demagogues, or self-important "loudmouths," and the like.

Each police officer should be required to report all incidents coming to his attention which involve minority group relations. There should be made on each incident a written report which should be forwarded to the designated officer of the department. Such a record should include what took place, what appeared to have caused the incident, where it occurred, who the parties were to the dispute and whether others became involved, and any other details of pertinent interest. This information should then be carefully examined by a person delegated by departmental administration.

A spot map can be of great value in indicating the locations and kinds of incidents that occur, and whether they are verbal, involved blows, or lethal weapons. They can also indicate to the police administrator the necessity for the assignment of additional manpower to areas where tension is great.

Any information received by the delegated person within the department which could conceivably be of interest or value to other agencies should be forwarded to them. The police department should also encourage other agencies to forward to the police reports on incidents coming to their attention.

Such strategically located persons as school teachers, community workers, ministers, transportation employees, housing directors and social workers can usually be persuaded to work in conjunction with officials from the police department to gather comprehensive and important information as to tension and possible developments.

SYMPTOMS

The law enforcement officer who understands the basis of human behavior leading to destructive riots will be in the fortunate position of knowing what to expect. He can recognize the signs of the impending explosion and apply effective measures to counteract it.

There are eight areas in which to look especially for the symptoms of the riot virus:

1. Opinions and sentiments.
2. Rumors—the verbal "milling process."
3. Racial frictions.
4. Demagogic groups.
5. Juvenile delinquence.
6. Police relations.
7. Economic and social conditions.

Some examples and pointers will indicate more clearly the kinds of symptoms that appear in these areas.

OPINIONS AND SENTIMENTS

Opinions are what we say we think about things, events, persons, or whatever. But sentiments are our deep and emotional likes, dislikes and drives to action. We can easily report our opinions, but our sentiments lie largely in subconscious areas of our minds. It is difficult for us to distinguish our own sentiments. It is consequently much more difficult to distinguish the sentiments of other individuals and other groups.

Opinion is always a "surface reaction" to ideas and issues of a public sort that are being discussed. In other words, it is what a person willingly tells a relatively unknown interviewer. Opinion is thus conscious, verbal, sometimes falsified to conform to "the right thing to say," inconstant, not too difficult to change within the limits set by people's sentiments, and rather easily measured.

Sentiment, on the other hand, is more emotional, less organized, and more stable. In other words, it is what we really feel towards another person, group, idea, or issue. People thus do not like to reveal their sentiments and, to a marked extent, do not actually put them into words or even understand the nature of these main springs of their thought and action.

The officer must listen to the opinions expressed by the people in order to gauge their sentiments. An expressed opinion might be an accurate reflection of a person's true feelings or it might be shaded somewhat by the person's ideas of what he thinks he really should say. In other words, people are often unwilling to reveal their true feelings or sentiments.

Nevertheless, when people, particularly the more rabid ones, begin to express themselves with less restraint, more vociferously, and with increasing bitterness, law enforcement officers should take note, for this is one of the danger signs. Telltale signs can often be found in the language used. Deprecating catchwords and phrases become more frequent and more derogatory. A noticeable testiness develops in the use of such terms which previously may have been employed in a somewhat jocular tone.

The minority or community press reactions to tension situations often bring to light a problem before it is otherwise evident. The office must be alert to and read all available publications, newspapers, tracts, pamphlets, for they will frequently give indication of the mounting tension. The headlines become more strident. The language used becomes more and more exaggerated. Law enforcement executives should arrange to get copies of such publications representing all points of view and should objectively study them for signs of significance.

Public demonstrations, meetings, rallies, marches, and even scribblings on sidewalks, billboards and the like should be watched carefully by law enforcement authorities. Such affairs not only indicate the saliency of the attitudes of the participants, but also the intensity and direction of those attitudes. What is done and said on such occasions is of great significance and may provide important leads to law enforcement in preventing open hostility. The law enforcement executive, in keeping his finger on the pulse of things, should arrange to be advised of activities of this type well in advance so that appropriate safeguards may be devised.

Law enforcement must know what organizations are active and what their programs are. Any programs or proposed action must receive careful study in terms of their effect on the community and in terms of possible retaliation by opposing groups.

RUMORS—THE VERBAL MILLING PROCESS

As people "mill around" in their ordinary day-to-day lives, rumors are common enough, rumors about all sorts of things. These rumors are largely random and seldom important beyond the individuals involved. But as racial tensions mount, the rumors that circulate take on a nastier and more purposive character. They cease being merely idle gossip with little or no basis in fact and become more biting and direct in their dynamic contributions to the more and more rapidly turning whirlpool of mob hysteria.

Rumors symptomatic of race riots generally go through three chief stages:

1. They begin with tales of alleged insults and discriminations, frequently traceable to subversive groups.
2. Then come stories of imminent violence, of arming by the other race, of the need to protect one's home and loved ones, of invasion from another city.
3. Finally one hears the crisis rumors, the inflammatory accounts of sex assaults, beatings and murders.

These rumor symptoms circulate with increasing rapidity in barber shops, beauty parlors, bars, church socials, in lobbies, business gatherings, union meetings and family conclaves, in face-to-face talks, telephone conversations, and even in rare instances over the radio and in the newspapers. The significant fact is that on the eve of race riots, rumors frequently bear the earmarks of artificial creation and abnormally rapid dissemination.

RACIAL FRICTIONS

Our sentiments toward others frequently contain both affection and hate, tolerance and detestation. When conditions are favorable, we treat a given person decently or even fondly. At other times, upon relatively slight provocation, blind fury may flare up between us. The police must watch carefully for evidences of a shift in race opinions caused by a shift in the underlying two-sided sentiments. As in personal relations, that shift may occur with what looks like relatively slight provocation, and such shifts from reasonable tolerance to blind riotous hate may begin to sweep our community. A sudden upsurge in open statements against the other race is a definite symptom of this emotional shift, a symptom that immediately precedes a riot. Also, the police must be especially alert to an increase in minor incidents of conflict, particularly by youths. They must watch for any unusual influx of outsiders with a subsequent buildup of bristling and jostling.

Here again, with respect to the symptoms of an approaching riot, the incidents are not as significant in themselves as is the inescapable fact that they begin to increase in (1) frequency; (2) boldness, and (3) violence.

DEMAGOGIC GROUPS

Groups of emotional anti-Negroes and of emotional anti-whites flourish and die out in many American communities. Often these organizations may be found to be operating under a code of high principles which are interpreted and twisted by some elements to serve their own personal interests. They actually breed prejudice and generate an emotion climate of intolerance and hysteria, of organizational sanction for aggressive activities.

In addition to breeding and sanctioning an atmosphere of intolerance, such groups also serve as the rumor-mills and propaganda-mills out of which the intolerant get their ready-made prejudices. Such organizations also provides leaders and rank-and-filers to jump into any riot situation the instant the "break" against law and order has occurred, for they will attempt to seize upon a race riot as an opportunity to demonstrate their power.

In searching for symptoms, we must know as much about such anti-democratic organizations as we can. Fortunately, long before they become effective, demagogues show themselves in public and thus expose themselves to ridicule, analysis, counterpropaganda and perhaps elimination. They cannot build their organizational power long in secret. They are ham actors who need notoriety. They are highly insecure people who have to convince themselves of their own importance through swaggering before a public. As a riot condition approaches, they move out more boldly into the open because they think they see greater acceptance for their views. Thus the police must watch for a sign that shows any progressive tendency of demagogic groups and known agitators to operate more openly and boldly; to propagandize against a group; to presume the existence of a greater degree of social acceptance for their views. He must also be alert to the appearance of threatening or derogatory signs, leaflets, pamphlets and "hate" literature in commercial and public places.

JUVENILE DELINQUENCY

The war aggravated the general trend toward family disorganization in our cities that has been developing in an alarming manner for many years. This is revealed in part by the high tide in juvenile delinquency. When police reports of arrests of minors begin to climb, when social workers discover more and more children left alone while parents work or play, an explosion is in the making.

Delinquency and crime reports include serious frictions between members of different racial, religious and cultural groups, but they also yield other valuable types of information. They tell especially about the character of current gang activities.

Sometimes there will be an increase in the number of incidents of violence or threats of violence. One incident or two in unrelated cases is not significant, but when violence breaks out in various parts of the city simultaneously or with regularity, it should be regarded as a strong indication of impending trouble of a more serious nature. As evidence of friction the reports on gang incidents may show an increase in frequency, boldness, and violence beyond seasonal expectations. Watch out for bloodshed and smashed store fronts, they may come next.

POLICE RELATIONS

Be alert to an increasing mistrust or resentment of the police.

This mistrust may be noted as a reluctance on the part of certain people to cooperate in furnishing information or discussing the situation. It will also show up in the press as increasingly biased or even demonstrably false accounts of police unfairness and brutality. Watch for more and wilder rumors of police unfairness and brutality and take effective action to scotch these rumors.

Another sign of significance is more frequent and bolder resistance to police. Mistrust and resistance may show up as an increase in nasty remarks to officers, as a sullenness or perhaps even refusal to obey police orders, an increase in the number of charges and complaints of alleged police brutality, or as outright physical resistance and attack—increase in antisocial youth and minority group activity involving malicious mischief and gang or group conflict, particularly if the juveniles of minority groups are involved.

ECONOMICAL AND SOCIAL CONDITIONS

The officer must be aware of social and economic conditions in his community. Congestion in housing and transportation facilities wears the nerves of everyone to the "jumpy" point. It can lay the groundwork for violence. Watch also labor conditions, particularly the unemployment situation, for competition for jobs will fan ill will. Economic frustration and dissatisfaction with status, coupled with a gradually changing social organization, have resulted in increasing irritation.

Chapter 6

RUMORS

INTRODUCTION

SPECIAL ATTENTION must be given to rumors, for they are often the forewarning of racial disturbance. In times of critical tension, they may contribute, indeed often cause, serious incidents. They can bring people to the scene of a relatively minor incident where they often proceed to act on rumor rather than in the light of the facts of the situation.

The relationship that exists between rumors and crowd and mob action is self-evident. Rumors may be likened to an electric charge spreading throughout the community and touching the emotional life of the people. They serve as a stimulant to motivate many innocent people for mob action. Without the inflammatory quality of rumors, the public seldom becomes aroused to the point where a race riot can occur.

DEFINITION

What is a rumor? A *rumor,* the dictionary tells us, is "a story or report in general circulation without any known authority for its truth." Traveling rapidly, it is supposed to convey information, but actually it is very often based on inaccurate information, on half-truth, or on no truth at all. More briefly, rumors are stories that masquerade as truth.

TYPES OF RUMORS

Rumors may be classified according to the human emotions that underlie them. From that standpoint, most rumors fall into one or more of three classes—fear rumors, hope or wish rumors, and hate rumors.

Fear Rumors

A fear (or bogey) rumor is one that arises from the widespread

[57]

fear that the thing rumored may be true. It is easy for listeners to accept rumors that seemed to give substance to their fears.

Hope or Wish Rumors

The hope or wish rumor is the reverse of the fear rumor. We tend to believe a story, even though it is unconfirmed, if we want to believe it, and if we want it to be true.

Hate Rumors

The most vicious and dangerous of all rumors, and one of the most widespread types, is the hate rumor. Since this type of rumor seeks to set one group against the other, and to destroy the basic unity of the American people, it is sometimes called the "wedge driver."

WHY DO WE HAVE RUMORS

Psychologists tell us that most of us, at certain times, unconsciously enjoy spreading rumors. There are many reasons for this, but these four stand out: (1) rumors seem to supply answers to important questions that need to be answered; (2) they furnish excuses for actions; (3) they relieve pent-up emotions; (4) they make the teller feel important.

THE DANGERS OF RUMORS

A question that naturally comes to mind is "Just how much harm do rumors do?" The best way to start answering that question is to ask yourself, "When I pass along a rumor, am I harmed?" The answer is "Yes, you are." Most of us rise or fall on the basis of our reputations—on what other people think of us. If people can depend on us and believe what we say, our reputations, and hence our chances of getting ahead in life, definitely increase. But if they find us habitually a "fall guy" for rumors, they can't depend on what we say and as a result our reputation suffers. We may enjoy being first with the "news," but we will be hurting ourselves if our story proves false.

In addition, rumor can hurt the person about whom it is circulated. Circulating a rumor that a certain person is a Communist or a foreign agent, a hard drinker, a wife beater, or a pervert, merely on the basis of hearsay and without conclusive evidence, may do that person and his family irreparable harm. It may lead to the loss of his job and his standing in his community. Many people who have had their reputations ruined by unfounded rumors have been driven to suicide.

RUMORS IN RACE RIOTS

We may state as a dependable law that no riot or lynching ever occurs without the aid of rumor. As racial tension mounts, the rumors that circulate take on a nastier and more purposive character. They cease to be merely idle gossip and become more biting and direct in their dynamic contributions to the more and more rapidly turning whirlpool of group hysteria. Rumor is found to enter into the pattern of violence at one or all of four stages.

1. The gradual building up of animosity preceding a violent outbreak is assisted by stories of the misdeeds of the hated out-group. One hears particularly that the minority in question is itself conspiring, plotting, saving up guns and ammunition. Also the customary run of ethnic rumors takes a spurt, thus reflecting the mounting strain. One of the best barometers of tension is the collection and analysis of ethnic rumors in a community.

2. After preliminary rumors have done their work, new rumors may serve as a call to rioting or lynching parties. They act like a bugle to assemble the forces. "Something is going to happen tonight by the river." "They'll catch that nigger tonight and whale the life out of him." If alert to the situation the police may use these "marshalling rumors" to forestall violence.

3. Not infrequently a rumor is the spark that ignites the powder keg. Some inflammatory story flies down the street, becoming sharpened and distorted at each telling. The Harlem riot was spread by means of an exaggerated story to the effect that a white policeman had shot a Negro in the back.

One such situation occurred in Detroit, Michigan in 1943 when the rumor was widely circulated among the white populace that a Negro had raped a white woman on a bridge leading to a recreational area on Belle Isle. Simultaneously, among the Negroes it was rumored that the whites had killed a colored woman and her baby on the Isle. While these stories had absolutely no basis in fact, their effect in mobilizing the passions of the people was tremendous. The fact that they were untrue did not make them any less provocative. Under the influence of the inflammatory rumor the trouble spread quickly.

More recently in both Philadelphia and Los Angeles wild rumors were circulated that the police had beaten and killed a pregnant colored woman. During the heat of the riot, rumors sustain the excitement. Particularly puzzling are the stories that appear based on hallucination.

CONTROL OF RUMORS

What an Individual Can Do

How can an individual check up on rumors and stop the spread of dangerous rumors? There are no sure answers, for rumors are as complicated as the human mind. But following are some suggestions that will help keep you rumor-wise.

Get the Facts

Get the facts. This is basic. Knowledge is the best way to offset rumor. If someone tells you something about which you have the facts, and the facts are at odds with his story, you can set him straight and squelch the rumor.

Getting the facts means getting all the facts. It means hearing more than a few words of a newscast and reading more than the headlines of a newspaper's account. Headlines are written to catch the eye and make you read what follows, but they are rarely able to give a complete story in themselves.

Getting the facts also means going to the source of facts, whenever possible. Moreover, getting the facts sometimes means waiting until the facts are announced by the proper authority.

Keep a skeptical attitude. Be "from Missouri" on the tall tales you hear. Ask yourself, "Does that sound true?" "Is it likely, in the light of other known facts?" Asking a few questions of the story-teller may help. If you can make the rumormonger question his own story, he may cooperate with you in trying to find out the facts.

Find out who brought the news. If you hear something that sounds as if it could be a rumor, ask the person where he heard the news and how he knows. Does he have reason to know what he is talking about? Did he hear or see the evidence himself or did the story come from a source of questionable reliability? If a startling piece of news can be traced to a well-known rumormonger, you will have good reason to doubt it.

Laugh it off. Ridicule helps kill rumor. Laugh down a foolish and dangerous rumor.

POLICE ROLE

Police experience indicates that efforts to track down the source of inflammatory rumor is seldom productive. However, officers can and should be on the lookout for rumors, for police officials must regard them as symptomatic. If rumors are plentiful, they should be reported. If they are then cleared through central police offices, they can become an effective barometer of the state of mind of the community and can indicate the likelihood of trouble in any particular area.

Each department should have a clearing house, possibly in connection with the local press, where rumors can be checked, verified, or exposed. It collects all the rumors it can get from interested citizens, from persons who monger their rumors to the clinic, and from men like bartenders who hear lots of idle talk. Then it investigates them, publishes them, refutes or corrects them, and incidentally, by showing that rumors are usually false, ridicules them.

Procedure in Handling Rumors

Don't repeat a rumor. A police officer should never repeat a rumor, even to deny it, as rumor is usually so much more sensational than fact that the latter is likely to be overshadowed. If he does pass it on, the hearer will probably add to the story and say, "I have it on the highest authority," since he secured his information from a policeman.

Stop the spread of the rumor. Check the spread by questioning the person attempting to pass them on and insist upon verification and proof. Make plain to the carrier of the tale the implications of his acts. A rumor stopped at any point can be of great significance in cutting short its network-like spread.

Counteract the rumor. The most reliable antidote for poisonous rumor is fact, and the officer should be on the lookout for rumor and facts to counteract it. The police should get the facts promptly and publish them as widely as possible. Cooperative relationships previously established with the press would be helpful here, but extensive use should also be made of civic organizations, minority group organizations, and other channels of information.

The department could keep a rumor bulletin board. That is a bulletin board on which apparently false rumors are posted, with the actual facts alongside. After a while the exhibit becomes ridiculous, because the board has on it so many rumors that contradict each other, as well as having already been disproved by publication of the truth.

SECTION II
ORGANIZATION AND GENERAL PROCEDURES

Chapter 7

GOVERNOR'S RESPONSIBILITY

INTRODUCTION

THE GRAVITY OF recent disturbances has been such as to be beyond the power of local jurisdiction to control. More and more often the governors of our states have been turned to for aid, and for leadership. When this demand is made, the governor must act with courage and determination. A needless delay may mean the senseless loss of life and destruction of property. To assure that he is able to act, the laws of his state must be reviewed to determine their adequacy. Next, a manual of procedure should be prepared. It will catalog the powers of the governor in the event of a disaster of either natural or human origin. The various forces at his command, i.e., the national guard, state police, state highway patrol, sheriffs' staffs and local police, and the condition and method of pressing them into service should be spelled out. The financial liability of the state and the individuals pressed into service should be defined. The command of the various units should be established.

The first step in the plan is to inventory the resources of the state. This inventory reflects the resources in personnel, communication, transportation, ordinance of each city, county and region. The completed inventory is compiled on a region, county and city basis so that it is possible to immediately pinpoint potential assistance. Together with any such inventory should be a roster of those to contact in the case of need. It should show the name of individual to be contacted, his home and business telephone and his first and second alternate.

ADVANCE PLANNING

It is not enough for the governor to know his legal rights and responsibilities. He must have a plan to utilize those powers when called upon to do so. This requires a plan.

The purposes of the plan are as follows:

1. To provide for the coordination of the dispatch and use of state and local law enforcement and national guard personnel and equipment whenever, because of enemy action, disaster, civil disturbance, or any other cause, a local law enforcement agency requires the dispatch to it of law enforcement assistance.

2. To provide for the coordination of law enforcement planning, operations and mutual aid on a state-wide, regional, operational area county and city basis, and to relate such plans to the overall state plan for civil defense and disaster operations.

3. To provide for a system for the receipt and dissemination of information, data, and directive pertaining to the law enforcement services between local law enforcement officials and state and federal agencies.

4. To prescribe a procedure for the inventory of all law enforcement personnel, facilities and equipment in the state.

To develop the plan and supervise its enforcement the governor should have a state-wide coordinator. If the state is large, he can be assisted by regional and area coordinators.

The coordinator should act as the clearing house for information on potential problems throughout the state. He should also establish liaison with all local police and draft tentative plans to be utilized in the event of a disaster. In particular, the question of command must be resolved so that when disaster strikes the responsible individual may immediately begin to function.

In the event of an actual disaster, the coordinator should immediately establish a command post and do all that can be done to activate the plan and call in the needed aid. The governor will then be ready to immediately act and give to the state the centralized leadership it must have in instances of state or regional disasters. His strong courageous leadership will go far toward gaining command of the situation and rapidly resolving the crisis.

NATIONAL GUARD

The governor must give special consideration in any plans to calling the national guard into action. In a major riot that is out of the control of the local police, he must not hesitate to call it into immediate action. In this field his chief coordinator will be the adjutant general or his designated representative. Again detailed treatment of the subject is found elsewhere in this book and is referred to here only to underline and stress the grave responsibility that rests on the governor. He must know his duties, powers, and the forces available to him. He must have established a plan and working relations with local government. He must have an intelligent network that will keep him apprised of all developments. But most of all he must have the courage to act and the ability to lead.

Chapter 8

DISASTER AND RIOT PLANNING

INTRODUCTION

A LAW ENFORCEMENT ORGANIZATION has a serious responsibility to its community. The citizens of the community expect prompt, intelligent, and efficient discharge of these responsibilities in time of emergency. The foremost objective of responsible law enforcement personnel should be to prepare both the organization and its personnel for immediate action.

No aspect of the program is more important than planning for the action to be taken before, during and after a disturbance. Unless the plan is thoroughly detailed in advance of the disturbance and unless it is founded upon realistic considerations in terms of availability of personnel and equipment, the operation will be doomed to failure. Regular review of all plans should be mandatory, with the further requirement that a report of such review plus recommendations for adjustments to current conditions be forwarded to the chief for his review and appropriate action.

Planning must provide for the action to be taken before, during and after disturbances. Thus it will cover three general phases: (1) the planning and training phase; (2) the alert phase, and (3) the operational phase. The planning and training phase encompasses all preparations that are made prior to the agency being alerted. Included in this phase are preparation of a department alert plan and standard operating procedures, preparation of tentative plans for probable areas of disturbances, preparation of riot control devices and equipment, instructions in riot control operations, and rehearsals with equipment.

The alert phase precedes actual commitment. It may be short duration or may extend over a period of days. During this phase the department or agency is fully prepared and ready to move. Weapons, ammunition, riot control agent munitions and supplies are given a final check. Individual officers should be briefed on the situation and mission. Other agencies, departments, organizations and individuals which may become involved must be alerted and briefed. The operational phase deals with the procedure, strategy and tactics applicable during an emergency.

STANDARD OPERATING PROCEDURES

Standard operating procedures—SOP—are designed to amplify, clarify and standardize methods of operation that are considered permanent procedures within the organization. Standing operating procedures are normally divided into two categories. Administrative standing procedures include, but are not limited to, matters such as food and water, medical aid, casualty reporting, basic loads of ammunition, riot control agents, re-supply procedures, vehicle distribution and usage and certain communications instructions.

Tactical standing procedures include, but are not limited to, matters pertaining to construction, defense and displacement of roadblocks, patrols, security, designation of and instruction for selected marksmen, plans for the employment of riot control agents and designation of personnel involved in such plans.

ALERT PLAN

The alert plan is the step-by-step procedure that is used to bring the unit rapidly to a state of operational readiness. The alert plan should be designed for implementation in the event of fire, disaster, or civil disorder. The details of the plan are based upon local operating conditions and should be revised through the result of experience gained in rehearsals of mission changes. Each individual affected by the plan must know his personal responsibility and the responsibility of his unit. Prior to departure for the scene of disorder or before a practice alert terminates it is important that officers in charge make detailed yet rapid inspections of their elements. The alert plan should cover the following:

1. Authentication procedures for the alert order.
2. Required actions by individuals.
3. Required action by individual sections of the organization.
4. Procedures for issuing special equipment, supplies, and material.

5. Vehicle preparation.
6. Security.
7. Administrative details.
8. Tentative briefing schedules.

The alert plan should be thoroughly understood by each individual police officer in the department.

OPERATIONAL PLAN

Tentative plans should be prepared for each probable operational area. Each plan should indicate an assembly area and routes thereto, locations of road blocks, observation posts, location of closest telephones, communications, a tactical plan, a patrol plan, temporary quarters for billeting and feeding police, and other necessary details.

Containment, isolation and dispersal areas should be identified, as there is little or no time to select these areas after a riot has started. Alternate plans are a must. Plans should provide for dispersing through the use of any or all means available. Necessary plans, maps, overlaps and sketches should be distributed to appropriate commanders. A reserve supply should be maintained.

WRITTEN PLAN

Although an organization may have the foresight to plan for anticipated situations, the value of such planning is of little worth if planning is not reduced to written form. Personnel with intimate knowledge of such plans may be unavailable at the very time it becomes necessary to implement the program. A written plan will furnish a documentary record which can be referred to as needed to refresh the knowledge of key individuals and can be used to indoctrinate persons who become replacements. Finally, any plan, if it is to be placed into timely operation, must be readily available at all times to those individuals having the responsibility of implementing it. Each individual affected by the plan must know the details of the plan, his personal responsibility and the responsibility of his department. He should also be prepared to replace his next senior.

SURVEY OF THE AREA

In planning for the riot control for a large metropolitan area, the city should be broken down into districts or precincts. Sectionalized and detailed maps should be obtained or made for each area. Each precinct or district should survey the area under its jurisdiction and maintain current information covering the following:

1. Characteristics of the population.
2. Areas subject to conflict between groups.
3. Shopping and business areas.
4. Points most susceptible to trouble.
5. Vulnerable points.

Vulnerable points are places to which personnel must be assigned to prevent looting or damage. Locations such as the following shall be considered vulnerable:

1. Liquor, jewelry, department and large chain stores.
2. Pawnshops.
3. Armories and other places where weapons or ammunition might be available.
4. Subway and elevated stations.
5. Powerhouses.
6. Bridges and tunnels.
7. Penal institutions.
8. Water gates.
9. Fire alarm boxes.
10. Telephone and communication centers.
11. Other important places.

Based upon such information the commander should prepare maps with colors and symbols indicating the following:

1. Special zone boundaries.
2. Control points.
3. Isolation areas.
4. Mobilization point areas.
5. Parking spaces.
6. Hospitals.
7. Temporary detention buildings.
8. Station houses.
9. Division office.
10. Other important locations.
11. Shopping and business areas.
12. Vulnerable points.

Copies of these maps must be forwarded to the field commander and made a part of his work papers for use in the event of an emergency.

PROBABLE PROBLEM AREAS

Responsible police officials through the evaluation of their community and its environment can predict with reasonable accuracy those areas which might be prone to experience civil disorders. Evaluation of intelligence information will indicate trends within the population and causes of public unrest. Each area selected as a possible disorder site should be reconnoitered with attention to locations of key facilities, primary and alternate routes of access and tentative areas available for the use of police forces. Maps and aerial photographs should be secured for the areas concerned, whenever possible. A brief outline of the probable nature and location of anticipated emergencies, including determination of the probable number of disorderly elements and the possible use of weapons by the rioters should be prepared.

Chapter 9

COMMAND

INTRODUCTION

ALTHOUGH THE overall responsibility cannot be delegated to subordinates, the delegation of some authority and responsibility to subordinates is essential. The extent to which authority and discretion in the event of a disaster can be delegated is largely a matter of good organization, administration and the chief's attitude toward it. If he insists upon being the source of all ideas and upon reviewing all decisions before they are executed, he will burden himself with such a mass of detail as will create a "bottleneck," seriously retarding the handling of disturbances. To avoid this he must develop leadership which will encourage initiative in the group to cope with the problem. He must determine the extent of the abilities and limitations of the "grass roots" leaders in the area and avoid surrounding himself with men who are too lazy-minded or timid to control fear-stricken people. These men must be free thinkers and not compliant or defiant thinkers. To accomplish this, a chain of command must be established, general and special staffs must be organized. Far in advance of any difficulty the chief must assign responsibility. A chain of command must be established. That plan should specifically designate the officers who will serve in various positions. In fact the plan must establish at least two complete command structures, for a prolonged emergency cannot be commanded by one man no matter how strong or capable. Fatigue will take its toll. The order should not only provide for two completely different commands to relieve each other at stated times, the plan must designate deputies for all staff and command positions. Each deputy will act as the assistant to his immediate superior and will act for him during temporary absences and replace him in the event he is unable to perform.

[73]

WARNING—STAY ON THE JOB

One of the upsetting developments in certain recent riots was the tendency for executive personnel to leave their headquarters and proceed to the scene of the emergency operations. In most cases this has caused a leadership gap in the making of decisions at the policy level. The decisions are delegated to subordinates or are left pending until such time as the executive can be contacted. Therefore it must be stressed that command level personnel shall remain at their operational point and perform the activities assigned to them. Should it become necessary for these individuals to leave the control center, they shall insure continuity of operation by the assignment of an alternate. This alternate must have full authority to act on behalf of his superior.

CHAIN OF COMMAND

There must be no question where command rests in the face of a disorderly crowd. The chain of command must be well defined and respected. Commanders at all echelons must make adequate provision for uninterrupted perpetuation of the chain of command. The succession of command must be prescribed for all contingencies ranging from the temporary absence of the commander to the loss of the commander and staff.

DEGREES OF DISASTER

In establishing a chain of command, it must first be recognized that there are varying degrees of disaster which require varying degrees of involvement on the part of the police. Thus, some standard of classification of the severity of a disturbance must be agreed upon, then a corresponding command structure planned.

We may begin by distinguishing between incidents, occurrences that are more or less ordinary routine police situations, and disasters, incidents which are of such proportions as to be out of the ordinary. Naturally all such evaluations must take into consideration background factors that could transform a relatively low degree incident into a disaster such as the attitude and relations of groups in the community, the area of the incident, and similar factors.

Incidents and disasters have been graded from the first magnitude through the seventh magnitude. All problems handled by the police department will fall within one of these categories.

Incidents

FIRST MAGNITUDE. An incident which requires only the attention of a patrolman or a squad will be considered to be of the First Magnitude. Examples are disturbances, minor accidents, theft investigations and other routine calls.

SECOND MAGNITUDE. An incident which requires field direction by a sergeant or detective shall be considered of the Second Magnitude. Examples are two alarm fires, major accident, homicides or investigation requiring a crime scene search, or an incident where more than two squads are utilized.

THIRD MAGNITUDE. An incident which requires field direction by a lieutenant shall be considered of the Third Magnitude. Examples are three alarm fire, injury necessitating hospitalization of police personnel, or any incident requiring two or more first-line supervisors.

FOURTH MAGNITUDE. An incident which requires field direction by a captain shall be considered of the Fourth Magnitude. Examples are explosion, plane crash, four alarm fire, minor racial disturbances and all other incidents which can be handled by personnel on duty assigned to the incident with a minimum of overtime.

FIFTH MAGNITUDE DISASTER. A chief officer shall authorize a rating of this magnitude when, in his opinion, the incident or disaster is of such proportions that it meets one of the following requirements: (1) will require a majority of on-duty personnel to work overtime to handle the situation, but does not require the mustering of off-duty personnel; (2) where field supervision and coordination of functions of more than one division is necessary for an extended period of time. Examples are incidents that include special events of sufficient size to warrant the rating. Disasters include five alarm fires, or higher, plane crashes, explosions, riots and other disasters that can be handled with on-duty personnel as set out above.

SIXTH MAGNITUDE DISASTER. The ranking chief officer on duty shall authorize a disaster rating of this magnitude when, in his opinion, the disaster is of such proportions that it will require partial mobilization of off-duty personnel. Examples are major explosion, commercial plane crash, large strikes causing riots, and other incidents requiring more personnel to handle than is on duty.

SEVENTH MAGNITUDE DISASTER. The chief of police, or the acting chief of police, shall authorize this rating when, in his opinion, the disaster is of such proportions that it will require a total mobilization of police personnel. Examples are tornado, flood, racial riots, major explosion, or any incident requiring complete mobilization of the police department.

As the magnitude of the incident or disaster increases, the functions and responsibilities increase in proportion and, therefore, higher ranking supervisors are designated to command, and the delegation of authority is more diversified. A point is reached when it will be mandatory to establish a separate unit to handle the problems involved, and thereby permit the department to carry on its normal functions without too much disruption. At that point the line dividing incidents from disasters is reached. This will be when an incident of the Fifth Magnitude is reached.

COMMANDERS

Chief or Overall Commander

The chief or his designated representative commands the resources of the police department and makes appropriate decisions concerning requests for assistance. His basic responsibility is to manage the resources of the department in such fashion that the field forces at the theater of operations receive adequate support and the portions of the city that are not affected by the unusual occurrence continue to receive police services commensurate with known and anticipated problems. He will have overall command of all operations, but not direct tactical command of the field units which will reside in the field commander.

Field Commander or Police Coordinator

The field commander, or police coordinator as he is at times designated, exercises control of resources committed to the unusual occurrence.

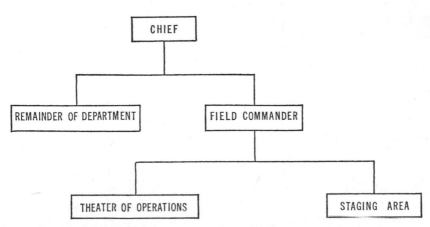

Organizational chart of top command in major disasters. The chief is the over-all commander responsible for the operation of the entire department. The police force is divided into two sections, one which conducts the regular police operation and another which concentrates on control of the disaster.

Scene Commander

The scene commander is the officer directly in command of a unit in the field. He must have the authority to take whatever action, in his judgment, is necessary at the time. The duties of the scene commander shall be assumed by the highest ranking officer where the disturbance occurs, and he will continue to so act until replaced by a superior. The scene commander is responsible for the following:

1. Coordination of scene activities.
2. Requesting additional personnel.
3. Deployed personnel.
4. Initiating proper tactics and techniques.
5. Establishing a scene command post.
6. Maintaining appropriate communications.
7. Promptly removing principals.
8. Determining circumstances for making arrests.
9. Carefully observing the legal requirements and restrictions.
10. Establishing necessary patrols and surveillance to prevent recurrence.

Any time a scene commander is replaced, the command post must be advised of the change.

Reserve Force Command

The staging area is an area set aside for the accumulation of men and material resources that will be made available for field assignment. It is under the command of the reserve force commander, or staging officer. All directives to the officers under his command are relayed through him except as his personnel may be properly attached to another commander. Reserve commander is responsible for the following:

1. Maintaining contact with the field commander to keep him advised of men and equipment available for use.
2. Organizing the units.
3. Dispatching units and equipment in accordance with orders from the commander.
4. Briefing the personnel. His briefing is based upon the information he received from the scene and includes the situation at the scene; the tactics to be used to restore the situation to normal; the formations to be used, and the point at which contact will be made with the crowd.

Squad Commanders

Close supervision by command officers is required at all times and at all locations where officers are on crowd control or riot duty. Certain men on each shift should be designated as squad leaders. Certain other men on this shift could be assigned to these leaders.

The squad leader will direct his units from the rear, where he can observe and supervise. The moment he makes the mistake of "plunging into the fray," with his men, he loses control of the action as he cannot see what is going on, and he becomes ineffective as a supervisor. Before deployment for riot duty, the second and third in command of each squad will be clearly identified so that there will be no loss of control in event of casualties.

STAFF

The staff consists of the officers who assist the commander in his exercise of command. Staff personnel may be characterized as divisions of the commander himself into specialized advisory seg-

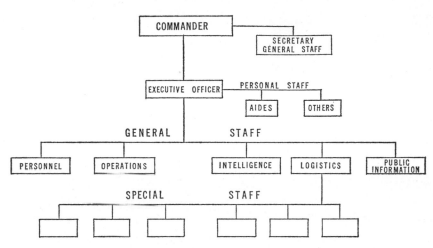

Organizational chart of the staff structure. The commander is assisted by a staff of specialists who concentrate on the various aspects of the problem. Each member of the general staff is in turn aided by his special staff.

ments. The staff is normally organized into functional sections which, together, embrace all functions of command.

Staff Functions

The staff assists the commander in his exercise of command by performing the following functions:

1. Providing information required by the commander to plan and conduct operations and bring to the commander's attention matters which require his action or about which he should be informed.
2. Making a continuing estimate of the situation for anticipatory planning.
3. Recommending policies and plans to implement the commander's desires and decisions.
4. Translating the decisions and plans of the commander into orders, and providing for their dissemination to the command.
5. Exercising necessary supervision to insure that the policies, intentions, and orders of the commander are executed properly.

The *general staff* consists of the commander, the executive, intelligence, personnel, logistics, operations and public information officers.

Each of these general staff members has a deputy and their own specialized staffs through which they operate.

Executive Officer

The executive officer is the principal coordinating agent of, and adviser to, the commander. He supervises and directs the staff to achieve unity of action. He may transmit the decisions of the commander to appropriate staff officers for preparation of the necessary orders, or he may transmit the decisions in the form of orders directly to those who execute them. He informs the appropriate staff officers of the orders he issues directly to commanders. He performs the following specific duties:

1. Formulates and announces policies for the general operation of the staff.
2. Supervises, directs, and coordinates the work of the general and any special staffs (those staffs devoted to specialized activities). This consists of activities of the sections within the general and special staffs; relations between the general and special staffs, and relations between the general and special staffs and subordinate units and agencies.
3. Keeps the commander informed of the situation; the situation relative to adjacent, supported, and supporting units; and the situation of the command as to location, strength, morale, training, equipment, supply, evacuation, and general effectiveness.
4. Represents the commander when authorized to do so.
5. Receives decisions from the commander and makes such additional decisions as may be required, or directed by the commander, and gives necessary instructions to the staff in furtherance of these decisions. Secondly, he allots the detailed work of preparing plans and orders, coordinates the resulting drafts, and submits them to the commander for approval. Also, he alerts subordinate units concerning the plan of the commander.
6. Insures that all instructions published to the command are in accord with the policies and plans of the commander.
7. By personal observation, and with the assistance of the general

and special staffs, insures that orders and instructions of the commander are executed.

8. Continuously studies the situation with a view to being prepared for future contingencies.
9. Review staff section reports prior to submission to the commander and forwards the required copies to higher headquarters.
10. Requires all staff officers to inform him of any information or recommendations given directly to the commander and any instructions they have received directly from the commander.
11. Secures from the commander information, recommendations, and instructions received or given as a result of the commander's contact with higher and subordinate commanders.
12. Insures establishment of liaison with adjacent, higher, subordinate, and supported units.
13. Supervises the operation of the command post.

Secretary of the General Staff

The staff should have a secretary. The secretary of the general staff performs the following duties:

1. Acts as office manager of the command post.
2. Maintains records of all activity of the staff during the emergency.
3. Receives officials visiting the headquarters.
4. Performs such other duties as may be assigned him by the chief of staff.

Personnel Officer

The personnel officer has responsibility in the field of personnel or manpower. He supervises the activation of personnel, both within and without the department, so that manpower will be ready for assignment in controlling the disturbance. He keeps a check on the deployment of operational and reserve units so that immediate reassignment may be made. All manpower requirements, present and anticipated, are routed through him, as are all orders regarding the movement of men.

Intelligence Officer

The function of the intelligence officer is to keep the commander fully informed on the disaster situation. He defines and measures the field problem and reports to the commander, so that an evaluation of the field problem can be compiled. This can only be done if there is a constant flow of intelligence as the direction and objectives of a mob can change instantly. He supervises map and photo procurement and distribution within the command. His specific duties normally include the following:

1. Production of intelligence. Directs the effort for the collection of information, and processing the information into intelligence, including recording, evaluation, and interpretation.
2. Use of intelligence and information. Disseminates intelligence and information to the commander, and to all others who need it, in the form that will furnish the greatest assistance and in time to serve their purposes. The forms normally used are intelligence estimates, periodic intelligence reports, intelligence annexes, tactical studies of the weather and terrain, summaries, reports and studies.
3. Counterintelligence. Plans and implements all active and passive measures designed to counter or neutralize hostile espionage, sabotage, and subversive activities. Plans methods and procedures for deceiving the enemy, and conducting counterintelligence phases of such operations.

Logistics Officer

The function of the logistics officer is to provide logistical support of all kinds to field forces. He assists the chief of staff in the planning and coordination of functions pertaining to supply, evacuation and hospitalization, transportation, service, and miscellaneous related subjects.

An additional responsibility of the logistics officer is to develop sources for obtaining material support from sources outside for his own department. This might relate to other departments within the city, other governmental agencies, or to private suppliers. In one sense, his responsibility is similar to that of the personnel officer in that he must provide the communication and transportation procedures so that material may be made available to field personnel at the proper time and place. His specific duties normally include the following:

1. Supply, i.e., determination of supply requirements; requisitioning, procurement, storage, security, distribution and documentation of supplies; allocation of combat weapons, munitions and equipment in critical supply; collection and disposition of excess, surplus, salvage and captured weapons and recovered stolen property.

2. Evacuation and hospitalization of the injured, sick and wounded.

3. Transportation and troop movements, i.e., transportation of units, personnel and supplies; control of movements to include selection of routes, highway regulation, and traffic control; preparation of march order annexes pertaining to regulation or control measures and other logistical aspects.

4. Service. Other logistical activities not covered by 1 through 3 above, including maintenance and repair of supplies, equipment, facilities, installations; property responsibility; sanitation, and food service.

Operations Officer

The responsibility of the operations officer is to use the intelligence gained by the intelligence officer on the nature of the problem and the information supplies by the personnel and logistic officers on the capability of his organization to develop a strategy for control of the unusual occurrence. Once the strategy is developed and approved by the executive officer and the field commander, it can be converted into missions for field supervisors in charge of the men.

It is the responsibility of the operations officer to monitor the progress of missions in the field, to measure them against the strategy and tactics approved by the executive officer and the field commander, and bring to the attention of the executive officer and the field commander any deviation from the instructions provided. Another function of the operations officer is to answer questions that come to him from the scene commanders concerning latest intelligence information and the nature of the mission to which the scene commanders are assigned.

Chapter 10

COMMAND POST

INTRODUCTION

R<small>ECENT</small> <small>HISTORY</small> has taught that it is essential to unify command at central locations. This is particularly true in a major disturbance when city, county, and state units are all involved in the action. If each agency establishes separate command posts, there will be a breakdown in communications and the exchange of intelligence, duplication of effort, conflicting policy statements, will be a waste of time resulting in confusion. This is aggravated if political antagonism exists between the various leaders, for the lack of communication will give rise to suspicion and petty jealousy. It cannot be overly stressed that in times of emergency the first consideration must be the restoration of law and order. There is no place for personal aggrandizement at the expense of society.

In disaster situations, two command centers will be established: (1) emergency control headquarters, and (2) field command post. The chief or his delegated representative is in charge of the emergency control headquarters, while the field commander is in command of the field command post. The emergency control headquarters will usually be established at police headquarters, as it is the best equipped to serve as the center of operations. The command post should be established at or near the location of the disturbance, to provide control, coordination and communications. It will be the control center for the entire operation. Through it passes all information, including the assignment of officers, equipment and any other directions necessary to coordinate the efforts of those men involved in a particular police problem.

A command post may be established by a supervisory officer when in his judgment the circumstances surrounding the situation require a base for radio communication or direct command control. Headquarters must be advised of the exact location of temporary headquarters and all telephone and other communication facilities available for use at the scene.

In a large operation, in addition to the command post established by the commander, each subordinate scene commander may establish a field post. The activities of each particular branch will be controlled from this field post. However, no independent action should be instituted without notification to the command post. The subordinate commanders shall assign a superior officer to the command post to maintain liaison. In addition, each commander shall constantly maintain direct contact with the command post by radio, phone, or other method of communication.

ADVANCE PLANNING

A list of potential posts based on a survey of possible trouble areas should be compiled in advance of any emergency. Plans should be developed for the establishment of a command post and for the staffing and equipping of the command post, in time of need, with a minimum of delay.

The following information concerning each of the potential command sites should be determined:

1. Primary and secondary routes of travel to the site.
2. Communication facilities available.
3. Medical facilities in the vicinity.
4. The names, addresses and telephone numbers of individuals to be contacted concerning the availability of such facilities.

LOCATION

The nature and extent of the emergency, and the facilities available will determine the location of a command post. The following factors will be considered in choosing a location:

1. Number of personnel to be mobilized.
2. Number of other agencies to be mobilized.
3. Availability of telephone service.
4. Number of anticipated casualties (dead, injured, displaced persons).
5. Availability of space for administrative and clerical work.
6. Probable time emergency will last.

7. Extent of emergency area.
8. Facilities for parking.
9. Distance from scene of actual emergency operations. It should be as close to the incident as possible without jeopardizing the purpose and function of the command post.

   In the case of a demonstration the command post should be located where a clear view of the demonstration can be maintained, but it should also be hidden from view. Usually some room in a building across the street from the demonstration area works well.
10. Convenience to other facilities, i.e., headquarters for other commands and agencies, press center, etc., if the emergency requires the establishment of separate facilities.
11. Freedom from smoke, protection from weather.
12. Removed from the escape paths of crowd.
13. Ingress and egress. It is desirable that the location of the command post be such it can be reached from more than one direction and by an unobstructed route.

Headquarters must be advised of the exact location of the command post and all telephone and other communications facilities available for use at the scene. In the event that the operation is of large magnitude or of long duration, a station house in the vicinity, a public building or any other building offering adequate facilities may be used. The best would be a city or county owned building; however, any empty building adjacent to the location may be used. Schools afford excellent facilities as they have ample open area for parking of vehicles and the assemblage of men; numerous large rooms that can be allotted to various staffs, often that have, in addition to adequate sanitation facilities, showers and kitchens. A word of warning: an elementary school has furniture that was designed for children, not adults, thus special equipment may have to be brought in.

MOBILE COMMAND POST

At times a mobile command post may be used. Its great advantage is its mobility, which allows flexibility in response to a fluid mob situation. Likewise, because such a command post is fully equipped, no time is lost in setting up and establishing the necessary communication outlets. It can be any type vehicle. Surplus military trailers, large trucks, converted buses, and similar units have been developed around their local availability and low original acquisition costs.

If the department is starting from scratch to set up a mobile command center, it is recommended that a truck-trailer unit be acquired. This enables all of the permanent installations to be installed in the trailer unit. The truck unit can then be "exercised" at regular intervals, since vehicles and motors deteriorate when standing inactive. Over a period of years this will prove to be the most economical and efficient system.

EQUIPMENT

As far as equipment for the command post, the important thing to bear in mind is the purpose to which it will be put. It will act as the nerve center of the entire operation. This means that it is basically a communications center.

It must have the extra radio receiving and transmitting equipment. The better type units will have a means to tie into local telephone lines in the area and carry auxiliary emergency, gasoline-powered plants. The more sophisticated will have closed television circuit facilities as well as standard television receiving sets. It should have a portable power supply, maps, lighting, data and reference material necessary in the direction, coordination and control of any major incident. If the command post is moved, notification should be given to all units and the new location shall be left at or near the old location.

SECURITY

The command post should be placed under guard and have available to it several areas of approach and exit. Road blocks should be used to seal it off and these should be manned by officers in sufficient numbers and armed with the necessary weapons to secure it completely from mob or public interference. This is necessary to prevent raids and also to prevent blockades of streets and avenues of exit and approach. Police headquarters and units located in the center of the city, where narrow streets are common, are especially vulnerable to a planned roadblock. Many times a single stalled vehicle or a staged collision at one or more critical intersections near the police headquarters will be sufficient to block movement of police vehicles to trouble areas. This is a tactic that can be expected in conjunction with any professionally organized riot action and must be foreseen and protected against. Fires, explosives, bomb scares, organized demonstrations and similar obstruction tactics may also be employed.

A perimeter guard should be set up so that the commander and his staff will be isolated and not interfered with in any way. A pass system should be initiated so that only authorized personnel will be allowed into the post. It is no place for curious sightseers who have no function and whose presence will merely complicate and confuse the situation. A log should be kept of all those who enter and leave the post. It should show the following:

Name	Organization	Destination	Time	
			In	Out

INTERNAL ARRANGEMENTS

Command posts are arranged to afford the staff maximum working facilities consistent with requirements for security and mobility. To save time and effort and to facilitate coordination, staff sections having closely related activities should be grouped in the same locality. Sections which have numerous visitors or process a large volume of messages should be located near an entrance to the building or area; sections handling considerable classified material need the protection of a location away from main entrances.

War Room

The war room is primarily an orientation, briefing and conference room. In a tactical headquarters, it may also serve as the combined operations room.

The purpose of a war room is to provide a single location within the headquarters in which the commander and chief of staff may familiarize themselves with the entire situation as it pertains to the command. It also provides a location where the commander or executive can assemble staff officers or commanders to provide them with all available information concerning the current situation. Another important use is to provide a centralized location where

A SUGGESTED ARRANGEMENT:

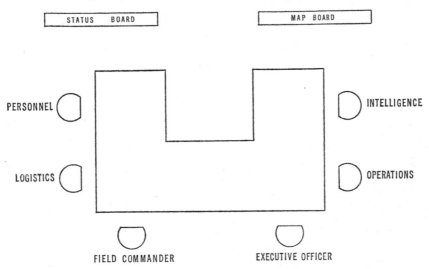

War Room. This is a suggested arrangement for a war room. It is used by the general staff for orientation, briefing, and as a conference room.

certain designated liaison officers may secure the latest information on the situation without disturbing the staff sections.

The war room normally is the responsibility of the executive. Adequate measures must be taken to insure security of the war room to include security control of the personnel having access thereto. Insofar as the physical arrangement of the room, there must be adequate space for all who work therein. This means that it should be large enough for easy movement within the room. It should also be as quiet as possible. Chairs and tables should be set up in such a way that the staff may confer as well as view the situation maps.

Situation Maps

One of the most important aids to the staff is the situation map. A situation map is a graphic presentation of the current situation. The staff must keep a situation map posted to date showing disposition and activities. Data should be posted on an overlay on the map as soon as received.

The use of an operations or situation map enables the police commander to monitor progressively a civil disorder as it develops. Timely posting of information relating to the situation can point up details that could otherwise be overlooked. The map picture of the civil disorder simplifies the commander's ability to accurately estimate the situation, make timely decisions, and issue clear, concise orders.

INFORMATION RECORDED. The information routinely recorded on an operations map includes the following data:

1. Locations of rioters.
2. Mob patterns of movement.
3. Possible mob objectives.
4. Locations of critical areas.
5. Mob dispersal areas.
6. Mob dispersal routes.
7. Police troop dispositions.
8. Possible positions for police barricades.
9. Police patrol routes.
10. Critical intersections.
11. Routes for traffic rerouting.
12. Areas which might prohibit the use of riot control agents.
13. Police routes of advance.
14. Police assembly areas.
15. Locations for police reserves.
16. Police control and communication points.
17. Possible positions for medical aid points.

TECHNIQUES. Operations maps should be kept at police command posts. Incoming information should be promptly posted by trained police personnel.

Instead of making different colored entries for different types of offenses, color should depict different hours of activity, thus, from 8-9/green, 9-10/blue, 10-11/red, 11-12/brown. In this way any pattern or movement is graphically portrayed. This occurred during the Los Angeles riot when the entries on the chart pointed like an arrow to the target of the rioter—downtown Los Angeles. Once the movement was spotted and the target anticipated counter measures were initiated. The entries show the type of activity, e.g., robbery, sniping, fire assault, by the use of a letter. In addition, there should be a notation as to the time of the event.

Communication Center

A communication center where all of the communication equipment is established should be close to the war room. It should be equipped with radio transmitters capable of contacting all the various units that may be committed, teletype, and telephones.

All information concerning the operation must be expeditiously transmitted to the command post, so that the commander may be cognizant of the current situation. This is essential so that an evaluation of the conditions present may be made, and necessary orders issued. All reports and messages received should be immediately taken to the officer for whom they are intended.

One telephone line should be kept open constantly between the command post and headquarters. The telephone lines at the command post should be used only between units for battle purposes. A bank of telephones should be pressed into operation to handle the flood of complaints and calls for help that will flood the department during the riot. These phones should not be used for communication between police units.

Because of the effectiveness of our mass news media, it is possible to learn much from them. To maintain contact with the source, a standard frequency radio and television set should also be installed at headquarters for monitoring news and other pertinent broadcasts or telecasts. In addition, a monitor system should be pressed into operation to intercept any radio messages by the rioters.

Public Relations Area

The public relations officer should establish an area in which the media of communication can be regularly briefed on the latest developments. Situation maps should be maintained for their convenience. A comprehensive, consolidated summary of information must be maintained and supplied other interested agency heads so as to give them an accurate, current digest of the situation that will permit them to take further appropriate action as required.

Personnel

Sufficient security service and clerical staff must be assigned to the command post to enable the commander and his staff to function effectively.

Equipment

A special package equipment for the command post should be prepared in advance and immediately rushed to the post when trouble begins. In addition to the communication equipment already mentioned, there should be bullhorns and walkie-talkies. Signs identifying various locations "Conference Room," "Communications," "Press Room," and distinctive colored arm bands which identify the assignment of individuals "Commander," "Staff," "Guard," will prove of great value.

Power—Standby

Each headquarters should have an emergency power source. The plan should spell out the availability of this source and the steps necessary to activate it. As the post will, in effect, be an office, all necessary office supplies such as typewriter, paper, pencils, etc., shall be delivered. Maps, standard plans, data and reference material should also be supplied.

Chapter 11

INTELLIGENCE

INTRODUCTION

A<small>N</small> EFFICIENT INTELLIGENCE operation is essential to cope with disasters, civil disturbances or demonstrations. Intelligence must be established as a continuing program to maintain a pulse reading on the population.

Intelligence secured prior to, during, and after the riot action is as vital to police as it is to the military on the battlefield. Prior intelligence enables the mob action to be faced with the proper forces and equipment to combat it. Intelligence during the action is essential if the police are to be able to tactically dominate and disperse the mob. Intelligence after the action is necessary to determine who the mob members were, causes of the riot, to identify leaders, and to forestall any recurrence.

Definition

Intelligence is information. Police intelligence may be defined as any particle of information, news, or advice which will assist the police in accomplishing their mission.

INTELLIGENCE UNIT

Each department should have an intelligence unit. The important factors in the establishing of an intelligence unit are the selection of personnel and indoctrination of each individual in the field of intelligence production.

The unit is the eyes and ears of the chief of police. It is the liaison between members of its own department, members of other police departments, and representatives of state and federal law enforcement agencies. If they are successful in establishing complete cooperation between department and within their own department, the results are tremendous. Instead of having only the few men and women in one section supplying intelligence, the department has many hundreds engaged in collecting data, exchanging information, and keeping cognizant of the trends, changes, methods, and improvements in the vast field of intelligence who now share their knowledge.

Qualities of a Good Intelligence Man

The qualities that should be possessed by an individual who enters the field of intelligence are the following:

1. Intelligence and education.
2. Perceptiveness about people.
3. Ability to work well with others under normal and difficult conditions.
4. Ability to distinguish between essentials and nonessentials.
5. Ability to discern between fact and fiction.
6. Inquisitiveness.
7. Ingenuity.
8. Attentive to detail.
9. Ability to express ideas clearly, briefly, and, very important, interestingly.
10. Personal and professional integrity.
11. Loyalty and dedication.
12. Discipline.
13. Professional competency.
14. Creativity.
15. Prudence.
16. Ability to understand other points of view, ways of thinking and behavior, even if quite foreign to his own.

INTELLIGENCE CYCLE

The intelligence cycle can be likened to a four spoked wheel which assists the police agency in efficient operation. The wheel of intelligence turns in perpetual motion. The four spokes that comprise the wheel are the four steps of intelligence: (1) the collection of information; (2) the processing of collected information; (3) the dissemination of resulting intelligence, and (4) the planning of the collection effort. In the organized intelligence program, these four steps occur continuously and simultaneously.

PLANNING THE COLLECTION EFFORT

Planning and guidance by police officials are necessary in the conduct of intelligence activities in order to maintain direction and continuity. Intelligence needs must be forecast in advance to allow sufficient collection time. This requires that intelligence and operations be integrated.

The first step is to determine what intelligence's objectives are and what information it needs, without regard to obstacles. Priorities are established among these objectives according to their relative urgency. Priority is given in the intelligence effort to those aspects of the situation which represent the greatest prospect of success and the greatest threat to the accomplishment of the police mission. Only after priority has been established is the question of obstacles examined.

Finally the subordinate collection agency, whether it be the individual police officer or separate unit, must be notified of the precise nature of information desired by their superiors. It is apparent that systematic procedures and effective communications are essential for collection and use of intelligence.

Essential Elements of Information

A fundamental prerequisite to an intelligence plan that is to be used in the event of a civil disturbance is the formulation of the essential elements of information. These are statements or listings of the specific items of information required by the commander at a given time, and are prepared by the commander with the assistance of his intelligence officer. They focus the attention and activities of all collecting agencies and intelligence personnel on the specific information desired. They state the current intelligence needs and form the basis for the intelligence collection plan.

Essential Elements of Information—Civil Disorders

The essential elements of information for civil disorders will include the following:

1. Probable time and location of civil disorders.
2. Probable cause of civil disorders and the events leading to the disturbance.
3. Types of individuals involved, ages, sexes, and affiliations, etc.

4. Classification of individuals or groups who might create or support civil disorders, such as age, sociological, economic and psychological background.
5. Estimated number of participants.
   a. Initial number.
   b. Anticipated reinforcements—by source.
   c. Types and quantities of weapons.
6. The leaders.
   a. Who they are?
   b. How they became leaders?
   c. Whether they are subversive?
   d. Are they spontaneous types, amateurs, or are they professional agitator types?
   e. The location of ringleaders and danger centers.
7. Known leaders of past civil disorders and present potentially troublesome social movements.
   a. Forcefully influential members.
   b. Professional agitators.
8. Probable assembly areas for crowds.
   a. Assembly areas where riots might occur.
   b. Assembly areas removed from site of disturbance.
9. Prominent organizations, individuals and news media who are friendly with the leaders and are supporting actively or passively the cause of the disorder.
10. Plans, activities, methods or operation prepared or used by disturbance leaders in the following areas of interest.
    a. Possible destruction of property.
    b. Possible interference with community utilities and services.
    c. Possible assaults on nonsympathizers.
    d. Agitation.
    e. Embarrassment to government.
    f. The direction of movement of the mob.
    g. Objective of rioters.
11. Disturbance activities.
    a. Passive resistance to control.
    b. Verbal displays.
    c. Violent acts.
    d. Physical resistance to control.

12. Degree of organization.
    a. Milling rioters.
    b. Organized mob front.
13. Routes available for police movements to crowd assembly areas or potential locations of civil disorders.
14. Location and nature of material and equipment available for use by members of the disturbance.
15. Location of arms, ammunition, explosives and volatile inflammables under control of rioters. Location of probable sources for such supplies if violence breaks out or continues.
16. Vehicles and other equipment.
17. Methods of identification they may have among themselves and their communication methods.
18. Location of unguarded material or equipment that could be seized by rioters, ammunition, arms and explosives.
19. Location of important buildings that may be used by rioters to assemble or as potential targets for destruction.
    a. Public.
    b. Government.
    c. Private.
    d. Food supplies.
20. Location of communications systems, transportation systems, public utilities, and stores of material and supplies subject to damage during civil disorder.
21. Routes of escape for rioters and routes which should be cut off by road blocks to prevent reinforcements arriving or the spread of the action to other areas.
22. Weather information and forecasts at estimated time of possible rioting and during the action.

Essential Elements of Information—Strikes

In the case of intelligence related to possible strikes the efforts are basically the same as for any anticipated civil disturbance. The type of information gathered, however, must be specific enough to contain certain essential items. These items are as follows:

1. Business name, address, and telephone number.
2. Business owner's name, address, and telephone number.
3. Name, address, and telephone number of president or manager.

4. Principal product(s) produced by the firm and whether essential to national defense.
5. Production (normal daily and present daily).
6. Total number of employees.
7. Name, address, and telephone number of union involved.
8. Union president's name, address, and telephone number.
9. Reason for the dispute.
10. Number of pickets and orderliness of activity.
11. Date of strike declaration.
12. Number and occupation of employees who will continue working.
13. Plant schedules for shifts, production shipments, etc.
14. Plant layout, exists, parking facilities, utilities, etc.
15. Nature of trouble anticipated.
16. Transit facilities in the vicinity.
17. Any other special hazards or items which may affect the number of police employed or the safety of police employed at the scene.

Essential Elements of Intelligence—Disaster

Preparatory intelligence planning for providing aid in the event of a disaster follows the same general pattern as the advance planning conducted in anticipation of a possible civil disturbance; however, essential information is more easily obtained. Speed in the collection of information of intelligence value is vital to the commander assigned the mission. In addition to the pertinent factors outlined above, the outline of a disaster intelligence study may include the following:

1. Location and nature of the disaster.
2. Sequence of events leading to the disaster.
3. Secondary disasters (such as fires or tidal waves which follow earthquakes).
4. Type and description of damage.
5. Preliminary estimates.
   a. Number of people to be supplied.
   b. Probable length of time for which supplies are required.
   c. Quantity and kind of supplies available locally.

d. Requirements for funds.

e. Requirements for storage.

f. Available means for distributing supplies.

g. Probable ability of local population, authorities and organizations to meet the disaster conditions, to include local resources of aid material and personnel.

h. Whether local authorities are making a maximum effort.

i. Probable extent to which other agencies are able to commit their resources.

j. Need for evacuation.

k. Effects on law and order.

6. Countermeasures taken.

7. List of facilities which may be of use in implementing disaster relief.

When the estimates of essential information needed have been developed, a plan for the collection of information is formulated by the commander or his intelligence officer. The estimates constitute the basis for orders, instructions, and requests governing the search for information. They do not impose limitations on reporting agencies, which, in addition to satisfying the requirements arising from the essential elements of information, must also report all additional information that comes to their attention.

COLLECTION OF INFORMATION

The collection of accurate information is the most difficult step in the successful operation of an efficient intelligence effort. To obtain accurate information, the police official must give careful consideration to two aspects which effect the collection effort; the sources of information and the means of collection.

Sources of Information

A source of information is considered to be the origin of the information. Generally, any police agency has access to numerous sources of information in the course of its daily activities. For example, valuable information can be developed through the sources listed below:

1. Local civic organizations.

2. Businessmen.
3. Social clubs, fraternities, and similar organizations.
4. Political rallies.
5. Parades.
6. Churches and religious groups.
7. Athletic and other public events.
8. Other community services.
9. Informal crowds.
10. Routine patrol. Special attention to unusual gatherings and actions.
11. Statistics—arrest patterns, crime reports, resistance, assaults on officers.
12. Special reports—use of force, shots fired, strikes, racial incidents.
13. Informants and contacts.
14. Television, radio and press, handbills, announcements.
15. Letters-to-the-editor columns.
16. Newspaper stories and editorials, special features.
17. Speeches and gatherings.
18. Television and radio panel discussions.
19. Rumors.
20. Members of a minority group, preferably leaders.
21. Liquor establishment employees.
22. Former or presently prominent athletes connected with the demonstrating class.
23. Welfare, recreation, or social workers.
24. School officials.
25. Teenage gangs, leaders and athletic groups.
26. Any group connected with the particular area.
27. Business persons in the area.
28. State, county and city agencies and officials.
29. Complaints received by the police or other government agencies.

Means of Collection

Intelligence information may be collected by either individuals or organizations. Police agencies throughout the world generally have several means of collection at their disposal.

Overt Police Intelligence

The word *overt* literally means "open." Thus overt police intelligence activities are those undertaken openly and without attempted concealment from public view. For example, the individual police officer routinely collects information in an overt manner while performing his normal every day duties. Indeed, it is he who can sense a changing attitude or notice that "something is different." Each police officer should be a listening post, alert to the changing attitudes in the community, and to do so he must know what is wanted, when it is wanted, and why it is so important. He should be encouraged to report facts, rumors, and other information he may obtain during both his on-duty and off-duty time.

The police officer must be taught what to collect, where to collect, when to collect, and why to collect. He must be thoroughly indoctrinated on the importance of police intelligence. The officer must be trained in the application of man's five basic senses of sight, taste, smell, touch and hearing to the collection of information. Training in the collection of information of police intelligence broadens the officer's understanding as to its importance in the detection and prevention of serious incidents. The typical police officer discards daily items of information that do not directly affect his immediate area of interest. However, what may seem unimportant to him may be of vital importance to the police agency. What the police officer is to collect is largely dependent upon information requirements formulated by his superiors; however, in the course of his duties he must evaluate all information which may be important to the collection effort. Where the officer is in doubt, he should report the information.

A police officer can never know too much about his area. This rule applies not only to his ability to collect information but also to the successful accomplishment of his primary mission—the enforcement of laws and the maintenance of order. He is, in effect, a walking storehouse of information. Specific information that the police officer should know might include all items listed below.

1. The economics or means of livelihood for the area.
2. Industrial interests of the people.
3. Cultural composition of the population.

4. Religious differences and beliefs.
5. Social aspirations of the group.
6. Fluctuations in the strength and character of minority groups.
7. Political beliefs.
8. Popular trends of the people.
9. Attitude of population toward international movement.
10. Individuals considered popular or influential with the people.

After gaining a thorough knowledge of his area and its inhabitants, the police officer must establish rapport with the people. The police officer then follows the general rules outlined below.

OBSERVE. Through observation the police officer is able to note accurately the occurrence, person(s), place, or thing that is related to the performance of his duty. The application of the ability to observe is important in overt intelligence. Observation should include the following points.

Patterns within the neighborhood. Generally, most neighborhoods develop standard patterns of operation or habits. The police officer must be familiar with these habits and note those happenings which do not fit into the normal scheme. When reported to superiors, information often can be correlated with other information to form a clear picture of an item of intelligence value.

Meetings and rallies. Assemblages of this type normally alert the police officer to the moods of the population. Often, leaders and organizers are readily identified and controversial subject areas clearly defined.

Athletic events and parades. The policeman can determine through observation, trends in nationalism, moods of the population, and the repressed feelings or sentiments of minority and majority groups.

Neighborhood businesses. Continuing observation will reveal changes in activities that could be the result of subversive pressure.

Strangers. The movement of strangers through the neighborhood when observed and correlated by further checks can disclose information concerning activities, associations, and interests which may be of intelligence value.

Listen. The police officer must be a good listener. In the successful collection of information he must listen to many things spoken by many people; things which would include personal problems, opinions, interests, gossip and grievances. He should listen to the conversations of people, speakers at meetings and rallies, and public expressions at informal assemblages. These particles of information collected from various sources may form an important intelligence picture.

READ. The police officer must read. His ability to comprehend thoughts and idea conveyed by literature is an important part of his effectiveness as a collector of information. He should continually review for intelligence value the information expressed on items such as handbills, newspapers, advertising, business signs and propaganda literature.

Patrolmen should make regular reports regarding intergroup relations and attitudes on their beats. A special form developed for these reports would provide for the recording of such information as the following:

1. Current stories about recent incidents (which might be real or rumored) showing either antogonism or liking for some other group of citizens, approval or disapproval of actions on the city government, including the police, etc.
2. Rumors of activities planned by neighborhood groups against other or outside groups or vice versa.
3. Complaints about any condition in the neighborhood or in the city which the people on the beat feel is disadvantageous to them or advantageous to some group they dislike.
4. Evaluation of the effects of any efforts being made in the neighborhood by individuals or organizations to change the attitudes of local people toward any other group in the city, either for better or for worse.

In addition to these general reports which would be periodically required of police in selected areas, all police personnel should have standing instructions to report immediately any sudden developments that might result in a serious clash. Such reports should be routed promptly both to top police officials and to the records unit.

Covert Police Intelligence

The word *covert* has the meanings of sheltered, covered and concealed. Covert intelligence refers to information collected by methods concealed from public view. Covert intelligence collection activities are considered secret. The collection of covert intelligence may provide vital information concerning causes of public unrest and subversive agitation within the community.

The essence of covert intelligence is access. Someone, or some device, has to get close enough to a thing, a place or a person to observe or discover the desired facts without arousing the attention of those who protect them. The information must then be delivered to the people who want it. It must move quickly or it may get "stale." And it must not get lost or be intercepted en route.

Undercover Police Officers

An undercover police officer is one who abandons his official identity as a law enforcement official and assumes an identity which will enable him to obtain information he would not otherwise be able to obtain. The assumed identity may merely involve the wearing of civilian clothing, or it may require very elaborate preparations. In either instance, the preparations should be sufficiently thorough to preclude compromise, to minimize any danger to the undercover police officer, and to insure the ultimate success of the undercover mission. Normally, undercover investigations should not be attempted if other means of obtaining the desired information can be utilized effectively. The police officials charged with obtaining intelligence data should consider the following factors before authorizing an undercover mission: the exact results required, the importance of the mission, the availability of planning data, the availability of qualified investigative personnel, the equipment and preparation necessary, the danger involved, the time available for completion of the mission, and the prospects for success.

SELECTION OF PERSONNEL. When it is decided that an undercover mission is the best means of obtaining required intelligence information, the best qualified police officer should be the candidate first considered for the assignment. The undercover police officer should be well trained and experienced in investigative work; he should be calm, mature and resourceful; he should be completely self-confident and feel certain that he can assume an undercover role successfully; he should be courageous and able to deal effectively with unexpected and emergency situations; he must be able to avoid intemperance in all its forms; and he should be ready and willing to accept the undercover assignment. For a specific mission, the selected police officer should be convincing in the particular role he will be required to assume. He will need a good memory if it is not possible to make notes; he must be proficient in any occupational area in which he may be required to allege competence; he should have the physical appearance and characteristics consistent with his role; and he should have the background, education, or training which will enable him to wear his role like a well-tailored garment. The undercover police officer should also be completely familiar with the background and ramifications of the total investigation so that he will be able to assess accurately what he observes while undercover.

In addition to the above factors, superior officers must consider the linquistic talents, the educational background, the hobbies, the athletic abilities, the religious background, and other aspects of the prospective undercover agent's total personality when selecting a man for a particular undercover mission.

BRIEFING. Prior to assuming an undercover role, a police officer must be completely briefed on the nature of the task he will be expected to accomplish. He should know as much as possible about his geographical area of operations, his expected contacts, and his reporting facilities and procedures. Obtaining the background information needed for this briefing before beginning an undercover assignment is essential for a successful mission.

PREPARATION OF COVER. A background or cover story for the undercover police officer will be necessary whenever he is required to infiltrate any organization or group of individuals. Every practical effort should be made to fit the cover story to the actual background of the undercover police officer. If it is even remotely possible that the fictitious background data of the undercover officer will be checked by members of the group being infiltrated, arrangements must be made in advance for prompt corroboration of the fictitious elements of the cover story.

REHEARSALS. The undercover officer, before embarking on his assignment, must rehearse his cover story carefully so that the fictitious elements appear to be genuine. He must also be certain to have on his person and in his personal effects only those items of clothing and equipment which are consonant with his cover story. Nothing which might connect him with the police agency should be taken on an undercover assignment.

INFORMANTS

General

Informants are persons who give information to the police. They are sometimes compensated for their services, but compensation does not necessarily imply payment by the police officer receiving the informant's cooperation. For example, an informant may provide information to the police for purely altruistic reasons. The confidence of informants must be scrupulously respected by the police.

Utilization

Informants are valuable only when they are in a position to obtain information of value to the police; good will or a spirit of cooperation is not enough. The police officer interested in obtaining information about action groups which might pose threats to internal political stability of a community will need informants who are members of such groups. For example, informants in politically conscious labor unions, student groups and political party executive committees will be most helpful.

Recruiting

Persons who have or can obtain access to information wanted by the police may be recruited as informants. Each potential informant must be approached carefully, with the officer furnishing the motivation best calculated to appeal to the individual. The officer may have to spend much time in careful cultivation of the prospective informant before making any direct approach. There is no universally effective recruiting technique; each officer must discreetly plan his approach after making a complete evaluation of the prospective informant and the type of information he may be able to furnish. The virtues of patience and perseverance are of paramount importance.

Placed informants, known as *"sleepers,"* can also be of great value to the police. These are individuals recruited as informants who infiltrate the action groups to be penetrated. Great care must be given to the selection and use of placed informants who may be compelled to remain without contacts with the police for extended periods of time while earning the confidence of groups penetrated. There is always a danger that placed informants will discard their allegiance to the police agency under the constant influence of new associates, so police officers must exercise caution when dealing with placed informants. The term *placed informant* can also be used to describe individuals who are recruited as informants and then placed in positions where they will come into contact with members of the action groups whose activities are of interest to the police. Barbers, cooks, waiters and maids are examples of this latter type of placed informant.

Special Considerations

Police officers should treat their informants with respect and should not imply by word or deed that informants are anything less than patriotic public servants providing valuable services for their countries. However, the officers should not confide in their informants nor discuss investigations with them. Often well-intentioned informants tend to assume control of investigations; police officers must guard against this development, particularly with informants who have been used frequently.

Protection of the identity of informants is the responsibility of the police officer. When confidence is implied or promised, it must be observed. Only by scrupulously observing all agreements made with informants can police officers hope to engender the confidence and enthusiasm that mark the valuable confidential source of information.

SURVEILLANCE

General

Surveillance is the investigative activity which consists of keeping persons, places, or vehicles under observation. While a surveillance may be conducted by informants acting in behalf of a law enforcement agency, use of the term is usually restricted to describing the clandestine observations conducted by investigative personnel.

Purpose

The surveillance technique of gathering information can be used effectively to obtain evidence; to locate wanted individuals by observing known acquaintances and haunts; to develop information about the activities of individuals; to secure a basis for the issuance of a search warrant; to check on the behavior of informants; to identify individuals frequenting or visiting a certain location or premises; to determine the nature of suspicious activities; to develop timetables or schedules of the movements of suspicious or suspected individuals, or to develop sources of information which may not be already known to the police agents.

Types of Surveillance

Surveillance may be maintained from fixed or mobile observation points. Observations may be restricted to visual observations; they may involve the use of a variety of eavesdropping techniques; or they may include a combination of visual and aural techniques. The use of still and motion picture cameras to supplement or supplant ordinary visual observations should be encouraged when possible.

Fixed Surveillance

In selecting a fixed observation point, police investigators should consider the possibilities for observation that various prospective locations provide. They should also consider the need for movement of technical equipment and the opportunities for its use, as well as the number of surveillants the job will require. A fixed surveillance post should be close enough to the target location or premises to enable the surveillants to identify persons entering and leaving; binoculars and telescopes can be used to increase visual range when necessary. A communications system should be installed so that the surveillants can maintain round-the-clock contact with police headquarters and with other surveillants in other locations. Naturally the type of neighborhood and the availability of good observation points will influence the selection of the surveillance post, as will the kind of intelligence information required. If concealment is impossible to achieve, it will be necessary to inaugurate a system of intermittent surveillance using a number of investigators who will walk or drive past the location or premises periodically to maintain the surveillance; it may be possible, too, in cases of this type, to conceal hidden cameras or eavesdropping devices to provide aural coverage when visual coverage cannot be maintained without detection.

Mobile Surveillance

In mobile surveillance, the police officers may find themselves on foot, in public conveyances, in automobiles, or using all three modes of transportation. When the purpose of the surveillance is to gather intelligence information covertly, the surveillants may use either a loose continuous surveillance, or a form of progressive surveillance in which the subject is discreetly followed for a certain distance each day and picked up the following day where the surveillance was discontinued previously. The progressive surveillance can be used effectively when the moving subject follows the same route daily; this type of surveillance will in time reveal the location of all premises visited by the subject.

REPORTING AND PROCESSING

Transmitting Information

Reports should be submitted as soon as possible after the collection of data. Speed in reporting is often essential if the collected data are to be of any real value to the police agency.

Advance planning for the reporting phase of intelligence activity is essential if speed is to be achieved. Informants, undercover men, and other investigative personnel must be thoroughly briefed on the means for rapid communication available to them. Radios, telephones, the mail, the use of drops and safe houses, contacts with messengers or other investigative personnel acting as couriers, and in-person communication using codes or signals are some of the means of communication that may be used. Selection of a particular means of communication for the transmission of a particular message should be determined by the circumstances. The type of message, the physical location of the sender in relationship to his intended receiver, the urgency of the situation, and the various means of communication available at a given time and place are some of the factors to be considered.

The Processing of Collected Information

Processing is a three-step operation which includes recording, evaluation and interpretation. Information is normally processed in accordance with priorities of importance. It is then correlated with other associated information.

RECORDING. Recording is defined as the reducing of information to some form of writing and the grouping together of related items. The information must be indexed and filed in such a way as to be recoverable on demand. The recording process simplifies the subsequent step of interpretation, rendering it easier to accomplish and more accurate in the end product.

ORGANIZATION FILE. The intelligence section should prepare and maintain a file on known organizations operating or existing within their jurisdiction which either historically, presently or potentially are of interest in this area of police operations. The following information should be collected and maintained:

1. Name, address and telephone number.
2. Regular meetings—dates and times. (Meeting place if other than headquarters.)
3. History and background of organization.
4. Purposes, goals and objectives of organization.
5. Membership.
6. Local police experience with organizations.
7. Local connections with national or parent organizations.
8. Press clippings about organizations.
9. Executive committee members and officers.
   a. Name, address and home telephone number.
   b. Occupation, address and telephone number.
   c. Personal history and background.
   d. Automobile and license number.
   e. Membership in other organizations.

Organizations are categorized in intelligence operations with background information concerning general area of operations and particular attention is devoted to the following:

1. Extremist organizations, both white and Negro, particularly those advocating force and violence.
2. Infiltration of other organizations by members of the groups indicated in.
   a. Extremist organization as a front.
   b. Activities of individual persons designed to breach security of informational sources available to the intelligence unit.
   c. Interlocking arrangements between various organizations, particularly resulting from dual membership.

AGITATOR FILE. The intelligence section should prepare and maintain a file on all known agitators. It should contain the following:

1. Name, address and telephone number.
2. Photograph.
3. Criminal record.
4. Affiliations, political and racial.
5. Techniques.
6. Evaluation: professional agitator, forceful follower, aggressive, passive.

EVALUATION AND INTERPRETATION

Evaluation

Evaluation is the critical appraisal of information wherein it is determined whether or not the information was obtained from a reliable source and is accurate and pertinent.

Interpretation

The final step in processing occurs when the significance of the information is determined with respect to what is already known. Conclusions are drawn as to the probable meaning of the evaluated information. Interpretation can be summarized as the concluded results of critical judgment, analysis and integration.

Evaluation and interpretation transform raw information into intelligence by establishing the pertinence of the information, the reliability of its source, the accuracy of its content, and, in addition, its significance in the light of prior intelligence. The police officer who collects the information must make the initial evaluation; he alone can provide an objective appraisal of the data source. He knows his informants and undercover agents; he knows their reputation for integrity, honesty, accuracy and good judgment. Without evaluation of the source of each bit of intelligence data, all data must be assumed to be of equal value with regard to accuracy and completeness.

More sophisticated evaluation of the data is the responsibility of the intelligence office who will be using the collected data for operational planning. These analysts will have access to all the intelligence information collected by the entire police organization. They will also have available data supplied by other law enforcement and intelligence agencies. It is they who will be required to construct the "big picture" from the bits and pieces of assembled information. They will be able to compare single bits of intelligence data with all other scraps of information that have been collected and reported to them. They will be able to make good judgments about the investigative units furnishing intelligence reports.

When the analysts examine the collected data, they will frequently see the need for additional investigation in specific areas.

SENSITIVE AREAS. As a result of information received, geographical areas of unrest may be delineated. Such areas are known as "sensitive" areas, and are always primary intelligence targets.

INDICES OF AGITATION. Any information which indicates a possibility of agitation, violence, or instability among the local population is made a special intelligence target. It is then analyzed in terms of cause and effect and is integrated with intelligence already developed. For example, attempts by civilians to collect weapons as indicated by an increase in the sale of weapons by pawnships or other vendors of weapons, would become an intelligence target and the subject of a further intelligence operation. Through police command channels, new data requirements will be transmitted to the investigative units able to assist in the problem areas, and the collection of intelligence information will continue with direction from the top command echelons indicating the areas of interest and concentration for each of the investigating units.

DISSEMINATION OF INTELLIGENCE

Information that has been processed must reach the users in time to be of assistance in the formulation of plans. The means and methods selected for dissemination depend entirely on the detail, pertinence and urgency of the information and its intended use. Police officials should carefully consider which branches of government may require processed intelligence information in consonance with the nature of the information. Intelligence indicating early occurrence of a civil disorder will require immediate dissemination so as to permit rapid planning and implementing of coordinated preventive actions.

INTELLIGENCE STUDY

The intelligence study is a presentation of all pertinent information which may be of assistance to the commander in making an estimate of the situation or in conducting an operation. The form varies according to the situation and the nature of the study to be made. The study, which is based on the latest information available, is usually prepared as far in advance as practicable, is supplemented by spot intelligence as the situation develops, and is revised when necessary.

Types

Intelligence studies that are made in preparation for potential civil disturbances are of two types. The first type, an advance intelligence study, is conducted to gather general information which may form the basis for the preparation of preliminary emergency plans applicable to a general area in the event of emergency. The second type not only included the intelligence gathered in the preliminary study, but also the information obtained in a specific locality where a civil disturbance is in being or may be imminent. The second type of study is made subsequent to the outbreak of the disturbance or where the potential of the disturbance is great.

A suggested outline for an advance intelligence study follows:
1. The area.
   a. Listing and evaluation of sources of information.
   b. Area subdivisions (physical, economic and political).
   c. Terrain (natural and artificial features).
   d. Predominating weather and climatic conditions.
   e. Key installations and facilities.

    f. Political factors.

    g. Sensitive portions of the area.

    h. Communication systems.

2. The population.

    a. Racial composition.

    b. Political complexion.

    c. Religious affiliations.

    d. Social structure.

    e. Economic conditions.

The following is a suggested outline of factors that may be included in the second type of intelligence study which is conducted as a continuation of, and supplement to, the advance study.

1. General considerations.

    a. Type of disturbance (political, economic and racial).

    b. Events leading to the disturbance.

    c. Psychological background of the population.

    d. Progress of riot (objectives attained to date, damage, etc.).

2. Ringleaders and important personalities.

    a. Personal data.

    b. Relation to events.

3. Disturbed elements of the population.

    a. Estimated number of rioters.

    b. Weapons and attempts to secure weapons.

    c. Immediate and projected objectives of rioters.

    d. Type of action and degree of violence to be expected.

    e. Capabilities of disturbed elements.

    f. Geographical location of sensitive areas.

4. Dependable elements.

    a. Organized and unorganized civilian groupings.

    b. Measures taken to counteract or suppress rioters.

    c. Capabilities of dependable elements.

    d. Courses of action open to dependable elements to curtail rioting elements.

    e. Security measures affected by dependable elements.

    f. Sources of information available to dependable elements.

Regular Meetings

At least once each week representatives of all units and departments should meet for an exchange of current information and an evaluation of what action should be taken.

INTELLIGENCE DURING
ORGANIZED MASS CIVIL DISOBEDIENCE

If it is learned that a particular group plans to violate laws and upset the peace of the community, every effort should be made to meet their challenges by maintaining law and order. This can only be done with advance knowledge of their plans.

Before any acts of civil disobedience, contact the group leaders and learn as much about them, their organization and aims, as is possible. During these times they will answer some questions and converse with the police, for they themselves will be interested in evaluating the police and learning as much as they can of the police plans and techniques. Indeed, they may look upon such a conversation as a battle of wits. The smart investigator would not try to overwhelm his subject with his intelligence. In this manner, the subject might be led into a much more revealing conversation. While they will talk, every piece of information possible about their background should be explored. Later they freeze up and become silent, for they must create the impression that the police are their enemy. A report on them should be written out to go into the department's case history of the organization.

As fast as the leaders are identified, a record check should be requested from all the places they will admit having been for any length of time. The information thus gleaned could indicate the type of person the police may have to deal with later. The identified leaders, regardless of what connection they have with the effort, are to be photographed.

If at all possible, when the local movement seems to be concentrating on such an organized effort, an informer should be planted or developed. He should be encouraged to be a familiar figure in the movement. This individual will be more valuable as an informer if he has some leadership abilities, as this will put him close to the decision making group. Indeed he should strive to be included in all of the group planning. He will get more inside information if he gains their confidence enough to be let in on the top level plans. The earlier this contact with the informer the better are his chances of getting into a good position for his work. After the movement starts, the task of securing a good informer becomes almost impossible. This type of work in this particular field will probably cost more than other general work of similar nature. It is a more valuable service because the community as a whole will be affected. The informer must exercise great secrecy in reporting his information and in getting his pay for his services. His pay should never be in the form of a check, for the obvious reason that in cashing the check he might reveal his connections.

Keep a watchful eye on meeting places and points of activity. A constant surveillance is important. Never put a lone officer on these surveillances if he must be near the gathering, or if he is at a point where the parties watched may observe the surveillance.

In order to obtain information and intelligence data at the scene of any threatened civil disturbance, certain members of the enforcing agency may be assigned to act as observers, their duties being to report their observations and to insure that the proper information is furnished to the commanding officer. The observations reported by them may greatly influence the action that will have to be taken in a given situation.

Men assigned to this duty should be in plain clothes and dressed to fit the occasion so that they can mingle with the crowd without attracting undue attention. No parts of their uniform should be worn while on this duty. The given situation will control the number of men assigned to this work.

Upon approaching the disturbance area, any vehicles used by the observers should be parked at the safest location available. The location selected should be some distance from the scene so that men will not be observed entering or leaving the vehicles.

Once at the scene of disturbance, the nearest available telephone offering the maximum security should be noted. Reports of conditions should be made periodically to the individual in charge and should include such information as the following:

1. Whether the disturbance is increasing or has lessened in intensity.
2. The size of any group, or opposing groups, if more than one.

3. The names of the ringleaders or persons who appear to be inciting or agitating the crowd (their description, dress or other identifying data); whether they are local persons or strangers; and the degree of success each leader seems to be having in handling the crowd.
4. Circulation and nature of rumors.
5. The types of persons who comprise the group or groups and their reaction to suggestions of violence; any bristling or jostling that is going on.
6. How armed, whether carrying concealed weapons, sticks, bats, wrenches, bricks, etc.
7. The types of placards or signs being used and the phraseology appearing on them.
8. The number of spectators, type, probability of disorders being committed by them, number of each sex, whether they are friendly or opposed to disorderly elements.
9. The equipment used by the leaders such as sound trucks or other vehicles, loud speakers without sound trucks, etc. (In reporting on vehicles, note the model, color, year, uses, occupants, registration number and other identifying data.)
10. Any conversation that might be overheard, indicating the degree of violence that may be expected.
11. Any attempt at intimidation, threats, name-calling.

In connection with reporting conditions by the observers, complete notes should be made until such time as the information can be written as a report. When there are stores located in the disturbance area, the observers should ascertain the types and also what merchandise they handle, keeping in mind the possibility of looting in the event the disturbance starts.

The observers should be mentally and physically alert at all times. They should not consort with the factions involved, except as it may be necessary to obtain information. They should not engage in any unwarranted conversation or social activity while on duty, except in extreme necessity to obtain information. All information and facts obtained by the observers should be reported without prejudice, bias, or partiality.

Intelligence Journal

All information pertaining to civil disturbances is recorded in an intelligence journal, wherein a correct day-by-day chronological record of events is maintained. A tentative evaluation of the information received is always assigned to each item which is entered in the journal.

INTELLIGENCE DURING A RIOT

Introduction

During the riot, the intelligence effort must not diminish; indeed, it must be intensified to provide the decision-maker with timely information concerning the rioters and their plans. Plainclothes officers and informants should mingle with the crowd and enter into the mob to gather intelligence, identify leaders, ascertain their plans, and if it is at all possible, photograph and record their commands and statements. In addition to providing timely information this will provide evidence for later court action. All possible means of observation should be used, aircraft, including helicopters, and ground observation posts established from various vantage points, such a rooftops and upper floors of buildings. A systematic interrogation of individuals connected with the mob in any way should be initiated prior to detention, as these persons may disclose valuable information.

If it is learned that a riot will be deliberately instigated, there must be an intelligence contact established with the militant group planning the action. This will be most difficult for the more serious riots generally cannot be anticipated because the planning or instigation is secret. Fortunately because there are few possibility of riot being instigated without considerable numbers of people having been preconditioned for a riot, the choice of those capable of inciting a riot is limited to leaders of special interest groups (labor, racial), conspiracy groups (communism), or vengeance groups, whose tendencies have been disclosed by previous episodes, and expressed views or attitudes. If informants cannot be used to reach them, some other means discussed under covert intelligence must be utilized.

Reconnaissance

Reconnaissance is the effort of field agencies directed toward obtaining information through observation of the enemy, weather, terrain and other environmental factors of the area of operations. It is also directed toward locating or verifying the locations of friendly units. To be fully effective, reconnaissance operations require freedom of maneuver and a favorable mobility differential over the enemy.

Reconnaissance efforts are directed toward gaining and maintaining contact. Information is obtained by stealth, if possible. Reconnaissance by fire or in force may be used when stealth is not essential. Reconnaissance by fire is used against suspected enemy locations to cause the enemy to reveal himself by movement or by returning the fire.

Reconnaissance in force is an attack by a sizable force to discover and test the enemy's strength, disposition, or composition. The commander directing such an operation must be prepared to exploit success. He must, however, consider that either the reconnaissance in force or by fire may disclose his own dispositions and provoke a strong enemy action.

Reconnaissance operations are facilitated by use of electronic equipment, search, interception, and monitoring of enemy communications. Mechanized reconnaissance units will prove extremely useful to screen the movement into disturbed areas of large foot, motorized or armored units. In addition, they will prove useful for extensive patrolling, especially where the area is large and the use of small tasks forces is used to hold prospective rioters in check. The mobility of reconnaissance units provide the commander with a useful unit to use as a mobile force to control outlying areas away from the scenes of the main disturbances.

Observation

Observations of activities of participants in disturbances are made from a number of observation posts. Observation aircraft, particularly helicopters, are valuable. The police helicopter should be activated to provide reconnaissance of the surrounding area, maintaining radio contact with the command post, to alert police of the movement of large groups toward the area, or the congregation of potentially dangerous elements on roof or other vantage points. As observations are made, reports should be made directly by radio to the commander or command post.

Motorized and foot patrols may be used as observers in areas where vehicles can patrol. Security of the men and vehicles involved will determine the extent of use of this source of information.

Manning Observation Points

In addition to verbal and written intelligence, visual observation is very important in an active or potential riot area. For this purpose, men can be sent to strategic locations such as rooftops, rooms overlooking critical areas, and into ground-level locations near the action scene. These must be mature and reliable men who will report accurately what they themselves see. They may be disguised and operate from concealed positions. Usually they will have to be capable of protecting themselves; if not, additional men can sometimes be sent with them for security purposes. The telephone is a natural means of quick communication with headquarters, but it is not always reliable in riot-torn areas where light and communications are the first targets of the more organized rioting elements.

Plans should provide for agents to mix with the rioters and learn their plans. At the outbreak of riotous conditions the unruly element will be loosely organized and undisciplined; its leadership will rarely be good; its armament and equipment will be inferior to that of the police. It will be difficult for the leaders to keep secret, or execute, a well-prepared plan. It should be possible to determine the plans of the rioters and take preventive measures.

Plainclothes officers and informants should gather intelligence by mingling with crowds and enter into the mob. The functions of these officers are as follows:

1. Identify leaders of group, spot trouble areas and ascertain the plan of action and its degree of armament.
2. Pass information through a contact man to field commander.
3. If dispersal order is to be given, these officers should deploy themselves on the opposite side of the crowd in order to hear the order and thus be able at a later date to establish in court that it was given in such a manner as to be heard by the mob.
4. In event of disturbance
   a. Observe actions of participants.
   b. Assist uniform officers only in the case of emergency.

    c. Follow leaders who leave scene.

    d. These officers may also make an arrest for a minor altercation, but should follow the suspect and make it away from the scene.

5. Photograph demonstrations and leaders from within the mob itself.

6. Record, by the use of concealed equipment, statement and commands of mob leaders and professional agitators.

Because of the undercover nature of an observer's work, reporting is difficult and delay in reporting is often unavoidable since it is usually necessary for an observer to leave the crowd to make his report. Further, significant action may take place during the observer's absence from the area of activity.

COUNTER-INSURGENCY INTELLIGENCE

Intelligence is the key to counter-insurgency operations. Without it the police are as a blind man trying to defend himself against a pack of wolves. With proper intelligence the rebels can be harassed, hounded and destroyed.

The first step is to learn the organizational structure, the area and method of operation, the source of supply and the leadership of the insurrectionists. The tools used to accomplish this are those basic to covert intelligence. Experience teaches that the best source of such information is the surrendered enemy.

How does one induce to surrender a person, so dedicated to a cause that he takes to the demanding cruel life of a guerrilla? There is no single answer, but certainly high on the list is disillusionment with the cause that led one into the rebellion. Certainly there is no greater breeder of disillusionment than the sense of defeat, the feeling that ambition has been frustrated. This is brought about by delivering crushing blow after crushing blow, by harassing and hunting the guerrilla in his own territory, with his own tactics, by destroying his contacts with the populace upon which he is dependent and without which he cannot continue to operate.

The government must, on the other hand, hold out some inducement. Surrender must be made attractive. Amnesty, land, rewards, are all lures to the disgruntled revolutionist. Most important, law enforcement must establish a reputation for living up to the terms set forth in their psychological appeals. Such a reputation will not be quickly established, but once gained, will pay rich dividends.

Although the informant is the most prolific source of intelligence, the other methods must not be ignored. Indeed, intelligence activities should include detection and penetration type operations such as the following:

1. Search and seizure operations.
2. Establishing and operating checkpoints and roadblocks.
3. Documentation of civilians for identification with central files.
4. Censorship.
5. Physical and electronic surveillance of suspects and meeting places.
6. Maintenance of extensive dossiers.
7. Use of funds and supplies to obtain information.
8. Intensive interrogation of captured guerrillas or underground suspects.

Special effort should be made to collect information that will lead to the capture of irregular force leaders, since they play a vital part in maintaining irregular force morale and effectiveness.

Dossiers on leaders and other key members of the irregular force should be maintained and carefully studied. Frequently the operations of certain of these individuals develop a pattern which, if recognized, may aid materially in the conduct of operations against them. Efforts must be made to obtain rosters and organization data of irregular force elements. The names and locations of families, relatives and friends of known members are desired. These persons are valuable as sources of information, and traps can be laid for other members contacting them. In communities friendly to guerrillas, some persons are usually engaged in collecting food and providing other aid such as furnishing message drops and safe houses for guerrilla couriers. Every effort must be made to discover and apprehend such persons; however, it may be preferable in certain cases to delay their arrest in order to watch their activities and learn the identity of their contacts. It is sometimes possible to recruit these persons as informants, thereby gaining valuable information concerning the irregular force organization and its communication system.

Overt Collection

A large part of the intelligence required for operations against irregular forces is provided by intelligence personnel, troop units and special information srvices assisted by civilian agencies and individuals. Reconnaissance and surveillance is an indispensable part of operations against the guerrilla elements. Great care must be exercised, however, so that such activities do not alert the guerrillas and warn them of planned operations. Reconnaissance missions, whenever possible, should be assigned to units with a routine mission which is habitually executed in the arca and which they can continue at the same in order not to arouse the suspicions of the guerrillas of forthcoming operations. Extensive use is made of aerial surveillance using all types of sensors, with means for speedy exploitation of the interpreted results of such coverage.

Every peace officer and soldier is an intelligence agent and a counterintelligence agency when operating against an irregular force. Each man must be observant and alert to everything he sees and hears. He reports anything unusual which concerns the civil population and the irregular force, no matter how trivial.

Covert Collection

Covert collection means are a necessary source of information. Every effort is made to infiltrate the irregular force with friendly agents. The most intensive covert operations possible must be developed consistent with time, available means and established policy.

Counterintelligence

Irregular forces depend primarily upon secrecy and surprise to compensate for the superior combat power available to the countering military force. Since the degree of surprise achieved will depend largely on the effectiveness of the intelligence gained by the irregular force, intensive effort must be made to expose, thwart, destroy, or neutralize the irregular force intelligence system. Counterintelligence measures may include the following:

1. Background investigation of personnel in sensitive assignments.
2. Screening of personnel.

3. Surveillance of known or suspected irregular force agents.
4. Censorship or suspension of civil communications.
5. Control of civilian movement as required.
6. Checks on the internal security of all installations.
7. Indoctrination of personnel in all aspects of security.
8. The apprehension and reemployment of irregular force agents.
9. Security classification and control of plans, orders and reports.

PRISONER INTERROGATION

A new phase of police intelligence which will play a more important role in law enforcement in the future, due to its greater involvement in counter-insurgency, is prisoner interrogation and captured document and material processing.

Interrogation Unit

Plans should be made to detail and interrogate persons who leave or are taken from the mob. Detailed interrogation of prisoners and inhabitants of the riot area is accomplished by the police who operate under the direction of the intelligence officer.

Phases

The purpose of interrogation is to develop information of immediate tactical importance to the commander, and to establish identifications and information concerning order of battle.

Responsibilities of Those Guarding Prisoners

Prevent prisoners from discarding or destroying any document not taken, or overlooked, by the capturing unit. Guards bringing up the rear will be instructed to collect any documents dropped by prisoners. Prevent anyone other than authorized interrogators from speaking with prisoners. Prevent anyone from giving prisoners food, drink, or tobacco prior to interrogation. Enforce silence among prisoners at all times.

Wounded

Examination of wounded prisoners by interrogator personnel may take place at any time during evacuation, if, in the opinion of the surgeon, such examination will not endanger the life of the prisoner. The fact that prisoners are wounded and a prisoner are two psychological aspects which make them quite willing to divulge information.

Dead rioters will be searched for documents and other items of information, as directed by the intelligence officer or his representative. Documents found will be tagged as to the time, place and circumstances under which found, and put into intelligence channels. Only a relatively small percentage of prisoners will be questioned in detail, based on a brief examination of all prisoners.

Reports

Reports are divided into spot, consolidated, special and periodic reports.

SPOT REPORTS. These are important items of information sent immediately to the intelligence officer.

CONSOLIDATED REPORTS. These are reports containing information gathered from a number of prisoners.

SPECIAL REPORTS. These may be reports of information obtained from one individual or pertaining to one special matter.

PERIODIC REPORTS. Periodic prisoner reports are a summation of information gained during a predetermined period. They have no special form, but are usually prepared in such a way as to fit easily into the periodic intelligence report.

Essentials of the Prisoner Report

ACCURACY. The report must be precise in its reference to numbers, locations, calibers or weapons, names and other details. If a question exists relative to the accuracy of any information, it will be noted in the report, and every effort made in future interrogations to verify the questionable statements.

BREVITY. There is little need for lengthy or detailed reports at tactical command levels. In an active situation the intelligence officer will have little time to read and evaluate such reports.

CLARITY. The report must be written in clear and understandable English. Foreign words and expressions should be translated.

TIMELINESS. The quality of timeliness is especially important in the interrogation reports prepared at lower echelons. The interrogator should furnish the intelligence officer any pertinent information with the least possible delay.

OBJECTIVITY. The interrogator is objective at all times. He must never inject his prejudices into his report, but simply state facts. If he "believes" or "doubts" various items of information, he so states in his report. Knowing the language and the mentality of the prisoner, he will be the best judge of the dependability of his information. When the facts he is reporting are in any way questionable, they are prefaced in the report by such phrases as "believes"; "claims to have seen"; "claims to have heard"; according to rumors"; "feels certain"; etc.

Captured Documents

A captured document is any piece of recorded information which has been in the hands of the enemy. Documents include maps, sketches, photographs, orders, tactical and technical manuals and instructions, code books, log books, maintenance records, shipping and packing slips and lists, diaries, books, newspapers, notebooks, service records, pay rolls, postcards and letters, the records of head-quarters, post and telegraph offices, and any written, printed, engraves, or photographic matter that may contain information relative to the enemy, actual or possible operations.

Handling

Proper steps will be taken to guard against destruction of documents by prisoners. Documents should be properly tagged to identify them with the prisoner from whom taken. They should be handed to the escort for delivery with the prisoner throughout his journey to the rear or exceptionally, when desired, for transmission through intelligence channels in advance of the prisoner. Thus the documents will be available, with the prisoners upon whom found, to subsequent interrogators.

Enemy documents may be found wherever the enemy has been. Many documents are found accidentally by an individual police officer. It is imperative that he be trained in the proper handling of such documents to assure that they are transferred to intelligence.

It is a command responsibility to place guards on enemy installations, immediately upon seizure to permit authorized personnel to make a detailed search of areas, and to prevent destruction or loss of any documents. Special attention must be given to all areas previously occupied by the enemy for partially destroyed or buried documents, including maps, letters, charts, cryptologic documents and orders. Captured documents will be tagged. The tag will bear the following information:

1. The capturing unit.
2. Where it was found (geographic location).
3. When it was found (time and date).
4. The circumstances under which it was found (e.g., loose on the ground, on a dead body, in an office or headquarters).

This last item is important because it assists in determining the validity and current importance of the document when it reaches intelligence hands.

Classification

All documents will be transferred to the intelligence section which is charged with the duty of examining and classifying.

Documents of immediate tactical value will be referred to as "A" documents.

Documents of strategic intelligence value will be referred to as "B" documents.

Documents of no military or strategic intelligence value will be referred to as "C" documents.

Untrained personnel should under no circumstances be authorized to declare a document "of no intelligence value." Some of the most innocuous-looking documents may contain fragmentary information which, when evaluated in conjunction with other sources, may lead to important indications or intentions of the enemy.

Priority of transmission to the commander will be determined by classification "A," "B," or "C"; "A" documents receiving highest priority. Documents containing information in both "A" and "B" classification will be studied carefully. Information falling in the "A" classification will be extracted for immediate use. The processing of documents must be so conducted as not to efface the originals or otherwise render them unsuitable for photographic reproduction.

Captured Materiel

Material must be secured for study by intelligence. Material includes supplies, stores and equipment of all types, including instruments, vehicles, clothing, weapons and ammunition. All captured and abandoned enemy material is of intelligence interest. Personnel responsible for the interrogation of prisoners must be fully cognizant of the importance of the intelligence to be derived from material. The examination and exploitation of documents captured with, pertaining or referring to, enemy material must be coordinated with the examination and exploitation of such material.

Chapter 12

DEPARTMENT MANPOWER PLAN

INTRODUCTION

ANY PLAN FOR action is centered around manpower. Manpower is a most important element for successfully maintaining peace and good order during strife. Plans must be drafted to assure the rapid assembly and deplorement of personnel and equipment in sufficient numbers to cope with almost any emergency situation. For maximum effectiveness, this plan must be activated as soon as possible.

EMERGENCY MOBILIZATION AND DEPLOYMENT

Plans should be formulated for mobilization of both the regular and auxiliary or reserve forces. It should include the following:

1. A listing of personnel designated for riot control assignments. Such listing should include information concerning their duty assignment (location and shift), their residence address and telephone number.
2. A system of notification for personnel.
3. A plan for transporting personnel to the trouble area.
4. A program for periodic briefing of personnel concerning their specific assignments.
5. Information concerning the identity of personnel trained, with the type of riot control training specifically set forth. It is most important that individuals with technical training (communications, photography, etc.) should be listed.
6. Dispersal of reserve personnel and equipment to assembly areas outside the potential critical areas.
7. Sources of reinforcement. Special categories of personnel such as doctors, nurses, ambulance attendants, dog and horse trainers, aircraft pilots, armored vehicles drivers and boat operators.

Determination of Need

The first step in any manpower plan is to determine the personnel requirements. The number of police personnel required should be based on an analysis of intelligence reports, reconnaissance, previous similar events, number of magnitude of potential problem areas and information by sponsors of the event. Such flexibility is gained by establishing various degrees of mobilization.

Types of Mobilization Orders

There are eight basic types of mobilization orders which may be issued for one or more specific departmental units. They may be issued singly or in groups.

Departmental Mobilization Orders

MO 1 mobilizes on-duty personnel for a departmental unit.

MO 2 mobilizes personnel of the departmental unit next due to report for duty.

MO 3 mobilizes personnel of a departmental unit last relieved from duty.

MO 4 mobilizes the emergency police reservists of one or more precincts.

Complete Mobilization Orders

CMO 1 mobilizes all on-duty personnel for the entire department.

CMO 2 mobilizes all personnel of the department next due to report for duty.

CMO 3 mobilizes all the personnel of the department last relieved from duty.

CMO 4 mobilizes all emergency police reservists.

Relocation and Reassignment

The relocation and reassignment of that portion of the manpower already on duty throughout the city or community is the first step in the massing of manpower in critical areas. Each shift should have a percentage of its men assigned to a reaction unit which will respond to any crowd problem that may arise during its shift. Emphasis should be placed on the establishment of a mobile reserve force with good communications.

It is desirable in advance of any trouble to organize squads and designate leaders on each shift. By having the group leader and his group selected from the same shift, they are more easily and quickly called in for action. There is a definite advantage to having these men in groups. It allows the commander to hold units in different degrees of readiness. One may be in reserve, any on standby and still another on alert. The commander also can call out any one of the groups without having all of them report. One entire shift can also be held over after duty hours without complete groups contained within the shift being broken.

Keep the group reporting as a unit during emergency operation so a minimum loss of time in special assignments will be experienced. The commanding officer can do his work much faster if he can issue orders for a unit to the group leader. He is thus relieved of the task of assigning specific tasks to everybody, thus he and his men can get much more work done in a shorter time.

Recall of Off-duty Officers

There must also be a plan to recall off-duty officers for assignment to the area of tension or to man those districts or beats left unattended by those sent to the mob or riot area. There are several ways to do this. To cancel vacations and days off will add considerably to the force. To activate two twelve-hour duty shifts and divide the men between just these two shifts will further increase the force, but that just about ends the potential of the police department. To simplify the division of the department personnel for twelve-hour duty shifts, it is better to concentrate only on the division and reassignment of one of the three shifts into the remaining two shifts.

Call-up Plan

A police department would do well to establish as a part of its routine procedures an emergency call list whereby off-duty policemen could be returned to duty as rapidly as possible. Sources of off-duty manpower will be utilized in the following order, sufficient to provide the requested number of police officers:

1. Recalling personnel from the off-duty relief within the affected district who are scheduled to report for duty on the next watch.
2. Recalling personnel from other districts as qualified in point 1. This notification to be made by telephone and teletype. This recall may be extended to any or all districts, bureaus, or units, until the required number of officers is obtained.
3. Recalling off-duty personnel from within the district affected who have last completed a tour of duty.
4. Recalling off-duty personnel from other districts and units as qualified in point 3.
5. If details must be maintained over a prolonged period, an administrative decision shall be made giving consideration to the following.
   a. Cancellation of off-days.
   b. Establishment of twelve-hour shifts.
   c. Obtaining manpower from other sources.

Degrees of Call Up

To preserve the energy of the police, it is well to establish degrees of call up. The first is the *alert*. The police are notified of the emergency and told to hold themselves in readiness. *Standby* requires the police to be dressed, equipped and ready to move if called. *Reserve* demands that the officer report to the designated reserve center to await commitment to action.

Notification

A systematic method of notifying officers must be established. One method is to divide the shift into groups, each with a group leader. The highest ranking officer of each off-duty shift should be notified of the mobilization. He will notify subordinate officers who will notify the group leaders. The group leaders will notify each member of their group. The number of individuals each person notifies should be kept to a minimum. In no case should anyone be assigned to notify more than eight persons.

The notification shall inform the officer of where and when he is to report. It is also advisable to designate the troubled area in order that he can skirt that area.

The officer will report as soon as possible to the designated staging area. At this point there must be a designated spot at which he will check in and receive his orders.

In the event of a major disaster, arrangements should be made to have a broadcast made by the radio and television stations on the disaster-warning network every fifteen minutes the first hour, every fifteen minutes the second hour, and every thirty minutes the third and fourth hours to call all police back to duty. After the first hour of this broadcast, the various districts and bureaus can begin notifying by telephone those officers that have not reported on duty. When emergencies of major proportions occur and it is evident that mobilization of the department is probable, members shall report at their assigned unit without waiting for an official notice.

Test Alert

Periodically and at unannounced times test alerts should be conducted on order of the police chief. When this type alert is involved, nothing further than completion of notification by telephone and execution of the form is necessary; physical response to a location is not required.

Actual Alert

When an actual alert is ordered, personnel will physically respond to the designated assembly point. The assembly point shall be clearly set forth in all communications and properly recorded in the appropriate space on the form. When personnel are notified of an actual alert they will be given specific instructions relative to reporting immediately to the assembly point in full uniform and completely equipped. At the conclusion of a test or actual alert, all forms will be collected by the unit commander and, accompanied by a covering report explaining any problems or unusual circumstances, forwarded to the police chief.

Pre-demonstration Mobilization

When possible, it is desirable to mobilize the police and assemble them at the scene of the expected violence prior to the arrival of the mob.

MOBILIZATION POINTS

The plan should designate the points for each precinct at which units will mobilize in event of emergency. Although this point will usually be the police station, it is wise to designate an alternate point to cover possible unforseen contingencies that may render the station unfit for this purpose.

A site selected as an additional mobilization point must be suitable for such use. It must be available at all times, have telephone facilities and space to accommodate reserves. A building should not be selected which might be used during the emergency for purposes incompatible with police operations, for example, a business to which the public would be allowed free entry even during the emergency. The location should be convenient to transportation facilities and the portion of precinct to be policed therefrom. Adequate parking space must be available.

The mobilization point area shall be divided into sectors for foot, mounted and radio motor patrol forces. Sectors for each type of patrol shall be numbered consecutively.

BRIEF OFFICERS

One of the common causes of mistakes made in handling demonstrations is the failure to instruct officers who are to handle situations. All police personnel should be informed personally as thoroughly as possible regarding the nature of the disturbance, its cause, origin or identity of the leadership, types and sources of violence anticipated, rights and limitations of the police and rights of citizens. They should know generally the tactical approach to be utilized and techniques likely to be employed. They should likewise be advised of the location of important points such as first aid locations.

PERSONNEL ASSIGNMENTS

Assignments of all members of the department shall be entered in the temporary headquarters log maintained at the scene. An accurate account of all department personnel and equipment must be kept at the staging area and forwarded to the field command post for inclusion in the log. The report will show the personnel involved and their assignments.

To utilize fully the varied skills and experience of the members of the department, assignments at an emergency shall be made, if possible, according to the particular branch or unit to which the member is permanently assigned. The assignment should contain the following:

1. Location to which they are to report.
2. Time at which they are to report.
3. All assignments should be listed and should show
    a. Location of command posts.
    b. Communication access to command posts, i.e., the telephone numbers, radio frequency and call numbers.
    c. List of the chain of command and designation of specific officer assigned to each position.
4. Each officer's assignment should be listed. This should include a designation of his commander, his area of responsibility, his duties, and any pertinent facts or the identification special trouble spots unique to his assignment.
5. His telephone number, radio band and call designation should be shown. If he is to be in a mobile unit, the particular vehicle should be designated.
6. Any special equipment he is to carry should be listed.
7. The assignment sheet should have a summary of telephone numbers, wave bands and call numbers.

Thus the officer not only has clear cut written personal orders but a knowledge of the placement, assignments and method of communication with all other units. When pertinent, charts and maps should be attached to the assignment order. All key points should be coded and the key included with the assignment.

IDENTIFICATION OF POLICE

Officers not in uniform must have a ready means of immediate identification. It is as necessary that they recognize each other as it is for the mob participants to recognize them. Any method which meets this criterion is acceptable. Probably the two most widely used methods are armbands and lapel badges. The armband may be used on the arm opposite the lapel bearing the badge. This affords the officer better identification from all angles. A combination of badge and armband offers a better means of identification than the use of either method alone. A riot helmet worn by the officer will also provide an excellent means of identification.

It may be necessary to issue passes to certain employees, as well as members of the press, to allow them to enter buildings and restricted critical areas that are cordoned off.

A further refinement of identification used extensively at command headquarters in recent riots was to assign various collor armbands to signify various staffs and functions. It was thus immediately apparent whether or not one was authorized to be in a given area, such as newspapermen at a closed strategy meeting of the top command where secret and confidential information was discussed.

POLICE AUXILIARY

In some instances special deputies or auxiliary groups have been found to be of assistance to the police. In this connection, if auxiliary police are to be used, they should be in a uniform recognized by the community as representing law and order. Special officers or reserves should be used to replace regular officers in traffic duty and in patrolling unaffected districts.

UNTRAINED CITIZENS

Don't use untrained citizens if it can be avoided. Nonprofessional persons, regardless of their good intentions and patriotism, usually prove of little or no value.

RESERVE

The commander should not commit his entire force to any operation, but rather he should maintain a reserve at the mobilization point. Reinforcements may be required if the size and fury of the mob is greater than anticipated. Replacements will be needed to replace casualties and fatigue cases and to reinforce weak areas. The reserve is also used to frustrate the efforts of agitators who attempt to divert police attention from the actual scene by causing other disturbances. If available manpower permits, the police commander should usually employ his forces by having one third in direct contact with the mob, one third as support units, and one third held in reserve. Reserves should be strategically located with respect to the crowd, its direction of movement, and the rallying point for striking forces. The field commander should be kept informed at all times regarding the status of reserves.

RIOT TRAINING

Introduction

Riot control training is combat training. Each police officer must be impressed with the need for this type of training and the importance of riot control duty. Training must be intensive and continuing and must reach all who will become involved, whether in the field or in a command position. Stress must be placed upon a disciplined response to orders, the maintenance of a correct objective attitude, even in the face of the most aggravating circumstances, and the need for teamwork of a very high order.

Training is not limited to the officer on the line. Both field and staff personnel at the command level must receive training which should include plans, organization, control, communications and coordination of combined operations, as well as the use of basic formations and weapons.

Types of Training

INDIVIDUAL. Plans for disaster operations call for police to perform certain duties. These police should be designated and should receive training in the particular duties that they are to perform. Each person should be trained so that he will know what he is to do and how to do it.

UNIT TRAINING. After individual officers have been trained to perform the specific duties, the unit should be trained to function as a team. This includes assembling at designated locations with appropriate equipment and practicing the operations called for in the disaster plans.

CONTINUOUS TRAINING. The officers must always be ready to assume their roles in disaster operations. In order to maintain a state of readiness, there should be periodic rehearsals of the operations set forth in the disaster plans. Staff personnel should observe the operations to note any deficiencies to be corrected and to determine the degree of proficiency of the training.

Each department should conduct yearly in-service training programs. The best results are obtained when such sessions are conducted just before the summer months, since this is the period in which the most trouble is to be expected.

Criteria

It is obviously impossible to recommend any specific training course that will suffice for all departments. There are certain criteria, however, which would serve as guidelines for the law enforcement executive or training officer in devising an adequate course. The first step would be formulation of the major objectives of the training. Next, the curriculum should be developed with careful consideration being given to both subject matter and method of teaching. Finally, some provision should be worked out for evaluating the results of the training.

Objectives

The major objectives of the training should include at least the following:

1. Greater understanding the sociological, cultural and psychological factors underlying the development and actions of mobs.
2. Development of an effective functioning unit which can be mobilized quickly to prevent or control outbreaks of violence.

The law enforcement executive should satisfy himself that the training courses accomplish the following:

1. Offers good understanding of the psychology of the formation and behavior of mobs and crowds.
2. Gives each man a clear understanding of the department's overall plans for preventing and controlling violence.
3. Makes each man proficient in operating the equipment available for use in these situations.

4. Teaches each man his specific assignment and how to carry it out.

5. Assures trained alternates for all key positions.

6. Renders each man so well drilled that he can function without error as a member of a team in the various formations.

7. Thoroughly indoctrinates each man to assure that he will not breach discipline nor lose his head and provoke violence.

8. Gives each man a knowledge of what legal weapons he has available—the statutes and ordinances under which he can take action.

9. Develops in each officer confidence in his ability to carry out his assignments effectively.

Courses

Courses which can be given include the following:

1. Special problems of minority groups.

2. Riot control tactics.

3. Police formation.

4. Characteristics and employment of gas masks, tear gas, riot guns and any other special equipment that may be utilized in a riot.

5. Laws and ordinances used in control of mobs and crowds and suppression of riots.

6. He must know his authority and its limits. He must know what legal tools are available to him and when to use them.

7. Informative lectures should be given to the officers concerning the causes of civil disorders, mob behavior, composition of mobs and the basic elements of mob action. The officers then will have an insight into the strong and weak points in a mob and will be better able to comprehend what faces them and how they can deal effectively with the problem. Motion pictures of actual riots should be used whenever possible.

8. Security.

9. Intelligence.

10. Police plans of a semi-permanent nature such as alert plans, standing operating procedures, loading plans, and others as necessary.

11. Map reading.
12. Communications.
13. Road blocks and barricades.
14. Physical conditioning.
15. Care and maintenance of riot control equipment.
16. Civil disorder prevention and the police civic action program.
17. Disaster control operations.
18. First aid.

Supervisory Personnel

In addition to the general training for all personnel, supervisory personnel should be taught the following:
1. Supervision of their units under extremely difficult conditions involving mob violence and rioting.
2. Setting up command post establishing protection from mob.
3. Planning.
4. Organization.
5. Control procedure and planning.
6. Communications.
7. Coordination of combined operations.

Training

Training should be conducted in classrooms and on the scene where possible. The program should be built around actual incidents. Right and wrong type examples should be used.

The conditions confronting the police in a crowd situation should be simulated in training. Police should be allowed and encouraged to attend and witness demonstrations and acts of mass civil disobedience which occur in other jurisdictions. In this way they fully appreciate the magnitude of the problem and what they will have to face.

Most of all, the officer must practice what he has been taught. Only first-hand experience can thoroughly imprint on men's minds the lessons taught by lecture. Training must include offensive and defensive operations for both daytime and nighttime operations.

Psychological Training

Riot control training is combat training. Police must be impressed with the need for this type of training and the importance of riot control duty. They must realize the necessity for absolute lack of partisanship and for perfect discipline, and that their strength lies in teamwork. They must learn to maintain an objective attitude, even in the face of the most aggravating circumstances.

Their training, including practical field experience, should give them a feeling of familiarity with their duty, the formation weapons, and tactics they will be using. Most of all, as a result of that training, the police should have confidence in their ability to control any disorderly assemblage and a sense of superiority in physical conflict. This confidence arises from familiarity with riot control formations having modern weapons and equipment, and from a realization that they have been properly trained. The officer who does not know what to do will usually be slow and timid, while the trained officer will be prompt, determined and courageous.

The police must be ready to act and must realize their importance to the maintenance of our society and our way of life. They must be convinced that they are right and that they can and will prevail. If a defeatist attitude drapes them, the battle is lost. They must have confidence in themselves, in their leaders and in their cause.

Training should include mental conditioning of the officer for mob violence by actual exposure to such situations. Police and small unit leaders, inexperienced in riot control duty, should be trained to adjust themselves to the noise and confusion created by large numbers of people facing them. They should realize that a mob may shout at them, insult them, or call them names. They must learn to ignore these taunts and not allow personal feelings to interfere with the impartial execution of their mission. Police must expect objects to be thrown at them but they learn to remain in formation and avoid thrown objects by evasive movements. They must never throw them back at the mob. Troops should learn to subdue their emotions and to carry out their orders determinedly and aggressively. They must be emotionally prepared for weird mob actions, such as members of the mob screaming and rushing toward them tearing off their own clothes, or deliberately injuring or maiming themselves. They should understand that the orderly execution of orders is part of the psychological force applied against the rioters.

All personnel should be trained in how to gather evidence, with particular emphasis on the need for a full documentation of the facts and circumstances of an arrest. A riot scene is a place of confused, fast-moving action and an arresting officer cannot place his reliance in his ability to recall, at a later time when the case goes to trial, the conditions under which he took the enforcement action, unless he has made basic notes and memoranda to refresh his recollection.

RIOT SQUAD

Introduction

Every department should give serious consideration to establishing a special riot squad. It should be a specially selected highly trained unit which will act as a nucleus for any force sent to the scene of a riot. It provides a mobile force of highly trained and specially equipped officers. This special detail will give stability to a larger contingent of lesser trained and inexperienced officers which may be used at the scene of such mob violence. Their employment in lesser disturbances permits the local patrol force to return to its normal duties.

Location

This unit should be as centrally located as possible to minimize the time required to field it at the scene of a disturbance.

Selection of Members

The methods of selecting members are the following: review of department personnel records, talking with candidates' past supervisors, and personal interview of the candidates. The following should be found in the members of this unit:

1. A desire to belong to the detail and a willingness to be away from home and to work long hours.
2. The candidates must have experience within the department, primarily in patrol functions.

3. Members of the unit must be young, tall in stature, in top physical condition, and physically capable of meeting the rigorous demands that will be made of them. It is axiomatic that all officers should keep themselves in excellent physical condition, for during times of major disturbances officers can be expected to work long and arduous hours of duty during which they will be subjected to extreme tension and hard physical exertion.
4. They must be calm and composed, with the ability to control and conceal their emotions, particularly their fear.
5. They must be able to maintain self-control.
6. They must impart to the crowd an intelligent, energetic display of confidence and an ability to cope with their responsibilities.
7. They should be impartial and unbiased, patient, alert and friendly.

Training

The members of the riot squad should be trained to operate as a unit and receive periodic drills in riot control. Intensive and continual training should be given in the following subjects:
1. Military drill and formations.
2. Law.
3. Crowd psychology.
4. Weapons.
5. Weaponless defense.
6. Special equipment
   a. Mobile command post.
   b. Generator and lighting.
   c. Ropes and barriers.
   d. Mobile kitchen.
   e. Photographic equipment.
   f. Communications—field telephones, walkie-talkies and loud speakers.
7. Industrial relations.
8. Fire survival.
9. Evidence.

10. Physical fitness.

11. Tactical principles.

All training should be presented by the best qualified personnel available, supplemented by the most up to date visual aids and handout material. Results of the training program will be tested through the use of field problems—written tests and critiques of actual operations.

Organization

Riot control units should be organized on a reserve basis for each shift of the day. Each member should be assigned a particular function or position on the riot unit of the shift which corresponds to his regular work shift. Alternate members should be appointed to cover vacancies caused by days off for illness, training or vacation. In the event of an emergency, the alarm should be transmitted by the most rapid means. Members of the riot control unit should proceed to a designated point near the scene, receive their riot equipment, which would be waiting, take their proper places and go into action.

The Commander

A permanent commander should be selected and assigned this unit. His full-time duties should consist of formulating plans to handle such situations and commanding the special forces in time of deployment. He should also be responsible for preparing and supplying the training unit with adequate instructional material and giving other technical support to all training in these areas of activity. He should supervise periodic drills in riot control. He might also prepare simple legal information with respect to the rights of officers and citizens. He should act as liaison officer with line commanders in matters involving planning for control of large disturbances.

INDIVIDUAL OFFICER'S CONDUCT

The police are most effective when they are able to attain and maintain the respect of the disturbing element. Thus the impression an officer creates by his dress, bearing and demeanor are of the utmost importance. The uniform should be complete and in good repair. The officer who is neat in appearance with a clean uniform is a symbol of law and order, and by his appearance will affect the crowd psychologically.

The office should create a favorable impression with his carriage and appearance. His appearance and manner must depict competence and confidence, sometimes beyond what he actually feels. To accomplish this he should maintain a soldierly bearing. He should stand and walk erect. He should not put hands in pocket, on hips, or folded on chest. When hands are not at his sides, they may be clasped at the rear in an "at-ease" position. He should not lean on a car, building, or other structure.

Speech

Because of the public position he holds, what an officer says and how he says it can have far reaching effects, particularly in crowd and mob situations. By controlling his voice and gestures he can exert a firm and steadying influence over those around him, especially at scenes of civil disorders or crimes of violence. His language and manner of speaking can be an aid to influencing those near him. He should use short, simple, positive and direct sentences. He should not use profanity nor indulge in sarcasm or irony.

Police officers must strenuously avoid the use of insulting terms and names. Some expressions which may be used casually without thought of offending are nevertheless offensive to members of minority groups and invariably antagonize the person or group to whom they are addressed. It is much worse to use a term that insults the group than to use one which insults the individual. It is, of course, absolutely essential that no insulting terms of any kind be used, but terms which refer to a racial classification or a racial group should be most strenuously avoided.

The police officer must be careful not to make any remarks or become involved in any action that could be seized upon and used to condemn him or his department. He must not joke with the mob, nor debate issues, nor become involved in any arguments, nor take sides, nor reply to taunts, nor repeat rumors.

The officer should maintain a stern, determined attitude and facial expression and remain aloof, impartial. He must be dignified. Dignity implies a state of being worthy and honorable. The police officer must remain calm and in control of his temper. He cannot get excited or jittery, for if he does his attitude will be projected to the members of the mob with disastrous results.

Guidelines for Action

The officer must respond immediately to supervisory commands. This is particularly true in a riot situation; but if an order is not understood, he should not hesitate to ask a superior to clarify it.

If he is required to leave his post for any reason, he should immediately report to a superior officer the necessity for leaving. If it is impractical to notify a superior officer before leaving a post, he should be notified as soon as possible.

When committed, each officer will keep the crowd under observation at all times. He should sweep the group with his vision when he is in an advancing or stationary formation. Confining attention to one person invites a response from him that may be abusive. The officer should watch particularly for carried parcels or objects. Mob members have been known to carry paper bags with broken bottles inside. The bag should be checked if any doubt exists. Whip antennas are used by rioters as weapons. These should be seized as evidence along with the rioter carrying it. All evidence must be marked. Glass, bottles, or bottle fragments within reach of the line should be smashed with the baton. The officer should report all objects that could be used as weapons: soft drink concessions with bottles, rocks at construction sites, beer cans in trash pickup points, etc. He should also report to the commanding officer immediately any information pertaining to a situation that might aid in dispersing the crowd.

When he acts, he should be firm and decisive but courteous. To avoid being guilty of unnecessary or rough handling of persons involved, he should use only that force which is necessary to maintain order, effect the arrest, and protect himself from bodily harm. "Hand-to-hand" fighting or individual combat must be avoided as far as is possible since police officers are almost always outnumbered. Supervisory control and unit action would be lost to the police department, thereby sacrificing our most valuable assets.

Never at any time should a single officer attempt to handle one rioter. The idea of individual heroic police action is not only unnecessary, it may be positively damaging and foolhardy. A police officer who attempts singlehandedly to subdue a mob or grapple with individuals puts his own safety in jeopardy. In the violence that then is bound to ensue, he merely stimulates the ugly tendencies of the crowd. It is of prime importance that such situations be avoided. They can be avoided if supervisory officers so arrange and instruct their personnel the reinforcements can be mobilized at any point in the shortest time possible and in numbers appropriate to the situation.

When making an arrest the officer must remember that he must be able to identify any person that he arrests and connect him with the crime with which he is charged. In order to do this, he must do the following:

1. Be prepared to testify concerning the acts of each prisoner.
2. Carefully note descriptions of persons arrested so as to be able to identify prisoners in court.
3. Record in memorandum book the name and description of each prisoner, and the facts of the case.
4. Deliver prisoners to patrolmen assigned to vehicles designated for transporting prisoners.
5. Give the evidence and the following information to the member of the force assigned to convey the prisoner:
   a. Name, sex and race of the prisoner.
   b. Location of arrest.
   c. Charge.
   d. Rank, name and shield number of arresting officer.

Mental Attitude

The officer assigned to crowd control must always act in a manner that insures impartial enforcement of the law, and affords to all citizens the rights guaranteed to them by the Constitution and the legislative statutes. The agitators will frequently try to force police officers into retaliatory measures not warranted by the situation by heaping upon them verbal abuse and insults. The police officer should expect such abuse and should ignore it. If he responds by an unwarranted use of force, the agitator becomes a martyr to the crowd and the ugly mood of the crowd is reinforced.

The difference between personal feelings or attitudes and official attitudes must be inculcated in every member of the force. There is no room in a police force for an officer whose emotions control the manner in which he performs his duty. An officer must be prepared to receive the jeers, taunts, or insults of demonstrators without resorting to physical force. His foremost consideration must be to demonstrate his impartiality to any cause except that of preserving the peace. An officer who transmits this attitude to the people with whom he deals is assured of an initial degree of success in his undertakings.

Group attitudes of police officers must reflect the same degree of impartiality desired of the individual. The chief asset of a police group in restoring order is the conveyance to the demonstrators that enforcement will be strict, impartial and certain. At no time should there be a display of uncertainty by a police group assigned to control a civil disturbance. The feeling of confidence or lack of confidence is quickly transmitted to the members of the crowd, just as the attitude of bias toward an issue is quickly transmitted. Partiality on the part of a police group merely adds a number of persons to one side of the issue or the other, and the stabilizing influence which should be effected by police control disappears completely.

Chapter 13

OUTSIDE ASSISTANCE

INTRODUCTION

M UTUAL AID PLANS with law enforcement agencies of surrounding communities, as well as with the sheriff, the state police or highway patrol and the state national guard, and any military units stationed in the area, should be made final at the earliest possible time. These plans should provide for the method of requesting assistance and the manner in which these forces will be utilized, so that such aid as the situation warrants can be requested and delivered at the earliest possible moment.

Coordination With Other Agencies

Plans must be made to assure coordination with and incorporation of federal, state and local agencies and public utilities, as well as with other police agencies in the area, in any disaster operation.

PLAN

Purpose

The purpose of liaison prior to any problem is to develop plans for the joint operation of the various agencies in time of disaster. It stands to reason that plans made in normal times will be more detailed, complete and efficient than those thrown together in the press of a disaster. Too, if everyone knows the part he is to perform, he is better prepared to act and can go into operation at the earliest possible moment. The plan should do the following:

1. Establish exactly what is expected of all agencies in any and all emergencies, for if these duty and responsibility lines are clearly established, there is little chance of mistakes.
2. Call for an exchange of information between departments. Information on "What NOT to do" is as important as "What to DO."

3. Allow each to learn the other's capabilities, limitations and what assistance they can expect from each other under emergency conditions.
4. Provide for the exchange of intelligence information, and to otherwise prepare to operate effectively.
5. Establish command responsibility.

Plan to Alert and Notify

The plan should include provisions for the alerting, briefing and coordination of efforts of other local, state and federal agencies. Lists should be compiled of the organizations and agencies that will be involved in the activities during emergency situations, together with the names, addresses, and telephone numbers of key representatives of such organizations and agencies who will be contacted.

CHECK LIST

Name	Address	Telephone	Time Notified	Person Notifying (How—telephone, wire, person)

Plan for Standby Preparations

Plans should call for other agencies to place their personnel on an alert basis, that is, advise all personnel either by radio or telephone to be immediately available for duty or standby basis—personnel to be in full uniform at a designated point ready to move upon orders.

Community Leaders

A designated officer must obtain and file the names, addresses and telephone numbers of municipal, county, and state officials, and persons prominent in the community who, in the event of an emergency, will address persons in the area of disorder. The leaders of the minority groups must be included in this list. Liaison must be established with them prior to any emergency and their assistance solicited and obtained.

MUTUAL AID AGREEMENTS

Past experience has shown that disasters and riots can reach proportions that are beyond the capability of local law enforcement agencies. When such is the case, it is necessary to reinforce the local police with additional resources, both personnel and equipment. Realizing this, prior arrangements should be initiated to provide the assistance required. Procedures should be established, command relationships agreed upon, jurisdictional and legal authority problems resolved, and any financial considerations clearly defined. Such agreements should be reflected in the city plan, with the established procedures outlined in detail for the information of all concerned.

State Mutual Aid Plan

The recommended method is to design a state-level assistance plan, such as the Law Enforcement Mutual Aid Plan of the State of California. This plan is designed to facilitate the mobilization, organization, and operations of the law enforcement resources within the state to most effectively minimize the effects of natural or war-caused disasters, to include riots.

The California plan is a combined civil defense, natural disaster and civil disturbance operational plan. As all three of these functions will require some type of outside assistance to the local police agency, such a procedure is feasible and workable. Although the specific procedures established may not be suitable to all states, the basic policies pertaining to the planning procedures accomplished for providing assistance from all resources located within the state are sound and adaptable to all states.

Purpose of the Plan

A sound state aid plan should be formulated to accomplish the following:

1. To provide for the coordination of the dispatch and use of law enforcement personnel and equipment whenever a local law enforcement agency requires law enforcement assistance from any other jurisdiction.
2. To provide for the coordination of law enforcement planning, operations and mutual aid on a state-wide and intra-state jurisdictional basis, and to relate such plans to the overall state plan.
3. To provide a system for the receipt and dissemination of information, data and directive pertaining to the law enforcement

services between local law enforcement officials and state and federal agencies.

4. To prescribe a procedure for the inventory of all law enforcement personnel, facilities, and equipment throughout the entire state.

Regional Mutual Assistance Agreements

Under certain conditions and circumstances, it may be advisable for two or more states to form mutual assistance agreements. Such would be appropriate where large, adjoining metropolitan areas cover two or more state jurisdictions. It would also be beneficial where a densely populated state is bordered by one or more sparsely populated states, where a majority of the population is centered in one or two metropolitan areas and state law enforcement resources are minimal. Such agreements need not be limited to civil disturbance assistance, but may include civil defense, disasters, and combating the interstate crime problem. Such a regional compact has been initiated in the New England States, the New England State Police Compact. This compact provides a basis for two much needed types of cooperation: (1) establishment and maintenance of a central file for the records relating to persons engaged in organized crime, and (2) emergency assistance to the state police of one state by the state police of another state. Although the New England Compact is limited to state police assistance, agreements between states could be expanded to include other state resources, to include State National Guards.

PROCEDURE

Size of Outside Units

If units are to be sent in from other departments, they should come in squad strength and be under their own squad leaders, so that they can function as a unit at the scene.

It is also suggested that instructions be directed to each area that personnel assigned be inspected in their home areas to make sure that they present an acceptable appearance while on the detail.

Organization and Identification of Units

Areas furnishing personnel should be instructed as to what companies they will be assigned, and instructed to furnish each vehicle assigned with a designated distinctively colored cloth to be tied to each antenna, to make company assignments readily identifiable by visual inspection. They should assign different colors for each company. This will enable command personnel to visually identify units of their respective companies. This is particularly important when commanders are dealing with large numbers of unfamiliar officers difficult to identify by appearance or mobile unit.

Automotive units of various companies reporting at the rendezvous point, should be instructed to report to a parking control officer who assembles various companies into predetermined locations, in order to avoid delay and confusion in assembling companies.

"Parking staff" type markers may be used to designate the parking area for each company. Colored flags corresponding to the colored tapes for each company, and including the letter designation of each company, are attached to the top of the staff and located at pre-determined positions. Areas should be assigned to companies prior to their arrival at rendezvous point, and a parking control officer assigned to direct area personnel to their designated parking position on arrival.

STATE NATIONAL GUARD ASSISTANCE

The magnitude of the Los Angeles, Cleveland and Chicago riots demonstrated the inability of the local police agencies to contain a major riot. The tax structure of our cities and counties does not permit the maintenance of reserves of police manpower sufficient to handle riots of gross magnitude. Even in lesser riots and large demonstrations, police manpower must be diverted from its principal duties of providing adequate police protection to all areas of the jurisdiction served.

It is therefore essential that a secondary source of well-trained, controlled and disciplined manpower be available to assist local authorities in the control of riots and demonstrations which are potentially or obviously beyond the capabilities of the local police forces. This legal and historical resource is the State National Guard.

Planning

Every local plan to control large demonstrations potential riots should include means by which the State National Guard can best assist local authorities during these contingencies, and how they can be readied to reinforce local police in a minimum amount of time. Training and rehearsal of the plan is equally important.

Mission

When military force has been called to aid the civil authorities, the troops should never assume the functions of the police unless the civil authority is completely paralyzed. The functions of the police and the military are entirely distinct, and should be kept so.

Policing of the entire city must continue, and this function should be performed by the local police agency, not State National Guard or other support forces sent to assist the local authority. The State National Guard should be employed in the immediate vicinity of the riot area, or engaged in security missions at such places as key utility facilities or other important buildings or potential targets for the rioters. Where the probability of a disturbance can be foreseen, joint task forces of police and guardsmen should be organized and trained together prior to being committed.

Request for the Guard

Application by local authorities for the Guard's aid should be made directly to the governor. To preclude undue delay in providing the assistance required, the establishment of a procedure whereby certain specified key officials may request and authorize employment of the State National Guard is recommended. This procedure should be documented in the appropriate plans and other legal documents, and be supported by pre-positioned, signed, and duly executed legal documents (i.e., proclamation). Individuals authorized to request State National Guard support, as planned for in appropriate plans, should include: the chief executive officer of the city and the police commissioner and/or chief of police. Although such requests would be directed to the governor concerned, in his absence or temporary unavailability, the lieutenant governor, the state attorney general, state adjutant general or state commissioner of police should be empowered to authorize commitment of forces designated for the area concerned.

Certain other facts about the National Guard are important to bear in mind when they are called upon for aid. Military commanders assign missions or tasks to *units* i.e., squads, platoons, companies, not individuals. When planning for State National Guard assistance, local police agencies should determine the strengths of the assigned units, and understand their organizational structure. Only by this method can the police planner gain an understanding of the capabilities and limitations of the supporting forces.

A request for assistance, and the granting of authority for this assistance, must be timely. Only when properly authorized and directed may a unit implement its alert notification plan. The time required to assemble the individuals and prepare to move to the objective area will vary with the units; a minimum of six hours should not be considered excessive. Plans should include alert and assembly time requirements; the decision to request State National Guard assistance should be based on this time factor.

Individuals concerned with requesting and approving State National Guard assistance must also understand the difference between *alerting* the State National Guard (or elements thereof) and *committing* the State National Guard. Planning should also be accomplished with a clear understanding of these two different situations or conditions in mind. Alerting the State National Guard merely gives advance notification and permits the unit(s) to begin actions required to reach the desired state of readiness. Commitment involves actual engagement, and is accomplished in conjunction with the issuance of a proclamation by the governor.

Command

In each plan, and for each contingency, it is essential that the command structure be spelled out in detail. While employed as the State National Guard, the governor may place it, or any part thereof, under the direction of such state or local officer as he may determine appropriate. However, if the State National Guard is federalized, said units are then employed by the Federal Government. In that case, when the units furnish assistance to civil authorities in domestic civil disturbances and disasters, the military commander is subject to no authority except that of his superiors. Thus, Federal troops used for intervention in aid of the civil authorities will be under the command of, and directly responsible to, their military superiors. They cannot be placed under the command of an officer of the state defense forces or of the National Guard not in the Federal service, or of any state, local, or Federal civil official.

Predesignation

National Guard units are located throughout every state in the nation. It is normal to find a preponderance of units in or adjacent to the metropolitan areas of a state. Such a circumstance favors using State National Guard forces to augment and assist local police agencies, as the metropolitan area is the most likely location for a riot to occur. It is these units, located in or immediately adjacent to a metropolitan area, that should be predesignated to assist the local authorities. These units will prepare specific plans based on the city plan.

The adjutant general of each state should designate those State National Guard units that will support a specific city plan. Prior to any units being designated, a city plan must exist, as this will serve as the basis for determining the amount and type support required. The state adjutant general will further designate the senior commander for the area and specify one unit as the area control headquarters. It is this commander and control headquarters that will initiate planning and coordination with the local authorities. Each will insure the existence of mutually supporting companion plans and will initiate revisions in existing plans as needs for revision and/or change become apparent.

Joint Maneuvers

To test the plan and develop working relations between the police and the National Guard, joint maneuvers and test exercises should be conducted.

Cooperation and Liaison

There must be complete cooperation between the military and both the local and state civil authorities. Usually the military commander will be from a different locality and will not fully understand local conditions or the psychological background of the disturbed population. The police, on the other hand, should know the ringleaders or agitators among the rioters, the estimated strength of the disorderly elements, as well as the temper and sympathies of the people. The police will have operatives and contacts who will be of great assistance in keeping the military informed of the rioters' plans.

Once the possibility of an immediate riot has been recognized, other departments and the National Guard should assign a liaison officer to the tension area. Information gathered prior to and at the time is of great importance in controlling the situation and must be made available to all. The liaison officer will maintain contact between the local chief and their departments, keeping their commander fully apprised of the local situation and possible developments.

Release of the Guard

In addition to the preparation of necessary procedures and documentation to request and obtain assistance from the State National Guard, procedures and required documentation are necessary for the release of the State National Guard. This recommendation should be a joint decision by local authorities and the area military commander, directed to the governor for appropriate action. This release from state duty may not apply to all units at the same time, but may entail a gradual reduction in troop strength as dictated by the circumstances. Once the riot has been dissipated and as local law enforcement agencies become capable of maintaining law and order, troops and other law enforcement agencies should be withdrawn accordingly, at least out of public view. This action will not only tend to relieve tension in the area of operations, but in other areas throughout the state as well. Employment of State National Guard forces and other law enforcement agencies for an unwarranted period of time could result in a recurring riotous situation fostered by such charges as "martial law," "police state," and other similar accusations.

USE OF THE FEDERAL ARMED FORCES

Basic Policies

In the United States, the protection of life and property and the maintenance of law and order within the territorial jurisdiction of any state are the primary responsibility of state and local authorities. It is a well-established policy of the Government of the United States that intervention with military forces takes place only after state and local authorities have utilized their own forces and are unable to control the situation; when it is apparent that the situation is beyond their capabilities; or when they do not take appropriate action.

Civil disturbance and disaster emergency operations and emergency military support of civil defense are primary responsibilities of the Army and collateral responsibilities of the Navy and Air Force. When emergency operations are undertaken, commanders of the appropriate military services will provide emergency military support according to previously prepared and mutually agreed plans.

Normally when a decision is made to intervene with military forces, the mission is assigned to the suitable available ground force nearest the point of intervention. The initial forces are relieved or reinforced, if necessary, by forces of another service on the basis of availability or qualifications to perform the technical operations required. Each service is responsible for providing, organizing, equipping, and training its forces for civil disturbances.

The ultimate mission of the Armed Forces in a civil disturbance role is to initially maintain or restore law and order, and then to assist state and local law enforcement officers to resume their normal roles.

Requesting Assistance

Application by a state for federal aid to its civil authorities should originate with the legislature of the state concerned or with the governor, when the legislature cannot be convened, and should be made direct to the President. This procedure, while seemingly involving excessive delay, insures that state officials have, in every instance, the opportunity to employ all state resources prior to requesting federal assistance. With today's efficient communication systems, there is little reason to fear that this procedure would be unduly delayed.

Command Authority

In the enforcement of the laws, troops are employed as a part of the military power of the United States and act under the orders of the President as Commander-in-Chief. When intervention with federal troops has taken place, the duly designated military commander acts to the extent necessary to accomplish his mission. In the accomplishment of his mission, reasonable necessity is the measure of his authority.

Federal troops used for intervention in aid of the civil authorities are under the command of, and directly responsible to, their military superiors. They will not be placed under the command of an officer of the State Defense Forces or of the National Guard not in the Federal service, or of any state, local, or Federal civil official; any unlawful or unauthorized act on the part of such troops would not be excusable on the ground that it was the result of an order or request received from any such officer or official. Commanders of federal troops, with the consent of the governor or other appropriate official of the state, may direct the activities of the state defense forces and State National Guard troops, which are not in Federal service.

Responsibility of the Military Commander

The military commander is subject to no authority but that of his military superiors. But he is ordered in case of intervention with federal troops to cooperate to the fullest possible extent with the governor and other state and local authorities and forces, unless or until such cooperation interfered with the accomplishment of his mission.

INTERESTED AGENCIES AND ORGANIZATIONS

Civil Defense Coordination

The plan must provide for the integration of civil defense personnel and organization, not only during an operation but into the planning and training programs. They should be kept apprised of plans and procedure for quelling of civil disturbances, set up by the department. They should be consulted regarding the purchase of equipment and supplies that may be obtained through the local civil defense organization. Agreement should be reached on general coordination of the police operation with civil defense operations, in case of riots or other disasters.

Fire Department

In the light of recent riots, special consideration must be given to close cooperation between the police and fire departments. In a riot of the type to be expected, fire bombs will be extensively employed to destroy for the sake of destroying, to destroy to cover all trace of one's guilt, to destroy to eradicate all evidence of one's indebtedness to the victim, to destroy, to distract police so that raids may be made in other areas. When fire units are committed, there is the danger that they will be subjected to sniper fire. The plan should recognize these facts and provide for coordinated action on the part of the police and the fire department.

Utilities

In drawing up plans, the police should contact the telephone, gas, water and electric companies to develop the basis for mutual assistance in emergency situations. Whenever use is being made of public utility equipment or fire equipment, precautions must be planned for the protection of civilian operators and equipment.

District Attorney

Not to be forgotten in this planning stage is the advice and counsel of the prosecuting attorney. All the police action in arresting law violators must eventually end with the prosecuting attorney endeavoring to present the evidence to a court of law. The efficiency of the police action will reflect in his success or failure to present a justifiable cause for the criminal charges against the defendant. Every police action planned or executed should keep that in mind. Therefore, he should be kept informed of plans and his advisory services solicited wherever technical influences are encountered. It is to his advantage also to make his services available and keep himself alert for action involving technical areas of trouble.

Schools and Parent-Teacher Organizations

School superintendents will see the wisdom of drafting and placing in the hands of teachers detailed emergency instructions. Interracial incidents within school buildings are becoming more common. Teachers and principals can do a great deal to calm excitement, to hold teenagers in school and release them in a wise fashion, to interpret to them the gravity of race conflict and the probable consequences of it, and to obtain parent and police collaboration when needed and possible. Teachers and schools can do much to help the majority of children and youth keep themselves under control. Through the children a great deal could be done to reach the adults at home. In every community, faced by possible race problems, there should be discussion between local civic authorities, leaders of racial groups and representatives of the schools as to steps which teachers would take in an emergency.

Parent-teacher organizations can also help. They can plan to escort children to and from school. They can insist upon the schools being kept open. They can stress the value and safety of keeping children in the schools where they normally get along together. And they can put pressure on the schools to emphasize both the short-run and long-range importance of education in promoting intergroup understanding and democracy.

Transport Companies

Transportation officials will recognize the desirability of working out emergency plans for crises. The bravery and common sense of streetcar and bus operators have saved thousands from personal injury in tense flareups. Such heroism and intelligence should be recognized, dramatized and rewarded.

The contributions that transportation officials and their employees can make to interracial understanding are great. Operators can be courteous and obliging to passengers without regard for their racial or cultural background. They can challenge passengers who make intolerant remarks or who get involved in disputes with persons of another race. These actions will place an emphasis upon fair play and understanding that will keep an atmosphere of intolerance from developing. Operators can also bring participants in serious incidents promptly to the attention of the nearest patrolmen.

The Clergy

Clergymen should use their moral authority and their courage to disperse rioters where possible and to rescue victims and provide sanctuary for those saved from the mob. Clergymen want to know in advance what they can do. They want to know, for example, how to set up local joint study conferences with the aid of national religious and interracial organizations. And they will want to learn the experience of others who have open church doors in riot-shaken neighborhoods. The chance of a mob pursuing a victim inside a church in a slum neighborhood is slight indeed. Ministers can also plan to show themselves to rioting mobs and to speak to them. A clergyman's presence is quickly sensed by mobsters and respected.

Management and Labor Leaders

Plant managers and union leaders are not likely to be confronted with more than minor incidents inside plants, but they can do a great deal to carry their influence beyond plant walls. Both can make it clear that they oppose race conflict. Then neither management nor labor can pin the blame or part of the blame upon the other. Union leaders, through shop stewards and educational officials, can mobilize union stalwarts to help avoid rioting. Management can use its plant loudspeakers, bulletin board, and, when appropriate, announcements through local newspapers and radio stations to strengthen the forces of law and order. Labor-management committees, where they exist, can work out emergency steps in advance and place them in operation with a minimum of delay. Most union leaders know, quite graphically, that race friction is poison to unionism, and management is fast learning that it is just as poisonous to industrialism.

Veterans' Groups

Veterans' groups can help keep peace by understanding the fundamental issues. They can also aid the civil authorities to enlist emergency patrolmen from the various racial groups.

Youth Organizations

Boy Scouts, Girl Scouts, Campfire Girls and other young people's organizations can plan to mobilize to aid school officials and parent-teacher groups. They can help to keep teenagers away from the riot area. They can get the younger children home quickly and safely. Older members can run errands. These groups are naturally even more useful in an effective long term program.

Make use of civil and service clubs and agencies. Men's and women's civil service clubs can aid in hundreds of ways to create as much sentiment against rioting and for decent interracial relations as possible.

Chapter 14

COMMUNICATIONS

INTRODUCTION

RAPID, EFFICIENT COMMUNICATION systems are mandatory in all phases of modern law enforcement. In all phases of an emergency operation, especially at its inception, communications are of the utmost importance. In riot actions, where the situation is changing from minute to minute, they are an absolute necessity. If the forces used to combat the rioters are limited, good communication equipment becomes all the more essential.

Communications must be provided between command and line officers. Officers on intelligence assignments must be able to communicate immediately to the command officers their findings relative to developments. As the mob surges back and forth, dangerous centers of action spring up, different individuals emerge as leaders, new victims are found by the mob, rumors fly around, looting may break out, groups of hotheads, juveniles, or organized agitators may be discovered arming themselves with bricks, clubs and the like. Such developments as these must be communicated to headquarters without delay.

PLANNING

Of major importance in communications, planning is the consideration that must be given to communications established with supporting forces such as the State National Guard. Appropriate and adequate communications must exist between all elements of the force engaged in the operation. The leader cannot control or direct the operation unless he can communicate with his subordinate elements; without control an operation is doomed to failure. Where equipment is not compatible (i.e., radios will not net together), prior planning must include provision for this establishment of relay stations, equipment exchange and frequency allocation.

[164]

A communication plan must be established to keep the command post and all subordinate units well informed of the situation on a twenty-four-hour basis. The plan must provide for the immediate dispatch of communication equipment for use not only at the scene but between the scene and command headquarters. Part of this plan must arrange to supply the protection to civilian telephone, teletype, telegraph and radio centers during emergencies.

One of the primary objectives of advance communications planning is to insure that supplementary media such as local radio stations, newspapers, sign-making firms and printing firms will support the police during civil disorders. Advance police planning should provide for appropriate standing arrangements for support from these or other media. Materials which may be written, printed, or recorded in advance include scripts, leaflets, and recordings. These materials must be prepared in the appropriate language. The psychological value of efficient use of all available communications media by the police should never be discounted.

FIELD COMMUNICATIONS

The maintenance of communications between the field commander and headquarters and the field commander and the police forces on the scene is the most important. A police commander employing his units against a mob must be able to continuously communicate instructions and orders to maneuvering elements. Orders will normally flow from field commander to platoon commanders to squad leaders to squads. The following methods may be employed to supplement the lines of communication to forces in the field.

AUDIBLE. The use of public address systems on police vehicles and use of portable sound amplifiers.

MECHANICAL OR ELECTRONIC. Handi-talkies and walkie-talkies.

PHYSICAL. The use of runners, patrolmen both on foot and on motorcycles assigned to the field commander to carry messages.

VISIBLE. Arm and hand signals.

In communications, it is obvious that speed of contact is important. For this reason, messages sent by motorcycle or foot should not ordinarily be used if a swifter means is available. But there are times when messages are the only means of contact. Likewise, messages which are necessarily long and complicated should be written and delivered by messenger service wherever possible; for under the stress of combat, oral messages are subject to distortion, especially if they are lengthy. The commanding officer should also always arrange to have assigned and accompany him individuals for use as messengers. Manpower must also be available to give security to the messenger to prevent the message being captured.

Signals for offensive action, retreat and formation changes should be developed. These may be either by sound or sight. Signals, such as whistle blasts, horns, sound systems and voice, can be utilized, but they must be used at times when outside noises, i.e., gunfire, do not drown them out. They must be strong enough to cover the entire area of the operation. In addition to hand signals, small pocket-size colored smoke grenades and colored flares may be used.

TELEPHONE

In an affluent and sophisticated society like the United States, ninety-five per cent of all requests for police assistance are made by telephone. Further, the person making the request is probably making his first plea for assistance. In times of emergency the problem is magnified, for many will call to inform the police of violence or to obtain information. Then, too, there are those who will call the police for the sole purpose of tying up the police telephone. Once their call is completed, they leave their phone off the hook and leave the public booth from which the call was made.

In an emergency, banks of phones must be established to handle incoming calls. Separate phones should be maintained for interdepartment and intradepartment communications. Lists of special and important numbers should be prepared and circulated to all commanders to facilitate communications.

Mobile Telephone

The mobile radio telephone can provide telephone communications to and from the temporary headquarters at the scene of an emergency prior to the installation of regular telephone service. Mobile radio telephone may also be used to supplement the additional telephone service after installation. The mobile radio telephone is not a private line and should not be used to transmit confidential messages as other persons subscribing to this service have receivers on the same frequency.

RADIO

Introduction

Skillful use of police radio equipment provides for greater operational flexibility and can be vital to the successful execution of a riot control mission. Using it the police can achieve the flexibility which is so essential to meet the guerrilla type of riot.

There is a great variety of equipment available for communications purposes. Radio equipment capable of being used ranges all the way from permanently installed central radio stations to small transceivers which are carried on the person. The exact nature of the equipment most serviceable varies with different local conditions. In some cases, transmitters in police cars will be adequate and, in some cases, devices such as handie-talkie sets may be needed.

Frequencies

Radio frequencies are allocated by the Federal Communications Commission on the basis of need, area and frequency availability. The police service is just one of the many emergency services, when considered in the overall community picture. Therefore, air space or frequency range assigned to police communications systems is limited. Consolidation of many separate agencies on one frequency is not uncommon. The result may be considered as both an advantage and a disadvantage. The advantage is in providing greater coverage area in transmission of emergency broadcasts and coordination in searches and pursuits. The disadvantage is in congested air time; there never seems to be as much time available as we believe there should be.

Communications

Police radio communications should be controlled through a central facility, known as communications. Portable hand-carried radio communication facilities must accompany riot police into the actual combat area. The more economical citizen-band short-range portable transceivers can be used to good advantage at the action scene. Messages for longer range transmission to headquarters can be relayed by the radio patrol cars on the perimeter of the combat scene.

On the scene where the counter-mob effort is being made, each tactical unit (squad, platoon, etc.) operating under the "on scene" commander should have direct "line of sight" radio communication with him. The officer in charge of field operations should be, when possible, at a point of vantage such as a roof top in a building where he can observe the entire action and control the tactical operations of his units.

Special miniature two-way radio sets that can be readily concealed on the person can be carried into the mob by undercover agents and used to keep the police advised of the location and plans of the leaders.

SECURITY

Police communication installations are prime targets for seizure or destruction by mob elements. They should not be readily accessible to the public and must be protected at all times. Normally their location should not be on ground floor levels. The higher they are located in the building, the less vulnerable they become.

It must be anticipated that unauthorized persons may monitor police radio nets or attempt to send false messages over the nets. Procedures used should be carefully prescribed. Continuous emphasis must be placed on requiring all police personnel to follow established security procedures. Messages must be authenticated. Adequate authentication instructions should be prepared for operators of communications equipment and for those who dispatch and receive messages. Simple codes should be used. The primary purpose for use of a code is to save time and to avoid confusion or misunderstanding. Frequency changes should be provided for where characteristics of radio equipment permit. Where several law enforcement agencies are involved in the same riot control operations, joint operating agreements may be necessary to avoid communications security problems. Such agreements could establish uniform security procedures, provide for exchange of communications liaison personnel and equipment, and clarify other matters deemed appropriate.

However, to minimize the danger of compromise, police codes, authentication systems, procedures governing frequency changes, and other highly sensitive matters should be published in confidential communications operating instructions. These confidential instructions must be periodically changed to avoid compromise. During actual riot control operations such changes may be required on a daily basis. Confidential communications documents must be rigidly controlled. Distribution and location of each copy can be regulated by means of control numbers and a receipt system. All police officers must be instructed to report expeditiously the loss or capture of a confidential document. Orders should be issued which place the police radio net on listening silence whenever the loss of such a document is made. An alternate set of instructions should be available for immediate distribution. Radio listening silence should not be terminated until each station in the police radio net has received a copy of the alternate confidential instructions.

Radio operators working in close proximity to members of the crowd or mob should use headsets for receiving and should use a low voice for sending. These precautions will help to prevent members of a crowd or mob from hearing the messages. Thought must be given to transmitting deceptive data if you are sure the enemy is monitoring your messages.

DISRUPTION OF ENEMY'S TRANSMISSION

More and more in the widespread guerrilla type of riot, the leaders of the rioters will rely on radio communications to direct the operations of their units. Every effort must be made to discover the transmitter and put it out of operation, or to jam it at critical times, or to pretend that you are the leader and transmit misleading orders.

Chapter 15

LOGISTICS

INTRODUCTION

IF THE POLICE are to be successful, they must have the necessary supplies and equipment. Poor logistical planning can and has seriously interfered with the effective execution of riot control planning.

The logistical problems encountered in crowd and riot control may be lessened considerably through advance planning. Logistical planning is accomplished to determine accurately the requirements for supplies, equipment transportation, shelter and other types of support needed by the police force engaged in riot control duty. Logistical planning for a civil disturbance or disaster includes planning for procurement, storage, transportation, distribution and evacuation of material and personnel; and for the acquisition, operation and disposition of certain facilities.

Logistical planning should outline actions to be taken. Plans should furnish detailed guidance in procedures for reporting supplies on hand, requisitioning, documentation, local purchases, shipments, issue and turn in of property; determining and meeting service requirements. Alternate plans should be prepared.

PLANNING

The supply problem should be discussed in detail with emphasis on the following:

1. Supplies available and under the control of state officials.
2. Supplies available from local government, welfare and civil defense organizations.
3. Supplies that are needed, but have no possible source of procurement other than a military source.
4. Allocation and issue of supplies.
5. Transportation of supplies.
6. Inspection and maintenance of equipment and supplies.

Preliminary planning, based on anticipated needs, must insure that sufficient quantities are on hand and ready for use at the appropriate time. Evaluation of resources should include the following:

1. Number of persons who will require assistance.
2. Period of time during which such assistance will be necessary.
3. Type of assistance that will be needed.
4. Essential priorities.

Inventory

An inventory of all riot equipment in the possession of the police department and other agencies must be made. It should show the type and quantity of the equipment, its location, the names, addresses and telephone numbers of those authorized to issue it, and those qualified to operate and those designated to utilize it.

Emergency Supplies Sources

Preplanning should consider the need for emergency supplies in the event the mob or riot situation extends over a considerable period of time. The source of such supplies should also be set forth, together with the names, addresses and telephone numbers of individuals who can make them available when needed. This will also effect economics, as extensive stockpiling is unnecessary when sources are documented.

Requisitioning and Earmarking

The commander should issue specific instructions for requisitioning and storing munitions, supplies and rations, and for earmarking them for disturbances and disasters. The plan should provide that normal riot equipment, along with extra armament, bullet-proof shields and vests, sniper equipment, gas masks, reserve supplies of chemicals and firearms, munitions, etc., should be assembled and kept "frozen" on a ready list for emergency issue as a package. This method insures that it will always be immediately available. If a special emergency vehicle is also maintained, these supplies can be stored in special built-in lockers and hangers.

The plan must provide that with issuance of mobilization signals certain department equipment will automatically be dispatched. All requests for additional department equipment shall be transmitted to the temporary headquarters. Prior to requests for additional equipment, the police coordinator should ascertain the number and type of equipment present at the scene so that unnecessary equipment will not be dispatched.

Before requests are made to outside agencies for equipment, consideration shall be given to the use of department equipment. All equipment dispatched shall be directed to respond to the staging area or temporary headquarters where record shall be maintained of its use. From these points equipment may be directed to locations where needed.

INSPECTION AND MAINTENANCE

Never overlook the fact that equipment must be maintained in tip-top working condition. There is often a tendency to put off checking equipment that is not in constant use. Corrosion, rust, moisture, heat, collection of dust and dirt are factors to be reckoned with under these conditions. Serviceability depends upon good maintenance. Therefore, there should be periodic inspections to make certain the equipment is always ready to use. This is emergency equipment and when needed there is little or no time to make inspections and repairs which should have been handled on a continuing basis.

INDIVIDUAL OFFICER'S EQUIPMENT

It is essential that enforcement personnel be completely equipped. It is equally necessary and should be mandatory that the men being used to combat a mob be personally protected against injury as much as practically possible. If the men are properly equipped, they will perform counter-mob tactics more aggressively, their morale will be higher, and their willingness to close with the rioters will increase accordingly.

Individual protective equipment for riot control should be durable, light in weight, and capable of being worn over long periods of time in hot, humid conditions without excessive tiring or discomfort. In close combat situations, a man instinctively strives to protect his eyes, abdomen and groin. If these areas and his head are protected by equipment he is wearing, he will perform in combat in a much superior and more aggressive fashion.

Psychological Effect of Specially Equipped Police

Some police officials take the position that when specially armed and equipped riot police whose very appearance makes them stand out from the public's day-by-day concept of the police uniform confront rioters, this will antagonize them. This is a limited viewpoint. Usually the opposite effect is achieved. When rioters, either real or potential, are confronted by police units who are obviously armed and equipped for "business" and any eventuality, the mobsters are more reluctant to commit violent acts. Many times the best psychological impact is achieved by concealing the special shock unit from view and only ordering it on the scene when the situation becomes critical. Many times the surprise show of specially equipped additional force will help tip the scales in favor of the police early in the confrontation.

FOOD AND SHELTER

Plans must be made to feed and/or shelter members of the police who are working prolonged shifts during the disaster. The utilization of a mobile kitchen should be considered. Plans should also provide for feeding men at their assigned posts or at massed points nearby. Use of mobile kitchens (from disaster response organizations, the Red Cross, Salvation Army, or private caterers) should be planned for serving hot meals, which are far superior to box lunches or sandwiches.

Lists of various caterers or established food vendors must be maintained, along with a statement of their capabilities. Delivery of food to men on assigned posts is to be considered. Scheduling of feeding may be planned on a "subject to change" basis. This will enable the men assigned to the problem to be fed substantial, hot meals. Such a program is essential for several reasons. One, the feeding in close proximity to the problem at hand keeps the maximum amount of personnel available, and secondly, the men will remain in better physical and mental condition when fed good, hot, palatable meals.

The effect on morale of such action during recent riots has proved beyond any doubt the value of warm meals.

Abnormally long hours under stress will tire the men, and if excused to return to duty in a short time, they may not have enough time to travel to and from their homes and still get sufficient rest. Provision should be made for a sleeping reserve that includes sufficient spaces, cots and bedding supplies, as well as sanitary and bathing facilities.

Chapter 16

TRANSPORTATION

INTRODUCTION

Transportation

TRANSPORTATION IS ONE of the most important elements to be considered in planning for police action of any kind. It is necessary to move individual officers and squads of officers rapidly from one place to another. Equipment must be transported. Prisoners and injured persons must be removed from the scene.

The plan should encompass loading and unloading procedure and the selection and establishment of appropriate points and alternative points for such activity. Likewise it should cover the use of reconnaissance and convoy plans to protect their movement. Plans should also be made to guard and protect the equipment while parked at the dispersal point. To keep transportation facilities usable, provision must be made to have available adequate supplies of gasoline or other fuel, tires and repair parts.

TYPES

Considerations

Factors to be considered include the suitability, maneuverability, vulnerability and reliability of the available means of transportation. The vehicles must be suited to the terrain and conditions under which they are expected to function. They must be adapted to the purpose for which they are to be used. They must be in good condition so they will function properly under emergency conditions.

Airplanes and Helicopters

Aircraft will prove an important adjunct in the control of widespread civil disturbances. One of the most important and effective uses for aircraft is reconnaissance. Helicopters, in particular, have proved invaluable in keeping the police advised of the location, movement and activity of the mob.

Aircraft may also help in directing troop movements, controlling traffic, providing air cover for marching troops, and maintaining communications between widely separated units. Aircraft may assist the commander in a civil disturbance in the same manner as in a combat operation. In an extremely serious situation, aircraft may assist armed forces in driving or keeping rioters off roads by engaging in strafing attacks or by dropping chemical agents, high explosives, antipersonnel bombs, or psychological warfare leaflets. They may be employed to spray tear gas during serious civil disorders.

Planes equipped with public address systems can be used to broadcast messages or proclamations to the rioters. Also, they can drop copies of the proclamation and other orders. These will also be suitable for traffic control during movement of troops into the disturbed area.

INVENTORY

A complete inventory of all available means of transportation should be made. If special-purpose vehicles are needed, the law enforcement executive should know where and how they can be procured. Arrangements to use such vehicles as ambulances, hearses, school buses, trucks and the like, should be planned before the need arises. There is usually little problem along these lines relative to fire department vehicles, but their use in a coordinated effort needs advance planning.

A survey of available facilities should be made and records kept of the names and telephone numbers of the persons to be contacted in the event the vehicles are needed in an emergency.

The designated officer should arrange with business concerns, located within commands, for the use of suitable transportation, such as trucks or buses, available day and night. A sufficient number of patrolmen qualified to operate these trucks or buses shall be designated on each platoon.

Each division should have transportation lists prepared. The lists will account for available trucks under the following captions:

TRANSPORTATION LIST

Trucks Available	Location	Telephone Number	Owner	Precinct	Assembly Point for Details

Transportation lists shall be checked frequently to assure that they are up to date.

PROTECTION

Equipment that is moved into the riot area should have portable fire extinguishers for use in the event of an attack with Molotov cocktails. The bodies of the vehicles can also be electrically charged to deliver a high voltage low-amperage shock to anyone who tries to touch the vehicle in order to stop it. The vehicle and those in it will not be affected. The driver can initiate and continue the shocking effect by holding down a push button switch on the dash. Such a device is not costly and will prove of great value when moving through dense crowds (who can be warned by the speaker system that the body is electrified) or when masses of rioters surround the vehicle and attempt to climb on it or turn it over.

TRANSPORTATION OF PERSONNEL

Police units must be prepared for rapid deployment in a riotous situation. It is imperative that police elements adhere to the principle of unit integrity during the loading of personnel in the deployment phase. Advance loading plans that have been rehearsed and proven effective should become standing procedure within the police unit. Exactly how the riot control group is to be transported should be determined beforehand so that this important part of the plan can become operated immediately when needed.

Since rioters can effectively delay the arrival of troops, movement planning should include the selection of routes to the scene of the disturbance which are believed to be shortest in distance and least vulnerable to danger. Movement planning for foot marches should include consideration as to the distance to be traveled by the police and their fatigue prior to being committed.

Movement by Air

Where deployment by aircraft is practical, advance planning should determine exact characteristics of available aircraft so as to properly plan loading. Plans should permit preserving the integrity of subordinate police elements enroute. Equipment and personnel weight must be calculated with a high degree of exactness. Special aircraft should be used so as to preclude the complications which could arise if units attempted to move piecemeal aboard scheduled passenger flights.

If movement is by air, there must be a central clearing house established for receipt of all information and orders and for the control of all aircraft so that they can be used to maximum capacity. In such situations, units to be transferred will often be spread over a large geographical area. It is apparent that only with central coordination can they be picked up and moved with the minimum expenditure of energy. All airports must be secured and protective perimeters established to assure the safe operation of the aircraft.

Movement by Rail

If personnel travel by rail, special trains should be provided to avoid subjecting civilian passengers to hard conditions and from retaliatory measures that might be taken against the police or troops. Use of cars in regularly scheduled trains can lead to serious complications. For example, special trains can preserve unit integrity. Also, they can be placed on sidings easily.

If there is danger of interference with the troops at the entraining point, guards should be posted to keep all unauthorized persons from the vicinity. Railroad trains should be run at reduced speed over portions of the track where interruptions may be expected. If there is reason to suspect that an explosive has been placed along the track, it may be advisable to push several flat cars ahead of the engine. The commander of the troops may assume control of the train when the military situation demands that he do so, but until such necessity arises he should leave the operation to the crew.

On reaching the vicinity of the disturbances, it will be necessary to proceed more cautiously. It may be advisable to detrain on the outskirts of a city and march the remaining distance. Detrainment, however, should be as near the bivouac area as practical, to reduce to a minimum the marching distance under possible hostile conditions. Detraining points should be so selected that personnel will be reasonably free from interference while detraining.

It may be necessary to dispose some of the first personnel to arrive to cover detrainment of later arrivals. Upon detrainment, personnel should take such formations as will enable them best to protect themselves against attack. Detrainment, however, should be with a minimum of public notice. If possible, action against the lawless elements should be deferred until fully organized. The supply situation may make it advisable for detraining personnel to carry a twenty-four hour supply of personal equipment and rations.

Motor Movement

The security of the motor column during the motor movement is the responsibility of the commander. Such protective measures will be adopted as the situation requires. To conserve vehicles and simplify parking and protection problems, squads should report to the area of the disturbance in as few vehicles as possible, each police vehicle or mobile patrol carrying as many officers as possible.

It is advisable that each squad have its own motor vehicle so that it is independent of other transportation. This keeps the unit intact, thus increasing its mobility and getting it into action faster. The movement should be in convoy.

It would be wise to transport the officers into the staging area several units at a time. Then if they were intercepted enroute to the staging area by a section of the mob, there would be less disruption of the police operation.

Security during a motor movement is increased by reconnaissance; advance, flank and rear guards; air observation; and the selection of a route which affords the most security.

The column should be preceded by an advanced patrol consisting of two or more vehicles. Flank and rear patrols will be dispatched when necessary. One or more advance reconnaissance patrols should operate ahead of the column. Their principal mission is to gain and maintain contact with the groups creating the disturbance and provide the commander with timely information as to the location, strength, composition and activities of the lawless element. Light vehicles equipped with two-way radio are suitable for this mission.

Each unit should have a simple, well understood, emergency plan. All convoys should be accompanied by security units assigned the task of clearing the route to assure uninterrupted movement through traffic and furnish additional security. The first unit to arrive should take up a formation suitable for protecting itself from attack and to furnish protection to the following units.

Detrucking

It is usually advisable to detruck in an open, sparsely populated area at a distance from the scene of the disturbance, and proceed forward on foot. Detrucking areas in the vicinity of the disturbance will be selected prior to the arrival of the column. The detrucking area should be out of sight of the mob, between the mob and its apparent objectively, reasonably close to crowd or mob action, and be secured prior to arrival of main body.

Sentries will be posted around the area to keep unauthorized persons at a safe distance. Sentries should not be posted singly, but should be comprised of two or more men. The troops detruck, assemble into tactical formations, are inspected, and equipment is checked before they advance against the mob.

PARKING AREA

An area must be designated for the parking of responding police units so as not to interfere with the overall operation. If possible, all vehicles used to transport officers to the scene should be parked in this area.

Motor vehicles must not be left unattended lest they be set on fire. A mob's ability to inflict damage to a police car is a means of increasing their bent toward destruction. They feel that they have overpowered the police.

A security plan for the motor park should be prepared, and sufficient number of men should be detailed to guard police vehicles and equipment left behind from acts of vandalism. Normally, the drivers constitute the security force. They may be reinforced as necessary. The following parking area regulations should be imposed:

1. Members assigned to the parking area must control the manner

in which vehicles are parked in order to prevent serious obstructions and delays.

2. If practicable, operators shall remain with their vehicles.
3. Vehicles shall be parked so as not to obstruct other vehicles entering or leaving the area.
4. Establish a parking pattern, for example, require all cars to angle park (45° angle) at the curb, or in rows at a forty-five degree angle in an open area.
5. At large emergencies the superior in charge should maintain a record of the location of cars parked and identity of the drivers.

MARCHING

Troops marching should take the same precautions that are taken during motor movement. Flank patrols or perimeter security should be employed to protect the unit during halts. Tactical formations are best suited for security elements of the command. Air observation of troops marching materially aids security.

MOVING THROUGH STREETS

When it is necessary to move in streets to reach the scene of disorders, use less frequented thoroughfares. Marching columns often provoke crowds into throwing missiles from sidewalks, windows and housetops. Even when the results are harmless, such acts inflame people and lessen their respect for the police. The marching of men through city streets filled with people should be avoided, as it will expose them to encirclement and attack while in the vulnerable exposed march order.

If it is necessary to march men through streets in order to reach an affected areas, and if rioting is general, the streets are cleared in front of the units. Under no circumstances are persons permitted to crowd the sidewalks while the police march past. Riot control formations are employed, however, only when necessary.

Personnel should march in the center of the street. Tactical dispersion should be adopted when required by the situation.

Columns of troops marching through city streets are secured by advance, flank and rear guards. Squads of the advance party march in single file on the sidewalks on each side of a street. The members of these squads observe the windows and roofs of the building on the opposite side of the street. Designated members should be prepared to fire upon persons who throw missiles or fire at the police.

When possible, units should avoid moving through streets with high buildings on either side. Canyons created by the location of flat-roofed, multi-storied buildings are a natural trap. Assaults from such elevated positions may be avoided by clearing the rooftops in the area. When adjacent units are marching on parallel streets, halts are made at street intersections until they have arrived abreast of the main body. Rear detachments should always be provided to prevent crowds from closing in on rear elements.

AMBUSH

Any police or military element that moves on the surface of the earth can be attacked from ambush. This includes columns and patrols moving on foot, motor convoys, railroad trains and river craft. The objectives of the attack from ambush range from complete destruction of the target to delaying a marching column and minor harassment. For guerrillas, the capture of weapons, supplies and equipment is often a major objective.

The idea of entrapment is fundamental. The trap is the killing zone into which the ambush party hopes that the patrol or convoy, or that part selected as the target, will move unsuspectingly.

In most cases, great care is devoted to the laying of an ambush. The thorough preparation may require days, during which careful reconnaissance of the site is made in daylight and measures are taken to assure the cooperation of the local populace. All movement is at night; most of the personnel of the ambush party may not move into the position until after midnight on the day the target is expected. The trap is laid, security detachments are positioned to guard the flanks and the withdrawal route, and local informants provide current information, on the approach of the target. The ambush may be sprung during the hours of darkness or in daylight. The victim, though in motion, is in the poor defensive posture of a column on the march, whereas the ambush part is immobile and ready. Weapons are generally positioned parallel to the road and sited to fire into the flank of the marching column after it enters the killing zone, leaving no part of it uncovered.

If the approaching column marches into the trap, the ambush party has the initiative. The ambush party develops instantaneously its full firepower potential, with all weapons firing at a rapid rate at targets looming just beyond the front sights. For a few moments it has a target that is vulnerable and almost helpless. After a few minutes of devastating fire, with destruction fairly complete, there may occur what is sometimes termed an assault by the ambush party. It is, perhaps, more in the nature of a mopping up, with designated teams moving into the killing zone to complete the destruction or to capture weapons. If there is any immediate danger of being cut off or pinned down and captured by superior forces, all elements of the ambush party will quickly withdraw to a designated assembly point to reform and move.

The ambush party has a tremendous tactical advantage. In addition to surprise, it can be reasonably certain of having an overwhelming advantage in volume of fire for a few minutes at the decisive point—the killing zone. Historically, the ambush has been a favorite and successful tactic of resistance movements in areas where those movements enjoy a measure of popular support. In such areas, the government controls little more than the localities it occupies in force. The routes linking these localities can usually be kept open by daily maintenance and mine clearing. Because the government does not control the terrain on both sides of the roads, however, it is impossible to eliminate the constant threat of ambush. To render lines of communications secure throughout extensive gray areas where the population supports the insurgents would require a heavy commitment of troops from the government.

The ambush enables the insurgents to overcome the severe overall disparity in numbers, firepower and technology between themselves and government forces. By operating under cover, by avoiding decisive conventional engagements with superior forces, and by exploiting their intimate knowledge of terrain and superior foot mobility, the insurgents can choose the time and place for brief concentrations to attack small government elements in transit. The ambush constitutes a major irritant to the government, a cause of serious losses, and a basis for persuasive insurgent promises of ultimate victory in their propaganda efforts to win more popular support.

The effectiveness of the ambush may also be measured in terms of the road mileage that the government is compelled to close to traffic, or over which security escorts are required. The gradual surrender of surface lines of communication has serious military and political implications. The abandonment of roads, especially in populated areas, generally leads to the prompt loss of such areas to insurgent control.

The ambush is not a war winner. It is a feasible small scale offensive tactic for insurgents who are strategically committed to the defensive because of their weakness. Its use, however, in combination with continued expansion of areas of popular support and recruitment of more guerrilla bands, tends to lessen government control. This, in turn, ultimately reduces the disparity in strength to a point where the insurgents can develop units capable of challenging government forces in a more conventional type of warfare that can lead to the latter's defeat.

Countermeasures

Countermeasures come under two classifications, protection and detection. The former aim is to neutralize the advantage of the ambush party when the ambush is sprung, and the latter is to discover the presence of the ambush party before the head of a column enters the killing zone.

Protective techniques include, among other factors, the organization and conduct of the march, use of specially equipped convoy protection units, immediate action drills, special weapons and air cover. An example of a protective device is special slip-on side armor for troop-carrying vehicles.

Clearly, the problem confronting the commander of the advancing column is to discover the presence of the ambush party before the head of the column enters the killing zone. Only then can he wrest the initiative from the ambush commander and abort the ambush by deploying and attacking it before the column moves into the trap.

There are two detection techniques which can discover an ambush before the head of a column enters the killing zone—security on the march and a reliable informant net. The degree of security of a column on the march may be regarded, roughly, as inversely proportionate to its rate of march. Security of the main body is achieved by the exposure of small detachments between it and a possible enemy on all avenues of approach open to that enemy. For a column temporarily halted, security is usually possible. But when the column is in motion, protection of the flanks is difficult to gain because offroad movement is necessarily slower and sometimes impossible. Too, there is no time to investigate the terrain in depth on either side of the road to assure that any ambush party lying in wait is flushed out before the head of the column enters every possible killing zone. This can be done, but only if the column is halted frequently, and it is a process which is painfully slow and unacceptably time consuming. Some means of detecting an ambush is needed that will enable a column to proceed at a reasonable pace.

Counterambush Action

A dismounted unit employs a formation that provides for all-round security while en route. March interval is based on the type of terrain, limits of visibility, size of the patrol, and to a certain extent on the means of control available. The interval between individuals and units at night is closer than the interval used during daylight. The interval is also great enough to allow each succeeding element to deploy when contact with the enemy is made. However, the distances are not so great as to prevent each element from rapidly assisting the element in front of it. The patrol leader is located well forward in the formation but not so far as to restrict his moving throughout the formation as the situation demands. Units are placed in the formation so they may distribute their firepower evenly throughout the formation.

Regardless of whether the unit is on foot or motorized, security to the front, rear and flanks is necessary. A security element is placed well forward of the main body with adequate radio or pyrotechnical communications. The security element is strong enough to sustain itself until follow-up units can be deployed to assist in reducing the ambush. However, if the enemy is not detected, it may allow the security element to pass unmolested in order to attack the main body. If this occurs, the security element attacks the ambush position from the flanks or rear in conjunction with the main action.

Flank security elements are placed out on terrain features adjacent to the route of march. They move forward either by alternate or successive bounds, if the terrain permits. This is often difficult because of ruggedness of the terrain and the lack of transportation or communications. The next best thing is moving adjacent to the column along routes paralleling the direction of march.

Rear security is handled similarly to frontal security, and plans are for the rear guard to assist in reducing the ambush, either by envelopment or by furnishing supporting fire. Aircraft above the column flying reconnaissance and surveillance missions increase security. In an ambush, fighter and attack aircraft can provide support. Communication between these elements is a must.

All available means of communication consistent with security are used to assist in maintaining control of the small unit. March objectives and phase lines may be used to assist the commander in controlling his unit. Communication with security elements is mandatory. Detailed prior planning and briefing, and rehearsals for all units, will assist in control. Alternate plans are made to prevent confusion and chaos. If the unit is ambushed, higher headquarters is notified as soon as possible to alert other units in the vicinity.

Counteraction

If the unit is ambushed, the most important counteraction is for all available personnel to return fire as rapidly as possible. It is incorrect to stop vehicles in the area that the guerrilla has chosen as a killing zone—unless forced to do so. The proper action is to drive on when fired upon, to stop only when past the ambush area or before running into it, and to counterattack immediately from flank and rear.

When vehicles are forced to halt in the danger zone, troops will quickly unload under the covering fire of the sentries, which should include smoke if possible, and will make for cover from which to join the attack against the guerrilla force. When trucks are required to halt, drivers halt their trucks on the road. They do not pull off onto the shoulders because they may be mined. Trucks used as lead vehicles are reinforced with sandbags to reduce the effect of mines. Where only the foremost elements of a unit are caught in the ambush, an immediate encircling attack is carried out by the remainder of the unit. Where the entire patrol is ambushed in open ground, an immediate assault is carried out by the survivors.

If the guerrilla ambush extends on a wide frontage and occupies a considerable portion along the trail or road, then a different tactic is called for. A small patrol, even with correct spacing, can be caught within the ambush. Sufficient room for maneuver is often limited, requiring an immediate assault mounted directly at the guerrilla. It is seldom possible or desirable to try and take up firing positions and exchange fire with the guerrillas as long as the patrol is in the killing zone. The patrol moves as quickly as possible to a position outside the killing zone, and then assaults the guerrilla position.

In action, when some troops are ahead of the danger zone and others are halted short of it, confusion may arise as to which group should initiate the attack. The party which has not yet entered the ambush should make this attack.

The best way in which an armored vehicle can assist in counter-ambush action is by moving to the danger zone to engage the guerrillas at very short range. In this way it can give good covering fire to our flanking attack, and afford protection to any troops who are caught in the guerrilla killing ground.

If the strength of the unit is adequate, envelopment is usually the most desirable method of attack. A holding element and an attacking element are designated in all plans. Each element is briefed thoroughly on its actions and alternate plans necessary to meet different situations. For example, a plan calling for the advance guard to be the holding force would not succeed if the enemy allowed this force to pass unmolested. If the strength of the ambushed unit prevents their attacking by envelopment, the plan should be to break out of the immediate area rapidly to minimize casualties. If a unit is surprised by the enemy, it tries to overcome him by returning all available fire immediately. This also allows the ambushed unit to deploy and maneuver.

An alert force, prepared to move by foot or helicopter, should be on constant alert for employment by higher headquarters in the event a patrol is ambushed, or for employment for other purposes. The alert force studies the plans for all patrols. By studying the routes, check points and designated helicopter land sites, and through means of communications, it can rapidly reinforce an ambushed unit. If ambushed, the patrol leader may request reinforcements. He designates his position by reference to check points, designated helicopter landing sites, terrain features, or smoke panels. If possible, he sends a guide to the place designated to guide the reinforcements into position. A system for rapid employment of alert forces, ensuring defeat for the guerrilla ambushes, makes the ambush less likely to be employed by the guerrilla.

The reorganization after an ambush involves the use of assembly points and plans for security. Care is taken to minimize the possibility of the enemy's pressing the attack during this period. All personnel, including wounded, equipment and supplies are assembled. If reorganization cannot be accomplished because of guerrilla action, it is accomplished after reinforcements arrive.

Chapter 17

TRAFFIC CONTROL

INTRODUCTION

A<small>NY DISASTER WILL</small> cause traffic problems. It is therefore essential that traffic control plans be prepared to insure uninterrupted movement of emergency personnel and equipment. To assure that there will be such advance planning and control when needed, a given officer should be designated as the traffic control officer.

TRAFFIC CONTROL PLAN

Plans should be developed for the following:
1. Halting or detouring automotive traffic around disaster areas.
2. Procedure to prevent the movement of troublemakers into or from disturbed areas.
3. Traffic routing so that roads will be kept open for passage of troops, firefighting equipment and other emergency personnel and equipment.
4. Supervision of rail, interurban and bus terminals, to prevent unauthorized individuals from entering communities where their presence might cause trouble.
5. Supervision and direction of movement of prisoners from collecting points to jails or stockades.
6. Establishment of emergency routes.

TRAFFIC CONTROL OFFICER AND TRAFFIC CONTROL HEADQUARTERS

In disaster situations, the officer assigned to traffic control will establish a traffic control headquarters, at a suitable location along the route sufficiently removed from the scene of the emergency. The officer in charge shall advise communications of the limitations imposed on traffic, requests for additional coverage along the route and the location and telephone numbers of the traffic control headquarters.

[189]

Adequate personnel assignments must be made so that all intersections along the route in the vicinity of the emergency scene are covered. The superior officer in charge of the traffic control headquarters shall maintain an accurate list of assignments.

Special instructions shall be given to the personnel assigned as to restrictions imposed on traffic and, if necessary, as to detours to be set up. Communications must be kept informed by the traffic control headquarters of conditions along the route and any changes in restrictions imposed on traffic.

When weather, visibility and terrain permit, and tactical considerations do not make it inadvisable, observation aircraft carrying traffic control personnel can be employed to good advantage in directing traffic. The purpose of aerial traffic patrols is to secure a more general picture of traffic conditions that can be obtained by ground supervision. In addition, two-way air-ground radio connection must be established between the aerial patrols and key points on the route of traffic. Airplanes should be equipped with public address systems for broadcasting information and instructions directly to traffic control personnel not provided with radios.

EMERGENCY RESPONSE ROUTES

In order to permit the prompt response of emergency personnel and equipment to the scene of an emergency or disaster, an emergency response route should be established from the scene to a point where traffic is moving freely and without congestion. To insure the prompt establishment of such routes in an emergency, for the advance knowledge by crews of radio motor patrol cars of the routes to be utilized, and for the effective policing of such routes when required, predetermined routes must be designated which will permit approach to within a short distance of an emergency in any section of the city. The emergency response route is established by combining the connecting route, designated by the superior officer at the scene, and the nearest accessible predetermined emergency route.

The superior officer in charge at the scene shall, when requesting the transmission of the rapid mobilization signals, inform the field command post of the connecting route that has been kept open from the scene of the emergency to the nearest predetermined emergency route. If practicable, he shall also designate an area for the parking of vehicles that respond in answer to the rapid mobilization signals. The commanding officer at the scene will police the route in the vicinity of the emergency and, as soon as possible, designate a superior officer to take charge of the route and supervise its maintenance.

When notified by the superior officer at the scene of the connecting route, the superior officer in charge at communications shall establish the emergency response route by combining the connecting route and the previously determined emergency route. In some cases because the predetermined emergency routes are one-way it will be necessary to designate different streets for approaching from different directions.

Communications must notify the field commander, the fire, hospitals and other departments and agencies involved of the emergency route. The location of this route will also be frequently transmitted by radio to responding units during the initial phase of the response.

When notified of the emergency response route, designated officers in precincts through which the route passes must assign radio motor patrol cars and foot patrolmen to patrol that portion of the route passing through the precinct. Preferably personnel and mobile units shall have been previously designated and shall respond in accordance with prepared plans in order to police these routes during an emergency. Particular attention shall be given to important intersections and locations where congestion may develop.

Personnel assigned to an emergency response route shall enforce applicable restrictions. In all cases they have the responsibility to see that there is no congestion along the route and that traffic, if permitted, is not an impediment to responding vehicles. If congestion develops, traffic shall be immediately detoured from the route by personnel assigned without awaiting specific instructions from superior officers to do so.

If it becomes apparent that the designated route is not adequate, due to construction or other obstruction, the member assigned to the route shall forthwith notify the communications which shall consult with the commanding officer at the scene of the emergency so that an alternate route may be selected.

TRAFFIC CONTROL

Vehicular Traffic Control

Nonessential vehicular traffic in and around an emergency area presents a problem of congestion which must be overcome in order to handle an emergency situation effectively. This condition may delay the response of emergency vehicles, congest the area of operations and require the assignment of additional personnel whose efforts could be better utilized in the actual emergency.

Vehicles already in the area prior to the arrival of the police cause unnecessary interference with the emergency forces. If necessary, tow trucks should be dispatched to assist in removing these vehicles.

Communications, upon being notified of the emergency, shall request radio and television stations in the area to broadcast a request that unauthorized persons avoid the emergency area and to advise motorists of alternate routes. This traffic must be detoured away from the scene to keep the roads available for emergency vehicles. Detour routes should be set up and maintained to keep traffic fluid. Necessary assignments shall be made by the superior officer assigned to traffic control to assist in the rerouting of traffic from the emergency scene.

Public Transportation

Bus routes which pass through the emergency area must be temporarily suspended and buses rerouted around the police lines. Notification shall be made to the transit authority or bus company concerned by the field commander.

SUBWAY OR ELEVATED TRAINS. Depending upon the nature of the emergency and the location of the facility the following action shall be taken regarding transit exits and entrances within police lines:

1. Close the facility if alternate facilities are available outside the police lines.
2. Establish a policed and barricaded route from the police line to the facility.
3. Request the transit authority or transportation company concerned to by-pass the station.

Assisting Emergency Vehicles

Emergency vehicles are seldom able to move rapidly in crowded areas because of the hazards created by unpredictable traffic. A motorist might not hear a siren, or pedestrians may cross the street along the route of an approaching emergency vehicle without realizing the danger of their action. These circumstances make considerable caution necessary on the part of the driver of the emergency vehicle, thus reducing his promptness in answering the call. Officers directing traffic at an intersection should therefore stop all pedestrian and vehicular traffic to assure passage for the emergency vehicle. Roadway obstructions such as removable "turn" signs should also be cleared from the path. A beckoning signal then given to the emergency vehicle driver will indicate to him that the intersection has been cleared. If the driver signals for a turn, an officer can acknowledge by motioning in the proper direction, indicating that the way is clear. This will also alert officers at adjacent intersections of the approach of the emergency vehicle.

Congested Locations

At points of heavy congestion, a plan to assist any emergency vehicle through the intersection should be prepared. For example, the supervisor of a street construction crew can be requested to stop any loud noises from such equipment as airhammers so that the siren of an approaching emergency vehicle may be more audible.

At a particularly crowded, one-way or "off-center-laned" street, the officer should act well in advance of the arrival of an emergency vehicle. The drivers in the least occupied lane can be directed by hand and whistle signals to a nearby lane or curb to provide clearance. After the emergency vehicle has passed, the displaced drivers should be allowed to proceed before other vehicles.

Parking Area

DEPARTMENT VEHICLES. The superior officer at the scene requesting the rapid mobilization signals shall designate an area for the parking of responding police units so as not to interfere with the overall operation. A member of the force should be assigned to this area to supervise personnel. A bullhorn will also be of use in this area.

PARKING AREA REGULATIONS. Officers assigned to the parking area must control the manner in which vehicles are parked in order to prevent serious obstructions and delays. If practicable, operators shall remain with their vehicles. Vehicles shall be parked so as not to obstruct other vehicles entering or leaving the area. The police must establish a parking pattern, for example, require all cars to angle park (45° angle) at the curb, or in rows at a 45° angle in an open area. At large emergencies the superior in charge should maintain a record of the location of cars parked and identity of the drivers.

Chapter 18

PHOTOGRAPHY

IMPORTANCE

Evidence and testimony presented by witnesses and officers should, whenever practicable, be supplemented by a few well-chosen photographs which tell the story of the crime in a vivid and understandable manner. Photographs speak for themselves! They leave an indelible impression in the minds of the judge and jury when determining what offense, if any, had occurred, the identity of the victim and the culprit, and the general circumstances surrounding the occurrence.

OBJECT

The object of the police cameramen is to record the criminal action and the faces of the criminals. Profiles are not desirable; neither are backs, clothes, feet, or pictures out of focus. They should keep in mind the motto of news cameramen, "Get meat in the pictures!"

Any time opposing groups come close to each other, the camera is a wonderful way to show their relative positions. Spectators may develop quickly into an opposing group. The cameramen are there to record the scenes. The best objective for the camera detail to keep in mind is to take pictures of everything that happens if it helps to show any part of the problem or related involvements.

USES OF PHOTOGRAPHY

The application of photography can be effective throughout the stages of crowd and riot control. It may be used in gathering intelligence data, planning, critiques, training, identification of participants and public relations.

In the event prosecution is instituted against persons participating in mob violence, photographs, especially movies, constitute excellent demonstrative evidence. It is indeed difficult for a defendant to refute the evidence a photograph provides of his presence and participation in the riot. There is much truth in the statement that a photograph is worth a thousand words. One glance at a photograph can convey a picture that words could never describe.

The further uses of camera equipment as a riot control technique is too often overlooked. It is a psychological deterrent in discouraging participation in the mob because it has a tendency to destroy the feeling of anonymity and create a feeling of anxiety, to help identify unknown participants. Many persons will feel safe while participating in a riot if they think their personal involvement will remain unknown and if they think they will not be singled out from other participants. When their presence is known or singled out, they have a tendency to withdraw because of a feeling of fear, anxiety, shame, embarrassment, or guilt. In short, they do not want to be identified with the unlawful violence and, realizing the camera will reveal their participation, they are deterred. The camera, therefore, can be of great assistance in controlling a mob if the individuals comprising it know they are being photographed.

Motion pictures and still photographs provide police with an invaluable record of the actions of a mob. They can be used effectively to identify criminal acts, participants and mob tactics.

Post Riot Control Utilization

Photographs taken during a civil disorder are useful in analyzing mob tactics for the development of future countermeasures. They are also useful in analyzing the effectiveness of police tactics and equipment. Riot photography provides excellent training material for police personnel. It also may be used to defend police commanders against charges of police brutality which are frequently made in the aftermath of a civil disorder. Riot photography assists in the modification or redesign of equipment and in the development of protective devices.

Having mob violence photographically documented makes possible an objective study of what has occurred. Sometimes photographs viewed later may reveal circumstances vastly different from impressions gained in the heat and excitement of the action itself. The films, upon study and analysis, may disclose areas where preventive action could have been taken, tactics which were not as effective as others, inadequate communications, misplacement of personnel, weaknesses or oversights in planning or execution of maneuvers, and other facts of significance for future guidance.

Planning

Vital, sensitive areas such as power stations, banks, and water works may require predetermined protective measures which can be rapidly applied during a civil disorder. Photography can assist in the determination of these measures. Through the use of aerial and ground photography, access and egress routes may be selected. The locations for barricades or police strong points can be selected by analysis of photographs. Photographs allow the police official to view the actual area of a projected operation in advance of his arrival. Aerial photographs lend themselves to use as maps.

MOVIES

Moving pictures should be taken of the demonstration while it is in progress, taking care to cover the leaders. Photograph every movement relating to the conflict, the demonstrators, the opposing groups, the spectators, the police action. Leaving nothing out of the photographs. Get movie shots of all concentrated actions and use color movie film wherever possible.

The movie camera operator should get mostly action shots. He should be close when the arrest is about to be made so he can have his camera running when the group goes limp. This type of shot shows the extent of their organization and their intent to resist arrest.

The movie camera operators will have a tendency to take short strips of action unless they are cautioned. During the handling of prisoners this is terribly important. They should make a practice of letting the camera run down before cutting off the motion. The moment it is cut off, the spring should be wound back tight. It is inexcusable to be caught with a camera almost run down. The most valuable shot of the effort might be lost.

The movie cameramen should concentrate on action shots generally, but occasionally there will be a need to single out an individual in a crowd. The telescopic lens can do this, and it is handy for use on short notice. Some cameras are equipped with zoom lens, but they are expensive and the telescopic lens will meet any requirement of police work.

During the arrest action, the movie camera should be kept working. Even if no trouble is encountered by the police in making the arrest, it may be to their advantage to have a record of their actions. The care they exercise to prevent injuries to the prisoners is sometimes important, especially when the reckless charges of brutality are made.

Date and Time

One method of recording date and time on the film is to use a calendar and clock. If a wall clock is available, hang a calendar by it. By using a pin or some type of movable pointer, designate the day involved and, of course, the clock will show the time. The practice of taking a quick ten-second shot of the calendar and clock before going out on a mission will save some tedious work later when the date and time is in question. The only trouble with taking this shot of the time is that it does not show a.m. or p.m., and also that nothing may happen at that time worth a picture. The method would perhaps be much better if the ten-second shot was taken after each episode where film was used. The only trouble with this would be in running the picture; the action would show before the date was specified. Whether the before or after method is used, it should be consistent. If the method was inconsistent, sometimes taken before the action and sometimes after the action, it might be more confusing than some other effort to point out the day and time.

PHOTO—ARREST LATER

If the police are unable to reach and arrest a group because of the large number they have to handle at a given time they can utilize the following procedure:

Photograph the group and observe it. Later identify the individuals by the pictures made. Get warrants for these subjects and make the arrests at the convenience of the police. These pictures can be used for later arrests if they are properly taken and processed and backed up with the oral testimony of the observers.

ARREST PICTURE

Still photos shall be taken of each and every arrest. This picture should clearly show the officers effecting the arrest and the person arrested. Every effort should be made to get frontal or side view shots of the arrested person. When the arrested person is turned over to the transportation officer, the technician can take a still shot of the person showing the transportation officers as well.

PROCESSING

The evidence technicians should stay at the scene of a public demonstration until released by the commanding officer in charge. Only in dire emergencies should the evidence technicians assist in the actual arrests.

After being released, he should return to the photo lab and remove all film from his cameras, and, with any other exposed film, place them in a protected container, properly marked for identification. The container should be plainly marked "Emergency Status, Develop at Once."

The officer assigned to developing and processing film should, upon receipt of such film, process it at once. All pictures, regardless of what size camera with which they are taken, should be processed in the regular 8" x 10" size. He should, without delay, process the standard mug shots of all persons arrested at the scene of a demonstration.

If possible, the photographer himself should develop the pictures and should stay with the picture he made until he gets the dried print and identifies both the print and negative with the proper department file number.

INDEXING AND FILING

After the pictures are developed and printed, they must be indexed and filed. A small gummed label is placed in the upper right hand corner of the negative. A number is then placed on this label, beginning with number 1 for the demonstration. Proceed to number each picture consecutively. A record of this negative is then entered on a pad. The lines on the legal pad are numbered in sequence at the extreme left margin. The entry should be made opposite the corresponding number. This legal pad is the master index of the picture file.

The number on the line at the extreme left margin represents the print and negative being processed. Continue on that line as follows:

No.	What	Date	Time	Cameraman
1	Marching line	10-14-64	14:00	Mark
2	Step, Cadillac Co.	10-14-64	15:05	Mike
3	Interior " "	10-14-64	15:45	Steven

The number assigned to this picture should also be placed in a corner on the back of all the prints made from that negative. At least three prints should be made of every negative at the first printing. The photographer should place the following information on the back of each print made from that negative:

1. Cameraman's name.
2. Date and time picture was taken.
3. Descriptive caption ("Pickets on Market Street").
4. What type of camera used.
5. Camera setting (shutter speed, lens opening).
6. Film used (sheet, roll, film pack).

When the suggested information is recorded on the back of each print, the entry should be made on the legal pad. The negative and extra prints should then be placed in a folder and filed in a letter file drawer or cabinet in its proper numerical position.

Place the picture in the file with its back side facing front. This will make the number show in the upper left corner and will facilitate location of it in the file. Repeat this procedure with every entry.

In all acts of civil disobedience sequence pictures are valuable. In preparation for trial a set of sequence pictures for each defendant should be prepared. A print of each picture in which he appears should be placed in his folder. He can be identified by placing a small gummed dot under his picture and placing thereon his arrest number for the event. When these dots are used, it is possible to remove them without injuring the picture; thus the print can be introduced whereas it might not be allowed if the police had written on the photo.

Chapter 19

PUBLIC INFORMATION

IMPORTANCE OF DISSEMINATION OF INFORMATION

Plans must be made for the dissemination of sound, basic and factual information concerning existing and potential dangers. The effect of insecurity and frustration is particularly severe if individuals are left in the dark as to the character of the situation. Through the direct use of public information mediums, the commander may do the following:

1. Facilitate operations by disseminating proclamations and instructions to the general public.
2. Assist in maintaining law and order as far as the situation permits.
3. Facilitate operations by disseminating proclamations and instructions to the general public.
4. Assist in maintaining law and order as far as the situation permits.
5. Counteract propaganda or prevent the dissemination of incendiary matter.
6. Keep the public at home or off the streets.
7. Provide a public information program giving a fair and impartial picture of current events.
8. Provide an orientation program explaining the reason for and purpose of the police action.

Sensationalism is to be avoided and the flash rumor method of reporting may become quite disruptive. Information should be factual, and rumor, speculation or unverified data should be avoided.

MASS MEDIA

The commander shall use all the public information facilities available in a given area, such as radio and television stations, local newspapers, news agencies, publishers or periodicals and books, posters and theatres.

Newspaper Coverage

Newspaper editors, being close to the tensions of a town, can make many helpful suggestions. They will also be willing, in most cases, to work out emergency steps that can be taken if a crisis develops, for newspaper editors have a sense of community responsibility. The editors should be kept informed of pertinent police activities.

The cooperation and advice of the minority press should be sought both as a means of securing facts and as a particularly effective technique for reporting facts back to the minority members of the community.

Radio and Television

Radio and television may be used as successfully as the press, thereby reaching a different section of the general public. In addition, radio lends itself to informal topical presentation and to developing points of emphasis. A predetermined central authority should begin feeding accurate information through available radio stations as rapidly as such information accumulates. Reporters over such systems of communication should have calm, flat, unemotional voices. The calm authoritative voice of a familiar radio announcer might be extremely effective in reducing confusion and emotional excitement, particularly if reassuring announcements are given about the arrival of rescue and relief teams.

Preparing Constructive Radio and Television Programs

Radio and television station managers will be glad to work out a series of announcements and general procedures for the control of news broadcasts during an emergency period. They will join in planning and producing programs to counteract the conditions causing riots. The public service division of national radio and television networks should be asked for special materials and recordings. Be sure that your station develops a series of spot announcements and interpretive programs ready to use throughout the crisis and also a well-formulated statement of policy for its newscasters on the handling of interracial tension reports.

USE OF LOUDSPEAKERS

Public address systems of sufficient power to be heard and capable of being mounted in trucks or aircraft should prove to be particularly effective in some of the following instances:

1. To deliver ultimatums of civilian groups.
2. To control civilians through simple instruction.
3. To disseminate factual information.
4. To direct traffic, evacuation, or dispersal of civilians.
5. To direct proposals to panic-ripe groups.

Since many confused anxious people may well be far from any functioning radio receivers, and since rubble, fires and other obstacles may very well stand in the way of ground vehicles with sound equipment, it would be desirable to use light planes, preferably helicopters, with sound casting apparatus, for the purpose of disseminating information, giving authorized directions, and counteracting overt panics should they begin to develop in any areas. Such data should be in simple, direct, factual terms, which can be assimilated as easily as possible by depressed, fearful and resentful victims of the disaster.

Preparation of Scripts for Broadcasts

Scripts for broadcast over a public address system are a type of psychological force. These scripts should be prepared in English and the minority language, if a foreign minority is involved. The force of the message must not be lost in translation. Scripts should be prepared for each major action taken by police. A plan should be drafted to enlist the aid of community leaders in making and directing appeals to the populace in the trouble areas.

INFORMATION CENTER

Scenes of disasters, particularly those involving a large number of injuries and deaths, will attract numbers of persons inquiring about missing relatives or property damage. These individuals and the public are concerned and want to know whether missing relatives and friends are alive or dead. Confusion and hysteria mount rapidly if their questions remain unanswered.

There are also other persons seeking to give helpful information.

The public information officer should establish an information center to which these persons will be directed. This center shall be established outside the police lines at a location which will not interfere with police operations.

The public information officer will designate an officer to take charge of the information center, and patrolmen will be assigned to handle clerical assignments, maintain order and act as messengers. Members of the missing persons unit will be assigned to question persons inquiring about missing relatives and friends.

The unit will have the following equipment:

1. Supply of 4 x 6 index cards.
2. Signs "INFORMATION CENTER."
3. Telephone facilities.
4. Clerical supplies.

Information

Information available on dead and injured persons, evacuees, property damage, etc., should be obtained from the command post on prepared lists. These lists shall be kept current by telephone or messenger service between the command post and the information center. Persons in the area having information concerning the whereabouts of possible victims, or persons inquiring as to possible victims, shall be requested to go to the information center.

Information obtained from persons regarding possible victims shall be forwarded to the command post. If the information center has no information regarding the person inquired about, a 4 x 6 index card shall be prepared containing the name and pedigree of the person sought and the name, address and telephone number of the inquirer and the relationship to the victim. This card shall then be forwarded to the command post, where it shall be inserted into the alphabetical file of the persons involved for possible correlation with a subsequent index card. This will assist in identification of casualties and notifications to relatives.

Inquiry File

A card file is to be maintained concerning missing persons sought, and shall include the name of the person seeking information, in addition to all other necessary information. The file is to be kept alphabetically according to the name of the persons missing. When information is later obtained on persons listed in the inquiry file, the card is to be removed from the file, and the proper casualty, dead body, or evacuee card made out, if this is warranted.

Chapter 20

PRESS

INTRODUCTION

Good relations must be established with news media as an aid to planning for crowd and riot control so that sensational reporting may be discouraged, rumors dispelled and misunderstandings corrected before further community tensions are created. Advance efforts must be made in this respect, since it is useless to attempt to change press relations from poor to good once a riot is in progress. Such a good relationship must already have been established. If it does exist, the commander will have a valuable ally who can help him obtain the cooperation of the public, which is of inestimable value to him during a riot. To gain it, it is the commander's responsibility to furnish sufficient news to the public to fully inform it of the true conditions surrounding the disorder.

By providing this service to news gathering agencies, the police department generally receives the advantage of accurate reporting by news agencies, and news gathering personnel are less likely to interfere with the effort of the police department to control the unusual occurrence.

INFORMATION OFFICER

To facilitate dissemination, a public information officer, preferably one who maintains liaison with the various news media representatives daily and knows them by name, their attitudes and their reliability, should be appointed from the commander's staff. Such a person would be able to develop a program of news dissemination to mass media and civic groups that would preserve the image of the force as a group sincerely interested in preserving the peace of the community. During the course of civil disorders, the information officer would be the sole source of information of news media. Commanders of civil disorder operations should never release information without coordinating such releases with their public information officer.

It is the information officer's responsibility to obtain complete and accurate information for release to accredited members of the press. It is also his responsibility to furnish accurate factual material for publication.

At no time should news releases be colored with defensive statements. Sources of information must be accurate and intelligence must be verified to prevent placing the police in an untenable position. Obviously, for the public information officer to be effective, it is necessary for the field commander to make information available to the public information officer as speedily as possible for prompt dissemination to the press.

At the scene of unusual events and emergencies where a large number of representatives of the press, radio, television and other news media respond almost simultaneously with the police, the scene commander should designate a press office to act as liaison and information officer until the arrival of the public information officer.

The duties of the public information officer are as follows:

1. Advise the commander and staff on all aspects of relations with the public.
2. Coordinate all public information functions within the command and supervise such functions within the headquarters.
3. Disseminate information pertaining to the command to appropriate information media in accordance with established command and security policies.
4. Plan positive and continuing public relations programs to gain and maintain public understanding, good will and support.
5. Maintain liaison with, receive and escort information media representatives, and assist them in obtaining material.
6. Observe and analyze trends in public opinion.

COORDINATION

The police agency press relations plan must be coordinated with all other municipal governmental agencies plans. Releases from one agency must be compatible with releases from all others, especially during periods of tension.

PRESS IDENTIFICATION CARDS

Identification cards should be issued to the press, so that they can quickly be identified and their movement authorized during a disturbance. Only news personnel with press credentials will be allowed in the special information service office.

PRESS CENTER

Early in the movement the police should set up a special press center where dispatches are released and inquiries answered. This will help prevent newsmen from roaming throughout the headquarters and bothering everyone with questions. Further, it will make it easier for members of the press to get all the information they are entitled to have. It will also provide a central spot where the press can check out the validity of rumors and other information, and facilitate the flow of press information without hampering the duty functions of various department personnel.

The press center should be located near the field command post within police lines, for speedy gathering and transmittal of information. The facility must be adequate to handle a large number of people with sufficient outside telephone communications to meet the demands of the news media. A direct internal line will be installed between the special press center and the field command post. All news media will be notified in advance of press arrangements.

Personnel

The public information officer or his representative will be in charge. He should have a special liaison officer plus a staff for telephone, messenger and clerical duty. The information section requires clerical supplies, "PRESS CENTER" sign, typewriter, tables and chairs and adequate telephone facilities for police use.

Operation

The press center shall be kept advised of developments. All police personnel on duty must be informed of the location of the press center. The representatives of the press will not be restricted to the press center, but will be permitted freedom of movement within police lines where practicable. However, where safety conditions, expeditious emergency rescue operations or similar police or emergency requirements demand, the movements of the press may be regulated in accordance with the particular situation.

Information

Information shall be channeled through the field command post from the temporary morgue, first aid station and other available sources. It shall be made available to the designated officer for release to members of the press.

Regular Press Conferences

The press center will report information to the news media as it is received. A situation map will be retained in the press center so they can maintain a graphic picture of the situation as it unfolds. In addition, the public information center could transcribe the more important field reports into hourly bulletins for issuance to the news media.

Whenever possible, the chief, the field commander and his staff and other department officials should be made available for interviews. In this way, officials can discuss the situation with the press without neglecting their primary duties. If possible, regular appearances of the commander could be planned. All interested parties would be served better than by chance contacts, which are difficult for both the commander and the press due to the demands of the situation.

GUIDELINES FOR PRESS REPORTING OF TENSION SITUATION

During recent riots the news coverage contributed to the magnitude of the problem. As a result of this the following guidelines for reporting of civil disorders and other events that may reflect public tension were prepared:

1. Avoid emphasizing stories on public tensions while the tension of a particular incident are developing. Ask the law enforcement agency involved whether the developing incident is designated as a disturbance of the peace or otherwise. Report the official designation of the incident.
2. Public reports should not state exact location, intersection, street name or number, until authorities have sufficient personnel on hand to maintain control.
3. Immediate or direct reporting should minimize interpretation,

eliminate airing of rumors, and avoid using unverified statements.

4. Avoid the reporting of trivial incidents.

5. Because inexpert use of cameras, bright lights, or microphones may stir exhibitionism of some people, great care should be excercised by crews at scenes of public disorders. Because, too, of the danger of injury and even death to news personnel, their presence should be as unobtrusive as possible. Unmarked vehicles should be used for initial evaluation of events of this nature.

6. Cruising in an area of potential crisis may invite trouble. It is suggested that reporters make full use of the law enforcement headquarters nearest such an area until a newsworthy event occurs.

7. Reporters who are at the scene of an explosive or potentially explosive situation should avoid reporting of interviews with obvious "inciters."

8. Reporters should inform in advance any person who is interviewed that the interview may be made public.

9. Scare headlines, scare bulletins and sensationalism of other kinds should be avoided in magazines, newspapers, radio and television.

10. All news media should make every effort to assure that only seasoned reporters are sent to the scene of a disaster.

11. No report should use superlatives or adjectives which might incite or enlarge a conflict, or cause a renewal of trouble in areas where disturbances have quieted.

12. Advisory data for discretionary use by newsmen should be written in calm, matter-of-fact sentences. This is for the purpose of avoiding inflammatory results from unintended public report of discretionary information. Honest and dispassionate reporting is the best reporting.

13. Reporters should not detail how any weapon is obtained, made or used.

14. Reporters should not identify precise locations of command posts of public officials, police, fire units, or military units.

15. Every reporter and technician should be governed by the rules of good taste and common sense. The potential for inciting public disorders demands that competition be secondary to the cause of public safety.

Chapter 21

MEDICAL FACILITIES

INTRODUCTION

Aɴʏ ᴅɪꜱᴀꜱᴛᴇʀ will require that prompt and adequate medical aid be supplied. To assure this in advance of any emergency, a medical officer should be designated and an emergency medical plan drafted. Planning for any type of disaster should include periodic liaison with medical authorities to enlist their aid and to impress upon them the need for accurate recording of treatment administered to demonstrators from a riot, etc.

MEDICAL OFFICER

As soon as news of a disaster is received, the medical officer is alerted so that preliminary steps can be taken to insure that adequate medical service, including hospital facilities, and personnel support services are available if needed. He will assume command of all medical planning and the supervision and direction of all medical operations. He will call up medical staff as needed and establish all medical facilities required.

MEDICAL MINUTE MEN

Teams of physicians should be organized by hospitals to provide twenty-four hour coverage at the scene of a disaster when twenty-five or more casualties are involved and existing facilities are unable to provide transportation to hospitals within a reasonable time. Each team should consist of three physicians. The medical team will carry such equipment as is necessary to provide immediate treatment without relying upon equipment in the police ambulances. The teams will be identified by their white suits and special emergency standards which they will affix to their car.

The request for help from the medical minute man teams is to be initiated only by the officer in charge of police or fire personnel at the scene of the disaster. Police radio will then contact the appropriate hospital for help and also request transportation for the medical team.

FIRST AID STATIONS

Plans should provide for establishment of aid stations manned by the minimum number of personnel necessary to give emergency medical attention to police personnel and civilians. They should be in close proximity of the tension zone. Plans should cover medical personnel, ambulance service, medical facilities, medical supplies, medical evacuation, casualty reporting, fatality registration procedures, and other appropriate considerations that may be considered necessary. Plans should be made to have oxygen equipment available, such as oxygen cylinders, inhalators and masks.

A sufficient quantity of medical supplies should be maintained to meet daily needs. However, consideration should be given to the location of additional supplies and equipment on an emergency basis. Personnel trained in first aid should be listed so their services can be obtained if needed.

The aid station should be staffed with police personnel sufficient to maintain order and perform the following duties:

1. Clerical.
2. Telephone duty.
3. Stretcher bearers.

The medical staff will consist of doctors, nurses and attendants. The aid station must contain all necessary emergency medical equipment to treat the particular type of injury to be expected from the particular disaster with which the police are coping. Ambulances must be available to transport the more seriously injured to more fully equipped hospitals.

In addition, adequate telephone facilities must be installed to maintain contact with the hospitals. The clerical staff must have everything needed to record the necessary information with relation to all those treated.

Tags containing appropriate information will be provided for use in identification of the injured and recording of the necessary information. A copy of the tag will be retained by personnel at the scene so that proper records can be made.

POLICE FIRST AID STATION

Establish a first aid station to supply medical treatment for police as soon as possible. It is very important that your men know that they will be taken care of if and when they become casualties. Do not permit those persons or medical units assigned to this task to be diverted by attending injured rioters. Have separate units for this purpose.

This station should be established close to the actual scene, in the vicinity of the ambulance parking area. It must be adequate in size and layout and capable of handling the number of cases anticipated.

PRIORITY OF TREATMENT

In a riot priority to medical treatment should be given to police over criminal participants, if all other things are equal. The police should be informed that this is the policy, for such knowledge will greatly enhance morale.

FIRST AID KITS

Each riot control squad should have first aid kits to treat minor injuries. These kits should contain eye solution for the treatment of injuries from smoke or gas in addition to the normal items.

AMBULANCES

In the event that ambulances are required at the scene the superior officer requesting the ambulances shall notify headquarters of the location where ambulances will report. The communications bureau shall direct responding ambulances to the above-mentioned location designating the emergency response route to be used.

The area designated for ambulances shall be used exclusively for that purpose to facilitate their response to and return from the emergency scene. This area shall be policed to prevent the entry of unauthorized vehicles and to prevent interference with ambulance dispatch.

Ambulance crews shall remain with their ambulances to insure immediate dispatch of ambulances when needed, except if their services are needed at first aid station, disaster area or otherwise directed by the medical superintendent.

If available, a walkie-talkie should be utilized to maintain communications between this area, temporary headquarters, first aid station and morgue to insure proper disposition of medical personnel and equipment.

A dispatcher must remain in the ambulance parking area to assist in the proper dispatch of ambulances. He should keep records of the hospitals to which the injured are sent, so that a more even distribution of patients can be worked out. Thus overloading of one or two hospitals will be greatly reduced. Hospitals are to be alerted when victims are sent it, so that they may be prepared to receive them. The information given should include number of victims, diagnosis and severity.

DISPOSITION OF INJURED

The following procedure shall be complied with in the care of injured persons at the scene of a disaster or emergency:

1. Members of the force shall render all reasonable aid to injured persons at the scene and assist the personnel of the department of hospitals in their duties.
2. The disposition of injured persons shall be the responsibility of the medical officer in charge at the scene. He shall decide which cases are to be treated at the scene, which cases are to be sent to hospitals, and which hospitals are to be used. In some cases, he may order that some injured persons be removed immediately without recording at the scene.

To provide an accurate record of all injured persons and their disposition, the following procedure shall be used.

PERSONS TREATED AT SCENE. Persons to be treated at the scene shall be taken to the first aid station for treatment. Patrolman assigned to the first aid station shall obtain the necessary information on these cases for the preparation of aided cards. These cards shall be immediately forwarded to the temporary headquarters for further action and filing. Persons at the scene claiming injury but refusing medical aid will be recorded on aided cards as above.

NOTIFICATIONS. When an aided case requires notification to a friend or relative the name, address and relationship of the person notified shall be entered on the aided card.

PERSONS TREATED AT HOSPITALS. As some persons may be removed or may depart from the scene prior to the arrival of police, the commander shall order a teletype message sent to patrol precincts to make a survey of hospitals within their commands to ascertain if anyone injured in the occurence has sought medical attention. Hospitals will be notified by precinct personnel to report any person claiming injury as a result of the occurrence. Members of the force shall be dispatched to these hospitals to obtain the necessary information. Members of the force shall be assigned to the hospitals in the area of occurrence to obtain the necessary information.

UNCONSCIOUS PERSONS. Prior to the removal of unconscious persons from the scene, a tag shall be prepared and attached to the victim. These cases will not be delayed at the scene from identification but will be accompanied to the hospital by a uniformed patrolman where the hospital authorities shall conduct the search. Information regarding the identity of these persons shall be obtained at the hospital and forwarded to the temporary headquarters. All necessary information obtained from the hospitals shall be telephoned to the temporary headquarters where aided cards shall be prepared and filed. When an aided case requires notification of a relative or friend, it shall be the responsibility of the temporary headquarters to cause such notification to be made.

Chapter 22

APPREHENSION AND DETENTION

INTRODUCTION

Apprehension, identification and detention are essential areas of any plan. In it specify the conditions under which the apprehension of rioters will be affected, the system of identification for prosecutive purposes, and the location of suitable facilities for detention, bearing in mind that there will be conflageration and collapse of buildings in case of disasters.

PLANNING

Plans must be made to anticipate the logistical problems of mass arrests. Plans must consider the possibility that arrests will exceed normal capability of secure confinement, adequate feeding facilities and normal transporting facilities.

Planning Transportation and Jail

If plans are not made for the proper transportation and booking of those persons who are arrested at demonstrations, serious problems may arise. This is true whether there are just a few or many arrests. Planning for the transportation and booking of prisoners in non-violent demonstrations or riots should include the following:

1. Personnel.
2. Vehicles to be used.
3. Routes to be taken.
4. Pre-loading procedures.
5. Loading of prisoners.
6. Identification of prisoners.
7. Handling of property.
8. Booking.
9. Medical treatment of prisoners.
10. Use of telephone.
11. Attorney's visit.
12. Feeding of prisoners.
13. Damage to property by prisoners.
14. Release procedures.

PERSONNEL

The officers selected to participate in the transportation and booking of prisoners who have been arrested for participating in a demonstration should be selected with care. Seasoned, thoroughly trained officers who are not biased or prejudiced will help to insure a successful operation. There must be an adequate number of officers available to handle the detail. If it becomes necessary to utilize reserve officers in the operation, they should be very closely supervised.

VEHICLES

Once the demonstrators or rioters have been taken into custody they must be removed to the place of detention. In most cases it will not be possible, nor desirable, to have them walk to the facility. If they are to be transported, some thought should be given to the type and availability of the vehicles to be used.

The vehicles used by the police come in a variety of models. This is especially true of the larger departments who in most instances have "paddy wagons," and in some instances, buses. The small departments are usually equipped with sedans and station wagons.

The paddy wagon is by far the most desirable vehicle to use in transporting prisoners who resist arrest or go limp. A prisoner who resists arrest in any fashion is extremely difficult to load into a sedan, station wagon, or bus. This process becomes even more difficult when the unloading must take place.

If it appears that many arrests will be made, and the prisoners will not resist, a bus can assist in expediting the operation. If your department is not equipped with a bus or paddy wagon, it is suggested that you arrange with the sheriff of the county, or a neighboring chief, who has this type of equipment, to assist you in the transportation phase of the operation.

A bus should not be used to transport prisoners who resist or go limp. Serious injuries can occur to the prisoners and the police during the loading and unloading process. The narrow entrance door of the bus and the step just inside the door, and the long narrow aisle which the prisoner must travel can be extremely troublesome if the prisoner does not cooperate one hundred per cent. The wide door of the paddy wagon and its limited capacity is the superior type vehicle to transport prisoners.

The vehicle that is used to transport the prisoners, regardless of what type it is, must be equipped with a two-way radio. A multichannel radio is desirable if more than one frequency is used by the department. It should also be equipped with a red light and siren.

SECURITY OF TRANSPORTING VEHICLES

The vehicle that is to be used to transport the prisoners should remain at a nearby location, not visible to the demonstrators at the scene of the disturbance. When it is needed it can be summoned via radio communication. The security of the vehicle must be considered. If the tires are slashed or obstacles are placed in the path of the vehicle, serious problems will occur. When the transporting vehicle is not in motion, an adequate number of officers must be assigned to act as perimeter guards around the vehicle. Once the transporting vehicle is in motion the security phase should not be relaxed. A sufficient number of officers must accompany the vehicle, regardless of the type, to handle any disturbance or problem that might occur en route to the custodial facility. An escort should also be provided. Motorcycles are effective when used for scouting and gathering intelligence such as road blocks or other obstacles that sympathizers might use to block the route of travel of the transporting vehicle.

Security will be increased if the vehicles are placed at strategic locations and moved into position so it will not be necessary to await their arrival after arrests have been made.

They should then be loaded and leave the scene as quickly as possible.

ROUTE

The route that is taken from the scene of the demonstration to the custodial facility should be selected with care. The most direct route with the fewest signals and stop signs is far more desirable than a route which winds through a residential area. The route may have to be varied if any efforts are made to interfere with the transportation of the prisoners. All traffic laws should be observed unless an emergency arises which would justify the need of using the red lights and siren. If the vehicle is driven too fast or in a reckless manner, a passenger could become injured and a civil action would probably be filed against the department.

PRE-LOADING

Prior to the time of loading the prisoners, they will have been properly identified by the arresting officers. Each person who has been arrested should be carefully searched to ascertain if he is in possession of any weapons or contraband. Policewomen should be used to conduct the examination of the female prisoners. All personal property and valuables should remain with the prisoner until he is received at the custodial facility.

The loading process, as well as the other phases of the operator, should be photographed. Both movies and stills should be taken. A documentation of the event is most desirable.

Each person that is loaded into the transporting vehicle should be accompanied by an "arrest identification card" or information sheet. Certain basic information must be on this sheet such as the following:

1. Name of person arrested.
2. Address.
3. Date of birth.
4. Sex.
5. Race.
6. Location of arrest (be specific).
7. Date of arrest.
8. Time of arrest.
9. Offense.
10. Arresting officer's name.
11. Single fingerprint—for identification.

This "tag" or card should be in duplicate so that the arresting officer will have a copy. In some situations, if more than one law enforcement agency is involved, several copies might be needed. Additional information that can be included on the arrest identification card will prove to be useful, especially if large numbers of persons are arrested, such as the following:

1. A space for comments.
2. Names of officers who removed or carried the prisoner.
3. Name of officer taking the identification photo.

4. Name of officer who took the fingerprint impression.

5. Transporting officers.

If a polaroid camera is used to take the identification photo at the scene of the arrest, this photo can accompany the arrest identification card and the defendant to the custodial facility where he will be formally booked. This assists materially in expediting the identification and booking process. Experience shows that some of the persons arrested at demonstrations do not carry any identification, and others will give fictitious names and addresses. One of the officers who will be riding on the transportation vehicle should be charged with the responsibility of having an arrest identification card, properly filled out, for each person to be transported in his vehicle. If the prisoners are being delivered to more than one custodial facility, the command post should maintain an alphabetical listing of the location of each prisoner.

Loading an uncooperative prisoner into the transporting vehicle can be a difficult task. Care should be used to prevent injuries to both the prisoners and the officers. If the loading process is done in a hurried fashion, confusion will prevail and someone is apt to get injured. The loading should be done in an unhurried businesslike manner, with only that amount of conversation that is necessary to get the job done. The news media will probably be present and everything that is said and done will be documented.

The prisoners should be segregated during the transportation phase as well as in jail. Segregation by sex and the segregation of adults and juveniles while transporting is a good procedure. A policewoman should accompany the female prisoners.

JAIL FACILITIES

Planning jail accommodations is a problem that must be considered. The inability of police to provide detention facilities hampers the effectiveness of the police in controlling a mob. It is impossible to determine specifically the amount of detention facilities that might be needed since the scope of the disturbance will dictate this need. A major consideration in the planning for possible detention sites is the determination of sufficient alternate sites so that when disorder arises, the location of detention facilities is not immediately adjacent the disturbance area. Congregation of demonstrators in such a detention area can create a serious control problem. At the same time, the site must not be so far as to preclude rapid transportation from the scene of the disorder.

Jails and prison camps in adjoining jurisdictions might handle a quantity of prisoners. It is well to provide for additional detention facilities, e.g., school gyms, and a special crew to man them as jails if the need is indicated. The state penitentiary and its field camp facilities are an excellent possibility. In more drastic situations some local government buildings may be pressed into use as a prison. Such an arrangement would require further considerations.

In the movement of prisoners to distant jails, the choice of individuals should be selective. Move the troublemakers, the leaders and the individuals who are likely to be the group organizers. It is more difficult to arrange bond or confer with key agitators if they are not in local jails. This practice will help to scatter their points of concentration and spread out their legal staff. This will help to slow down the incidence of law violations.

Thought should be given to the availability of a building in your area which can hold 500 to 2500 people. Many areas have temporary housing facilities available at fair grounds, 4-H areas, or camp areas. Stadium dressing rooms, convention halls, unused sections of public buildings and vacant schools may be available. Contact should be made with the local office of the civil defense agency for suggested areas. The location of the building will be of considerable importance. The further away it is from the center of town the less trouble you will have from outside interference from the news media, visitors and other demonstrators. If possible, prisoners should be unloaded inside the facility away from public view.

Booking

Upon arrival at the custodial facility, and prior to the formal booking, the prisoners should be informed as to where they are, what is expected of them, and what is going to happen next. The booking process should be complete and no shortcuts should be taken. A complete set of fingerprints and the standard identification photo of all persons arrested should be made. If the prisoners are not going to be released immediately, all property and valuables should be taken from them for safekeeping and the proper receipts issued.

If large numbers of prisoners are booked, an alphabetical listing should be started immediately. Numerous telephone calls are usually received during and after a mass arrest and a system must be established that will provide immediate information relative to who has been arrested and who is in custody.

Interviews

Time permitting, all adult prisoners should be interviewed. This will give a true picture of the people with whom one is dealing. A short list of questions should be prepared and the interrogation should be done by the detective division. The questions should pertain to the prisoners residence, previous arrests, organizational membership and other similar questions designed to develop general intelligence information.

Medical Treatment

It is not unusual to have a prisoner claim brutality and complain of alleged injuries. A doctor should be available to examine all prisoners who claim an injury or request medical attention. Officers should also be alert to refer the doctor to any person who appears to be injured or who is ill. Adequate records should be maintained by the doctor regarding the type of treatment rendered and medication dispensed. If a doctor is not available at the custodial facility, an injured prisoner should be promptly taken to the hospital for examination and treatment. Obviously a medical examination of those arrested will go far toward completely refuting any charge of police brutality. Sanitation and cleaning will be of importance, as an epidemic of any type would be disastrous.

Telephone Use

As most codes provide that an arrested person is entitled to certain telephone privileges, a written record should be maintained of the telephone calls so that the prisoner cannot claim at some later date that he was denied this right.

If large numbers of prisoners are arrested, the telephone facilities that are adequate in your day-to-day operation may prove inadequate in handling the increased volume of calls by the prisoners, attorneys and the public. The telephone company can assist you with this problem. Portable "pay telephones" can be installed, on a very short notice, by the telephone company.

Attorney's Visit

The right of the defendant to an attorney must be recognized. A record should be maintained relative to visits by an attorney. It should include the attorney's signature, and the date, time and length of visit. If a telephone call is made by an officer, for a prisoner, requesting an attorney, this action should also be documented.

Feeding

The prisoners should be fed at the regularly scheduled feeding times. However, if the arrests are made at a substantial time after the last meal, a sandwich and a cup of coffee or some light snack can do wonders to create a better relationship between the officers and the prisoners. If large numbers of persons are arrested and the facilities are not adequate to feed the prisoners, arrangements should be made with a catering service for food.

The feeding of the inmates is of the utmost importance. It should be decided how many meals a day the inmates are to be given and how they are to receive them. The building may have the necessary cooking facilities, or it may be better to prepare the food in the regular jail and take it to the inmates. If the food is to be transported, the arrangements for this should be worked out in advance. Food is a very important agent in determining the morale of the prisoners. Some of the inmates may require special diets which will add to the feeding problems.

Violence and Damage of Property

Any prisoner who violates any law during the transporting or custodial phase of the operation should be charged with the offense. It is not unusual for demonstrators to commit an assault or battery upon an officer. There has been evidence of damage to transporting vehicles and places of confinement by the prisoners in past operations.

Release

Prisoners may be released only upon proper authority. In handling large numbers of prisoners, extreme care must be taken to insure against releasing the wrong prisoner. Identification by fingerprints is ideal. If an impression was made at the time of arrest, a set of prints taken when booked, and a single impression taken at time of release, a comparison of the prints can be made which will prevent the mis-identification of any prisoner. The prisoner's property must be returned to him at the time of release, and the booking officer should have the prisoner sign a receipt showing that he received all of his property and valuables.

Chapter 23

PROPERTY PROTECTION AND CONTROL

SHUTOFF OF FACILITIES

When Ordered

THE SHUTOFF OF certain utilities may be directed by a responsible official of the department or agency concerned, or in an emergency by the field commander on the basis of information available that such action is necessary. Prior to such action, concurrences should be obtained from the other departments at the scene in order not to hamper operations.

The area involved in the shutoff may encompass several blocks or an individual building. If the affected area is large, the field commander may direct the use of public address trucks and helicopters equipped with public address systems to make public announcements throughout the area concerned.

Notifications to Residents

All residents and commercial occupants in the affected area should, if possible, be notified prior to the actual shutoff of gas utilities and instructed to extinguish pilot lights and turn off appliances. Before service is resumed, residents will again be notified.

Responsibility for Shutoff

The department or utility company concerned shall be responsible for discontinuing service from the street if a large area is affected. When restoring service, care must be exercised that hazards are not created, such as an explosion hazard from open gas jets, a flooding hazard from open water outlets, etc.

Other Notifications

In the event that it becomes necessary to shut off utility service in large areas, notifications shall be made to the field command post prior to the shutoff if possible which shall in turn notify interested agencies and news media.

Entries of service shutoff shall be made in the field command post log including the following:

1. Type of utility.
2. Area affected.
3. Addresses of buildings affected.
4. Name and identity of official ordering shutoff.
5. Location of shutoff, i.e., location of main valve or terminal, etc.
6. Notifications made, including identity of person notified and agency concerned.

PROPERTY DAMAGE SURVEY

If an emergency occurs which involves a great amount of property damage, the immediate area of the emergency and adjacent areas shall be surveyed by members of the various departments and agencies concerned to ascertain the damage caused by the occurrence and to determine the possible hazards which may have been created by such damage. The survey shall include the following:

1. Name and address of each person sustaining damage or loss.
2. Business name, if any.
3. Nature and extent of damages or loss.

All information obtained as a result of these surveys shall be reported to the field commander and entered in the field command post log. This information shall be used to determine the adequacy of present details and equipment, additions required, the location of police lines, whether evacuations are necessary and other problems that may be encountered.

EVACUATION

Because of damage caused by an emergency or disaster, specific buildings in an area, or an entire area, may require evacuation. Actual damage or potential hazards must be considered. The lack of sanitary facilities, utility services or other health hazards may necessitate evacuations. Serious consideration shall be given to the following, prior to issuing evacuation orders:

1. The area to be evacuated. This may include the area of actual damage and the area of potential danger due to drifting gases, radioactivity, subsequent explosion, etc.
2. The approximate number of persons to be evacuated.
3. The sick, aged and infirm.
4. The probable period of evacuation.
5. Temporary shelter, food and clothing, if necessary.
6. Transportation, if necessary.
7. Necessary instructions to be given evacuees on such matters as clothing to carry, securing premises, etc.

Search and Security of Evacuated Buildings

Buildings that are to be completely or partially evacuated must be thoroughly searched for persons remaining in that part of the building declared to be unsafe. Search teams shall be informed and assigned to search each building.

A systematic search shall be made of all rooms and other areas to assure that all persons have left the premises. Special attention will be given to assure that children, aged, infirm, or bedridden persons, or persons living alone, do not remain in the building. Insofar as possible under the circumstances, an accurate record shall be maintained listing the buildings searched and the identity of the officers assigned.

EVACUATION RECORD

Address	Type of Buliding	Floor	Assignments
201 W. 57th St.	4 story apt.	Basement & 1st floor	Sgt. Smith
		2nd, 3rd & 4th floors	Sgt. Joyce
203 W. 57th St.	2 story pvt.	All	Sgt. Casey
205 W. 57th St.	3 story apt.	All	Sgt. Ahrens

Evacuees File

Information regarding all evacuees, and persons relocated, shall be entered on an index card, listing the following:

1. Identity of persons.
2. Address of persons (including apartment number).

3. Address of relocation.

4. Agency involved (Department of Welfare, Salvation Army).

These cards shall be marked across the top "EVACUEES" and, when completed, shall be forwarded to temporary headquarters for inclusion in the file alphabetically with aided cases and persons inquired for.

In addition, a list shall be prepared in duplicate containing the above information. The original copy shall be forwarded to the information center, the duplicate shall be kept.

Security must be established and maintained to prevent unauthorized entry into the evacuated buildings. This will include the assignment of uniformed personnel to the front, rear and roof, if practicable. The assignments will be the responsibility of the superior officer in charge of the evacuations. A list of assignments shall be forwarded to the temporary headquarters.

Potential fire hazards should be eliminated in these premises: gas burners, electrical appliances in use should be turned off. In addition, inspectors must determine whether the evacuated buildings are fit for habitation. Circumstances may indicate the necessity for shutting off utility service in the evacuated buildings to prevent fires, floods, or other hazards. This operation should be performed by the various utility company representatives on the scene. In the absence of sufficient personnel from utility company emergency crews, the police officer in charge of evacuations may direct personnel assigned to evacuation teams to accomplish this additional safeguard.

Entry of the fact that utility service has been shut off at any location shall be made in the log. If water is shut off in any building or area, notice shall be given to the fire department officer at the scene.

Whenever utility service has been shut off at the building source; main valves and switches, service shall not be restored by police personnel. Persons in charge of such premises shall be notified to request restoration of service by utility company personnel concerned and to take necessary precautions to prevent damage from open sources within the building: gas pilot lights, open faucets, etc.

Buildings found unfit for habitation shall be guarded from the outside by uniformed patrolmen. They shall prevent unauthorized entry into said building and prevent the removal of any property except upon authorization of a superior officer. An entry of this assignment shall be made in the log.

Unsafe Conditions

Unsafe conditions such as holes, dangerous areas, unsafe buildings, etc., shall be safeguarded to prevent possible injuries. Barriers, rope or manpower shall be utilized for this purpose.

Valuable Property

Valuable property left unattended by the owner shall be safeguarded at the scene until removed by the owner or invoiced to the property clerk. A concerted effort shall be made to have the owner safeguard the property. If the property is claimed by the owner at the scene, a receipt shall be obtained and filed in the log.

Prevention of Looting

At the scene of a large scale emergency or disaster, property and evidence may be strewn over a large area, and must be protected. It is the responsibility of each member of the force present at the scene to prevent tampering with evidence and to guard against looting. This also includes "souvenir" collectors. The proper control over police lines and the check points through the lines will assist in safeguarding property and evidence by excluding unauthorized entry into the area. If necessary, specific assignments shall be made for detectives and uniformed personnel to guard particular areas against the possibility of looting.

At the scene of an emergency, an officer shall be assigned to be responsible that all property recovered at the scene is collected, safeguarded, itemized and finally disposed of as indicated below. An accurate record of all property shall be maintained at the temporary headquarters.

Property Found on Bodies

Property found on a dead body shall remain with that body.

Property found in the vicinity of a body will not be considered as necessarily belonging to that particular body; however, as this property may aid in the identification of the victim, a careful record shall be maintained of its proximity to the dead body for notation on property voucher including a description of the property, the serial number of the body near which it was found, and its position relative to the body.

The bodies, with the property found thereon, shall be placed in a body bag or shroud at the scene for removal to the morgue. At the morgue, the bodies will be searched by the patrolman or policewoman assigned with a detective from the missing persons unit under the supervision of a sergeant or other superior assigned from the patrol precinct in which the morgue is located.

All property removed from the body shall be listed in the patrolman's memorandum book and the entry shall be initialed by the supervising superior. The listing of the property removed from the deceased, shall be forwarded to the precinct of record which shall be the precinct in which the city morgue is located. Other copies shall be placed in a property clerk envelope and then sealed. The envelope containing the vouchers shall remain in the custody of the sergeant supervising the search until he is relieved when it shall be turned over to and receipted for by the relieving sergeant. The property and related vouchers shall remain at the morgue, available for viewing and possible identification. When the property is no longer required at the morgue, it shall be forwarded with the related voucher to the precinct wherein the morgue is located for invoicing to the property clerk.

Personal Property Found at Scene of a Disaster Other Than a Riot

Personal property, other than that found on the bodies, shall be collected at the scene and delivered to the superior officer assigned to property recovery. Prior to delivery of this property the officer finding same will make careful notation in his memorandum book of the description of the property and the exact location where found including serial numbers of bodies in the immediate vicinity and position relative to such bodies.

The superior officer assigned, assisted by personnel of the missing persons unit, shall carefully sort the property. Property of no monetary value, such as operators' licenses, identification cards, etc., which may aid in the identification of victims shall be listed separately and forwarded to the city morgue and delivered to the superior officer assigned there. Other personal property will be listed and forwarded to the precinct of occurrence for invoice to the property clerk.

If property is scattered over a wide area it may be practicable to indicate the location of found items on a precinct map. If a smaller area is involved, a sketch of the area indicating location of bodies and items of property found may be helpful in establishing the identity of dead and unconscious persons.

Cargo

All cargo and similar property found at the scene shall be collected, tagged and safeguarded at the scene and recorded pending removal to the precinct of occurrence where it shall be invoiced to the property clerk.

Aircraft

If possible, the parts of the aircraft should not be disturbed. Readings on the instruments should not be interfered with nor the instruments themselves moved. Subject to more important emergency needs, personnel of the Federal Aviation Agency and Civil Aeronautics Board should be permitted to check the instruments and parts of the aircraft prior to moving.

After a search of the parts of the aircraft for victims, property and evidence, the parts and equipment of the plane should remain in the same position pending completion of examination by the Federal Aviation Agency and Civil Aeronautics Board. A receipt shall be obtained from the contractor removing the parts from the scene. This receipt shall be filed in the headquarters log.

RIOT EVIDENCE

In the event that rioting occurs and looting follows as a result, there will be a problem of handling property recovered. This recovered property can be classified into one of the two following groups:

Evidence

Articles seized by the officer when actually making a physical arrest. This as well as any other physical evidence gathered at the scene will be tagged and properly marked and held as evidence pending disposition of the case. A photograph of the property and the suspect who was in possession of it should be taken at or near the time of his arrest.

Unclaimed Property

Unclaimed property may be defined as articles of value which will be found strewn about the streets and in the immediate area surrounding the scene of the riot. The owner is unknown or unable to be contacted. Such property will be classed as unclaimed property to be held awaiting an owner. This type of property will pose the greatest difficulty in handling.

Whenever possible, evidence should be transported with the prisoner from whom it was taken. If not, unclaimed property will be held until facilities are available for transporting it. Each item should be tagged and a notation made as to the location of its recovery and the name of the officer recovering it.

The scene commander will determine by reason of the amount of unclaimed property to be handled whether or not the physical facilities at the station will be adequate to store and handle same with security. If in his judgment his is possible, this will be his first choice. Unclaimed property will be conveyed to the station by whatever vehicles are available at the time.

In the scene commander's judgment, the volume of unclaimed property is such that it would impose a restriction on the operation of the station an alternate repository must be available. The scene commander will insure that an officer is detailed in the storage area to preserve all unclaimed property and prepare an itemized list of same. At the conclusion of the incident, detectives will attempt in so far as it is possible to ascertain the owner and notify him that the property will be made available to him.

SECTION III
FORMATIONS AND WEAPONS

Chapter 24

RIOT CONTROL FORMATIONS

INTRODUCTION

FEAR IS OFTEN created within individual members of a mob who find themselves in the path of an advancing, armed, determined and organized force of uniformed officers. This is the psychological intent of riot control formations.

Riot formations are modifications of military combat formations. Such a modification was necessary as infantry combat formations are not fully effective against civil disturbances. Those combat formations were designed to accomplish the military objective—the distruction of the enemy force. This is not the mission of the police or the military in a riot situation. Rather, the object is to disperse the rioters with the minimum number of casualties. There are also certain very practical considerations.

The skirmish line fails to develop the strength needed. The skirmish line may buckle and break when operating against a determined group of rioters. Small military units, deployed in line formation, will find difficulty in concentrating sufficient strength to overcome a sudden attack. The converse is true of riot formations. They become stronger when resistance is encountered, as pressure against the leading men will force other elements of the unit closer together.

Riot formations also are designed to provide more accurate control by platoon and squad leaders of specially trained policemen in dispersing disorderly crowds.

They also serve several important psychological ends. First they force the police officer who is basically individualistic by temperament, training and profession to function as part of a unit. Obviously this is essential in a riot situation, for alone the police would be isolated and crushed. By being trained to act as part of a unit, the officer is preconditioned for the new problem that the mob presents.

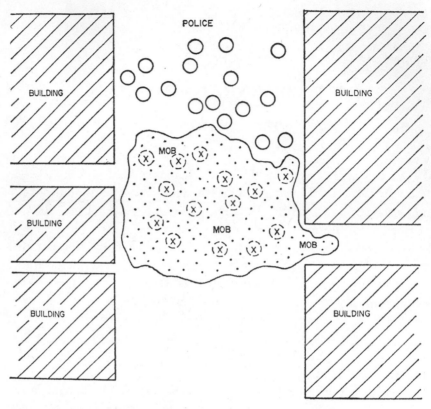

A loose formation of police which fails to present the mob with a closed wall of resistance will be circled and absorbed by the mob. The individual officer will be surrounded and subdued.

Secondly, the movement of the police as a unit impresses the mob members. They are reminded that their wild action is directed against the organized society in which they live and which must continue to exist if they are to live as a human being, rather than revert to the status of predatory beasts. The unit movement also impresses them with the power and organization that they must meet and defeat if they are to prevail. Naturally the use of formations in a civil disturbance is contingent on the nature of the emergency, the specific situation, and the personnel and equipment available.

The fundamental formations used in dispersing disorderly crowds and unarmed mobs are the wedge, the diagonal (to right or left), and the line. Other effective formations may be obtained by doubling, extending or combining the basic formations. These basic formations were selected primarily for their simplicity, flexibility and adaptability.

SQUAD COMPOSITION

The organization adopted should be developed along military lines, i.e., squads, platoons, companies and battalions. A squad, which is the best unit, can vary in number but usually consists of a total of twelve men, ten line men, plus a squad leader and an assistant squad leader. The minimum element or patrol used in riot duty should never be reduced to less than three men. Such a group is conducive to the following:

1. Unification of effort.
2. Efficiency.
3. Cooperation.
4. Protection.
5. Support of each individual.
6. Successful achievement of objective.

There are some who advocate a total of six men to a group, the number assigned to a group being six merely to eliminate the wide span of control. Also, six men can be transported in a car to remote locations without crowding.

A method being used in one modern, large metropolitan police department employs an eight-man squad, consisting of personnel assigned to normal patrol and predesignated as squad members. When the alert is sounded, personnel assemble at a designated point out of view of the impending trouble area. Equipment is secured, and a squad assembles in two units, each unit consisting of four men and a patrol car. A sergeant is in one vehicle and is the designated squad leader. The next senior officer is designated the assistant squad leader and rides in the second vehicle. Units thus formed are committed as squads, platoons, etc., deciding on the amount of force considered necessary. Their spontaneous, planned, organized arrival at the scene accomplishes the show of force, and the organization is such that these units are prepared to deploy in the various riot control formations.

ADVANCE ORGANIZATION

The squads should be organized in advance and the men taught to work together as a unit. Naturally the establishment of squad and platoon groups does not necessarily mean that such units will be assigned as a complete unit to another area for emergency. Commanders should, wherever possible, assign personnel as a complete working unit rather than small pieces of different squads. When group unit assignment is impossible and men are assigned to another area for crowd control or other emergency duty, the host commander of such area shall insure, through his staff, that imported personnel are immediately organized into working squad and platoon units by integration with local troop personnel. Organization of personnel into squads should follow these steps:

1. The host commander or his staff officer will assemble all non-commissioned officers.
2. Squad leaders and assistant squad leaders will be designated for each squad.
3. Each squad will consist of no more than twelve men including the leader and assistant. Squad leaders will build their squads with taller men next to the leader and down the file according to height. Assistant squad leaders will be the last man in the squad file.
4. Squads will count off, leader number one, etc.
   a. Each man will look to right and left to recognize his position in the squad. Remind him that this will be his permanent squad position.
   b. Squad leaders will obtain each man's name and position number and furnish this information to the platoon leader. Rosters will be compiled from these lists for assignments to duty.
5. Brief the squad leaders and squads on the course of action and what is expected of them. Squad leaders and assistants are responsible for the performance of their men, therefore they must fully understand the assignment and insure that their men do also.

Where additional men are assigned in excess of the number needed for squad assignment, these men should be utilized as platoon specialists, i.e., first aid, fire extinguisher, tear gas, etc. Men on such assignments must be familiar with the equipment to which they are assigned.

After briefing of squad leaders and men, the briefing officer will distribute post assignments to squad leaders. Squad assignments and rosters must be furnished the commander as soon as possible.

RESERVE

Each formation should have a reserve, which will serve under the officer in command as he dictates, to meet the demands of the situation. Members of this reserve can be used as messengers, to reinforce the line, replace wounded, perform special missions, handle prisoners, or perform other essential tasks. It is never advisable to commit all the unit reserve to the action, if this can possibly be avoided.

In a police action against the mob, it is best for the commander to have the firepower of the unit (small arms such as rifles, carbines, sub-machine guns, etc.) in the reserve part of the formation. This gives him better control and enables him to make more efficient use of these arms when necessary. When the men in the front against the mob, who may be armed only with batons and grenades, know they are backed up by firearms, they will perform with more aggressiveness and confidence.

The reserve should be equipped with first aid equipment. In an action, cuts and bruises and lacerations are to be expected. Mob members will hurl rocks, bottles, and other types of missiles at police. The unit should contain, within itself, first-aid kits for prompt treatment of wounds. It will also be advisable to carry, in addition to the normal medical first-aid supplies, some sort of eye-wash preparation. If the police operate without eye protection, they must expect to suffer this sort of injury. The reserve should also be equipped with a fire extinguisher for use in the event of a fire bomb attack on the riot squad.

INTERVAL AND DISTANCE

Interval is the lateral space between elements and distance is the space between elements in column. The normal interval and distance

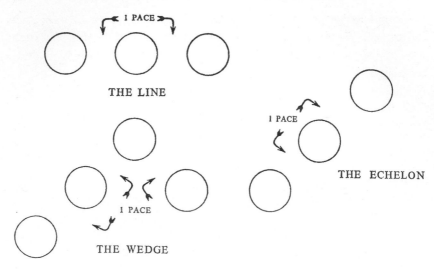

THE LINE

THE ECHELON

THE WEDGE

Interval and distance. The normal interval and distance is one pace.

between men in riot control formations is one pace (30 inches). The interval and distance may be adjusted to meet particular situations.

In any echelon formation with normal interval and distance, the angle made by the formation and the route of advance will be approximately 45°. The angle formed by the two wings of any wedge formation will be approximately 90° when normal interval and distance are used.

CADENCE

The normal cadence for movement into and assembly from all riot control formations is double time (180 steps per minute).

The normal cadence for movement of troops while in any riot control formation is at quick time (120 steps per minute). While in the on guard position, the cadence is approximately 60 steps per minute. For psychological effect, an on guard step may be executed by accentuating each step on the left foot with a resounding step.

For the "shuffle step" the police take the "on-balance" position with the knees slightly bent and the weight of the body equally distributed on the legs. At the same time officers will slide their left foot forward. The right foot will then be moved up to a position immediately to the right and rear of the left foot. The cadence of this "shuffle step" is 75 to 80 steps per minute.

Troops move in a slow, steady and determined manner. Changes in formation should be made with smartness and precision. Cadence may be increased or decreased at the discretion of the unit commander to meet varying situations. As soon as the crowd begins to disperse, the police should bring the cadence to a faster pace so as to discourage regrouping action.

MOVEMENT OF FORMATION

When moving against a crowd to disperse it, squads should move forward deliberately, permitting the crowd sufficient time to comply. Remember even a willing crowd can only move slowly. Persons in the rear must be given a chance to disperse. The line of advance must be decided on ahead of time and an escape path provided for the crowd.

Where the crowd does not actively resist the officers, the riot sticks should be held in a horizontal position applying pressure to the mid-section or chest area of the crowd member. Against the more truculent members the pressure can be applied to the throat or face area. It is important that squad members do not make comment or engage in arguments with crowd members.

Officers should not enter into individual encounters with any person in the crowd. If attacked, the officer should attempt to shoulder the assailant inside the formation. A more effective method is for officers on either side of the assailant to grasp him by the arms or shoulders and jerk him quickly through the line. Once inside the formation, the attacker can be taken into custody by the squad leader and his assistant or members of the close support squad. Handcuffs should be used when necessary and arrestees removed quickly to a mobile patrol wagon, which is close to the formation.

If attacks against squad members become general and attackers attempt to grasp the riot sticks, squad members should quickly shift the stick to the jab or thrust position, moving forward slowly against the crowd while employing the stick in a series of short rapid thrusts at the stomach area with a quick recovery. The same rules, of course, govern the use of the riot stick as apply to the regular police baton: they are to be used in self defense or to effect an arrest, and no more force to be used than is necessary to effect the arrest.

A cardinal rule is never to commit the units too deeply into the crowd so that they may be cut off. If this possibility develops the units should withdraw slowly. Officers should never turn their backs on a crowd but withdraw with their faces to the crowd.

All movements should be done on command and quickly to take advantage of the surprise element. The field commander should choose his own time for attacking and not permit his men to become provoked into premature action by name calling or abuse. Two way contact between platoon commanders and the field commander should be maintained by handie-talkies if necessary.

Where many arrests are anticipated, arrest teams, extra prisoner vans and other equipment should be in close support of the riot unit. Provision should be made for rapid handling, by units other than personnel of the riot formation, transport, and arrest procedures so that the persons involved can be immediately removed from the scene, while the special riot unit faces the crowd and maintains control. Delay in handling this type of police function can result in further incitation of the crowd to violence.

RETREAT

If a retreat becomes necessary because of an unforseen change in the situation, this retreat should always be made in formation, slowly so as not to give any indication of panic, and with the men facing toward the mob. Any situation that will indicate panic on the part of the police units will only encourage the mob and make it more aggressive.

SQUAD MEMBERS

Squad Leader

The squad leader is the most important member of the riot control squad. The ultimate success or failure of the riot control mission is dependent upon his reactions and judgment. In all squad formations the squad leader sets the unit in motion and regulates its pace. The squad leader should be an exceptional man with a reputation of intestinal fortitude. There is no place in crowd and riot control enforcement for uncertainty.

Position of Commander and Leaders

When in column, the commander at each echelon normally assumes his position at the head of the column. When in riot control formations, squad leaders and their assistants and platoon leaders and their assistants, take positions in the rear of the assault elements of their respective units where they can best direct and control their units. Each leader's exact location in that area is flexible. It is the position from which he can best perform his mission of direction and control.

Assistant Squad Leader

The assistant squad leader is second in command of the squad. He assumes command in the event the squad leader is incapacitated and acts as a reserve to fill any gaps in the squad.

Apex Man

The apex, base or point man of the riot control squad should be selected with great care. He must possess a quality of judgment, discipline and be in top physical condition. The apex, being the first member of the squad to make physical contact with the crowd, should be the largest in stature. The size and other traits as mentioned above have a tremendous psychological effect on the crowd. In the accompanying charts he is the number two man.

SQUAD FORMATIONS

Squad Line or Line of Skirmishers

DEFINITION. The line is a broad front formation that is continuous without gaps, with the blanks anchored to obstacles or protected by reserve elements.

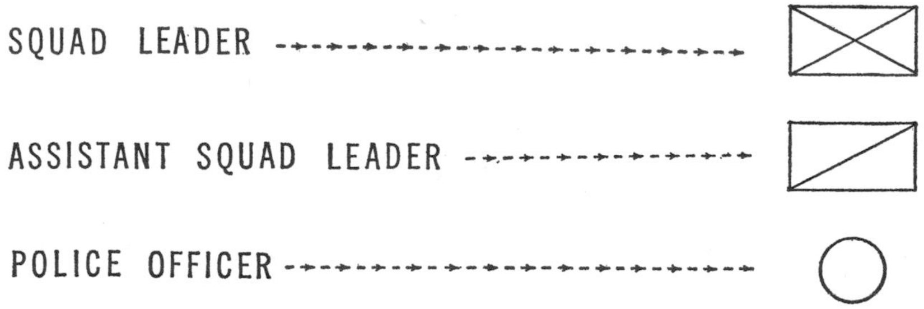

SQUAD LEADER

ASSISTANT SQUAD LEADER

POLICE OFFICER

Key to symbols used in illustration of riot control formations.

SQUAD LINE

Use. *Defensive Line.* The skirmish line is suitable for confronting the mob for a display of force and for denying an area to a mob. This formation is extremely successful to block an entrance. The use of barricades will aid police substantially in maintaining such a line.

Offensive Line. Offensively it is used to push or drive a mob straight back or across an open area or up a city street. It is also useful in driving a crowd from an enclosed area such as a court yard, as well as driving a large body of people from an open area.

Command. "Squad as skirmishers. Move." If the commander

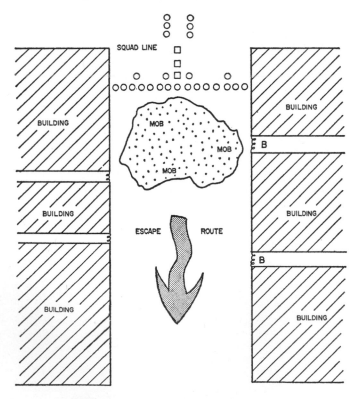

The squad line used to push back a mob.

desires, he may designate a specified number of paces between men in the formation by so indicating in his command, i.e., "Squad as skirmishers, two paces, Move." If no interval is specified in the command, the unit will automatically assume a one-pace interval.

SIGNAL. The squad leader will signal for this formation by raising both arms to the side until both are horizontal, arms and hands extended palms down.

EXECUTION. The apex man (number two) will then take a position indicated to him by the squad leader. All even numbered officers shall then position themselves to the right of the apex man, and all odd numbered officers shall position themselves to his left.

Diagonal (Echelon) Right or Left

DEFINITION. The diagonal is a slant line formation.

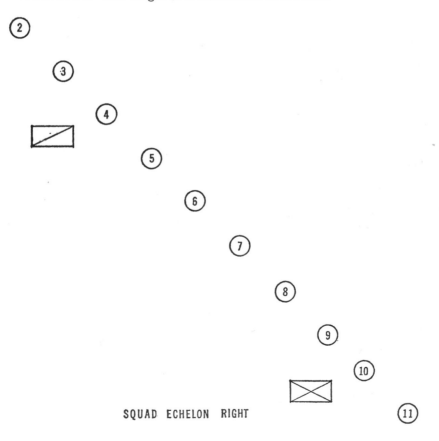

SQUAD ECHELON RIGHT

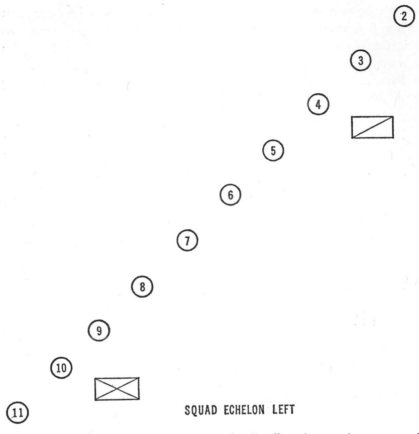

SQUAD ECHELON LEFT

Use. Used to achieve a "snow plow" effect in moving a crowd to the right or left.

The diagonal formation is suitable for clearing a mob from the side of a building, enclosure or wall. It is also useful for turning the direction of a crowd as the diagonal will force the group into side streets or open areas enabling the attack force to split the mob into segments for easy control. The diagonal is also useful in extending either or both sides of a wedge. It is best employed where a wall, building line, or obstruction exists to prevent the crowd from spilling in around the end of the formation.

Forming a Right Diagonal

COMMAND. "Squad Echelon Right, Move."

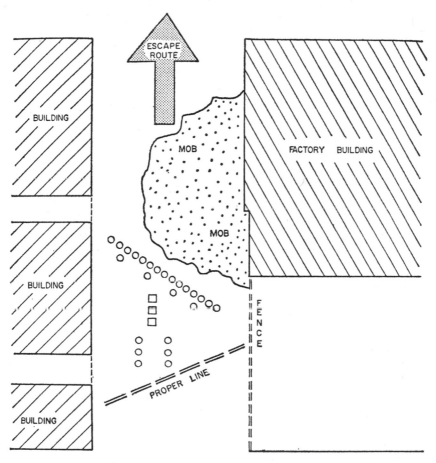

Proper and improper use of the diagonal. The top diagonal in this diagram situation is improper. It is not tight against the fence, rather sufficiently removed from it to allow segments of the mob either to climb over it or to pass around the left side of the diagonal and encircle the formation. The bottom diagonal, on the other hand, will prevent this and will pry the mob away from its target.

SIGNAL. The squad leader signals for this formation by facing the unit being signaled, and extending his right arm downward to the side at an angle of 45° below the horizontal in the direction in which the unit is to be echeloned, palm to the front; extend the left arm upward and to the side at an angle of 45° palm to the front.

EXECUTION. The apex man, number two, will then take a position indicated to him by the squad leader. All other officers shall then take positions one pace to the right and one pace to the rear of the number two man.

Forming a Left Diagonal

COMMAND. "Squad echelon left, Move."

SIGNAL. The squad leader will face the unit being signaled and extend his left arm downward to the side at an angle of 45° below the horizontal in the direction in which the unit is to be echeloned, palm to the front; his right arm should be extended upward and to the side at an angle of 45° palm to the front.

EXECUTION. The apex man (number two) will then take a position indicated to him by the squad leader. All other officers then take positions one pace to the left and one pace to the rear of the apex man.

MOVEMENT INTO MOB. The first officer entering the crowd forces some of the members over into the path of the second officer. The second in turn forces the rioters into the path of the third and as the police formation passes through the crowd, an entire segment is separated. There should be in reserve, following the diagonal line, a sufficient number of reserves to plug any gap that might occur. These reserves can also be used to subdue and remove any person who attempts to grapple with an officer in the line. After the segment has been separated from the main body of the mob, the line can then turn and force the section farther and farther away from the scene of the riot. Other units can then enter the crowd as a line or can take over the dispersal of the already separated segment.

Wedge

DEFINITION. The wedge is an inverted V shape formation.

USE. *Offensive.* The wedge formation is the normal formation for offensive action against a crowd or mob. It is best used for breaking the disorderly group into segments or clearing a street intersection. This formation is also used very successfully to penetrate a crowd, to apprehend an agitator or rescue a trapped officer.

Defensive. The wedge may be modified into a diamond for all-round security in the event the mob threatens to engulf the squad.

CAUTION. When the police are greatly outnumbered, a wedge

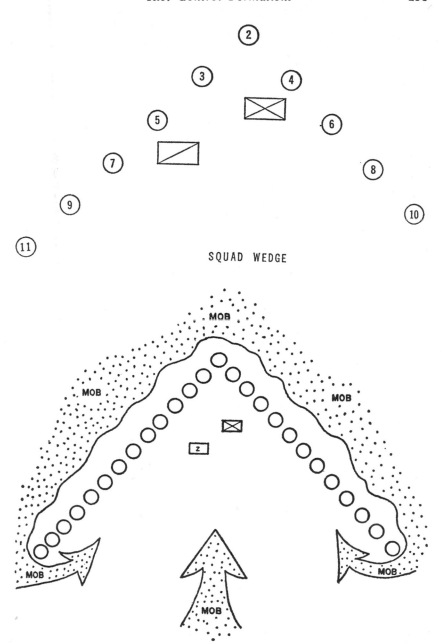

SQUAD WEDGE

A wedge that moves too deeply into a large mob is in grave danger of being outflanked, surrounded, and thus destroyed as an effective formation.

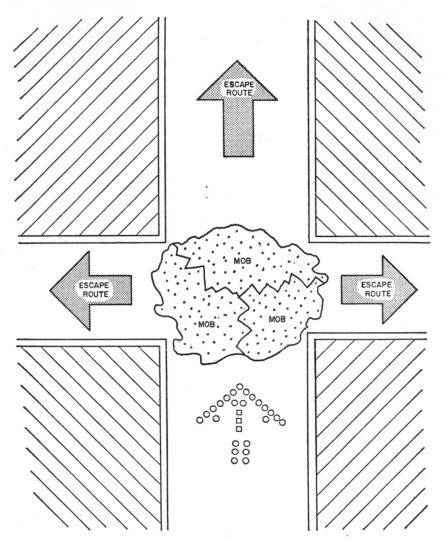

The use of a wedge to shatter and disperse a mob.

should not be driven into the mob as this could result in their being surrounded by the mob.

PENETRATING THE MOB. When the squad wedge moves toward the mob, the officers will be facing ahead. However, as the squad penetrates the crowd, it may be necessary for the officers forming the sides of the wedge to close the gap between each other and to face outward from the formation toward the mob. The numbers nine and ten men would then face the rear, walking backwards, in order to protect the squad from an attack from behind. The squad leader should remain inside the wedge so that he can direct the squad and maintain custody of arrested suspects while the squad withdraws from the crowd.

TAKING PRISONERS. When the formation reaches the individual to be apprehended, a gap is opened and the individual is pulled inside the formation. The gap is then immediately closed.

WITHDRAWING THE WEDGE. When the wedge has driven into a crowd and a prisoner has been taken into custody, it will be necessary to reach a point of safety as soon as possible.

If the mob is small, this can be accomplished by continuing forward to the opposite side. Usually, however, the crowd will be sizeable and will necessitate the wedge withdrawing along the same route it advanced. To effect an orderly withdrawal, the wedge should retain its shape and merely move backwards. If considerable opposition is encountered, while withdrawing, the officers on the flanks should daw together slightly to harrow the formation.

COMMAND. "Squad wedge, Move."

SIGNAL. The squad leader will signal for this formation by extending both arms downward and to the sides at an angle of 45° below the horizontal, arms and hands extended palms down, as shown in figure.

EXECUTION. The apex man (number two) will then take a position indicated to him by the squad leader. All even numbered officers shall then take positions one pace to the right and one pace to the rear of the apex man, and all odd numbered officers shall take positions one pace to the left and one pace to the rear of the apex man.

PLATOON FORMATION

Introduction

The formations utilized by the platoon are the same basic formations employed by the squad and the same principles are applicable to both. The only distinction is that a platoon has three to four times the manpower of a squad and is thus capable of utilizing squads in various types of support positions which increase the defensive effectiveness of the platoon as well as its offensive striking power.

Composition and Command

A platoon may consist of three or four squads. The platoon leader is in command of all squads in the platoon. In forming all riot control formations from the column, the platoon leader moves out to the right or left of his platoon and faces it when giving his commands. As he gives his preparatory command, he points to the approximate location at which he desires the platoon to form. If he does not point, the formation is formed immediately in front of the column. The platoon leader should pause between his preparatory command and command of execution to permit each squad leader to issue a preparatory command to his squad.

Types of Support

1. General—one or two squads remain in column behind formation.
2. Lateral—one of two squads move to the right and/or left to protect the flanks of the formation.
3. Close—one of two squads move forward to take up positions between the men in the assault element to strengthen the formation.

During riot control operations, the platoon leader may rotate his squads in the leading or assault elements to give a squad or squads a rest. The platoon leader may also relieve any two squads in the assault element by forming a like formation with the support squads and have the support element pass through the leading element. This procedure is frequently necessary when gas masks are put on for a chemical attack.

MOUNTED FORMATIONS

Horses are very valuable in controlling mobs. An officer on a horse has a psychological advantage in that he is elevated above the mob participants and is looking down on them. Then, too, the horse acts as a barrier between the officer and the mob and affords protection to the officer. By merely turning or heading the horse into a mob, the officer is able to turn or divide them. Mob participants realize that an animal is insensitive to their feelings and desires. They are uncertain as to what it will do. They know that if the animal becomes frightened, it may injure them.

When sufficient mounted men are on the scene they should be used as the spearhead of the formations. All that has previously been said about the use of the various riot formations can be applied with even greater effect by the mounted unit.

However, the unit shall not be considered as bearing the entire burden of handling the situation. Foot squads must be assigned to follow behind and provide close support to the mounted unit. Their function will be to take prisoners into custody and assist any rider under attack by rioters. Other foot squads can be used to disperse segments of the mob split off by the mounted unit, or for any other necessary purpose.

Officers on foot shall be observant of the actions of rioters to forestall any attempts to disable or injure the mounts. Knives, icepick and nails have been used in the past to disable or injure the mounts. Marbles or ball bearings thrown on the ground can cause a horse to slip and fall.

The mounted unit should attempt to maintain its formation acting together as a unit. It should avoid being split up into individual groups and should not commit itself too deeply into a crowd so that it is likely to be surrounded and cut off.

A suggested formation for one squad operating in conjunction with two mounted men is the following:

A diamond shaped wedge is formed by one squad with the Squad Leader, the Assistant Squad Leader and No. 10 man inside the wedge to handle prisoners taken into custody. Riders operating in front of and on the flanks of the diamond go after violators and turn them over to the members of the foot squad which then removes the prisoners to the wagon. This type of action may be used to advantage while working in the rear of crowds to break up rock throwing gangs.

VEHICLES AND POLICE FORMATIONS

Employment of Vehicles

The mobility, armor and armament of armored units make them particularly effective in the suppression of a civil disturbance. They are capable of crushing street barricades and obstacles; their armor renders them invulnerable to small arms fire and missiles; and they create a psychological effect that is of value in controlling an unlawful crowd or mob.

To counter the rioters tactics of employing vehicles against police formations, it may be advantageous to employ vehicles with the foot officers in riot control formations. The vehicle should be located at the apex or center of the formation being employed where it can be quickly maneuvered to block the oncoming vehicular assault on the formation. They should be employed only over terrain for which they are suited. By using vehicles, the police gain three distinct advantages over the crowd or mob, mobility, fire power and shock action. Vehicles also can give the police a wall of protection against those who employ vehicles to run them down, as was done during the Watts riot. Trucks can also be used as a gun platform or as a base to release riot control agents.

Vehicles employed in mass are effective against a mob when there is sufficient space for the vehicles to maneuver and for the mob to move. Vehicles should be protected by the placement of barbed wire or heavy mesh wire on the front, sides and top.

Vulnerable Characteristics

While vehicles add strength to any formation, they have certain vulnerable characteristics that cannot be overlooked. Tracked vehicles can be disabled by jamming iron bars and similar weapons in the "bogie wheels." Tires of wheeled vehicles can be punctured or slashed with pointed or sharp instruments. Headlights and windshields can easily be smashed and radiators punctured with numerous weapons. Brake and fuel lines can be cut or broken with numerous weapons. Open or unguarded areas on vehicles can be attacked with home-made bombs, stones, Molotov cocktails, and other missiles.

Precautionary Measures

Windshields of vehicles should be removed or completely depressed to horizontal position. If windshields are made of safety glass, they offer some protection while in an upright position to occupants of the front seat with minimum danger of injury from glass fragments.

Shields or mobile barriers can be constructed of wooden or metal frame strung with barbed wire and mounted across the front of vehicle.

Vehicles should always be used in conjunction with foot-troops— never alone. Police in the formation should be pressed tightly against the front corners of each vehicle to prevent rioters from attacking the sides and rear of the vehicles. In addition to the protection that is afforded by supporting foot troops, the occupants of the vehicles may be protected by covering vulnerable portions of the vehicles with mesh wire or similar suitable material. When vehicles are halted, troops defend them with rifles and bayonets. If a vehicle breaks down, two other vehicles should be used to protect it. The troops form an island of defense until they receive further orders.

Armored Vehicles

These should be employed when available and practical because of their much greater psychological effect as well as the greater protection they will afford the occupants.

Armored vehicles of the scout-car type may be employed in a similar manner, when less force is required to attain an objective. In addition, they are utilized in reconnaissance and security missions, for messenger service, in tactical support of the infantry, and as carriers.

Chapter 25

WEAPONS

INTRODUCTION

THE POLICE HAVE the mission of enforcing the laws and maintaining the peace. When a riot occurs, the mission of the police is to restore and maintain order. Decisive control measures are absolutely necessary for the successful accomplishment of this mission. Sound judgment dictates that only the minimum force necessary be used against rioters; to do otherwise may unnecessarily jeopardize life and property.

To aid in achieving this goal, a priority of force should be predetermined by each police agency based on the weaponry and equipment available to that department for employment in riot control duty. But within this broad framework, the field commander must be given the authority to use whatever he deems is warranted by the facts as he knows them.

Police on riot duty should never have specific instructions as to the limit of force that they may use. The commander should be instructed and empowered to use the necessary amount of force to subdue the mob and control the situation.

FIREARMS

The most extreme action which a law enforcement officer can take in any situation is the use of firearms. Firearms should be used only after all other measures for controlling the violence have been exhausted. Officers should never fire indiscriminately into a crowd or mob. Volleys of live ammunition normally should not be fired over heads of rioters. Such extreme action may result in injury or death to citizens and may erupt into a prolonged and fatal clash between the officers and the mob.

Decision to Utilize

The commander at the scene should make the decision regarding the use of firearms. The decision should be based on evidence that lethal force is intended or is being used by members of the mob.

In extreme emergency situations it is much better to plan in advance to use firearms as a last resort. The commander should let the mob know it, and put no restrictions on the men and their use of firearms at the proper time and signal, once the action has begun. Police and troops should never be sent into action without ammunition or armed only with blanks, or with orders not to use their guns.

In the past, the officer in command has maintained control of the ammunition and issued it when the situation became critical. This practice lowered the morale of the men and indicated a lack of discipline. Ordinarily it is difficult to issue ammunition hurriedly to the individual men while they are in contact during a riot. More than that, if the mob ever finds this out, they will be encouraged to attack, and in such a situation the police, powerless to defend themselves, will be mauled.

An officer should never fire a weapon while running. It takes only one carefully aimed shot to kill. When the target is visible, he should stop, take up a firing position and make the first shot good.

Snipers

The possibility that the police will be subjected to sniper fire cannot be overlooked. A sniper must be dealt with rapidly and severely. If permitted to remain effective, a sniper will not only pin down the police force, but he remains a threat to human life, police and citizen alike. This problem is not solved by police officers, crouched behind any means of protection available, firing their service revolvers, or shotguns, aimlessly at a building or rooftop. Such action is not only ineffective, it endangers lives and pins down units, preventing them from accomplishing their mission.

Selected marksmen should be stationed at certain strategic points from where they may control and survey the area. Such personnel should be selected on the basis of their marksmanship, good judgment and cool headedness. They should be equipped with telescopic rifles and should be instructed to fire at any person directing lethal force against the police. The selected marksmen should shoot to kill such persons.

Display of Firearms

The display of weapons can have a definite effect upon the mob, but that effect may be either beneficial or detrimental to the police. If the mob believes the weapons will be used, their display will have a deterring effect. But the display of firearms in the hands of the police, before their use is justified, will antagonize the mob and thus complicate control of the situation and further incite the mob, which is well aware that the police are unlikely to utilize such weapons. Likewise, the manner in which weapons are displayed may aggravate the situation.

The display of a weapon as a bluff is a dangerous practice. If the officer's bluff is called and the crowd moves in, he may be forced to fire into the crowd or withdraw, thereby losing respect and authority; or stand his ground and be forced to protect himself in some manner.

If it is necessary to employ a weapon in a crowd to effect an arrest or in making a shakedown, care should be used to holster the revolver as soon as the suspects are in custody or the situation is under control. Prolonged display of weapons has an adverse effect upon citizens witnessing the incident.

Weapons

The choice of arms and equipment is governed by the features of the area in which the riot occurs. Normally it is a congested section of a metropolitan area. In the immediate area there will be many innocent victims trapped in the action or in their homes or business establishments. Many obstacles are encountered in these built-up areas. Fighting normally takes place at close quarters. There are usually many firing positions giving good cover from fire.

This suggests that the weapons should be light, of relatively short range and low penetrating power so as not to rip through the wall and kill some innocent bystanders. Further, the weapon should have high volume of fire or great spread of impact. The shotgun best meets these requirements.

The shotgun has a distinct psychological effect on persons who believe it may be used against them. The muzzle of this weapon, when viewed in the hands of a police officer, may look as big as the open end of an empty oil drum. This psychological effect can, in many instances, be used to good advantage without need of actual firing of the shotgun.

Although the gun is not designed for use as a weapon for close-in fighting, it can be used as such when necessary and the man armed with it is in close contact with the mob.

Indeed, in the guerrilla type of riot, the shotgun must be used both as a weapon for firing and a club, for part of the mob will surge through the streets often making personal contact with police units while at the same time others will throw missiles or fire weapons and attempt to flee. To try to control such a mob with a riot stick and a revolver is useless. A shotgun, with or without a bayonet, will serve the function of both weapons. Care must be exercised in selecting all riot guns to assure that they are equipped with special riot stocks designed to take the strain exerted upon them when used to deliver body blows.

The Pistol and Revolver

The combat use of these weapons is practically limited to distances of not over fifty yards. In the hands of an untrained shot, the pistol will not prove an effective weapon. With constant practice, it will be found that the short barrel and the speed with which single rounds can be fired enable the firer to engage targets rapidly in different directions and render it a very useful weapon for close-quarter fighting.

Submachineguns

The submachinegun is accurate only at medium ranges, and, in reality, fills in the gap between the hand gun and the rifle. This gun can be fired from the hip or the shoulder. Its accuracy is comparable to a rifle up to 200 yards, depending on the type of ammunition used. It can also be used from the hip most effectively at close quarters, under poor light conditions, or when time is not available for an aimed shot, or burst, from the shoulder firing position.

Rifles

A well-stocked police arsenal should always include a number of rifles for possible use in riots, road blocks, raids and other special situations. The caliber of these rifles may vary with individual choice, but they usually will be .30 caliber or over.

As in the case of the submachinegun, the rifle should only be used by men who have had training and practice with it, even though this may limit its employment to a few selected individuals. From the standpoint of ammunition supply, combat effectiveness and training, it is best to have shoulder weapons standardized so they are all of one type and caliber.

BAYONET

Troops armed with either the rifle, riot shotgun or carbine should have their bayonets fixed whenever they are facing a mob. Not normally used in police service, but available, is a bayonet which may be attached to the riot gun. Its value cannot be doubted. The mere presence of a bayonet in the hands of an officer has a deterrent effect. Those who are sure an officer will not use a gun are unsure of whether or not he will resort to a bayonet. More than that, they will undoubtedly resolve any doubt in favor of an affirmative answer to the question.

Railway-type, long burning fusees can be very successfully used in military tactical formations for riot control. They can be wired to the bayonets and ignited. This presents a strong psychological and physical effect in dispersing the mob when the formation advances. This tactic is especially weird and effective at night. If the supply is limited, fusees can be best used on the apex of the wedge and flanks of the tactical formation.

THE BATON (RIOT STICK)

The police baton, riot stick, or truncheon, is probably the most useful, yet least dangerous, force which may be employed against disorderly persons. The baton is not intended as a weapon that each man uses, as he sees fit, to engage in a series of individual contests with separate rioters. It is a team weapon to be employed by disciplined police or military units.

The baton's psychological effect is probably its greatest value. A crowd or mob may defy police armed only with lethal weapons because they are aware of the normal hesitancy of the police to open fire. Therefore, they are likely to challenge the display of firearms as a bluff and continue or even increase the tempo of the disturbance. On the other hand, the sight of police advancing in formation and wielding the riot sticks instills in the participants a definite respect because they know that the police will make vigorous and unhesitating application of these weapons. When correctly used, the stick can inflict acute temporary pain without serious injury. The proper use of the baton should be so thoroughly learned that the proper use of it becomes automatic. The baton can be used both as an offensive and a defensive weapon. However, it is primarily an offensive weapon.

Reminders

1. The baton is not a club.
2. Proper use requires courage, footwork, strength and good direction.
3. The baton is primarily an offensive weapon.
4. The baton, when carried in a military manner, is an emblem of law and order and adds to the officer's appearance as an agent of his department.
5. The baton is valuable for close in as well as distance fighting.
6. Defensive techniques are developed to enable the officer to survive an attack, to counterattack, and gain advantage without seriously injuring the opponent or endangering his own life.

CHEMICAL AGENTS

While chemical irritants are not a solution to all disturbance control problems, they are useful weapons. They are a humane, effective means of achieving the greatest temporary incapacitation of a riotous group with the least permanent injury to its members and to the police. Not only do they cause the mob to flee and temporarily render its members helpless, they also shock the majority into a clearer perspective of the consequence of their acts, for the majority of any hostile crowd is usually composed of people who, although temporarily angry and dangerous, are generally law abiding.

Warning

The use of gas is a highly technical matter and should be done by persons skilled in its use. They should be thoroughly familiar with the performance specifications as set forth by the manufacturers, and aware of the dangers of misuse.

In the majority of disorders, civil officers and troops have encountered rioters in the open. When this happens, it is usually extremely difficult for the police to maneuver in order to approach the group from the direction of the wind. Unless there exists a favorable wind, it is not easy to drift gas clouds down on the rioters.

Aftermath of Use of Gas Contamination

The aftermath of heavy gas concentrations used in cities and heavily populated areas is always a problem for the police. The contaminating and irritating effect of CN can remain for days.

Gas fumes or particles spread by any of the standard means of dispersion are no respecter of property or persons. Odor of tear gas will adhere to the person, clothing, furnishings, or fixings for long periods of time, if the concentration has been a heavy sustained one. Humid, wet climatic conditions will cause the odor to linger much longer.

Washing the person and clothing plus fresh air and wind will eliminate the gas effects relatively quickly on individuals and objects in open areas. Confined areas, such as where a grenade has been exploded indoors or a barricade projectile fired inside a room, present special decontamination problems. Rooms, rugs, draperies and furnishings that have been subjected to heavy tear gas concentrations often require special decontamination measures by professional firms specializing in this type of work.

Advantages

Advantages of chemical agents may be summarized as follows:
1. Creates confusion among rioters.
2. Disperses them and facilitates the making of necessary arrests.
3. Most humane method of breaking up unlawful assemblies which cannot be dispersed without the use of force.
4. Effective method in preventing property damage, serious injury and bloodshed.

5. The hazards of hand-to-hand encounters between police and rioters may be minimized or avoided.

Disadvantages

1. The indiscriminate use of gas may arouse resentment to otherwise acceptable police procedures.
2. Affects innocent.
3. Impedes police operations, especially with change of wind.
4. Not generally effective if the rioting mobs are so widely spread out on a number of the city streets utilizing hit and run techniques.

Uses of Gases

Although gas is usually used to break up and disperse a mob, it may be used to achieve other ends.

DENYING AREAS TO RIOTERS. When an area is to be denied to rioters, a blanketing gas cloud may be produced over the area. Baseball grenades are especially well suited for use in denying small, confined areas to rioters because the fusing time is very short and dispersal is instantaneous. Mechanical gas dispersers may be used effectively in denial operations and a large area can be covered rapidly with a limited number of personnel.

SPLITTING A MOB. A narrow gas cloud thrown across the center of a mob tends to split it. This procedure is advisable in areas where there is no path of retreat to the rear for the rioters, or when the supply of riot control gases is limited.

ATTACKING A BUILDING. When rioters are barricaded within a building, the building itself may be blanketed with a gas cloud, provided that the windows have been shattered. Smoke may be used to cover the approach of police who may throw grenades directly into the building. The burning type grenade should not be used where combustibles are present because of the intense heat generated by the grenade and the danger of starting a fire.

GAS AND SMOKE. The combined use of a heavy smoke screen, as contrasted with the small amount of smoke from a grenade or shell, and gas will have a devastating physical and psychological impact on the mob. Together they cut off the individual from the mob and panic him into a realization of the gravity of the situation and his individual responsibility.

SMOKE

Uses

Smoke may be used for the following purposes:

1. Screen police movements.
2. Determine the direction and velocity of the wind.
3. Block off and deny a mob.
4. When used under conditions favorable to the formation of chemical clouds, it will create a certain amount of confusion among crowds and assist in their dispersion by disrupting visual contact between members of the mob and disrupt communications between leaders and rioters and nullify psychological influences of novelty, contagion, imitation and the force of numbers.

Colored Smoke

In this regard, the employment of colored smoke, green, red, orange, can have a great demoralizing effect upon the mob. Non-toxic irritants which effect the nose and throat, usually causing coughing by the individuals subjected to, or staying in, the concentration likewise helps to disperse the mob.

Colored smoke will produce a greater initial psychological impact than white smoke. Certain colors seem to have more dramatic impact than others and result in a more rapid dispersion of the mob. Caucasians are said to have a greater reaction to brilliant green smoke than to white smoke. Negroids and Latins are declared to be most affected by brilliant red, which is associated with blood.

Colored smoke is formed by particles of volatilized dye. When these particles are carried along in the smoke cloud they adhere to persons and clothing or whatever they touch, producing a sometimes indelible stain. As most mob and riot actions take place during hot and humid weather when there is a great deal of perspiration, the colored smoke particles will stain the light colored clothing usually worn in warm weather. Stains will be especially noticeable on neck bands, collars, and shirt cuffs. Such stains are often of great assistance to the police in later identifying mob participants after the violence has been quelled and the rioters dispersed. The staining effect of colored smoke must be considered by the commander when he makes a determination to use colored smoke.

There is a possible toxic effect if a person is subjected to a long stay in a heavy, sustained, colored smoke concentration; this hazard does not exist with white HC. However, in normal open field or street conditions the amount of toxicity is not considered to be dangerous. There will be a much more toxic effect if individuals subjected to a prolonged colored smoke concentration are located in confined areas or buildings. This fact must also be carefully considered by the officials responsible for employing tactics dictating its use.

WATER

Water from a fire hose may be effective in moving small groups, in moving groups on a narrow front, such as a street, or in defending a defile (including a narrow passageway) or roadblock.

Water jets are also useful in defending personnel, equipment and mob objectives, provided there is a sufficient supply and equipment for providing the necessary pressure. The personnel and equipment in this operation must be protected by police formations.

Water may be employed in two ways: as a flat trajectory weapon utilizing pressure, or as a high trajectory weapon employing water as rainfall. The latter method is especially effective during cold weather, but in the warm humid weather that usually prevails when a riot occurs, it loses much of its effectiveness.

In conjunction with the water, a harmless dye can be mixed into the stream for possible later identification of the rioters, but more important, for the psychological effect the color spray will have on the rioters. This procedure has several obvious disadvantages, however, since it dyes all, both innocent and guilty. This can further inflame the crowd. The use of invisible ultra violet dye would be better.

Hoses attached to hydrants are obviously limited to their length plus the distance the water is projected. This shortcoming is overcome by the use of a large water tank and a powerful water pump mounted on a truck with a high pressure hose and nozzle capable of searching and traversing and will enable the police to employ water as they advance.

Consideration in Utilization

While water may serve to dampen not only the bodies, but the spirits as well, of the riotous group, certain problems have been experienced, such as injuries, heart attacks, loss and damage to the hoses.

There is a great deal of physical pressure behind water from a fire hose or water thrower. If the stream is received full in the face or other vulnerable area at close range, serious injury can result. However, at a distance this force is dissipated.

If used in a business area, there might be unnecessary property damage. Storekeepers who have nothing to do with the situation other than the fact that their stores were in close proximity to the riot are made to suffer. Further, water under such pressure is hard to manage.

Fire hoses pose the following problems: distance restrictions (from hydrants, from pumpers, etc.) and protection, for if they are used they must be guarded (the entire length) because rioters cut and damage the hoses and injure firemen. Over and above that, should the rioters gain control of the hoses, they could raise havoc with the police.

If it is decided to use fire equipment, arrangements should be made with the responsible fire department official. Naturally, while this fire fighting equipment is in use or on standby at a riot, other areas would be denied their use, possibly resulting in unnecessary fire loss. Nor can the danger to that very expensive equipment be ignored in determining whether it should be used.

Recent use of water by this method has resulted in adverse publicity and in some areas has become synonymous with "police brutality." Insofar as the image of the police department is of concern, employment of such force is not advisable.

DOGS

Police dogs have proven their value in crowd control on many occasions. The trained police dog, by his very appearance, will exercise a subduing influence on persons who fear animals. If the dog is snapping and snarling on command while being held on the leash, he will evoke fear from within the mob. It is this fear which makes the use of dogs so advantageous in law enforcement. The psychological effect of the appearance of the dog clears people from his path, for the member of the mob realizes that while a police officer is human and has a human reluctance to inflict violence on his fellow man, a well-trained police dog has no such reluctance.

These dogs have also proved their worth in protecting handlers who have been struck down or injured. In more than one instance the dog has stood guard over its prostrate partner and by so doing saved him from further harm at the hands of the mob. But we must also recognize that the use of dogs to confront the mob or demonstrators in the past has served to increase resentment and ill feeling on the part of the public in general. The dog, being the animal that it is, is incapable of rational thought. Rather it is trained to react instinctively to given stimuli. The rioters are aware of the animal's weakness and can be counted upon to play upon them, as they have in the past, in this way embarrassing the police and gaining unjustified sympathy and support.

Thus it is that a tremendous disagreement exists between police over the use of dogs. Almost all agree that dogs can be employed effectively at roadblocks, in the guarding of key installations, and by foot patrols operating in an area previously cleared of rioters. But many are convinced that dogs should not be employed when confronting the mob, particularly during the show of force phase, when their presence could serve to furnish the "spark" which would ignite the riot.

Others claim that the mere presence of the dog and its psychological effect is sufficient to control the members of the crowd. They assert that in a riot situation dogs have been used in various capacities. Teams of dogs formed into squads and moving in riot formation can effectively move and break up a crowd. Here the normal procedure for the use of riot squads in disbursing are utilized. In particular the importance of avenues of escape must be stressed.

Teams can also be used to break up the back of the crowd and peel off the flanks. The dog handlers should, as they advance, be accompanied by other uniformed police protecting them on the rear and flanks. These officers will make arrests, transfer prisoners to patrol wagons, and perform other functions. Rather than employ the teams in the front ranks they may be employed as a back-up or flank guard for standard police riot formations. In this case if the column is continuously penetrated by the mob, canine teams will be brought forward and take positions immediately behind the column. Their use in this way avoids the harmful publicity that has so frequently followed their use, while at the same time utilizing fully the psychological effect by showing their availability in close proximity to the action.

The resolution of this problem is up to the individual commander. He alone is aware of the temperament in his community and the degree of training of his dogs and their handlers.

SOUND

Sound plays an important part in organizing and maintaining a mob, and by the same token can be used to break up the mob. Just as savages used war dances, chants and drums to build up emotions and capture the individuals attention and hold his loyalty, present day agitators and organizers employ chanting, rhythm-beat, slogan-shouting, hand clapping and singing to induce mass hypnotism. It is a basic means of controlling large masses of people, who, having lost their individuality, become subject to commands of the mob leaders and blend into the mob mass.

The police must break up this sound control. This can be done by removing the source—a method particularly effective against mechanical noisemakers, loud speaker systems and cheer leaders. A second method is to break the pattern with a counter sound barrage directed over police public address systems. This counter attack may consist of music, noise, sirens and messages.

Equipment is now available which emits a pulsating, penetrating sound equal to 120 DBM at thirty feet. This sound volume is so intense that organized agitation is broken up. Thus the hypnotic effect established by rhythmic beats, chanting, slogan shouting is neutralized, and as a result the mob leaders lose one of their most

effective tools in the control of the unified crowd and mob self incitation. If a mob advances toward the operated amplifier system,
the piercing sound causes extreme pain in the ears, and it can be
expected that signs, banners and weapons would be discarded in
order to free hands and cover the ears.

SECTION IV
CONTROL PROCEDURE

Chapter 26

CROWD CONTROL

PROBLEMS OF CROWD CONTROL

Introduction

T̤HERE ARE SEVERAL PROBLEMS inherent to crowd control. Police officers must be familiar with these problems, recognize them immediately, and be prepared to initiate timely remedial action.

Overcrowding

This problem is best controlled by the establishment of shutoff lines. These lines should be laid out and manpower and facilities assigned in advance so that upon a signal the shutoff can be established. Three principles are applicable in the establishment of a shutoff line:

1. It should be established at a point where the people who are unable to gain access to the area can be turned back without creating a congestion problem.
2. It should be established at a point where the physical features tend to channel the flow of pedestrians to its narrowest width.
3. It should be established at a point far enough beyond the crowd to prevent the shutoff point being overrun by the normal crowd.

Room for police to maneuver must be provided between the edge of the crowd and the shutoff point. Communications should be established between police at the shutoff point and at the crowd. Portable radios are excellent for this purpose. Consideration should be given to the establishment of an overflow area for accommodating those who wish to remain in the vicinity even though they may not be able to go to the main assembly area.

In the event the overcrowding already exists in the area (a beach or amusement park), police must insure the arrival of transportation prior to the management closing the area. Arrangements must be made to refund ticket monies and other such actions to eliminate situations that could cause trouble. An announcement of procedures to be followed should be made to the crowd.

Panic

Panic is the fear of the unknown. In a crowd panic can be highly contagious. Floods, fires, serious accidents, fights, or other critical emergencies may occur with such shocking suddenness that man's reasoning processes are suspended and panic results. There is only one truly successful way to control panic—prevent it. Nothing should be left undone. Plans for panic prevention should include the following:

1. Separation of crowds into smaller groups by establishment of aisles, barricades, shut-off lines, and other restrictive measures.
2. Provision of sufficient exits so that the area can be quickly cleared.
3. Strategic placement of uniformed police throughout the area so that prompt preventive or control action may be taken.
4. Inspection of the area before the crowd gathers to assure that no explosives, fire hazards, or other panic-producing conditions are present.
5. Adequate protection of light control switches to include provision for auxiliary lighting.
6. Provision for keeping exits clear. Width of exits should increase as the distance from the center increases.
7. Assurance that control personnel are thoroughly familiar with the evacuation plan.
8. Assurance that doors open outward and that revolving doors are not used.
9. Provision of a public address system.

Drinking

Use of excessive alcoholic beverages, especially among youths at beaches, has resulted in mob violence on several occasions. To control the sale of alcoholic beverages at the scene is not sufficient, as liquor is often transported to the scene by the various individuals or groups. The intake, as well as the sale, must be closely observed and controlled. In addition to lessening inhibitions, causing fights and over-zealous activity, the containers provide the individuals with weapons, to use against each other, or in consort against police.

Clashes Between Opposing Groups

Whenever possible, opposing groups should be segregated. Political meetings or those concerned with labor disputes are good examples of controversial gatherings where this system would be applicable. This involves assigning each group to a specific area. Equally desirable locations and equal opportunity for publicity should be provided. If possible, a different departure time should be given each group. In more confined areas, such as at beaches and amusement parks and where the varied opinions represented may be readily identified, different tactics must be used. In such instances assignment of plainclothes officers or detectives should be made in the crowd to identify leaders or potential troublemakers, determine plans of the group and enable prompt action in the event of disorder. If possible, groups so identified should be dispersed in different locations, exit routes and transit facilities policed, and shutoff lines established.

Criminal Activities

A crowd presents an ideal environment for pickpockets, sex offenders and similar criminals. All police personnel should be fully instructed in the *modus operandi* of these types of criminals. Plainclothes personnel should be assigned who are experienced in detecting pickpockets, dope peddlers and degenerates. Assignment of policewomen in civilian clothes is very effective in detecting sex offenders.

Sickness and Injury

First aid stations should be strategically located in coordination with health and other responsible agencies. The emotional tension normally associated with a crow situation and the necessity for standing or walking in a congested area creates an atmosphere in which some people become ill. It is good practice to pre-position an ambulance or patrol car equipped with emergency medical supplies and equipment to care for the sick and injured.

Lost Children

Provision should be made for the security of children who become separated from their parents. A shelter should be provided which should be under the supervision of a policewoman. Toilet facilities and facilities for the children's amusement should be provided. Communications should be established so that information regarding lost children may be quickly disseminated.

Traffic Congestion

Traffic congestion causes tempers to rise and is conducive to accidents. Accidents cause further congestion. A simple plan involving a minimum degree of control should be established to facilitate flow of traffic. Traffic must be diverted in order that vehicles will not flow through the crowd area. Detours should be established a considerable distance from the area involved. Communications should be maintained between these outlying detour points and traffic headquarters so that a complete detour may be instituted. In the interest of public relations, detour routes should be adequately policed. Traffic stoppages should be prevented by tracing traffic density for a considerable distance from the area occupied by the crowd. Consideration should be given to temporarily changing traffic patterns at the conclusion of an event in order to accommodate the mass exodus of vehicles. Widespread publicity should be given to all traffic plans and detours. Where applicable, full advantage should be taken of automobile radios and radio stations to broadcast traffic news.

GENERAL PRINCIPLES OF CROWD CONTROL

Introduction

A crowd is an essential prerequisite to the formation of a mob. Further, in all situations where there is an assemblage of many persons, there always exists the possibility that some incident could turn an otherwise peaceful crowd into a mob. The objectives of the police are the preservation of the peace and the protection of life and property. The methods used to gain these objectives will necessarily vary, depending upon the reason for the assemblage, and the crowd's actions after having assembled. But there are two cardinal principles which are universally applicable—get there first and in sufficient force.

Planning

The handling of a crowd may be divided into two stages—preparatory planning and the actual field procedure. The problems and procedures to pursue in planning to handle any unusual situation are discussed in detail in another chapter, therefore only a few observations will be made at this time.

The first step in planning for control of a crowd is to obtain all available facts and rumors. Information of planning value may be classified as factual or hearsay. Factual information includes the time and location of the event, the purpose and sponsor of the event, and the physical features of the area. Hearsay information consists of expected attendance, climate or atmosphere of the event, anticipated presence of opposing groups, the psychological background of the expected crowd, and any expected trouble or disorder. This is the intelligence phase of planning.

The next step is to plan the physical control of the event. This includes coordinating activities with sponsors, other municipal agencies (transit system), and management of the establishment. Problem areas should be identified, a traffic plan prepared, and personnel requirements determined. The equipment required will depend upon the information obtained and the type of control measures decided upon.

And finally, provision must be made for a reserve force, properly organized and equipped, to respond rapidly should the situation deteriorate beyond the capabilities of the committed control forces. The reserve force should be in the riot control uniform, and when committed, furnish a surprise *show of force*. In this early stage, their timely appearance could, and has, provided the psychological factor necessary to stall momentarily the threatening situation and permit the committed control force that time necessary to regain control. By proper planning and the application of sound judgment, a riot or mob violence will be averted.

Field Procedure

The following are some of the general principles that apply in handling a crowd. All officers should be in position before the arrival of the crowd. Officers should be employed in pairs, or at least close enough for mutual support, when on patrol or holding a crowd or mob in a line. A communication system between all police units should be established and maintained throughout the action. All equipment, public address systems and vehicles which may be needed should be available and in proper functioning condition.

Crowds can be directed and controlled only if they can be communicated with and the requests or orders of the police made known. This cannot be done by voice alone. Modern police departments must have powerful mobile and portable voice projectors for this purpose.

The general principles for handling a crowd are as follows:

1. Establish definite boundaries for crowd and maintain them for it is far easier to restrain a crowd than to push it back. Barriers have a definite beneficial psychological effect in restraining a crowd.

2. Persuasion tactics have long been used by mature, experienced police officers. These tactics are not fixed but depend on the officer in charge, his knowledge of crowd psychology, the type of crowd, and the individual make-up of its members. The persuasion tactic involves getting the crowd to control itself and cooperate with police. The crowd must be prevailed upon to remain orderly and not become antagonistic to the police or to police desires. It is far easier to maintain control than to restore it after losing it to an aggressive or riotous crowd.

3. Isolate and quickly remove causes of tension, such as hysterical individuals, disorderly drunks, law violators, and those who attempt to incite a riot.

4. Break up and disperse a milling crowd before the crowd becomes hysterical and aggressive.

A large nonviolent crowd that must be dispersed should be seperated as fast as possible. This can be done by cutting off segments around the edges, setting up exit areas, and by a combination of persuasion and physical police maneuvers.

A crowd has no consistently definable front or rear and can focus its attention in any given direction, at a moment's notice. However, it will normally have two long and two short sides, whatever direction it is facing. To break through, break up, or break out of a crowd, it should be penetrated by police units at the narrowest point on the longest side.

HANDLING SPECIAL CONTROL SITUATIONS

Special Events Crowds

Crowds attending various types of special events have certain characteristics or pecularities which, if thoroughly understood, can be of material assistance in crowd control planning. In such a crowd, the behavior of the individual is controlled by a guidance pattern such as established seating arrangements and physical accommodations, as well as established rules of accepted and expected behavior. These have been laid down for the purposes of such occasions. It is possible, however, for such a crowd to become unruly and aggressive. For example, the familiar throwing of pop bottles at the umpire or the quarrels that break out in the stands at a football game are evidences of the tendency to throw off the restraints and develop aggressive characteristics. These tendencies are curbed by a rigid and scrupulous enforcement of the rules and regulations. The opportunity to throw objects can be greatly limited by seeing that all liquids served are in paper cups rather than glass bottles or tin cans. It eliminates the chance that one excited individual who thoughtlessly hurls a pop bottle will be blindly imitated by others.

Crowds attending athletic contests are generally divided by team loyalties. Feelings often run quite high and arguments are frequent. Usually these arguments are of a "safety-valve" nature of little or no concern to police. Fights based solely upon the progress of the game or activity are usually settled quickly without material harm or damage. Indeed, the police officer is likely to get assistance rather than opposition in breaking it up. Where the crowd consists of large factions of the followers of each of the contending teams, and especially where they are differentiated on a racial, national, or religious basis, the situation is much more dangerous. Here the conventional crowd can easily split into very dangerous aggressive crowds in conflict with each other.

Experience with high school student rioting at athletic events illustrates how conventional crowds get out of hand. The situation becomes especially serious only when it is deliberately disregarded by authorities. Ignoring such incidents serves to legitimate violence, so that it becomes the expected thing. Those youths craving violence eagerly attend the events in order to enjoy the exhilarating experience of engaging in violence. At the scene, police tactics consisting of displaying concerted force, which inhibits would-be rioters, and picking out and removing the leaders of the violence, curb them before they can get out of hand.

Drinking of alcoholic beverages is usually the greatest problem at such events. The following is a guide for handling the situation:

1. Have PA system make announcement of prohibition of drinking.
2. When there is a violence, weigh all factors such as the danger of precipitating a major disturbance before making an arrest.
3. The annoying person should first be requested to leave.
4. If he refuses, remove him as quickly and as quietly as possible.
5. If an arrest is necessary, request the assistance of additional officers.
6. Act quickly and remove the offender from location immediately.

Recreational and Sporting Events

A number of recent riots and disturbances have occurred in connection with recreational or sporting events. There are certain common characteristics evidenced by all of them. They are as follows:

1. An influx of outsiders into a small town or circumscribed amusement area.
2. The number of outsiders was large relative to the number of local inhabitants and control personnel.
3. The outsiders were distinguished from locals by some common feature such as an intense interest (e.g., motorcycling), an age group (e.g., college youth), place of residence (e.g., urban areas), race, etc.
4. The distinction between locals and outsiders was often made more visible by differences between the two in dress, appearance and language.

The specific conditions under which exuberance and rowdiness exploded into rioting seemed to be the following:

1. Recreational, service and control facilities were flooded by

overwhelming numbers of visitors who were then left at loose ends, ready for any kind of "action."

2. Ineffectual, often provocative attempts at control and expression of authority.
3. Development of a sense of group solidarity among members of the crowd.

Often the locals, including the authorities, contributed to the developing cohesion by treating the visitors as a homogeneous mass, attributing negative characteristics to them as a class, labeling them for example as "hoodlums" or "young punks," and then treating them accordingly. The effect of opposition or attack is an increase in group cohesion.

The first step in controlling such a crowd is careful planning. To do an effective job, the police must know how many will be present, the character of the elements in the crowd, and the activities planned. The police must have a basic understanding of the character and emotional makeup of the crowd. The police must also realize that indiscriminate harsh treatment of all the group would confirm the latter's sense of persecution, increase group solidarity among them, and go far toward creating the very cohesiveness that the police do not want.

Any local sponsoring group should be contacted well in advance to close liaison developments. They must be persuaded to take part in the actual control effort. Not only should they refrain from participating in or serving as passive audience to rowdiness, but they must help actively in identifying potential trouble areas, keeping police informed of large group movements.

In these planning sessions one matter of utmost importance is to insure that there will be adequate facilities provided. The exact nature of these facilities will be dictated by the nature and duration of the event. Further, the schedule of events should be thoroughly planned. There must be enough to keep the crowd constantly involved and thus eliminate the milling which is an essential part of the evolution of a mob.

The plan must provide for a police force of sufficient strength, mobility and training to move quickly into any situation and bring it under control. Certainly in dealing with certain of the outlaw motorcycle groups the police have learned that the display of overwhelming force, and more important, the resolve to use it if necessary, is the greatest deterrent to criminal activity.

Political Rally

Crowds at political rallies are definitely partisan. Such meetings are usually orderly and peaceful. But tension is caused by the injection of a controversial issue about which audience members have strong feelings. Some rivalries become so intense that delegations may march into a meeting in progress and attempt to disrupt it. The master of ceremonies may then signal the band to strike up America, followed by The Star-Spangled Banner, thus immobilizing the intruders. Often this will at least prove a partial counter-action and reduce greatly the impetus of the attempt. If the demonstration continues in force, however, and a repetition of singing or an appeal for fair play fails, there is probably no recourse but to adjourn the meeting. Since the audience came to hear the speakers, such an ending is apt to react more against the opposition and hence serve the ends of the party intruded upon. Gallery booing constitutes a like threat to decorum and may be corrected by a threat on the part of the chairman to clear the galleries.

Often the opposing party may "pack" meetings or send agitators to disrupt proceedings. Early identification of these individuals and subsequent assignment of police in close proximity to them will greatly curtail their activities. Party leaders who have the support of the crowd should be called upon to give assistance to any police efforts or make any announcements of a police nature. Through this action, possible resentment may be avoided.

Youth Groups

Incidents in resort areas of the nation have shown the volatility of youth groups. These groups are generally very expressive and desirous of expressing their disdain for authority or convention. The slightest provocation has turned these expressive crowd into aggressive crowds. Leadership evolves quickly from within such a group and once a cause or issue is born, the crowd becomes an impulsive and emotional mass of humanity. Crowds such as these are most difficult to handle.

Preparation is of the utmost importance in handling such groups.

The experiences of various communities have shown that the expressiveness of these groups can be controlled to some degree if the groups are aware of the sureness of positive police action.

Aggressive Crowd

These are the groups that must be observed from their inception and to their conclusion by a police agency to avoid unlawful assemblies, routs and riots. To control, the police must use as many men as necessary and be sure they have proper equipment. In controlling, bear in mind that this is the type of crowd that can develop into a mob.

If agitators or leaders are attempting to excite the mob, try to make them aware of the fact that they are under observation. Separate them from the crowd if possible. The key to handling such a crowd is to disperse it promptly and prevent regrouping.

Parade

Where parades are used as a form of demonstration by political, religious, economic, student and other groups having intense emotional feelings, a basis of potential civil disorder exists. Parades in connection with holiday celebrations or festivities are less likely to produce violence unless the preceding period of time has been marked by intense agitation or other signs of public unrest. Normally the persons viewing the parade constitute the crowd. It is a friendly type crowd that requires only minimum policing.

Planning is essential to proper control of parades. In order to achieve it all cities should have ordinances requiring parade permits. In this way the sponsors must put the police on notice in advance of the planned parade and further must show that they have organized it and can control it. The government also has the opportunity to impose reasonable conditions necessary to properly control it so as to protect life and property. The application should contain a detailed proposed plan for the parade including the following:

1. Sponsoring organization.
2. Date of parade.
3. Time—starting and termination.
4. Formation area.
5. Line of march.

6. Disbanding area.
7. Police escort.
8. Reviewing stand.
9. Purpose of parade.
10. Type of parade.

The police must consider the following in making plans: The units that are to participate; assembly and dispersal areas; routes; time; escorts; traffic control; security cordons; signal communication; supervision of performanc and dispersal. The police should work with the organizers to iron out their plans for the event and suggest any changes that may be advisable.

Printed instruction for the participants in the parade are most helpful in avoiding confusion. They should include general instructions, designation of what can and cannot be done. The following are some of the items and areas to cover:

1. Time of march.
2. Cadence of march.
3. Route (maps should be attached).
4. Intervals.
5. Divisions
   a. Marshal.
   b. Assembly area (maps should be attached).
   c. Dispersal plan.
   d. Units composing each division.
6. Reviewing stand
   a. Location.
   b. Precedure of unit.
7. Flags.
8. Bands—music.
9. Signs.
10. Deportment.
11. Parade headquarters.

Information Sheet

In addition an information sheet keyed to each unit and division can be distributed.

Physical Inspection of Area

A survey of the streets may be necessary in order that all marching units, bands and floats will be aware of the distances available in connection with the size of their various units. Staging areas must be determined, located and surveyed. Assembly areas must be arranged and surveyed. The dispersal area has to be adequately planned to insure no backup of units would interfere with the movement of the parade. The parade route is reinspected twenty-four hours before the parade to note conditions requiring special attention or change of plans.

One overall police commander must be designated to direct all police units involved in the parade. The area affected by the parade should, for purposes of command and control, be divided into sectors. A parade sector includes that part of the parade route between designated streets, and the railroad terminals, bus routes and terminals, and elevated and subway stations located within one block either side of the parade route between such designated streets. However, a parade sector which includes the formation area or the dismissal area shall also include all streets and avenues within the boundaries of such formation or dismissal area and all transit stations or terminals within one block of such areas.

Each section shall have a commander. He shall select a headquarters in his sector and notify headquarters of his location and telephone number.

There should be constant communication between the commander and the section commanders. The sector commander will notify headquarters when the parade enters and leaves his sector and if there is any accident, arrest, unusual delay or incident, etc., connected with the parade.

Modern communication facilities are of course absolutely essential for the relatively smooth flow of units into the interspersing point, their assembly in proper parade order, and for checking throughout the parade on each unit in each division.

Organizing and Controlling the Parade

The parade units are organized in the assembly areas. Once the parade units are delivered to their respective assembly areas, their means of transportation are moved to their assigned dispersal areas. Within a matter of minutes following arrival at their transportation, the parade units should be loaded and en route from the area.

It is the responsibility of the sponsors to supervise this activity. Police units should be present to give assistance if needed.

The units are fed into the interspersing point from their assembly areas, and the proper joining of the elements of each parade division in their respective parade order is coordinated at this point. It is imperative that police be spotted at this point to prevent any tie-up that could pile up the entire parade. Once the parade is under way, the responsibility of the police is to see that the time schedule is maintained.

Accurate timing of each unit in the parade is the key to the successful completion of the parade within a reasonable length of time and on time. The cadence and step for all marching units should be set. The police should prevent special maneuvers or exhibitions to avoid large gaps between parade contingents. The parade should be kept moving. The command car which leads the parade can be paced to help accomplish this objective. In case of protest marches, it has been found that the television and movie car which always leads can be relied upon to control the pace of the march. When it speeds up the marchers will do likewise, for fear that otherwise they will not be photographed. Police units must pay particular attention to the dispersal area to prevent any congestion that might cause a back-up and disruption of the parade.

Control of Traffic

Sufficiently in advance, the commander should have "No Parking Today—Police Department" signs posted, and assign members of the force to prevent parking in the formation and dismissal areas and along the parade route. Parking may also be prevented within one block either side of the parade route.

The sector commander at the formation area will dispatch a motorcycle messenger ten minutes before the start of the parade to notify the other sector commanders that the parade is about to start. Sector commanders then exclude vehicles from the parade route and do not permit pedestrians to walk on the roadway or along the parade route.

Pedestrians should be passed out of the route at the nearest intersection. Arrangements should be made to permit pedestrians to cross the parade route at breaks in the parade.

Members of the force assigned to divert traffic should explain courteously to persons diverted the alternate routes or the most convenient way of reaching their destinations. Police officers should be assigned to specific locations. They should, whenever possible, receive written orders in addition to oral briefings.

The individual officer assigned to policing a parade has the responsibility of maintaining order and protecting the spectators. If the officer's post is along the line of march at a parade, he should face the crowd whenever possible. In this position, he is best able to watch the spectators and anticipate any problems that might arise. At the same time, he can be alert for such criminals as pick-pockets working in the crowd. Otherwise if he spends his time watching the event, his effectiveness is lost, as he becomes merely another spectator.

One of the first things an officer posted along a parade route should do is to see that the children are seated along the curb line in front of the crowd and behind any ropes or chains. If he suggests to the parents that their children will be able to see the event better from the front of the crowd, he will usually receive quick cooperation from the spectators. After the children have been seated along the curb, people in the rear of the crowd who push forward will find that they meet active opposition from the parents who will resist being pushed toward their children.

Spectator Control

The officer's duties in controlling the crowd include the following:

1. Preventing persons or organizations from joining the parade at other than formation area.
2. Preventing unauthorized persons or vehicles from entering police lines after the start of the parade.
3. Preventing spectators from standing near excavations, or climbing on structures, trees, poles, etc., or from using barrels, boxes or other portable stands.
4. Preventing movement into the street as other spectators will follow those who successfully press forward.
5. In the event ropes are used, preventing surging against rope.

6. Preventing spectators from overcrowding.
7. Keep open a passageway along the house line for persons who wish to leave or enter the parade area.
8. Preventing the sale of programs, flags and other commodities inside police lines.
9. Protecting fire alarm boxes and other property.
10. Cooperating with parade officials in removing from the parade any banners, signs, etc., of an offensive, derogatory or commercial nature.

To accomplish this, spectators should be directed to the area where the officer wishes to have them assemble. Their cooperation usually can be obtained by explaining to them the reasons for forming in a specific location. Requests that they move to another area should be directed to individuals, not to the crowd as a whole.

The officer should not permit any unauthorized person outside barriers or lines established for control of the crowd. If one spectator is permitted to stray beyond such lines, others may follow, making the officer's task more difficult.

If the spectators start congregating at an intersection where the officer is posted, he should attempt to move them toward the middle of the block by suggesting that they will be able to see the event much better there. Then it will be easier for the officer to clear the intersection in an emergency, and traffic congestion at the breakup will be alleviated more rapidly.

The officer can gain the crowd's respect and cooperation by being friendly but firm. He should be good natured and display a sense of humor without trading wisecracks with the spectators. Orders should be given in a clear, audible voice, loud enough to be heard over the noise of the crowd, but without shouting.

Safety of Spectators

An officer must take positive steps at special events to insure the safety of spectators. Small children often run into the street when such animals as horses are passing. By preventing children and other nonparticipants from wandering outside the barriers or into the street, officers will reduce the possibility of someone being stepped on by an animal or being injured by a parade vehicle. Spectators should not be allowed to surge against the ropes or other physical barriers. If these barriers should suddenly give way under the pressure of the crowd, people could be seriously injured.

Salute the Colors

The National Colors belonging to the units represented at a parade usually will be massed at the head of the parade. Only this group of flags need be saluted by the officer. However, smaller groups of colors that follow may be saluted if the officer's immediate attention to the crowd is unnecessary, but he should not try to do so when it is necessary to perform police duties. When the flag is within six paces of an officer, he should face it and give a hand salute. The salute should be maintained until the flag has passed at least six paces beyond the officer.

Sightseer Crowd

A sightseer crowd is a spontaneous crowd that gathers out of curiosity from nowhere at the scene of an exciting event, or unusual occurrence, such as an accident. The crowd is curious, cooperative and anxious to assist. Those in the crowd usually have no other purpose or preconceived ideas connected with such events. Because they are motivated by curiosity, the makeup of these crowds changes constantly due to individuals losing interest. Failure of such crowds to undergo this change should warn the police that some influence, possibly one which could lead to trouble, is retaining the crowd's interest.

Rapidly eliminate the cause of the attraction or center of interest of the crowd, if possible. If it is movable, get it out of the area. If the cause is immovable or an event rather than an object, the procedure should be to disperse the crowd and keep it moving. It must be remembered that a heavy concentration of police itself creates curiosity and attracts a crowd.

Traffic Accidents

Parking by curious drivers is the greatest problem. If possible, prevent parking in the immediate area. Parking at a distance discourages many onlookers from returning to view the scene. Establish traffic control an appropriate distance on either side of accident. Smoking must be prevented. The scene should be preserved for purposes of collecting evidence.

Disturbances and Crime Locations

This crowd is potentially dangerous and can become agitated or hostile. For this reason, it is perhaps the most difficult type of minor crowd control problem. Indeed, bloody riots that erupted in several of our cities in recent years were triggered by such crowds.

The first step is to make reconnaissance of the disturbance. If necessary, call for reinforcements. Determine if a crime has been committed.

1. If it is a misdemeanor, take a report or arrest depending on circumstances.
2. If it is a felony, make arrest if possible.
3. In other cases, contact witnesses immediately.

Isolate disturbing parties and witnesses. If an arrest is made, remove the prisoner from area as quickly as possible. Officers must not become isolated in a hostile crowd.

Fires

The purpose of police at the scene of a fire is to assist and make the firemen's job easier. Crowds attracted by this type of event are much easier to keep back at the outset than to push back or clear out later.

Hysterical people present at the scene should be isolated. The crowd must be kept from the rear of the premises and from unsafe places. Officers must be alert for looters. Personnel should be assigned to prevent looting, maintain fire lines, watch for new flareouts of flame and to prevent curiosity seekers from endangering themselves.

Surveillance of the crowd should be maintained and special attention paid to those who are overly interested in the fire. If possible, pictures of the curious crowd should be taken for study by arson investigators and possible future criminal prosecution.

The member of the force first on the scene shall do the following:

1. Immediately send an alarm or make certain that one has been sent.
2. If the fire is not in view from the fire alarm box, station a responsible person at the fire alarm box to direct the fire apparatus to the fire. If this cannot be done, remain at the fire alarm box.
3. If the fire apparatus does not arrive within a reasonable time, send another alarm from a different fire alarm box or notify the communications bureau of the borough.
4. Proceed to the fire as soon as possible.
5. Warn occupants of the burning building, drop fire escape ladders and assist occupants to the street.
6. Close all doors to deprive the fire of oxygen. However, if a stairway is on fire, open the scuttle or door to the roof to prevent mushrooming of the flames through apartment doors.
7. Report the fire to desk officer and, if necessary, request assistance.
8. Report action taken to a superior officer arriving at the scene.

When fire apparatus responds, members of the force at the scene should establish fire lines in front of and, if necessary, behind the building. Fire lines should be extended beyond the fire department apparatus and beyond any hydrant which is in use. If a high pressure hydrant is in use, the fire line should be extended fifty feet beyond the high pressure hydrant.

Members of the force should maintain fire lines with discretion in order not to interfere unreasonably with the rights of persons living or working therein. No unauthorized person should be permitted within the fire lines or to enter burning buildings or buildings adjacent thereto.

PROTECTION OF DIGNITARIES

Introduction

More and more in the handling of crowds the police are being called upon to protect dignitaries from assassination. The police must be prepared to supply that protection. This requires a knowledge of the problem and the techniques which are most effective.

Basic Causes of Assassinations

The majority of assassinations or attempted assassinations are basically caused by revolutionary, economic, ideological, psychological, personal, or mercenary factors. In some instances several of these factors may simultaneously be involved.

REVOLUTIONARY CAUSES. Individuals or groups who aspire to overthrow a government may seek this goal through selective assassinations. The revolutionary aspiration itself may be the product of economic, ideological, psychological and personal factors, or some combination of these considerations.

ECONOMIC CAUSES. An assassin is motivated by a belief that his victim is responsible for currently unfavorable economic conditions or will create such conditions adversely affecting his country, a certain group, his own family, or himself.

IDEOLOGICAL CAUSES. Assassinations may be adopted as a means of removing individuals having political or other views considered intolerable by fanatical opponents.

PSYCHOLOGICAL CAUSES. Along with other causal factors most assassins are suffering from some degree of mental derangement, fanaticism, or emotional instability.

PERSONAL CAUSES. Assassins may be motivated primarily by intense personal feelings, such as rage, hate, jealousy, or a desire for revenge.

MERCENARY CAUSES. The assassination is attempted for monetary reward; however, the assassin's sponsor may himself be motivated by one or more of the other causal factors previously discussed.

Nature of the Assassin

Assassination plots usually begin in the mind of a discontented individual who has reached the conviction that the only solution is to kill the person he considers responsible for his difficulties. This type of individual may have no legal basis or means of taking action against, for example, a highly placed political or military figure. The assassin will attempt to gain advantage by the use of surprise. He will endeavor to select the best opportunity by seeking information about his intended victim. For example, through reconnaissance, shadowing, inquiries of servants and neighbors, magazine or newspaper stories, and radio announcements, the assassin may gain a detailed knowledge of the habits and movements of the individual marked for death. The assassin may not be discouraged or deterred by observance of strong security measures. If the assassin attacks and is foiled but not captured he is likely to try again. Difficulties for a security force are increased by the fact that an assassin may not have distinctive features, that he may not fear capture or death, and that he may even desire to become a martyr. Moreover, the assassin may have one or more accomplices. Many potential assassins are suffering from severe mental disorders. They may experience hallucinations, delusions and obsessions. Demented cranks who are suffering from delusions of persecution are particularly dangerous.

Command

Central direction and unity of effort are of special importance because of the nature of this assignment. The officer in charge should be designated full responsibility for all phases of the security mission. Responsibility for each component phase of the security plan must be clearly defined.

Control of Advance Publicity

The security of the protected party may be placed in serious jeopardy by undue publicity. Where considered necessary, police officials should seek the cooperation of the press and other public relations media in minimizing this danger. The consequences of making public the details of an itinerary other than those deemed absolutely essential may gravely endanger the effectiveness of police security plans. Those aspects of an itinerary made public should receive particular scrutiny in police planning. In some cases absolutely secrecy may be essential to the success of the police mission.

Intelligence

Intelligence plays a key role in the security plan. All available information channels should be utilized for information of potential danger areas. Hostile groups must be investigated so that their plans are known. Potential troublemakers should be categorized under graduated security priorities and kept under constant surveillance.

Planning

Every phase of security must be carefully planned in advance. Absolute and complete protection of a dignitary against assassination or other types of attack is seldom possible. The goal is to minimize the chances of success of any contemplated attack. The privacy of the dignitary must be considered, and care should be taken to avoid his embarrassment.

Police planning must strive for simplicity yet be thorough enough to consider every probable contingency. At the same time security arrangements and plans must be flexible enough to respond to sudden changes in the protected party's itinerary or in emergencies. For example, weather conditions and mechanical failures (including failure of lighting systems) are two ever-present potential hazards. The unexpected arrival of large numbers of visitors is another situation frequently encountered. Last minute changes in the schedule of events occasionally occur. The security must be sufficiently flexible to cover these and many more eventualities.

Factors to be considered in planning include the following: composition of the party protected; the itinerary (routes, modes of travel, time factors, division of security responsibilities, engagements, eating and sleeping stops and refueling points); defense areas; security personnel and equipment requirements; coordination matters (including methods for cross-identification of various security agency personnel); communications; secrecy requirements; public relations; security post designations; advance screening and reconnaissance needs; emergency procedures; alternate plans, and miscellaneous administrative matters such as eating and sleeping arrangements for security personnel. Additional pertinent factors considered in this planning include importance of the protected person, political attitude of the local population, distances involved, and duration of the security mission. Consideration must be given to the prevention of accidents and the possibility of attempts to kidnap the protected person.

In preparing security plans one of the first steps is to obtain pictures, maps and floor plans of the areas involved. Aerial photos in addition to shots of key buildings taken from various angles are helpful. Maps showing the locations of buildings involved should be prepared and the area concerned surveyed, and street obstructions and dangerous vantage points indicated. Security routes should be selected, mapped and arrangements made for their policing at all times. Communications must be planned to keep all units in constant contact.

Manpower needs must be estimated and assignments made. The protective unit is assigned the job of personally accompanying the dignitary. It should be composed of alert, intelligent, resourceful men. They should be trained to cultivate a sober, relaxed appearance in public, for to be effective they must be as inconspicuous as possible. To achieve this end, they should dress conservatively in dark, well-tailored clothes, unless other apparel is dictated by the time and the place. These men should be in top physical condition and should be highly skilled in the art of physical defense and in the use of various firearms.

Mobile Reserves

The ability to shift reinforcements quickly from one spot to another has proved a boon to police work through the years. It is of equal value in security situations and plans must include it. During the presence of the dignitary it will be on constant alert. Whenever the situation requires added forces, the commanding officer at the trouble spot requests additional men from the mobile reserves. The plan should also provide for the replacement of this mobile reserve when it is committed to duty so that a mobile reserve will always be available.

Press

Special arrangements must be made to handle the members of the news media that will be attracted by the presence of the dignitary. A pass system must be established and passes issued to accredited newsmen.

Security Plan

The complete security plan should be prepared in the minimum essential number of copies and given a carefully limited distribution.

Each copy should be assigned a number for positive control purposes. Security agencies or other vitally important officials receiving copies should be required to adhere to a receipt system established by the agency preparing the plan. The preparing agency should habitually destroy all notes, drafts, used carbon paper and copies containing errors or not required for use. Only completely trustworthy typists should be used. Coordination of the entire plan should be limited to those individuals or agencies considered absolutely essential. Individual knowledge of the plan should routinely be restricted to what he has to know to carry out his particular duties.

Operations Center

A special operations center may be established to handle all the operations. At it two blackboards are maintained, one showing the identity of all the visiting dignitaries, with a list of their current residences. Blackboard No. 2 carries their immediate whereabouts, so that a quick glance reveals the location of each person.

Another chart lists the current deployment of each of the mobile reserve units. On another board, the permanent details and motorcade assignments is shown, with changes noted as they occur. A map of city streets is also kept up-to-date with pins appropriately marked showing the whereabouts, by street of the dignitary.

A log containing date, time and serial number every message received from field units or other sources pertaining in any manner to the security operation should be maintained.

Rumors and reports, incidents and allegations, fact and fancy, will be phoned in to the operations desk. The information should be recorded and affected units or individuals quickly apprised of the message. Every movement of the dignitary will be called in by the police at the scene and units along the planned routes swiftly alerted. Pickets and partisans congregating at areas housing the dignitary should be reported to the operations desk and police reserves speedily dispatched where required. The arrests of disorderly demonstrators and injuries to police or pickets should be called in and duly chronicled.

Communications

A strong line of quick communication is imperative. A communications network that enables instantaneous contacts between all units of command must be established. Telephones should be installed for outgoing and for incoming calls. Mobile observers equipped with radio equipment should be placed in the field at strategic locations to maintain constant touch with headquarters. The lead car and the rear car of each motorcade should carry two portable walkie-talkies, one operating on a confidential frequency between front and rear; one set on a restricted frequency for direct communication with headquarters. Plans should provide for the quick replacement of dead batteries in portable radios or effect rapid repairs.

Protective Techniques

Protection requires teamwork. Success depends upon the cooperation and assistance of others. The failure of one individual may nullify the efforts of an entire organization. Although it is impossible to devise protective techniques which are totally foolproof, all personnel should be trained for the ideal system and attempt to approach that system insofar as circumstances permit. Protective personnel must be rehearsed to assure that in an emergency, despite the excitement and emotion, they will instinctively act correctly.

Site Inspection

All areas to be occupied or visited by the protected person should be surveyed in advance. The procedure that is used for building inspections must be complete. In many instances, the dignitary is lodged in a building occupied by numerous other guests. The officer in charge and his advance party must use common sense and sound judgment in establishing the best security possible under existing circumstances. In some instances, the advance party can improve security plans by arranging for a separate house, separate floor, or wing of a hotel as a billet for the official party. Normally, billeting arrangements are included in the itinerary prior to the start of the protective mission. Proper building inspection entails a thorough examination from roof to basement. Detailed plans, such as engineering drawings or blueprints of the building, should be obtained. Rooms and hallways are measured visually and compared with the dimensions indicated on the building plan to locate any hidden passageways or alcoves. Each room is examined systematically. Walls, ceilings, and floors are mentally divided into three-foot squares and each square minutely examined for cracks, evidence of recent repairs, or any unusual features. Suspicious areas should be explained satisfactorily by reliable operating or maintenance personnel. All doors are opened; all furniture is carefully examined; and drawers are removed as a check for concealed compartments. All wires leading into or leaving the various rooms are traced and all devices connected with them identified. Heating radiators, plumbing, pipes and similar equipment are carefully examined for dummy installations. All locks and locking mechanisms are inspected. After the inspection is completed, the room or building is secured until used.

The areas around the residence of the dignitary should be thoroughly screened. Rooftops, rear yards, windows, nearby stores and buildings must be checked and kept under constant surveillance. Police should be assigned to strategic spots on rooftops and points of vantage. Persons carrying packages near the areas must be stopped; the contents of their bags checked. Suspicious individuals should be questioned and license plates of suspicious vehicles noted and checked.

Temporary headquarters should be set up at the dignitary's residence. Direct phone lines to police headquarters must be kept open. Waste receptacles and other portable objects should be removed where feasible, and fire alarm boxes watched. Shelter areas for the public may be established in nearby buildings in case of need. Adequate lighting must be assured

Physical Protection—Rings—Zones

Physical protection consists of a series of protective rings or cordons, each complete in itself. These defensive rings may be composed of security personnel, physical barriers, or both. An example of this type of security is the protection established around a house designated as a residence for a dignitary. A number of walking patrols around the grounds would comprise the first protective cordon. A series of fixed posts covering entrances would form the second ring. Security personnel stationed within the house would form the third echelon of protection. The depth of the protective forces and the degree of security established will be governed by the factors considered in the planning stage. In general, there will be a greater numerical concentration of these guards close to the dignitary than farther off.

This kind of defense, concentric and in depth, does not mean that there are rings of human beings completely encircling the dignitary. It is enough that the guard keeps every means of approach under surveillance. The natural protection given by a series of three concentric walls in any building is considered sufficient for most purposes. The protection of such walls is augmented by guarding their entrances.

A "frozen" zone through which no unauthorized person is permitted to travel must be established. Every doorway through which an intruder might enter—no matter how obscure or apt to be "forgotten" the section of the house may be where the door is—must be fully guarded. There must be a pass system for the staff members and frequent visitors. Food suppliers should be checked and food selection and handling should be controlled. Mail and packages should be fluoroscoped or inspected. Periodic inspection should be made of premises for safety hazards, lethal devices and sufficiency of security equipment. Adequate communications should be maintained. All possible emergency situations should be considered.

Packages

All packages addressed to the residence for use by the dignitary should be fluoroscoped and gone over with sound detectors by a bomb squad in safety zones. The post office and railway express will cooperate by alerting the bomb squad to all packages addressed to that address.

Dinners

At dinners and receptions given at hotels, operatives should be stationed strategically throughout the premises guarding doors, stairways, anterooms, powerlines and switches. A detailed systematic search of the ballroom and hotel rooms must be conducted, after which the area is sealed off and a security guard maintained.

During the dinner, plainclothes officers should be stationed at vantage points and among the audience so that they constantly can keep all present under surveillance. This is best done by allotting specific areas to each man. These areas should overlap to assure that there will be no blind spots.

Motorcades

Motorcades pose one of the greatest security problems. History has shown how simple it is to tie up traffic with an accident or a stalled vehicle. Once the motorcade is trapped, it is an easy prey for a well-organized mob.

To overcome some of these problems, primary security routes should be established. Alternate routes must be mapped for emergencies. These routes should avoid all traffic. Sharp turns or other features requiring slowdown should be avoided. These routes should be the shortest routes between the points of travel.

Heavy police details, buttressed with barriers, should be stationed along the routes. Overpasses and other areas overlooking the route must be policed and cleared during passage of the motorcade. Tow trucks should be near at hand in case of automobile trouble, or if a vehicle should be deliberately abandoned in the path of a motorcade. Routes should be divided into sections so that detours may be expeditiously placed into operation with minimum effect on normal traffic flow.

When emergency situations, such as fires or watermain breaks, erupt along the right-of-way, the caravan diverts to a secondary route. The new course should be radioed to headquarters.

On occasion, dignitaries suddenly decide to visit a place not on the known agenda—a site not already policed. If further security protection is thought necessary, mobile reserve forces should be alerted and immediately dispatched to the scene. If necessary, the motorcade should be slowed to allow extra time for reinforcements to get to the scene.

Cars to be utilized should be procured from a reputable source and be in excellent mechanical condition. They should possess ample power and be able to travel considerable distances at widely varying speeds without difficulty. Drivers should be well trained and reliable, and thoroughly familiar with the route they are to follow.

A commander should be designated for the motorcade. He should have the authority to summon additional units when needed. He will usually drive in the lead car. The motorcade will have special protective cars in addition to the vehicles of the official party, all of which must be identified and cleared with the commander. Observers in an advance vehicle should precede the motorcade by approximately one-half mile to report hazards and unusual conditions. An escort vehicle should precede the protected vehicle. This escort vehicle should be followed as closely as possible, consistent with driving safety, by the protected vehicle. Whenever possible at least one member of the protective detail should be in the protected person's vehicle. The protected vehicle should be followed by another escort vehicle. If the protective vehicle is to go at a very slow rate, protective ranks of officers may walk abreast of it on both sides.

The protective force should have all of the armor they may need to meet any emergency including tear gas, submachine guns, shotguns, rifles, gas mask and bulletproof vests. There should also be personnel who are experts in judo, wrestling and physical defense who can handle belligerents where weapons would be dangerous or not recommended.

All security units in the convoy should be radio-connected on a closed circuit within themselves. Continuous radio contact will also be maintained with police headquarters. Time of departure and destination is radioed to headquarters. Time of arrival is also transmitted to headquarters.

Part of the escort shall form a rear guard to prevent unauthorized vehicles from joining or interfering with the official party. The rear guard should notify the officer in charge when all vehicles of the official party have entered the police lines. Before the motorcades rolls, motorcycle officers will speed on ahead to alert patrol forces assigned along the route. Additional protection with limited manpower may be effected by notifying the routine patrol force to converge on the route in their respective areas at the time the motorcade begins.

Loading and Unloading

At the points of loading and unloading of the motorcade all light switches should be guarded, personnel security-screened, buildings and vantage points checked for snipers and secured. The commanding officer at the point of arrival should set up a restricted area about

fifty feet square at the entrance to the stand or hall. He should assign
members of the uniformed force closely aligned on three sides of this
area. Only authorized persons should be permitted in this area until
after the distinguished persons have arrived or departed.

Press cards, shields, etc., will not be accepted as identification for
admittance to the restricted area through police lines. Representatives
of the press, newsreel, television, etc., and security police forces must
show evidence from those in authority that they are assigned there to
duty in connection with the event.

When the dignitary arrives, the police should form an unbroken
passage from the entrance to the place provided for the official party.
Only the official party and the detectives or other security forces
assigned to that location shall be permitted to enter this passage.
The loading should be completed as rapidly as possible and the
motorcade should leave immediately to afford maximum protection
to the dignitary.

Crowds

Extremely large crowds should not be permitted to assemble too
close to areas containing dignitaries. Such a crowd, solidly packed,
can prove dangerous even though the intent is not present.

It is a cardinal principle of protection never to allow the dignitary
to stop his car in a crowd if it can possibly be avoided. Even a
friendly crowd can, and often does, get out of hand in a second.
And when it does it is a hydra-headed, idiot juggernaut pressing on
its adorned object in a manic frenzy. It could crush him to death and
trample him underfoot in its blind love.

The pressure of those in the rear, pressing toward those in front,
near the center of interest, is often irresistible and will break police
lines and barricades. A human wave effect takes place, forcing those
in the front to advance against their will, thus endangering the police
and dignitaries concerned.

A vacant buffer zone should be established around the area where
the dignitary will be. Other vacant buffer zones may be established
throughout the crowd to break it into segments and afford an open
area which can be used to absorb the pressure of forward movement

and the human wave effect emanating from within and from the rear. The larger a crowd, the greater opportunity a would-be assassin has of slipping in and getting close to the dignitary. And the greater opportunity, too, such an assassin has, amid the confusion created by such crowds, of plotting other types of dangerous mischief—severing a cable on an elevator car, weakening a chandelier over a table, starting a fire, etc.

Pickets

All picketing is controlled so that physical contact between rival factions will be averted. Police wooden barriers can be used to segregate the antagonists. Pickets must be kept on the opposite side of the street from any dignitaries so that they will not endanger the safety of the dignitary or spark an unfortunate incident. Passage of official parties must be arranged so they will not be required to move through or pass pickets. Pickets should not be allowed to carry signs with poles, which might be used as weapons. Plainclothes officers should circulate among the pickets and keep advised of all their plans.

Individual Officer

The individual officer should use the following guide for handling himself in such situations:

Be constantly alert and vigilant.

Face spectators all the time, particularly on dignitary's approach and passage of motorcade. Don't divert attention to salute.

Constantly survey spectators, windows, rooftops, setbacks and similar vulnerable points.

Be particularly vigilant at stops, slow downs and turns of motorcade.

Closely observe all persons in possession of packages and suitcases, handbags, etc., or acting suspiciously. Request identification if circumstances warrant.

Note suspicious autos in area. Note license number in memo book.

Advise commander on scene.

Know means of identification worn by secret service detectives, working press, etc.

If assigned to rooftops, don't lean over parapet or ledge.

Station self to observe rooftops, windows, etc., above and below you.

Report any suspicious dangerous activities immediately.

Chapter 27

DEMONSTRATIONS AND CIVIL DISOBEDIENCE

INTRODUCTION

THE INCREASING FREQUENCY with which demonstrations and civil disobedience are resorted to as weapons of social conflict makes it imperative that all police departments be prepared for such an eventuality. Ironically, the more effective the professional department may have been in establishing a climate of legality and mortality, the more vulnerable is that jurisdiction to the exercise of the tactical weapon of civil disobedience. This is not to say that such a department, itself, is vulnerable in the sense that it will suffer any loss of prestige or will fail to cope properly with the problem, but the very fact that law and order is likely to be maintained, despite these major disruptions, tempts those who would use these tactics.

RESPONSIBILITY OF THE POLICE

The police are the representatives of the government—a government of laws, not men. They have a sworn duty to enforce the law—impartially, objectively and equally. This duty must be performed. History teaches us that the failure of the police to perform their duty will not only invite disrespect for the law and encourage its violation but will be detrimental to police morale and the public's respect for law enforcement. Nor can they allow the law to be compromised. Any attempt to do so will be interpreted as a sign of weakness and the signal to push further, with immunity.

These principles apply as equally to demonstrations and civil disobedience, irrespective of the merits or demerits of the cause espoused by the participants, as they do any other police problem.

This means that at the scene of any public demonstration the police must and will maintain an attitude of complete impartiality and neutrality and enforce all laws with equal vigor, whether the violator be a demonstrator or one demonstrated against. No bias can be

[307]

tolerated or shown. Rather, the rights of all citizens must be respected and upheld.

The police must therefore clearly define for all what that police function is. Everyone must understand that the police recognize and respect the right of the people to express their views on matters of public concern. But, the police have neither the authority nor the responsibility to adjudicate or solve the social and legal problems which inspire demonstrations and acts of civil disobedience. Rather, the duty and goal of law enforcement at public demonstrations is to maintain the orderly balance between the individual's right to demonstrate peaceably and the right of others to be secure in their lives and property.

The police are aware of the social significance of the surge for equal rights. They have and will continue to recognize, respect, and protect the rights of all to assemble peacefully and express their views on matters of public concern. Obviously, this is a delicate and a difficult job but it is one in which an alert and well trained police force can be a credit to itself and to the community which it serves.

NON-VIOLENT, DIRECT-ACTION DEMONSTRATIONS

A demonstration is a public assemblage of persons exhibiting sympathy with or opposition to some political, economic or social condition or movement. The intent of demonstrators is to persuade by focusing attention on a problem or problems, and the persons or establishments against which action is directed, and to publicize the procedure or beliefs of the organizations and persons participating.

Demonstrations must be distinguished from crowds and mobs in that they are: (1) organized; (2) have leadership; (3) participants are well disciplined; (4) participants are orderly and non-violent, and (5) action is legal.

The means utilized by the demonstrators to express their views are the picket lines, parades, meetings and rallies. Demonstrations may be staged at a single location, or may be held simultaneously at various points; indeed, numerous simultaneous demonstrations may be held throughout the nation; indeed, throughout the world.

Rather than looking on a peaceful or lawful demonstration with fear and horror, it should be considered as a safety valve serving to prevent a riot. He who makes peaceful demonstration impossible makes violent revolution inevitable.

CIVIL DISOBEDIENCE

Civil disobedience has been defined as "refusing to obey the relations between the citizen and the state as regulated by law." Another definition declares that civil disobedience is the deliberate public violation of the law, with every expectation of arrest, as a protest and in order to dramatize one's sympathy with or opposition to some political, economic or social condition or movement.

It is thus apparent the term *civil* is highly inappropriate. *Criminal* disobedience would be far more accurate. Civil disobedience may be based upon belief in the unconstitutionality or immorality of the violated law, or upon the desire to influence official action or major changes in our society. In addition, other groups, with less noble purposes, use the trappings of nonviolent civil disobedience to further their own ends. The understanding and identification of the problem are essential for the alert police executive who would guide department policy in this most sensitive area.

PUT COUNCIL AND BOARD ON RECORD

When demonstrators begin to threaten the peace of the community, there is sure to be some speculations on what to do. The council or the governing body or top elected officials of the community may begin to hold meetings to discuss the problem.

The police should advise them of the position of law enforcement. They should be warned that laws will probably be violated in mass action. As these leaders know, the community cannot afford to advocate the compromise of law and order when to do so means turmoil. They will support the police.

The position of the governing body supporting impartial but firm enforcement of the law and maintenance of law and order should be publicly proclaimed prior to any disturbance. Naturally such a declaration of support should not embrace the details or techniques to be utilized by the police, as such action would unduly restrict the effective operation of the police, for it would be impossible to envision every potential problem that might arise.

PREDEMONSTRATION OPERATIONS

Introduction

The key to successful control of demonstrations is the same as that for riot control—intelligence, planning and communication. No single procedure can be established for all demonstrations as they will vary in their nature and the problems presented because of the character and number of the participants and the atmosphere in which they occur. Thus, any plan must be sufficiently flexible to adjust to the situation as it develops. Nevertheless, there are general principles that have proved applicable to all situations.

Demonstrations Coordinator

Every department should designate a given official to receive and coordinate all information relating to demonstrations. It will be his responsibility to evaluate this information and keep the chief or designated demonstration command officer fully apprised of all pertinent facts.

Know About Demonstrations

In order to police a demonstration properly, it is essential that the police know of it in advance. The first step in planning for control of a crowd is to obtain all available facts and rumors. For this reason liaison must be established with the numerous groups in the community that frequently resort to this method of achieving their ends. Their assistance must be enlisted.

It should be a rule that whenever any member of the department observes or is informed of the existence of any public demonstration or of any proposed demonstration, he should immediately notify a designated member of the department.

There will be groups that will not cooperate. To learn of their activities, it will be necessary to keep surveillance on their meeting places and develop informants who can keep the department advised of their plans.

A record and pictures of known demonstrators should be maintained and the men of the intelligence and special squads taught to identify them by name.

Information Needed and Why

Each specific act of civil disobedience is carried out by the participants with a definite end result desired. If the purpose and propensities of the group are known, the task of the police will be much less difficult. To evaluate the potential of the demonstration resulting in civil disobedience, you must have knowledge of the individual that participates. What motivates him? Is he a beatnik—a civil libertarian—a pacifist—an anarchist—or is it "*the* thing to do?" The following pertinent facts should be learned prior to the demonstration so that appropriate plans may be prepared:

1. Exact location or route of march.
2. Time and duration of demonstration.
3. Schedule of events.
4. Within what jurisdiction or jurisdictions—city or county— the demonstration will be conducted.
5. Activities planned.
6. Purpose of demonstration.
7. Estimate of attendance.
8. Character and temperament, psychological background, of those to participate and those expected to attend.
9. Likely climate or atmosphere of the meeting.
10. Sponsoring organization.
11. Names and description of leaders, monitors, marshals and coordinators.
12. Identity of potentially antagonistic groups and anticipated presence of an opposing group.
13. Expected trouble or disorder.
14. Physical features of the area. Information pertaining to entrances, exits, transportation facilities, and other physical features which may affect operations is best secured by an on-site inspection under conditions similar to those which will exist at the time of the event. Maps, sketches and photographs should be obtained.
15. Outside supporters, names, mode of travel, point of arrival.

No Advance Information

If the demonstration is in progress, when first called to the attention of the police, an immediate and thorough reconnaissance of the scene should be made, and a report shall immediately be submitted as soon as pertinent facts are obtained. The report should contain the location and disposition of the demonstration, the sponsors, number of onlookers and such other facts as are readily available.

Confer with Demonstrators

Do not avoid contact with the demonstration leadership. Seek out the actual leaders of the group sponsoring the demonstration, as well as the merely nominal organizers, and confer with them. Go to them, don't ask them to come to the station. Discuss the proposed event, potential problems, and possible tactics of control. Resolve problems that are likely to cause discontentment. Explain the position of the police and impress upon them the following:

1. The police recognize and respect their right to protest or demonstrate against a social custom or condition.
2. Their demonstration must be conducted within the limits of the law with respect for the rights of the rest of the community.
3. Impress the leaders with their responsibility to society to respect its laws and to maintain peace in the community.
4. The groups should be encouraged to enforce discipline in their own organizations.

Request plans for the demonstration and all needed information. If their proposed plans are in conflict with the law, so notify them and further inform them of the consequences of any violation. Advise them of shortcomings or defects in their plans, such as lack of time or facilities to handle the group.

Assist them in developing a plan that complies with the law, and see that it provides for methods of internal control, health facilities for the demonstrators, arrangements for feeding, availability of adequate transportation at the appointed time, and any other measure that will prevent a peaceful demonstration from deteriorating into mob violence.

Establish the Ground Rules

It should also be agreed up by both police and demonstration leaders that no resistance would be offered by demonstrators. The leaders should back this up by assigning captains and monitors to police their own lines to make sure participants are bona fide demonstrators and are acting according to previously prescribed rules of conduct. These "policemen" are of inestimable value in maintaining order during the demonstrations. Their role also served to strengthen liaison between their people and ours.

The importance of this tactic is to place the responsibility for conducting a lawful, peaceful demonstration squarely on the shoulders of the leaders of the demonstration. The police control technique is then to deal only with the leaders of the demonstration or their appointed monitors, and not with the mass of individuals.

Two points deserve special consideration as they can be handled at this point and will prevent much trouble at the demonstration. First, the demonstrators must be made to realize that the use of liquor by persons involved in demonstrations must be restricted as a preventive measure. The intelligent leader recognizes that an intoxicated demonstrator is not only hard to handle but reflects adversely on the cause; therefore, he will cooperate.

Secondly, it is well to regulate the diameter and length of the poles or supports of any signs or banners to be carried. The poles should be of small diameter and of fragile material such as light wood. This will prevent these same poles or supports from being used as effective weapons in case a riot ensues. Finally, as a result of this conference you will be able to evaluate these leaders and determine the degree of discipline among the ranks. Liaison should not stop with one meeting; rather, to provide efficient communication between the police and the demonstration leadership, a specified police officer should be assigned to act as liaison officer to the rally leadership.

Out-of-Town Demonstrators

When out-of-town groups conduct the demonstration, the police must identify the group, its motives, its leaders and its temper, its route and time of arrival. A permanent inter or intra state intelligence system with other police departments will be most valuable, and should be included in initial plans.

Arrangements should be made with out-of-town police departments in the area to keep the affected agency informed on the movement of buses and private cars and the number of persons involved. Are the buses full or half full? Are they sponsored by large companies or organizations, or are they private? And in both cases, are they under the control of their drivers? Determine their routes of entry to the city. How far have the buses come? Will they be staying in town overnight? And have accommodations been arranged?

It is best to stop such buses at the city line and escort them to parking areas. The police should explain why they have been stopped, and the reasons, namely, that the police are cooperating and want to help. The names of the bus driver and the group leader, their sponsor, the number and license of the bus, and the address of their home organization should be obtained so the police can contact them in an emergency. Most important, the police should explain the local laws and regulations to the visiting demonstrators.

Confer with One Demonstrated Against and Affected Persons

When large demonstrations and marches are going to be held, liaison must also be established with various civic groups and businesses that might be affected or inconvenienced by the demonstration. They should be informed of the probable actions of the demonstrators, the constitutional rights involved that the police must protect, and certain phases of the overall police policy requiring this course of action. Proper liaison with these groups is important to the successful outcome of the police action. Police should also confer with those against whom the demonstration is directed, i.e., employers in case of union picketing.

In some instances there will be counter-demonstrators. They too should be contacted and conferred with in advance. In the case of counter-demonstrators, demonstration areas should be agreed upon, the police objective being to keep the opposing groups separated from the demonstration group. Details should include time, type and extent of the counter-demonstration.

The conferences with those affected are important for in civil disturbances involving business and industry, the police cannot function alone, they must interact with management. The police cannot arrest for trespassing unless business policy makers wish to prosecute.

Too often the police have difficulty in locating an individual empowered to make management policy decisions. The policy maker may be unavailable and those in charge do not desire to make a decision. Often those present are not empowered to make that kind of a decision. Seldom are policy statements available for use of those in charge when top management is absent. Consequently, demonstrators are allowed to roam at will and confusion results.

The police officer must be cautious to protect himself against the attitude of the proprietor. At that moment the owner may only see that his establishment is being used in a manner to disrupt his normal business. He may be sincerely determined to rid himself of this undesirable situation. The next day he may appear at the trial and testify just as sincerely as he wanted the action to be taken by the police. But alas, those trials are not held the next day. It may be a long time before the final trial is held.

Many things may happen during the wait for the trial to be held. Many situations may develop. Other similar business establishments may submit to the demands of the groups and force this owner to change his attitude. Some high official may approach him and underwrite a 50 per cent increase in his business if he will submit to the demands. His convictions may have a weaker influence on him than on his pocket book. Many things may happen to cause his attitude to change. Then, when the trial is held he may want to ease off on prosecuting. He may want the charges dropped. If he is an unwilling witness, the case will likely be washed out. In either instance much damage is done to the prestige of law enforcement.

To help avoid these problems the police should confer with those against whom the demonstration is directed, i.e., employers in case of union picketing; explain the position and policy of the police, stressing the impartiality of the police, and make it clear that no violation of the law by either side will be tolerated.

If criminal acts are planned by the demonstrators or are likely to occur, representatives of management and their legal counsel should be fully advised of the threat. As certain acts when committed in a public place are not a crime until the owner has withdrawn his implied consent to enter or if he ratifies them by refusing to bring charges, it is essential that at this conference a firm understanding be reached as to what action will not be tolerated and when the assistance of the police will be requested.

When it has been clearly established between the police and the complainant as to what law is to be enforced, it is next agreed that any subsequent arrests shall be faithfully prosecuted by the complainant, and that at no future time shall he accept nonprosecution of the arrest as one of the terms of any agreement with the demonstrators.

Joint Conference

At times it will be beneficial to arrange a joint meeting with the leaders of various groups. Naturally the advisability of such action depends on the extent of the antagonism and the temperament of the various leaders. The police act as mediators and introduce community leaders or those against whom the demonstration is directed to the leaders of the protesting organization. Working together they establish the legal limits and the rules to be followed. The police should request their mutual assistance in maintaining law and order, but must avoid giving legal advice to either side. Rather, they should be instructed to seek counsel on non-police matters.

Arbitration of Differences Through Conferences

At the outset of a civil disorder, police officials should immediately encourage the conduct of conferences in which responsible community leaders are participants. The objectives of these conferences are to analyze the situation, plan actions designed to resolve differences, and discuss the likely actions of the participants. Initial arbitration conferences should be conducted before human passions are highly aroused and while the police agency still enjoys a favorable public opinion. During the opening period of the conference, police officials should emphasize the necessity for the maintenance of law and order, and the means that will be used to accomplish this end. Police officials do not take sides in any discussions. They simply stand on the firm ground of promoting the restoration of order.

Coordination

A designated officer should be charged with supervising all coordination with other agencies and departments. If the plan involves the calling in of outside police help, this should be coordinated in advance with the other agencies concerned. This may call for meeting with all chiefs in the area to discuss interjurisdictional problems which might arise during a demonstration.

In particular, the district attorney, prosecuting attorney, city attorney, county counsel should be contacted and a working arrangement established. Preferably a representative of the prosecuting agency should be present at all briefings and at the demonstration, particularly if arrests are contemplated.

PLANNING

The proper planning of the control of a demonstration is of immeasurable value in controlling it and in averting a riot. Planning involves development of a standard crowd control method or procedure. It should supply broad outlines of policies for every known potential hazard, and preliminary plans to meet any emergency. The mere existence of a plan helps by eliminating confusion and makes for consistent decisions.

Command

Any planning will have as its key a definite chain of command. Don't let too many commanding officers make the top decisions. Authority must be firmly established.

Any such plan should provide for alternate commanders for those instances where the demonstration may continue for a protracted length of time. Plans should be made for the orderly transfer of command to the succeeding shift, which will include an up to the minute briefing on all development present and anticipated conditions. Consideration should be given to assigning a staff psychiatrist to be present and always on hand to assist the command staff in evaluating crowd conditions and the application of the appropriate principles of crowd and mob psychology.

Chain of Command

The plan should divide and firmly designate responsibilities. Thus at the scene of a demonstration the following divisions may be established.

PERIMETER DIVISION shall be that unit charged with the responsibility of establishing a perimeter to separate the curious from those committing acts of civil disobedience. It shall clear all ingress and egress routes and aid the arrest team whenever necessary.

TRAFFIC DIVISION shall be responsible for overall routing and movement of units into and prisoners out of the area.

THE ARREST DIVISION shall be that organizational body, operating within the perimeter of the disturbed area, which is specifically charged with the responsibility of the following:

1. Accumulating the immediately available evidence of violations of law by individuals.
2. Carrying out of conditions precedent to arrest, where applicable, for violations of law, and informing individuals to be arrested of the charges against them, and other pertinent advice.
3. Arresting individuals who have violated penal provisions of the law.
4. Delivering arrested individuals, together with photographs and documents taken and/or prepared in connection with such arrest, to the transportation and removal division.

INTELLIGENCE may mingle with demonstrators, gathering documentary material distributed or used by demonstrators, and recording demonstrators, announcements and other material data.

SUPPORTIVE, OR BACKUP DIVISIONS will be taking additional photographs and motion pictures and gathering any physical evidence available.

TRANSPORTATION AND REMOVAL DIVISION will receive arrested persons and their identification and arrest forms, and their attached polaroid photographs from arrest team personnel, and index-fingerprint said arrested persons, conduct quick searches of their persons and load arrestee into vehicles and remove them.

JAIL DIVISION shall be responsible for the handling of the mass of arrestees.

Communication Center

A special communication center should be established if the demonstration is of sufficient magnitude to demand the deployment of substantial units from various agencies. This requires selection of uniform wave bands for radio transmission with ultimate bands and codes designated well in advance.

The local telephone company's assistance should be enlisted to install all needed extra telephones. Particular thought should be given to the use of mobile phones by key personnel.

Traffic Plan

Because of the many special traffic problems which are certain to be imposed by the influx of a large number of participants for a rally, a coordinated effort must be made to establish a complete traffic plan, including routes, parking areas, control points and police escorts.

Traffic circulation plans should be prepared indicating entrance and exit routes, bypasses, detours, parking areas, and routes for emergency vehicles which need a safe fast route into and out of the area for police and emergency vehicles. A special traffic plan for a major rally would provide for the following:

1. Bus parking areas adjacent to the rally area.
2. Control points and escorts to direct and escort incoming buses to proper parking areas.
3. Plans to maintain at the master control point a central registration of the locations of various buses.
4. Prohibited parking in danger areas.
5. Advising rally leader parking could not be provided for private automobiles bringing participants to the event, and request them to advise their participants to come to the city by common carrier.
6. Furnishing rally leadership with maps and directions for finding fringe parking areas for those participants who might disregard warnings about lack of parking within city.
7. Establishing booths at city entrances to direct private automobiles bringing participants to city to the fringe parking areas.
8. Arrange rerouting of transit buses and other traffic.

Special Equipment

Cranes for impounding automobiles and buses should be available in the event of stall-ins. If a stall-in is anticipated, extra tow trucks should be obtained and stiff fines imposed for the stalling or abandonment of a car.

Law

When the tempo steps up, the police must have the law at their fingertips for snap decisions are required. In order to aid the officer on the line, a list of state law and local ordinances related to the expected problem should be prepared by either the prosecuting attorney or by the police. If the latter course is pursued, ask the prosecutor to review this list and suggest revisions.

This list should contain the code number of the law and a brief statement on the elements of the violation. It should be mimeographed for quick distribution to all officers. However, only one official list should be circulated. It should come from the chief's office. No other possibly conflicting lists should be prepared or circulated by any members of the department. This list should be kept up to date if injunctions are ordered, or if someone comes up with a particular law that has been overlooked.

COLLEGE DEMONSTRATION PLANNING

Extreme student agitation, frequently accompanied by acts of violence, is not uncommon in European and South American countries. A number of our schools have already experienced it to varying degrees during the past two years and there is every reason to believe that this type of revolutionary activity will spread to other campuses throughout the United States in the foreseeable future.

There are certain unusual characteristics which are found in college demonstrations and which should be given special consideration for planning and operational purposes.

1. The demonstrators for the most part are relatively young, many of them being juveniles, and are inexperienced and immature. They are intelligent and the majority come from good homes and respectable parents.

2. Although most of the rebel group is composed of students, an appreciable number are nonstudents and as such are not subject to the school rules and disciplinary procedures.

3. The motivation may differ widely for individuals within the group. Some are idealistic and firmly believe in the group objective; some are pulled along primarily by the mob spirit; some become disillusioned and would like to withdraw but are afraid to do so for fear of group condemnation; some are mere dupes who have been captured by propaganda; some are merely looking for excitement; and finally, some are outright revolutionaries who adhere to communist teachings and are determined to overthrow academic control through the domination of students and faculty if possible.

4. Regardless of the nature of the group objectives, an effort will be made to justify them on the basis of U.S. Constitutional freedoms and rights.

5. School authorities abhor bad publicity and endeavor to keep their problems within academic circles. They exercise a highly protective attitude toward students and are not particularly sympathetic to police problems involving students. Their approach to student rebellion is through negotiation and compromise, and they will go to great lengths to avoid confrontations.

6. An appreciable percentage of the faculty will be sympathetic to and encourage the rebels, and some will actually participate in their demonstrations. It is probable that there will be a sharp conflict in opinion between many faculty members and school administrators as to proper action in resolving the conflict.

7. Students will have continuous support from sympathetic lawyers who will be present at their demonstrations to provide legal advice and representation. Left-wing or communist-oriented attorneys will most likely participate.

Since the success of college demonstrations depends upon the preconditioning of the minds of the persons who are to participate, they are seldom spontaneous. The objectives and plans of the organizers are outlined well in advance through meetings and rallies and by a continuous flow of propaganda in the form of handbills and posters.

It is essential that personnel be assigned to maintain a continuous observation of campus activities. The identity and background of student organizers should be known since it may well provide a clue as to the action which can be anticipated. Rallies and meetings should be attended and published material carefully studied. If possible, contacts with responsible students should be established to provide a continuing source of information regarding campus response to the agitators. Finally, liaison must be maintained with other governmental agencies which may be concerned with potential disturbancies so that there will be an exchange of mutually beneficial information.

Planning

First, it is imperative that all questions of jurisdiction and authority on a given campus be resolved. Some schools are public and some are private. Occasionally there may be a concurrent jurisdiction where both the city police and the college police have a joint law enforcement responsibility. There must be a clear understanding about which agency has primary jurisdiction and responsibility.

There should also be conferences involving the police agency and its legal representative, lawyers representing the school in question, the prosecuting attorney and the judge or judges of the courts in which arrested persons will be tried. The purpose of such meetings is to settle questions involving the legal authority of the police to take action; to decide in advance what charges will be placed against students arrested for specific acts; to outline the police procedures which must be followed in effecting arrests if successful prosecutions are to be sustained; and finally to establish bail schedules for specific violations or to provide other means of releasing persons who are taken into custody. It must be determined what actions on the part of demonstrators constitute a violation of law for which an arrest can be made, as contrasted to those violations of school rules and regulations which are not of direct concern to the police and for violation of which only school disciplinary procedures can be invoked.

It is also advisable to confer with school administrative officials so that there is a clear and mutual understanding of the role of the police if called. School authorities should understand that when conditions become so serious as to require the mobilization of police forces on the campus, and violations of law occur, the decision regarding what action will be taken must rest with the police official in charge at the scene.

SCENE PROCEDURES

Prevent Demonstrators from Rioting

During a demonstration persons who are grouped together with a common intent respond emotionally and collectively to the same stimuli, therefore they are the preconditioned crowd that is the first step toward a mob.

Police must keep demonstrators in line. Generally, control measures which emphasize the individuality of persons on the scene and cause them to think that they are recognized and known will lessen the group violence potential.

Individual Officer

An officer should expect and be prepared to resist verbal abuse designed to bait him into intemperate violent action. Most of all, he must realize that the political, philosophical, and mental makeup of many of the persons who engage in the so-called "nonviolent" type of demonstration is such that they are apt to misinterpret or place improper emphasis on what the police say or do. Regardless of how well the job is performed by the police, there will usually be some false charges or allegations made by one or more of the defendants. The officer should act in the following manner:

1. There should be no unnecessary show of weapons. Guns and batons should not be displayed in a provocative way, as such action will merely incite antagonism and foster conflict.
2. Do not bluff.
3. Avoid bodily contact.
4. Keep outside of crowd.
5. Observe spectators rather than event.
6. Identify and watch crowd leaders or potential leaders.
7. Employ crowd psychological factors to advantage.

Tension

Regardless of how courteous and how well prepared and conditioned the officer is who has to deal with these demonstrations, he finds himself taunted by the persons participating in acts of civil disobedience. This is why it is so necessary to select officers very carefully who have a full understanding of the whole picture, and are thoroughly briefed on what to expect; and that it is most important that they remain completely and totally impartial. It is particularly difficult for the Negro officer assigned to demonstrations. He has to be prepared to take the most of the abuse, being taunted and referred to as "Uncle Tom," "Judas," "Handkerchief Head," etc. Baiting by spectators should outwardly be ignored; however, such spectators should be kept under surveillance as potential leaders of disorders.

During these more tedious incidents, the police supervisory personnel must be extremely alert for high tension among the police officers. Officers themselves should be alert for the welfare of their fellow workers. Any signs of nearing the breaking point should be noted and prompt action taken. A word of caution or a friendly gesture may be the needed restraint that could prevent a foolish act on the part of a fellow officer.

Scene Planning for Event

Visit and inspect the scene in order to know the layout and access routes of a proposed demonstration prior to the demonstration whenever possible. A reconnaissance of the area should be made and maps or sketches prepared indicating potential problem areas such as transportation terminals, hotels, parking areas and buildings housing offices of various groups identified with the crowd situation.

Close off areas of potential danger and those from where it will be difficult to remove a sit-in demonstrator, i.e., lock cars in a display room, close cigar stand and shops in hotel lobby, close off second floor areas.

Preventive Measures

If a large rally or parade is planned, all other events which would demand large commitments of police, or which might conflict with it and thereby generate problems, should be cancelled. In this way the police can avoid conflicting traffic patterns and diversion of police manpower from rally details to the other events. Likewise, the closing of stores and offices in the affected area should be encouraged, particularly if violence is anticipated.

Barricades

At the scene of the demonstration, maintain police lines outside the building where the demonstration occurs to prevent interference with the external transportation of arrested persons to detention locations and to control crowds that gather to observe and in some cases to harass and obstruct the police operation. These perimeter lines around the building keep demonstrators on the outside from interfering with the arrest process and to act as a reserve squad.

Rope, when used to establish a boundary line, establishes a fixed line that the crowd can actually see, and when properly advised of the consequences of crossing beyond such line, crowds tend to respect it. However, positive police action, arrest if necessary, should be taken should someone violate the boundary. Ropes will be effective against the docile nonaggressive crowd. However, if a crowd is hostile and has a unity of purpose or plan of action, ropes will be of no avail. Due to the bulkiness of the necessary amount of rope, stanchions and barricades that would be needed to effectively close off an area, prior arrangements will have to be made for the storing and for transportation to the location which it is to be used.

DEPLOYMENT OF MANPOWER

There are two methods of deploying the police at the scene of a demonstration. They are the *show of force* and *strength in reserve*.

Show of Force Approach

As the name implies, this method concentrates the greater portion of available manpower at the scene. Generally officers act as a barricade between two opposing factions. It has the following advantages:

1. May be used to gain immediate control of a bad situation.
2. Effective in discouraging misconduct among demonstrators.
3. Discourages misconduct because of the recognized strength and organization of the police.

But it suffers from these disadvantages:

1. Officers assigned to long tours of duty on the "battle line" where they may be subjected to baiting and sarcastic comment by demonstrators.

2. The majority of police strength is exposed to public view. This permits demonstrators to evaluate police strength more accurately. Eliminates the "ace in the hole."

Generally, it is the conclusion that the show of force is a good technique to use in the following circumstances:

1. Demonstrators are few in number.
2. Demonstrators are inexperienced in conducting demonstrations.
3. Danger of destruction of property is imminent.

Strength in Reserve Approach

Only a token force is at the scene to indicate that the activity is being policed, but in short order it becomes obvious the bulk of the police strength is being held in reserve. Those at scene might be high ranking officers, line supervisors and three or four policemen. Coverage should be strong enough so that a mischievous demonstrator, or heckler, would believe he would be caught if he were to commit a violation of law, and yet not be of sufficient strength to guarantee him immunity from conflict if his heckling gets too vociferous. The advantages of this system are the following:

1. Does not "tip the hand" of the police and permit accurate evaluation of police strength.

2. Permits greater turnover at the line of conflict and thus shorter tours of duty for concerned officers (officers not subjected to as much abuse).

3. Enables field commander to introduce greater flexibility and mobility into operation.

Its disadvantages are that demonstrators may start fights and/or cause other disturbances and adequate force will not be present to prevent it or to arrest the offenders. In other words, there will be a delay between the triggering event and the arrival of reserve officers.

It is the general conclusion that when demonstrators are numerous, experienced, well trained and properly disciplined the Strength in Reserve approach might be a proper stratagem.

If no arrest is to be made, because of the wishes of the owner or administrator (victim), police force should not be obviously present at the scene.

Following is the deployment of manpower which has proved quite effective.

1. A radio equipped police car should be stationed adjacent to the scene and frequent descriptions of the situation broadcast to headquarters.

2. Traffic officers seal off the locality if the demonstration is a large one and divert traffic in much the same way as they do at a large fire.

3. Plainclothes officers circulate the scene to find and relay information on the situation and any impending change of tactics on the part of the demonstrators.

4. *Photographs.* Plainclothesmen photograph the demonstrators using movie and still cameras, in the street outside the premises before they enter; as they enter and while they are inside the premises prior to arrests. They also photograph the arrest and removal procedure.

5. *Recordings.* Plainclothes officers carrying portable tape recorders enter the premises at the same time as the demonstrators. They record, for later court use, the tumultuous sounds of the demonstrators. When announcements are being read they place themselves near the rear of the demonstrators so that it can later be shown that the warnings were issued in everyone's hearing.

6. *Reserve.* Sufficient uniformed officers are held in reserve, out of view, to meet any eventuality. They are not moved to the scene until it is time to make arrests. In this way the officers are fresh when they go into action, whereas, if they were subject to constant and prolonged harassment their nerves would be frayed and their tempers taxed. When they do appear, they should march in smartly and give an immediate impression of discipline and organization.

INTELLIGENCE AT DEMONSTRATION

Officers in plain clothes should circulate throughout the demonstration. Officers should take pictures of speakers, pamphlet distributors and other key figures, and collect the literature which is distributed. Note the general nature and context of speeches and remarks directed to the crowd, the reaction of the crowd. The police should listen to the demonstrators who may want to talk to them, for often in this way the police have obtained advance knowledge of the plans of the demonstrators.

PHOTOGRAPHY

The importance of camera coverage cannot be overstated. Pictures are essential to a successful prosecution; but, over and above that, they refute charges of police brutality and depict for the public the true facts. Cameramen should arrive at the scene of the demonstration in advance and check lighting conditions and distance to assure top quality photos. It is most important to photograph the following:

1. All demonstrators, particularly all principals associated with the demonstration.
2. The general area and crowd as well as any ensuing action.
3. Any person appearing intoxicated or acting in an unusual manner.
4. All vehicles used in the demonstration.
5. The picket line to show any infringement on another property other than the subject of the demonstration.
6. All demonstrators. Prepare a mug book on demonstrators which contains a complete record on said demonstrator and his activities.

Sound motion pictures should be taken of the demonstration while in progress and of the arrests and removal. Special care should be given to record the action and words of the leaders and monitors.

Still and motion pictures should be taken of the scene, giving particular attention to agitators and unlawful acts. This procedure is effective in gaining and preserving evidence and furnishes valuable assistance in investigating particular offenses. These pictures supply a means whereby officers may refresh their memory in case preparation, and furnish convincing evidence for presentation in court. The taking of pictures generally has a salutary effect upon individual members of the crowd, as they realize a visual record is being made of their conduct.

Movies are the skeleton of a case. Their shortcoming is that they are not always before the jury, but must be projected. Still shots, although lacking motion and sound, have the advantage of being constantly before the jury.

BRIEFING

Briefing of assigned personnel should never be sketchy. Each man should know the exact role he must play in the control effort as it is related to the roles of others in his unit. Plans should be made to brief all officers and other involved agencies and departments on the general techniques to be expected from the demonstrators, and on the proposed police procedure.

Command personnel should report to operational headquarters well before the start of operations, in order that they might be completely briefed prior to the arrival of the personnel assigned them. To attempt to brief both commanders and their personnel immediately prior to the beginning of operations results in sufficient time to properly brief, supply and assemble personnel.

To facilitate briefing of command personnel, as well as field personnel, it is recommended that a large map of the area involved, with acetate overlay, be prepared showing the anticipated location of the demonstration, march, or other gathering, and proposed deployment of enforcement personnel. This map will augment the map attached to the plan, and will provide an aid to the briefing officer. An enlarged photo of all leaders should be posted as fast as the pictures are available and the persons identified.

Advance orders given to police officers should be timely, complete, and in writing. Orders should be accompanied by a map, sketch, or overlay of the individual's assigned area of responsibility. The chain of command and the communications net must be thoroughly understood by police officers. The location of facilities such as the communications center, first-aid station, and lost-children shelter should be included.

Orientations should also include a review of the essentials of crowd control training. General premobilization briefing should stress not only formal procedures as outlined hereinafter, but should emphasize the fact that all conversations and talk, whether with arrestees, demonstrators, or one another, or other persons at the scene of action, should be limited to only that which is absolutely necessary to carry out arrest procedures and to communicate necessary information. An officer should never discuss or argue the issue with the demonstrators. He should make it clear that it is not his function to pass on the social or economic issues involved, and that he is not aligned to either side. The demeanor of all personnel should reflect courtesy, objectivity, and the absence of levity and/or hostility. The briefing should include detailed orientation as to identification procedures to be used by personnel in plain clothes. Personnel of the arrest division shall have been specifically trained and briefed in their particular functions, preferably well ahead of any specific occurrence in which they are used as a division or team.

Written Plans

When practical, written operational plans should be prepared and distributed. Such plans will supply the members of the department with knowledge of the proposed operation and the policies, plans and objectives of the department. The operational plan should be divided into the following sections:

1. General—a general summary of the problems, the organizations involved, potential danger.
2. Assignments of personnel.
3. Operation.
    a. Reporting.
    b. Uniform.
    c. Deployment.
    d. Arrests.
    e. Transportation.
    f. Special equipment.
    g. Daily journal.
    h. Telephone numbers.
4. Communication.
    a. Methods.
    b. Call numbers.
    c. Code.
5. Relief and messing.
6. Requests for ambulance, first aid, tow trucks and fire trucks.
7. Command post.

Attached to the plan should be organizational charts, maps and other pertinent material.

PREVENTIVE ACTION AT THE SCENE

Confer with Demonstrators

The officer in command of the intelligence unit or other officer under his command should personally talk to the leader of the demonstration, identify himself, and explain the position of the police. He should hand to the leader a copy of the previously prepared sheet entitled "Laws Governing Conduct of Demonstrators" and should answer any questions related thereto. He points out that as the leader he is accountable for the conduct of his followers, and asks the leader to help control the crowd. It would be well to record this conversation or at least to make a notation of it and the time.

It may also be well to advise the demonstrators formally, as a group, of the pertinent law and caution against its violation. This statement should be made with a radio amplifier on a police car or have a battery-powered portable megaphone. Located at the fringe of the group with either of these facilities, the commander can turn up the volume until he is sure to be heard. Photos of the announcement and a sound recording should be made. The message needs to spell out very briefly the laws controlling such a demonstration. The duty and responsibility of the police should be made clear.

The demonstrators should be told that if they break no laws they will not be arrested, but if the specific law or any other laws not mentioned are violated, they will be arrested. If they do not heed this message, the fact that they were warned will be good evidence against them. The warning should be repeated at least once. The message should end with the question, "Did all of you people understand what I said?"

TACTICS—DEMONSTRATIONS

The basic approach of the police in handling demonstrations is clear. Police must give demonstrators all possible physical protection, from time of arrival until departure. The ideal way to accomplish this is to isolate the area and protect persons and property within it. The area in which the demonstration is to be conducted should be clearly established and if possible divided off by the use of barriers. Divide sidewalk longitudinally into two areas by use of ropes and standards—this permits free flow of traffic during the course of the demonstration and still allows the demonstrators room to function.

Crowds should not be allowed to form. Near areas of expected trouble everyone should be kept on the move; thus preventing even small groups from congregating. If all small groups can be rapidly dispersed, there is usually little danger. If groups with opposing view-points are expected, the areas should be cleared of any trash cans or loose objects that can be thrown or used as weapons. Building sites with plenty of such "ammunition" lying around should be blocked off and made secure.

When opposing groups are gathered, the danger is that the conduct of the police will signal to one side or the other they are free to use force and violence. Such conduct by the police will also act as a signal to the group that it must protect itself. Therefore, all persons observed committing acts of assault and battery, aggravated assault, destruction of property and other serious offenses should be arrested.

March

If the march is legal, it should receive all the police protection needed to protect it and to maintain discipline. Lines marching on the sidewalk are reasonably easy to guide into desired areas. Their anticipated turns can be blocked or their movement guided by the casual position of police manpower. They will not walk into the standing police officers. The leader can best control his followers if he keeps moving, so he will usually turn rather than stop.

Some officers should be sent to the rear of the moving line. They must follow in order to prevent some antagonist from picking on the stragglers. These marchers are people and they must be protected, especially at the rear of the line since that spot is an ideal place for a riot to commence.

If the march is along a highway, a buffer zone should be set up between the marchers and traffic. If the march assumes the proportions of a full parade down city streets, the normal parade procedures for the control of participants, spectators and traffic should be put into operation. This means that the participants themselves should establish monitors to control the marchers. Police observers should cover the entire line of march and keep the command constantly informed of the developments.

If there is danger that the marchers will be attacked along the line of march, reserves should be kept ready to move to any area of trouble. In addition to a fixed reserve at a static point or points, roving mobile reserves may be utilized moving parallel to the march and converging on trouble spots. If the danger is extremely great, the police may flank the marchers with mobile police units to discourage attack as well as to repulse it.

TACTICS—CIVIL DISOBEDIENCE

Acts of mass civil disobedience pose very special problems for the police. The law is being openly violated. Those participating in the acts are flaunting their criminality in the hope that they will be arrested, for they realize that a mass confrontation with the police and mass arrests will make their activity more newsworthy and thus assure the broadest possible coverage.

When the motivations and plans of the demonstrators are known, the police are in a position to utilize a variety of tactics. Thus the police may deny access to an area, or isolate and ignore the demonstrators, or disperse, or arrest and remove them. The mode of action selected should be that which appears most likely to protect society.

Access can be denied in various ways. Manpower and the threat of arrest are the methods most often utilized. To be effective, the police must not only have the manpower to carry out the assignment, but must be prepared to do so. In denying access to an area, physical barriers should be utilized whenever possible to supplement manpower. The barrier may consist of normal police barriers. In certain instances concertina barbed wire can be used effectively. Foam, utilized in fire fighting, and other chemicals, can present a formidable barrier.

Dispersal

Closely akin to the tactic of denial is that of dispersal. In the latter instance, the civil disobedience group is dispersed. There are situations where this is the wisest tactic, for instance when the group is on the verge of being transformed into a mob or when it is of such a magnitude that all other action is impossible, or where intelligence indicates that the leadership must have arrests to maintain the loyalty of its wavering following.

In the past, the use of this approach has at times generated the most adverse publicity for the police and brought forth an avalanche of charges of police brutality. Thus if it is followed, great discretion and care should be utilized in executing the plan.

Isolate and Ignore

As the intent of those engaged in civil disobedience is to gain publicity for themselves and their cause by a confrontation and arrest, the police can often best serve society by isolating and ignoring the demonstrators. Thus a demonstration intent on blocking traffic can be met by a plan which diverts traffic around the area of the blocking. The area in which the demonstration is being conducted is cordoned off. No attempt should be made to move or coerce demonstrators, through arrest, use of fire hose, or tear gas. They are allowed to protest to their heart's content. Naturally a sufficient number of officers should be detailed at the scene to protect the parties involved and to observe the conduct of participants and nonparticipants.

Encourage Demonstrators to Leave

Mass arrests impose a severe strain upon the finances and manpower of both the police and the courts. The objective should be to make as few arrests as necessary, not as many as possible. For this reason, demonstrators should be urged to leave the scene of their own volition and should be given every opportunity to do so. It is recommended that during the entire time that arrests are being made, the police continue to urge people to leave and that this choice be given to each violator before he is actually taken into custody. Experience has proven that many of those involved had either been misled by propaganda or outright lies, or had not fully realized the many implications involved in an arrest. In addition, many are truly frightened and wanted to leave and needed only slight encouragement to do so. If the police take their time and fully inform the demonstrators of the consequences of their acts, an appreciable number will leave of their own accord.

Arrests

Arrests, followed by successful prosecution, are by far the best method of maintaining law and order and a respect for law and order. The first question to be answered will be, "Who is to be arrested? Only the leaders? All those participating?" Although it is desirable to arrest all malfactors, there are times when only the leaders can be arrested because of the sheer number of those committing acts of civil disobedience. The leaders recognize this and therefore do everything possible to turn out as huge a crowd as possible. They also develop second and third command teams to replace the arrested leaders.

At other times an attempt to arrest, in a given emotionally-charged environment, may lead to mob violence. Officers are only human and their badges and uniforms represent authority, but their actions under potentially violent circumstances can lead to more violence or bring about a lessening of tensions and dispersal of mob groups.

Avoid Picayune Arrests

Because an arrest to the demonstrators is the successful climax of any protest demonstration and will be interpreted as a denial of the right to demonstrate, the officer must be discreet in making arrests for intoxication or minor breach of the peace. He should have the demonstrators' group leaders or coordinators remove any visible intoxicated persons or undesirables. When this can only be accomplished by an arrest, the officer should be tactful in executing the arrest and have a responsible person from the group (leader or coordinator) sign the criminal arrest complaint affidavit.

ARREST PROCEDURES FOR CIVIL DISOBEDIENCE DEMONSTRATORS

Introduction

Mass violations cannot be treated with blanket arrests. The simple making of mass arrests is relatively easy, but at the trial convictions are based not on evidence of many people doing illegal acts, but on evidence of one individual violating the law. Without that evidence there can be no conviction.

Every arresting officer must be prepared to prove who he arrested, where and when and for what violation. In the confusion of a large demonstration, particularly at night, there must be careful teamwork by all officers to promote a smooth technique and to have a complete and accurate record of all action taken. It is most important that convictions be won in court. If they are not, more violations will be encouraged, and resistance and defiance will increase with each successive incident of a similar nature.

The problem of making arrests under some circumstances may be difficult or impractical, and any one of the following courses of action may be indicated.

IMMEDIATE ARREST. Follow normal procedure for an on-view arrest and remove prisoner to a safe place as quickly as possible.

DELAYED ARREST. When an offender has committed an offense and the size of the crowd or other circumstances prevent an immediate arrest, he may be kept in view, followed and arrested when it may be safely accomplished.

COMPLAINT AND WARRANT. When neither of the above are practical, and sufficient identification can be obtained, a complaint and warrant may be sought from the court.

CITIZEN'S ARREST. Certain jurisdictions believe that all arrests of demonstrators for trespass should be made by the owner of the building or his agent; or the person in lawful possession of the real property should make a private person's arrest since the passive type of sit-in is not an emergency, and instantaneous action is not generally necessary.

Procedure

When the field commander is satisfied that the law violations do exist, that the names of discommoded citizens have been obtained, appropriate pictures taken, and all necessary evidence accumulated, he shall take the following steps.

1. He shall personally approach the leader or leaders of the demonstration and identify himself.

2. He shall explain the law violations which are being committed. If the mimeographed handout on the law has not been distributed, he should do so at this time.

3. He shall suggest that the leaders disperse the crowd without police action.

In the event the leaders do not comply with the suggestion, the field commander shall then seal off the area so no one can enter and join the demonstrators.

Decision to Arrest

Only one person says when and where to arrest. In relatively small cities or communities, this person would be the chief of police. In large areas or under other circumstances, this person would be someone designated by the chief. This will assure that arrests will not be made until the police have evidence to prove the charge and obtain convictions.

A second reason is to confine the decision on what specific charges are to be made to only one person. In this way the charges against individuals in mass arrests will be fairly consistent.

Timing to Arrests

Civil disobedience demonstrators want arrests. Arrests are the climax to the demonstration. Being arrested at the height of their activity with the mass going along has a tendency to emphasize the cause of the protest. The real reason for the arrest, the violation of the law, is lost in the emotional tension of their activity. They usually have little concern about being arrested on the day of their action, but on the next day or subsequent days they don't want to be arrested. To arrest them when they don't really want to be arrested results in more serious thought on law and the consequences of the violation of the law.

If no arrests are made at the time the offense is committed, but, rather, warrants are issued, they should be executed in such a manner as to get the most psychological benefit. The individuals may be arrested at their homes at a time when the family is there. The arrest could be made just before the weekend or just before a holiday. The seriousness of what they have become involved in should be brought before their friends and family. If the troublemaker is arrested with a large group of his fellow troublemakers, there is very little stigma attached to it. If he is arrested alone without the benefit of fanfare, it presents the unlawfulness of the act in a different light.

Order in Which Demonstrators Are Arrested

Insofar as is possible, the first persons subject to arrest shall be those who are leaders of the demonstration or who were responsible for the disobedience. But there may be instances where this procedure will not be to the best interests of the police, for at times it may be desirable to allow the leaders to remain so that they can restrain their followers who might otherwise pose a serious threat of violence.

Watch agitators who try to get out. Be alert for those who seek to drop off when arrest seems imminent. The arrest of this type of agitator is much more important than that of the majority of the marchers. Usually they have a knack for organizing and inciting a march and are probably deemed more valuable to the effort if they can avoid arrest.

Location of Arrests of Marchers

The arrest should be made when the group is in a straight line. It should not be made when a part of the line bends around a corner or extends across a street intersection. The reasons are obvious. Select a spot where there is a maximum of building wall flush with the sidewalk, and try to keep from blocking doorways as much as possible. When the arrested line extends across a doorway immediately place a security guard in the doorway. If the group is moving toward a more ideal location such as a government building entrance steps or a large lawn, guide them into this spot before making any arrests.

Organization

Normally arrests will be made by the police. In order to accomplish this in the most expeditious manner organization, teamwork, planning and training are essential. The divisions to be established have already been outlined and will not be repeated. Special accent will be put on the organization of the arrest division for it will be the key to the success or failure of the operation.

Arrest Division

The arrest division shall be that organizational body, operating within the perimeter of the disturbed area, which is specifically charged with the responsibility of the following:

1. Accumulating the immediately available evidence of violations of law by individuals.
2. Carrying out of conditions precedent to arrest, where applicable, for violations of law, and informing individuals to be arrested of the charges against them (and other pertinent advice).
3. Arresting individuals who have violated penal provisions of the law.

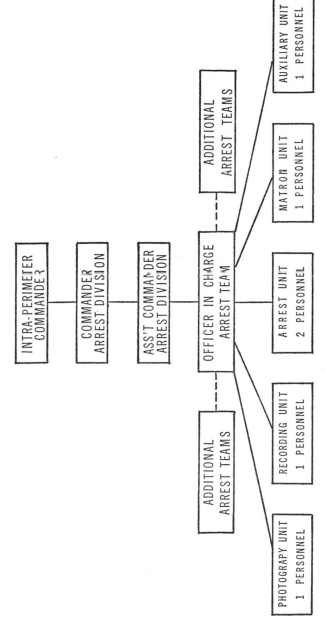

ORGANIZATION OF ARREST DIVISION

DIAGRAM OF ORGANIZATION

INTRA-PERIMETER COMMANDER

COMMANDER ARREST DIVISION

ASS'T COMMANDER ARREST DIVISION

OFFICER IN CHARGE ARREST TEAM

ADDITIONAL ARREST TEAMS

ADDITIONAL ARREST TEAMS

AUXILIARY UNIT 1 PERSONNEL

MATRON UNIT 1 PERSONNEL

ARREST UNIT 2 PERSONNEL

RECORDING UNIT 1 PERSONNEL

PHOTOGRAPY UNIT 1 PERSONNEL

4. Delivering arrested individuals, together with photographs and documents taken and/or prepared in connection with such arrest, to the transportation and removal division.

Selection of Special Police Arrest Squads

Each department should have a special police unit which will be used at the scene of demonstrations. It should consist of younger personnel in good health. Other desirable features of such personnel are alertness, tact and diplomacy, and a high degree of emotional self-control. Each officer must be an individual who can be depended upon to remain cool when present in a riotous demonstration. An officer whose dossier shows numerous arrests for resisting arrest should not be chosen, nor should one be selected whose disability file shows back injuries or hernia because he will be doing much lifting. An officer who has expressed strong feelings regarding racism or minority should not be used. The rugged "fighting cop" is needed in many spheres of law enforcement but not in this specialty. The cool taciturn officer who can be depended upon for implicit obedience to difficult orders is the kind needed for this new kind of police work. If arrests are expected, check the officer's conviction record to see how well he testifies. A top witness is a must.

The officer must be taught effective but harmless methods of arresting and removing limp, struggling and other types of uncooperative subjects. Techniques should be developed in simulated sit-in situations so that each officer, in addition to learning his job, also learns how it feels to execute it. Much effort should be devoted to insure that arrests are made carefully and with no more force and effort than needed to accomplish the police objective. Arresting officers should be instructed to avoid any provocative language or action and to conserve as much energy as possible to reduce the chance of personal injury due to exhaustion. The squad should spend a great deal of time in practicing procedures in connection with the physical handling of those to be arrested.

Arrest Team

All arrests should be made by the arrest team. Its composition and the duties of its members follow.

OFFICER-IN-CHARGE of the arrest team is in direct charge of personnel of the arrest team. He supervises fulfillment of procedures established and/or necessary to the gathering of evidence and identification of arrestees.

RECORDING UNIT OFFICER. Whenever the arrest unit is about to commence an arrest, he records all proceedings preliminary thereto, and continues to record all proceedings thereafter in connection with such arrest, including the voice of any matron or matrons participating in the arrest.

THE PHOTOGRAPHY UNIT (one officer). He photographs each person arrested from a distance of no more than ten feet. Each picture shall plainly show the following:

1. The person arrested.
2. The recorder.
3. The arresting officer and his assistant.
4. The number identifying the person arrested.
5. The immediate environment of the person arrested.

THE ARREST UNIT (TWO OFFICERS). They separate and remove persons to be arrested from other demonstrators.

THE MATRON UNIT (ONE WOMAN). If the person to be arrested is a female or young juvenile, the policewoman or matron steps in and replaces one of the two arresting officers during the arrest procedure.

THE AUXILIARY UNIT (ONE OFFICER). He assists the arrest team in the entire operation. In particular, he shall assist the officer in charge of the arrest team in supplying information and identification cards in sequence.

SEPARATORS. Extra officers should be available if needed to assist in separating an arrestee who violently resists arrests. Their duty is to unhook locked arms and legs and remove the arrested person from the group.

Uniforms and Identification

All members of arrest teams shall, whenever possible, be in uniform. Where this is not possible, distinguishing badges, insignia, or other agency identification shall be worn conspicuously. But belts, gun, stick, cuffs or anything that can be grabbed should be removed. Bolt cutters should be available in the event the demonstrators chain themselves together or to some fixed object.

Although the arrest team as described above has proved extremely effective, there are deviations from it that have worked equally well. Thus, some teams consist of only the officer in charge of the arrest team, two arresting officers, a photographer and any back up officers needed to make the arrest and removal. The procedure followed by these teams is as follows.

The officer in charge designates the person to be arrested, after which the arrest team moves in and removes him. He is transported to a designated spot where his picture is taken together with the arresting officers'. At this point his name is obtained and recorded on an arrest card together with those who are to be transported with him. When the transportation vehicle is full, the single card is to be taken to headquarters by the two arresting officers who book the prisoners. These officers are replaced by a new arrest team. This method is faster than when individual cards and recordings are made, but obviously lacks the degree of individual identification of that system.

Regardless of which type of arrest team is used, it is apparent that either is far superior to the old mass cattle drive type of arrest. The use of the team minimizes the number needed to make the arrest, and even more important, it reduces the number of police that must appear in court to testify. This latter saving in manpower would alone be enough to justify its use. Most of all, the use of this system assures identification of the violator, which under the old system proved the greatest block to successful prosecution.

Mass Arrest Procedures

Insofar as possible, arrests for refusal to comply with a dispersal order will be made only upon direction of a command or supervisory officer. Members in plain clothes in the crowd will not make arrests. Their responsibility is to point out violators who are to be arrested. Preferably arrests will be made by an arrest team.

There is a well-established procedure that should be followed in handling these mass arrests. First uniform officers should establish and maintain a perimeter. The curious should be separated, kept back and crowd broken up. If the violators are in a buliding all entrances should be secured. No one should be permitted to join the demonstrators. Police group leaders with specific assignments should begin to get their tasks done. Spectators are to be cleared from the area leaving only the police and those to be arrested. Traffic should be detoured from the area and the transportation vehicles moved into place. Ingress and egress roads must be cleared so that police can move in and prisoners can be moved out without interference. When all is in readiness the commander will give the command to proceed.

ANNOUNCEMENTS. The first step is to request the demonstrators to leave. The failure to obey provides a uniform charge for all persons who are to be arrested after being ordered to leave.

The reading of the statements must be done with the use of amplification to insure that everyone present hears the orders. The statements should also be recorded on two or more recorders placed as far distant from the speakers as possible. During the aforementioned activities, it is well to take still photos as well as motion pictures of all the activity possible.

At the scene of mass civil disobedience, such as a hotel, auto agency or some other legitimate, lawfully operated business establishment, the complete cooperation of the management is necessary. The manager of the premises must notify the demonstrators that they are trespassing and disturbing the peace. This is done by the reading to the group a prepared statement as follows:

> I am ———. I represent the management of these premises. Your actions are causing a disturbance and interfering with our business. You are not welcome here and are here against our wishes. I request and order you to leave immediately, and if you do not, I shall request the police to arrest each of you.

The purpose of this announcement, of course, is to allow management to rescind any implied invitation to enter and to form the *corpus delicti* for trespass and disturbing the peace. This is followed by a police announcement. This second announcement is read by an officer immediately following the prior announcement:

> I am ———, ———, and I represent the Police Department of the City of ———. I hereby notify you that your actions constitute violation of ——— [state code section violated and general nature of law violated].

I therefore command you in the name of the People of the State of ——
to disperse, and if you do not disperse, you shall be arrested for violation
of the following offenses: [state code sections violated and general
nature of the law violated such as:

407 P. C.—Participating in an unlawful assembly;
409 P. C.—Refusal to disperse;
415 P. C. —Disturbing the peace;
602j P. C.—Trespassing;
148 P.C.—Resisting arrest, if applicable].

The demonstrators are then informed by the police officer that they
have four separate and distinct alternatives:

1. They may leave the premises immediately, and are urged to
   do so and avoid arrest.
2. If they choose to remain and continue to violate the law, they
   will be arrested, in which case they may exercise the following
   options:

   a. They may walk to the wagon with an arresting officer.
   b. They may go limp, and be carried.
   c. They may resist, and the resistance will be overcome.

They should also be assured that if they are arrested they will be
prosecuted. They can also be notified that bail is set at so much for
each offense. It should also be clear that those who refuse to submit
to arrest and walk out of the building or who physically resist arrest will
be charged with an additional count of resisting and the bail will be
increased accordingly.

Those who wish to leave should be allowed to do so, but no one
should be permitted to join the demonstrators. The more that leave,
the less problem in arresting, and the less likelihood of violence. Those
who are under a doctor's care or are recovering from illness or injury
are asked to inform the officers so that they can be moved from the
building.

The commanding officer shall wait a reasonable length of time for
compliance. This nullifies the defense that the person arrested did not
know that he was violating the law. It also provides the casual on-
looker and the so-called "victim of circumstances" an opportunity to
leave the area to avoid arrest, and builds the case against the offenders
in the presence of arresting officers and competent expert witnesses.

If, after the second order, members of the crowd still do not disperse, the commander must order the arrest of all remaining in violation of that order. It should be stressed that time is not important in making arrests of civil disobedience demonstrators. There should be no haste.

The Arrest

The officer in charge of the arrest team designates the individuals to be arrested. However, in his absence or inability to act, one member of the arrest unit, previously designated, performs this function.

When making an arrest, the arrest unit (together with other members of the arrest team involved) approaches the person to be arrested. One of the members of the arrest unit, previously designated, states to the person to be arrested:

> You are in violation of —— (stating code sections violates and names of offenses). You are requested to please leave —— [Identify premises or area which is the subject of any trespass or unlawful assembly].

If the individual complies, the arrest unit permits him to leave.

If there is noncompliance, the designated officer of the arrest unit states:

> You are under arrest for —— [stating code sections for which the arrest is made and names of offenses].

The other member of the arrest unit then holds in front of the arrested person's chest and under his chin (or, if this is not possible, in some other appropriate position relative to the person) a previously prepared identification and arrest card received from the officer in charge, arrest team, or auxiliary unit in such a way as to permit photographing of same and the arrested person. This card bears the number assigned to the person. It must be of sufficient size and color to appear clearly in the photo which is taken. The photo of the arrested person and the arresting officers is then taken.

The designated member of the arrest unit then asks such questions of the arrested person (name, etc.) necessary for completion of the identification and arrest card details pertinent to this stage of the proceedings.

The other member of the arrest team records the name and address of the individual, and any other information elicited, on the identifica-

ARREST IDENTIFICATION CARD

NAME _____ RACE _____ SEX _____ AGE _____

TRUE NAME _____

ADDRESS _____

WHERE ARRESTED (Be Specific) _____

ARREST # _____

( ) 148 RESISTING ARREST
( ) 242 BATTERY
( ) 243 BATTERY/POLICE OFFICER
( ) 245 A W D W
( ) 370 PUBLIC NUISANCE
( ) 404 UNLAWFUL ASSEMBLY
( ) 409 REMAINING PRESENT/AFTER WARNING TO DISPERSE
( ) 415 DISTURBING THE PEACE
( ) 416 REFUSING TO DISPERSE UPON LAWFUL COMMAND
( ) 602-j TRESPASSES UPON LAND ENUMERATED: MISDEMEANOR
( ) 602-o REFUSING OR FAILING TO LEAVE A PUBLIC BLDG. AFTER HOURS.
( ) 602.7 REFUSAL OF UNAUTHORIZED PERSONNEL TO LEAVE COLLEGE OR
       UNIVERSITY PROPERTY

DATE _____ TIME _____

PHOTOGRAPHER _____

F/P TAKEN BY: _____

ARRESTING OFFICER(S) _____
(Name and Badge Numbers)

TRANSPORTATION OFFICER(S) _____

COMMENTS: _____

RF INDEX F/P _____

Arrest identification card. One side will contain in large print the number assigned to the arrested person. The reverse side contains blanks which are filled in at the time of the arrest and give a complete record of the offense for which the arrest was made, by whom it was made, and the identity of person arrested.

tion and arrest card, together with the charges for which he is arrested and a brief statement of the facts thereof, and the names (or other information identifying them) of those taking part in the arrest procedure. He receives the polaroid photograph and either staples it to the card or sees that this is done. Both officers of the arrest unit then separate the arrested person from other demonstrators.

The designated member of the arrest unit then requests the person: "Will you please stand up and walk with us?" His compliance with this request shall be entered on the identification and arrest card. If he resists, resistance must be overcome. One method of raising and moving him is by using the tips of the longer middle finger, to exert a lifting, in-and-upward pressure at the base of the ear, against the nerve centers. Few individuals can resist this tactic.

He is then removed from the area to the point previously established for his transfer to the transportation and removal team. At the beginning of such removal, if the arrested person is a female or young juvenile, the matron or policewoman shall replace one of the arrest unit officers.

Only one member of the arrest unit should question or converse with the arrested person; the other member is responsible for carrying out the procedures set forth above with respect to the identification and arrest card.

The arrest unit shall turn over the individual and his identification and arrest card, with the picture attached, to the transportation and removal team at the point or place established for that purpose.

Danger of Going Too Fast

When a mass arrest is to be made, the police action should be deliberately slowed down. It must be stressed again that there is a danger in moving too fast with arrest. This danger cannot be overlooked. The quality of the arrest may be impaired. The identity of the individual may be lost for proper court trials. The officer in a hurry builds up tension: He may unintentionally injure someone, or he may put himself in a compromising position. He may forget the training he has received that he must treat each arrest as an individual case. He may not consider that excruciating circumstances are different with each person. He may forget that the eyes of the world are upon him through the hovering television camera and searching eyes of the civil rights investigators.

Identification Cards

To aid the officer in his note taking, it has proved beneficial to prepare standard forms that will speed up the process and establish uniformity. One such card merely contains the names of the arresting officers and their star numbers, plus designation of the various offenses usually involved in such actions. The location, date and time of the arrest are noted. The officer merely checks, or preferably initials, the offense charged. The names of those arrested are placed on the back of the card. As only one card is made for each wagonload of prisoners, six names will appear on each card. There is also space on the back to note the attitude of the prisoners, the times received at the booking facility and the time received at the jail.

A more detailed card is as follows:

IDENTIFICATION CARD

```
        )
        )
        )
        )
        )                          #_____
        )
        )                          Case #_____
Rt. Index Finger )
        )                          Arrest #_____
       Location_____

       Date_____Time_____
       Name_____
       Address_____
       Offense
       (  ) 407 PC Unlawful assembly
       (  ) 409 PC Remaining in an unlawful assembly after request
            has been made to disperse
       (  ) 415 PC Disturbing the peace
       (  ) 416 PC Refusing to disperse upon lawful command
       (  ) 602J-PC Trespassing
       (  )
       (  )
       (  )

       Arresting Officer_____
       Comments: (continue on reverse side)
       _____
          OFFICERS INITIAL:
Arrest Team      (       )       )      Photographer  (           )
Removal Team     (       )       )      Fingerprint   (           )
Transportation   (       )       )                    (           )
```

This latter type should be printed on buff cards so that when photographed they will not reflect light and injure the quality of the picture. The cards should be approximately 5″ x 8″ in size, numbered in sequence on one side in figures not less than three inches in height. In this way the card can be used to show the ID number in the picture. The arrest form fulfilled three purposes: (1) to insure adequate information for a complaint; (2) to provide a handwritten report which the officer could use as his original notes when called upon to testify in court, and (3) to identify defendant by name, number and fingerprint.

Additional copies of these arrest identification cards can be prepared with a copying machine. In each case one can remain with the arresting officer, one with the prisoners, one be sent to the district attorney, and one retained by the arresting agency.

Transportation Officers

Once the arrest team has completed its job with a given individual, he is turned over to a transportation team. A team of transporting officers removes the subject, taking also the arrest identification card to which the polaroid picture is attached. The officers lead, drag, or carry the arrested person to an identification desk en route to detention. At the identification desk, the arrest identification card is reviewed for accuracy and completeness and the defendant's right index fingerprint is placed at the top of the card. All arrested persons are searched at the identification desk, en route to the temporary detention room. All women are moved to private quarters and searched by policewomen.

If the defendant goes limp or resists, every effort should be made to photograph the act of resistance. This step is desirable, but is not necessary. The photograph serves to support the officer's testimony concerning the defendant's deliberate attempt to obstruct the officer in the performance of his duty. Dragging the subjects is preferable to trying to lift the limp bodies. Admittedly this procedure is undignified, but it is probably the most humane since there is less chance of injury to the subjects and to the officers.

Young children should be removed by policewomen whenever possible and should be transported in patrol cars—not patrol wagons. It must be stressed that the clearing of an area should be slow and methodical with every consideration being displayed for the safety of the demonstrators. Kindness and courteous consideration of the demonstrator is of the utmost importance. Indeed the demonstrators will often expect—actually have been led to expect—violence on the part of the police. When they are confronted by calm, relaxed, patient and gentle police, they are unnerved.

Problems Involving Police Personnel

The favorite technique of demonstrators is to go limp and require physical removal by the police. Their objective is to make the law enforcement task as difficult and time consuming as possible. This is extremely tiring on police personnel and provision must be made for frequent relief periods. The arrest and removal squads should be rested about every thirty minutes.

After an extended period of handling both limp and resisting prisoners, and of being exposed to a continuing barrage of taunting and insulting remarks by the demonstrators, officers not only become physically tired but their tempers become badly frayed. To prevent any thoughtless retaliation or excessive use of force, a reaction which the demonstrators are trying to provoke, supervisory officers should be in constant attendance at all operational scenes and assure police behavior which will be beyond reproach.

For numerous reasons, it is probable that more police personnel will be mobilized than are required at any given time. Those being held in reserve should be stationed at some location other than at the immediate scene of arrest and removal. A large group of officers merely standing by at the scene will only tend to increase the friction which exists between the demonstrators and the police.

List of Arrested Persons

When the first arrest is made, a list should be started. Each person arrested should be added to this list. The identification and records files should be searched on each one, and his past criminal record should appear with his name of the list.

Evidence

Those at the scene must never become so engrossed in the making of arrests and removel of the demonstrators that they forget to secure and retain physical evidence. Signs, handbills, recordings and pictures made by the demonstrators themselves should be held, as they may prove invaluable at the trial.

When picketers and banner-carrying demonstration marchers are arrested, each banner, poster or sign carried should be marked before the bearer and the article are separated. The name of the bearer, the date, the time, the location of arrest, and the officer's name should be written on the item. If the bearer refuses to give a name, place his right index fingerprint where his name would have been written. Use an ink pad or portable fingerprint pad. Bind all the signs carried by this particular group together and date them. They should be stored just as other personal property. This is important evidence, especially so if the message printed on the sign is insulting, controversial, or discriminating. Signs that can be pinpointed to the defendant are of particular interest to juries.

Identify each poster with the bearer. Use the fingerprint method already described or use the polaroid camera along with the fingerprint method. Take a picture of each individual with his or her sign. Give the picture to the arresting officer, and as he puts the fingerprint on the card, he can also put it on the back of the picture. Get the officer making the arrest in the picture also if possible.

RECORDS AND REPORTS

Records

Complete and accurate reports concerning the details of the entire incident are essential, therefore plans must be made to record the case history as it happens in detail. A running log should be kept of the disturbance during the event. This is similar to an investigator's case history. The responsible person assigned to this task must record facts only. This document should be rather detailed: what happened, where it happened, date, time, how many involved, routes traveled, phrases chanted, what they did, all recorded in sequence. The wording on signs they used, how many arrested, is also recorded. Other personnel should be aware of this officer's assignment so they can report facts to him.

While supervisory officers are responsible for preparing administrative reports, all officers, irrespective of assignment or duties, should maintain accurate notes in their memorandum books relative to their participation in the operation. These memoranda will provide the basis for divisional reports, case preparation and court presentation.

Case File

A case file must be prepared on each individual arrested which will contain the following information:

1. Identification reference sheet, police photo and prior criminal record, if any.
2. Pertinent background information that might be useful in any cross examination.
3. Photo of subject with arresting officers.
4. Photos of subject showing his activity at the scene of the act of civil disobedience.
5. Copy of police report covering the arrest.
6. Names of witnesses, and a brief resume of the area of their testimony.

After Action Report

The after action report is a narrative of the highlights of the operation. It is written as soon after the completion of the mission as is practicable. Notes taken during the operation serve as a basis for compiling this report. Emphasis is placed upon difficulties which were encountered and the procedures necessary to eliminate them. Recommendations for improvement concerning planning, coordination, personnel and equipment are written in detail. A file copy is retained for use in improving future operations.

The police report on the specific act of civil disobedience is one of the most important facets of the successful prosecution. Whether we arrest one individual or 500 people, one master police report should be made covering the whole incident from beginning to end. The report must be accurate regarding the chronology of events and must cover thoroughly all the areas of the different violations of the law that contribute to the civil disobedience. Other incidents that result in arrests at the scene of mass civil disobedience, but which are not directly related, should be handled separately and covered by individual police reports by the officers involved.

THE CRITIQUE

This is the final stage of the crowd control mission. It is conducted to provide all participants with a clear, concise and objective idea of what was done correctly and what was done incorrectly. Intelligent, tactful and constructive criticism is necessary to improve operations. The critique can be most effective if held as soon as practicable after the mission is completed. Its success depends upon the flexibility with which the officer in charge employs it. He should criticize individuals in private and praise them in public. Participants should leave the critique with a favorable attitude toward the security mission and a desire to improve the next one. Examples of personal initiative or ingenuity, types of errors and proposals for corrective action should be specified. Personnel should be encouraged to participate in the controlled discussion and led to feel that the critique is a period for learning rather than a time set aside for criticism of their performance.

Critique Planning

The critique cannot be planned as thoroughly as other phases of the mission because the points to be covered are influenced directly by the performance of personnel. Advance planning can include the time and place of the critique and the general outline to be followed. The officer in charge can insure complete coverage of essential elements by following a general procedure similar to the outline below.

RESTATE OBJECTIVE OF THE MISSION. This will enable participants to start on a common ground. This is necessary because the participants who were concerned with a particular aspect of the subject may have forgotten the overall objective.

REVIEW PROCEDURES AND TECHNIQUES EMPLOYED. In this step summarize briefly the methods used to attain the objective. A critique could introduce, in addition to discussions, a showing of film taken during the disturbance, chalk talks in the form of drawing the scene, discuss techniques used by the demonstrators and by the police and perhaps a visit to the area for an on the scene replay.

EVALUATE PERFORMANCE. This is the most important part of the critique. Using notes taken during the operation, the officer in charge discusses strong points, identifies weaker ones, and makes suggestions for improvement. He must be careful not to "talk down" to the group. All remarks are sufficiently specific and impersonal to permit all personnel to profit from the experience.

CONTROL THE GROUP IN DISCUSSION. The person in charge should clarify the points he has mentioned and guide group discussion of other relevant topics which arise.

SUMMARIZE. The critique is concluded with a brief, comprehensive summary. The person in charge can suggest study and practice to overcome deficiencies.

THERE WILL BE A TRIAL!

The gathering of intelligence prior to the act of civil disobedience, the physical arrests, the sound recordings, the still and movie photography, the preparation of statements to be read, the transportation of prisoners, the processing and the incarceration of prisoners are all accomplished in a pre-planned, slow and deliberate manner for one reason and one reason alone. That reason is to present to the district attorney a lawful arrest on each individual committing civil disobedience, with legally gathered and presented evidence that cannot be refuted.

CHARGES OF BRUTALITY

Regardless of the care with which police operations are conducted, there will be charges of brutality and unnecessary violence. This should be anticipated, and the police should take steps to protect themselves. First, there should be a doctor available at the area of temporary detention and also at the final detention area, which may be the city or county jail or a special facility set up for this purpose. These men should not only be highly competent and of unquestioned integrity but, in addition, should have no immediate affiliation with any of the law enforcement agencies involved in order to avoid an accusation of bias or prejudice. Not only should they give medical treatment to any person who is injured, but should also examine any individual who claims injury as the result of the arrest or transportation procedures.

Second, the police operation should be carried out in the full glare of publicity. Permit accredited representatives of the press, radio and television to observe all police operations, the only restriction being that they not interfere with the work being carried on. The operations can also be observed by representatives of the governor's office, the county board of supervisors, the board of regents of the university, representatives of the state legislature, and the mayor. Not only does such observation curb the inclination of any officer to lose his temper or become overly energetic in handling a prisoner, but in addition it makes it extremely difficult for a demonstrator falsely, but successfully, to claim brutal treatment.

The press should be placed in an area where they can observe, but not interfere. It is recommended that a high ranking officer be assigned for press liaison, to provide information and to handle unusual conditions such as requests to interview specific prisoners. He should also have the duty of insisting upon proper press behavior and of removing any individual who acts in an objectionable fashion. Particular attention should be given to representatives of the left-wing press who may attempt to give a completely untruthful report of the proceedings.

Chapter 28

LABOR DISTURBANCES

INTRODUCTION

THE BASIC FREEDOMS guaranteed by the Constitution of the United States give workmen the right to refuse to work under conditions believed to be unfair. These same freedoms give the employer the right to defend his employment policies and work standards. Such disputes at times will become most bitter. This is because a labor quarrel is concerned with fundamental human rights. It is a contest between the worker, who seeks a living wage, and management, which is endeavoring to obtain a fair return on its invested capital. To both sides, then, the issue involves standards of living, prospects for security and, to a certain extent, the very right to live.

OBJECTIVES

The first step is to recognize the objectives of the parties involved. Labor will resort to a cessation of operation of a plant or industry in order to pressure management into granting demands. To accomplish this, the union will resort to the following:

1. Picketing premises.
2. Preventing and discouraging employees from entering.
3. Preventing and discouraging the movement of raw materials or finished products into or out of the plant.
4. Subjecting employees who enter to embarrassment and harassment.
5. Slow down the operation of the industry.

Management, on the other hand, has as its objective the maintenance of operation of plant or industry. To do so, it will try the following:

1. Encouraging employees to resume work.
2. Maintaining free ingress and egress of raw materials and finished products.

3. Replacing striking employees.
4. Attempting to limit picketing and other union activity by injunction.
5. Maintaining at least partial production.

The police have as their objective the following:

1. Maintenance of law and order.
2. Protection of life and property of all parties.
3. Protection of civil rights of all involved in the public interest.

The police can realize these objectives only if they are instilled with the attitude of neutrality and the responsibilities of their duties.

INTELLIGENCE

A distinct advantage to the police in controlling strike disorders is that normally the conditions related to the problem allow the gathering of intelligence well in advance of the actual disturbance. This permits the formulation of plans of action if and when a disturbance occurs and also alternative plans to cover exigencies. The following general areas of inquiry and suggested check list should prove of assistance in procuring this information.

Initial Strike Report

The first information needed is knowledge that there is or will be a labor dispute. Every department should have a definite plan for reporting a strike, preferably long before it commences. This plan should assign the responsibility for making such a report and designate the individual who is to receive such reports. The report itself should contain the following:

1. Name, business address and telephone number of employer.
2. Name and address of union, union local number, affiliation and telephone number.
3. Kind of business.
4. Number and occupation of employees involved in the dispute.
5. Reason for the dispute.
6. Date strike declared.
7. Number and occupation of employees who will continue to work.
8. Number of pickets.

9. Trouble anticipated.
10. Kind of strike (sympathy, wildcat, lockout, secondary).
11. Any additional factors which would aid in determining the number and kind of police details required.

Detailed Dispute Report

The next step is to learn the pertinent facts relating to the disagreement and the parties involved. The checklist is as follows:

I. Disagreement
    1. When does the current contract expire?
    Date ——; Hour ——.
    2. When will the strike begin?
    Date ——; Hour ——.
    3. Reason for dispute
       a. Economic (salaries, hours, conditions).
       b. Improper conduct of one of the parties.
    4. Status of negotiations if possible.
    5. Expected duration.
II. Employer
   A. Identification
     1. Name.
     2. Address.
     3. Telephone.
     4. Liaison Representative.
     5. Home address.
     6. Telephone.
     7. Products manufactured.
   B. Nature of employer
     1. Single location.
     2. Multiple locations.
     3. Subsidiaries.
     4. Parent.
   C. Plans
     1. Will the struck facilities be operated?
     2. What will be the extent of operations?
     3. Total number employees and an estimate of workers who will report despite strike.
     4. Time of arrival and departure of employees who will not strike.
     5. Transit facilities and routes used.
     6. Entrances and exits used by employees.
     7. Time when merchandise is to be received or shipped.
     8. Meal periods for employees and whether they eat on the premises.

     9. Exits, entrances and routes used by employees during meal periods.

    10. Special hazards or other conditions effecting police duty (e.g. loose debris that might be used as missiles).

D. Physical plan

    Location and nature of struck premises.

E. Security

    1. Security or protection officer.

    2. Address.

    3. Telephone.

    4. General security plan.

F. General attitude

III. Union

A. Identification

    1. Name and local.

    2. District or region.

    3. National.

    4. International.

B. Union profile

    1. IIistory of union conduct in past strikes.

    2. Character of members

       a. Skill.

       b. Seniority.

       c. Wage level.

       d. Education.

C. Officials

    1. Name of president, secretary, strike manager.

    2. Address and telephone (business and home).

    3. Picket captains (address and telephone).

    4. Command post (address and telephone).

D. Equipment

    1. Sound trucks.

    2. Public address systems.

    3. Permits for use required.

E. Picketing

    1. Number of pickets.

    2. Locations.

    3. Times.

    4. Captains.

F. Tactics

    1. Marches—when; where.

       a. Caravans.

       b. Motorcades.

    2. Harassment.
    3. Boycotts.
  G. Financial arrangements
    1. Feeding.
    2. Housing.
    3. Benefits.
  H. General attitude
III. Physical survey; if it appears that there may be violence, a survey should be made showing
    1. Location of the plant, number of exits and entrances, loading platforms, etc.
    2. Other buildings or locations which might be affected by the dispute.
    3. Time of arrival and departure of employees who will not strike.
    4. Transit facilities and routes used.
    5. Entrances and exits used by employees
    6. Meal periods for employees, and whether they eat on the premises.
    7. Exits, entrances and routes used by employees during meal periods.
    8. Time when merchandise is to be received or shipped.
    9. Special hazards or other conditions affecting police duty.

Evaluation of Reports

Once the basic information has been gathered, it must be assembled and evaluated and a preliminary assessment made of the possible severity and duration of the strike. In addition to basic identifying information, it should evaluate the following:

1. Nature of dispute.
2. Nature and history of the relationship between the parties.
3. Nature and temperament of parties
  a. Employer.
  b. Union.
4. Capacity of parties for disorder
  a. Employer.
  b. Union.
5. Degree of threat to public place
  a. On part of employer.
  b. On part of union.
6. Need for police action to protect public.

Distribution of Reports and Orders

The evaluation and all reports should be given to the officer designated to supervise the labor dispute. He will be responsible for determining what further police action must be taken. He will assign and brief officers who are to participate. He will notify all police units and all other departments and agencies of the city, state and national government which may be effected. He is responsible for planning whatever liaison is established.

PRESTRIKE CONFERENCE WITH PARTIES

The designated officer will contact and confer with both sides before there is an open conflict. This call, made prior to the time of the dispute, is at a time when pressure is not on either party. Such meetings are not concerned with anything save public order, and that tenor should immediately be set by the police official. Meetings should be held separately with each party but each should know the other has been contacted.

The police must explain the function of the police and the policy of the department—the methods of maintaining law and order— protection of life and property—and the protection of civil rights in the public interest make it clear that it is not the function of the police to establish a strike zone nor to limit the number of pickets. All parties must be made aware of the promptness and vigor with which indicated police action will be taken. They must be made to realize that police interference in a strike process is limited to the control of conditions which constitute violations of the law and interfere with the peaceful pursuits of the community.

Ground Rules

Experience shows that if all parties concerned know exactly what is going to happen on the street at the scene of a strike, there is little likelihood of misunderstanding which might lead to trouble. The parties must be warned that the following ground rules apply:

1. That force or violence will not be tolerated.
2. That the law will be enforced with strict impartiality.
3. That the rights of the public using the streets and sidewalk will be protected.

4. That unlawful conditions or acts which lead to disorder will not be tolerated.
5. That the employment of professional bullies and thugs will not be sanctioned.
6. That activities of professional agitators will not be allowed.
7. That no parties to the dispute may use language or manner of address which is offensive to public decency or may provoke violence.
8. That the rights of striking employees to conduct orderly picketing will be fully protected in accordance with the circumstances and conditions existing at the location.
9. That the number of pickets to be permitted should be established and adhered to.
10. That striking employees may picket in the vicinity or in front of the place of employment to
    a. Persuade those still employed to strike.
    b. Persuade those considering employment not to do so.
    c. Inform customers about the labor dispute.

The pertinent law should be pointed out. The police should solicit the cooperation of all parties in maintaining peace. If possible, agreement should be reached on the methods to be used. Should these methods be contrary to the public interest, the persons are so informed. Discuss and establish the ground rules and let the parties themselves enforce the laws at the scene. It is also desirable that the parties to these agreements by also the ones who enforce the law at the scene of the dispute.

Even more important is the establishment of mutual trust, for experience shows that the one thing that determines which will prevail, peace and tranquility, or strife and turmoil, during a labor dispute, is distrust by all parties concerned. Management does not trust labor—labor does not trust management—and neither trust the police.

Coordination

Arrangements should be made for maintenance of close relations during the disturbance. The union, management and the police should designate definite individuals who will be responsible for keeping the others advised and for receiving communications. In a large organization with a formal security force, the director or manager of security will usually represent the employer on this matter. The strike committee chairman or chief picket captain can act for the union.

PREPARATION

The police must prepare for a strike long before it begins. It has proved beneficial to assign to an officer or section the responsibility for handling all labor problems. His responsibility is to develop and maintain liaison with labor and management prior to any conflict. He must impress both with their positive duties: first, to act in a manner that avoids the kind of situation which converts a strike into a battle and secondly, to cooperate with public enforcement authorities who must actually police the public aspects of the dispute.

Such close relations will not be established by a mere casual visit. On the contrary, the designated labor officer should attend as many business and social functions as he can, and get to know the people involved, because by understanding the labor movement, its goals and motives, he, in law enforcement, can do a better job.

PLAN

Manpower

There must be established a specific chain of command with particular officers assigned to perform designated duties and with well defined authority. The plan must further provide for necessary manpower for all emergencies.

Routes

Whenever possible, management should be persuaded to limit the number of entrances to the struck premises, thus minimizing the points of contact which generate disorder, and further allow the police to concentrate their forces at these few key points. In selecting routes and access points to premises within several police jurisdictions (a plant cut by county or city lines, for example), preference should be given to the route through the jurisdiction with the largest force as it is better able to meet the great manpower demands of such disturbance.

Logistics

For a large police group it will be helpful to consider a self-contained supply system. This would include storage facilities for personal gear such as rainwear, and also canteen vehicles, communications vehicles, mobile command post and, if not otherwise readily available, temporary sanitary facilities.

Toilet Facilities

Arrangements should be made for toilet facilities away from company premises.

Command Post

If a large force is used, arrangements for a command post in the immediate vicinity should be made. It should never be located on or within the facilities of the parties involved.

Communication

Because the employer will have regular names and designators for gates, lots, roads and other interior locations, known to the striking workers as well, police should be given a detailed map or plan of the premises in which all such data are set forth. Police commands and orders can then use the same language and the risk of error or misunderstanding be lessened. If the employer has a security organization, the strike deployment can also be indicated so that the police commander knows where all enforcement resources are located.

Log

The police log should contain a complete record of the entire action. All arrests, incidents and matters of special interest should be recorded. In addition to showing police action, a periodic check of the number of pickets on each gate should be entered on the strike log. This indicates trends in union strategy, and assists in planning for future utilization of strike personnel. The time for picket counts will be designated by the Strike Commander, and the count on each gate will then be relayed to the command post for entry on the log.

Training

Special attention should be given in police training to the unique problems of labor relations. This should include a knowledge of the rights and interests of both parties to such disputes, the duty of law enforcement, the problems and methods to be employed. Much can be learned from films of other labor disturbances in the same community. The sight of other police officers in action will convey more of the chaotic, fast-paced strike action and the pressures it produces than mere discussion would. It will also portray the manner in which typical strike connected violence is perpetrated.

CRITICAL PERIODS

Certain critical periods exist in any strike situation. The first few days are critical periods. At this time the tone of the strike is not determined, and the labor and management strategy, and the number of pickets to be utilized, is not known. At the very offset both labor and management will endeavor to use the police for their best interests in carrying out their objectives.

It is also during this period that drinking may occur at the scene. Union officials and management will quickly assess the type of enforcement that is exhibited at the scene. If they feel that the police are unbiased and intend to maintain law and order, there will be little or no trouble. By the same token, if they recognize that the police department is biased, and not too sure of itself and its duties, it only follows that an attempt will be made to take advantage of this apparent weakness.

Each succeeding Monday is a critical period, as usually a show of strength is made at this time. The second Monday is more critical, due to failure of strikers to receive their usual pay checks. One of the most critical periods arises when some strikers start back to work, as this often develops into physical clashes between strike-breakers and persons on the picket line.

PICKETING

Whenever a union calls a strike, it is the normal procedure to establish pickets or a picket line outside of the struck facility. Picketing is patrolling by union members or sympathizers near an employer's place of business to publicize the existence of a labor dispute, to persuade workers to join the work stoppage, and to discourage customers from buying or using the employer's goods or services. The purpose of its establishment is to advertise and publicize their dispute with the employer.

The right to picket peacefully and truthfully is one of organized labor's lawful means of advertising its grievances to the public, and, as such, is guaranteed by the Constitution as an incident of freedom of speech. Thus, peaceful picketing is permitted during either the daytime or nighttime. It is the duty of law enforcement to protect the rights of pickets to establish picket lines and to uphold their right to picket legally.

Illegal Picketing

The constitutional guarantee of freedom of speech extends no further than to confer upon workmen the right to publicize the facts of an industrial controversy by peaceful and truthful means. In case of resort to acts of violence, physical intimidation, use of threats, force, or false statement, picketing loses its character as an appeal to reason and becomes a weapon of illegal coercion. Picketing becomes illegal if it blocks streets and roads or interferes with the free and immediate use of the sidewalk or with ingress and egress to any place of business.

Placards

Placards of any size may be carried while picketing. The use of placards in labor disputes in congested areas where pedestrian traffic is heavy, such as downtown areas, poses a problem. It is suggested that the union official be made aware of the inconvenience to the public. The usual practice is to call on the concerned union and request that sandwich-type signs (the width of the body) be used. If it is alleged that placards or banners are of a defamatory nature, redress is in the civil courts.

RELATIONS WITH PICKET CAPTAINS

When a strike develops and a picket line is established, picket captains are selected by the union to supervise the activities of pickets. Normally, a picket captain will be in charge of a group picketing a given gate or location. Picket captains are usually responsible persons, selected for leadership and their ability to supervise people. In most cases, they are willing to work with law enforcement officers at the location of a strike. The police commander should contact each picket captain and make himself known, and explain what is expected from the picket captain and the pickets and also explain what the picket captain can expect from the officers detailed to that particular location.

Many persons on a picket line for the first time make the assertion to the police that it is "illegal to cross a picket line to go to work." These persons are quick to accuse the police of strike-breaking when a demand is made for police protection to enter a struck plant. These misunderstandings can be mitigated, by obtaining the assistance of union officials in explaining the law to their followers.

The police should seek a common agreement regarding the methods to be used by the union. Should the methods planned be contrary to the public interest, the union official should be informed.

Each officer assigned should attempt to establish good relations with the picket captain and yet avoid fraternization. Officers assigned to a particular location should advise the picket captain that he will be held responsible for the activities of those under his supervision. If an incident arises, or it is apparent that a dangerous situation may arise, the matter should be discussed with the picket captain and he should be encouraged to handle the problem if at all possible. In many cases, this will eliminate the need for the intervention of law enforcement in order to handle the situation.

Instructions are given to the pickets most effectively when given through their picket captain. Thus, whenever possible, the police should ask him to give any instructions needed. Knowing the picket captain will also aid the officer in many other difficult situations. If the lines have to be crossed to speak to management, the beat officer can inform the picket captain of his intentions and also speak to him on the way out. By doing this, much ill feeling on the part of the pickets can be eliminated.

DEPLOYMENT

The deployment of officers at the scene of a strike of disturbance depends upon the particular situation. If no attempt is made to operate a facility or engage new employees there is little likelihood of any difficulty. While this occurs quite often, it is not always the case. The problem is primarily with the facility that does operate under strike conditions and does attempt to engage new employees.

If the preplanning was properly done, the police will know when the strike is to begin, how many people will be involved, what the perimeter is, where the likely skirmish points are located. Means of access to the struck premises will be reduced to the fewest, and all unnecessary vehicle and pedestrian traffic will be curtailed. All these steps will permit concentration of police resources at the trouble spots. But at the same time, this concentration will amplify violence potential at the key points. Thus, the decision on strength of police commitment is extremely important. Particularly during the crucial period, strength must be sufficient to meet all demands. A force large enough to sustain the first wave of possible violence should be mounted and maintained until the character of the strike becomes clear. If the size of the original force clearly settles the issue of enforcement capability, the pattern of the subsequent days will more likely be peaceful, and "on-line" personnel can be progressively reduced.

Gates normally used by workmen to enter and leave a plant should be given the most attention. Particularly, the beginning and closing of the workday is extremely important at these gates. Parking lots are also a potential hazard. All gates must be covered with adequate personnel, and each gate or post must be assigned a number. A chart of the effected area should be maintained at the command post and assignments and deployment of police units shown.

A schedule of shift changes must be kept at the strike command post and full personnel strength, less reserve, must be placed on the post at shift changes. If potentially dangerous locations are observed, the strength must be increased at these particular posts.

Muster Time

If a strike is effective at midnight at an enterprise whose normal day shift begins at seven-thirty A.M., striking day workers will probably start arriving at or a little before the time they would normally report to work. If the day population is the biggest at that enterprise, the violence potential will be serious beginning at about seven in the morning. In this type situation the pickets who first report at midnight are generally a token force and the situation can usually be controlled by personnel normally available or in reserve for that police tour. But the major resources must be "on the line" in time to meet the major threat in the morning. This should include time to assemble, form, hear orders, draw equipment and redeploy to post.

Motorized Equipment

Motorcycle patrol in both directions on public streets bordering the struck premises tends to keep the street open and to discourage the blocking of cars. The noise and speed of the machine as well as the immediate presence of the officer on it have a restraining effect. Thus, two motorcycles may effectively do what a dozen or more "point" assignments would not.

Relief

Periodic relief must be established for each man assigned to a post. A reserve must be maintained in order to re-enforce the man assigned on post in event of serious trouble. The reserve must only be committed as a last resort.

BRIEFING

Prior to being assigned to duty at the scene of a labor disturbance, the police should be briefed as fully as possible on the parties involved, their past relations, the issues, the area involved, the boundaries, the history of this dispute, the current situation and anticipated developments. The briefing should stress the impartial attitude that police must maintain and point out dangerous pitfalls that should be avoided so that the wrong impression will not be created.

OFFICER'S ATTITUDE

At all times the officer must be absolutely impartial and neutral. Impartiality and neutrality are the key to successful performance of police duties at the scene of a labor-management dispute. The police are always placed in the middle. Each officer must realize the position that he represents in any strike situation; that he is in the middle under constant observation by both labor and management. Therefore, it is necessary to maintain an attitude of strict neutrality and impartiality at all times.

How can the officer be impartial and neutral? The first step is to remember that the police are not supporting or opposing the strike. The officer's purpose in being at the scene of a labor-management dispute is to protect life and property and preserve the peace.

To assure that the police maintain that attitude, they should never under any circumstances talk over the merits of the strike with anybody. They have no reason to discuss the merits of the strike. By so doing, it will give the disputants a reason to believe the police are taking sides. Most important, if they are drawn into an argument, they may henceforth mentally associate with the side they defended in their discussion.

Next, they must never try to give the impression, by their actions, that they favor either side, for action speaks louder than words. This is not as simple as it may appear as there are innumerable small things that will give the impression of a lack of impartiality.

Some of these outward indications of sympathy, such as smirks, gestures or wearing a campaign button on the uniform, are apparent as is the resentment they will generate. Others are more subtle, but equally harmful. Some of these are the following:

1. Giving instructions to the disputant about injunctions.
2. Parking on property where dispute is in progress.
3. Receiving of gifts of gratuities, such as coffee, doughnuts and sandwiches, from either labor or management.
4. Eating either with union or management personnel.
5. Drinking coffee or eating in restaurant where disputants also gather.
6. Allowing plant guards to assist the police on public property.
7. Fraternizing with either pickets or company guards.
8. Acting immediately after speaking to a disputant or taking a complaint of some sort, thereby giving the impression you are taking direct orders from the disputant.
9. Leading persons with police vehicles when asked for directions.

The officer will be the center of attraction and must, therefore, act in the manner expected of a policeman. He must not only be, but must also appear to be, alert at all times when on duty. He must conduct himself in a judicious, calm manner, for excitement is contagious. When orders are given, he must obey and execute them with snap, confidence and precision. He must be firm and impersonal in his actions, rather than indifferent. When it is necessary to take any action that might be misinterpreted as favoritism, it is wise to explain fully why the action is necessary.

CONDUCT AT THE SCENE

Methods of Visiting and Observing the Picket Line

The number of visits per watch will be determined by the commander who will be guided by the size of the picket line and the probability of disturbances.

How should such visit and observation be made? Usually the beat officer can make his observation from across the street or a short distance away from the pickets themselves. Such a position offers several advantages. Standing next to the pickets prevents the officer from seeing the overall picture. From a distance, the officer will be better able to pick out the agitators circulating in the crowd. Likewise, remaining in the background, the police department is not likely to become the center of controversy. The officer standing close to or alongside the picket line will attract the attention of the general public. Standing a distance away and observing lessens the opportunity for the officer to become involved in unnecessary conversations. This does not mean that the officer should not converse with the pickets on occasion if necessary. It will often be of great advantage to know the pickets. Indeed, when visiting the picket line, at predetermined times, the beat officer should make it a point to talk to the picket captain. Sometimes an occasional chat with a picket is advantageous, of course, this should never be overdone. This will lessen the tension and the pickets will become aware that the officer patrols his beat and makes periodic checks. In this manner, the pickets are not aroused when the officer appears each time.

Certain other precautions should also be taken. Thus, the police should never show up at the picket line in force at any time to obtain information. One person can do this easily. Showing up in force creates excitement. Nor should the police drive onto or park on the property of the employer. Rather, police cars should be parked on the public street away from the point of friction and the police should walk to the scene.

Conversations with Participants

There are not any set rules to follow when speaking to the disputants. The officer must use discretion and common sense. To
guide him in this, there are certain suggestions of conduct that have in
the past proved effective.

The officer's conversation with members of either faction involved
in the dispute should be limited primarily to the picket line captain
and the ranking company official. When officers engage in conversation with pickets, or persons representing management, the other
parties present will not know what they are talking about but will
wonder what is being said, even though it may be a casual remark
about the weather, and may get the wrong impression. A professional
agitator in the crowd could seize upon this act to shout "See there,
the police are against us." The risk is even more pronounced if the
officer engages in conversation with friends or neighbors who may
happen to be on one side or the other. Thus, conversations are best
kept at a minimum to prevent giving the impression of, or giving
rise to any claims of, bias by either side.

Care must also be used to avoid confusion, therefore, speak slowly
and firmly so your words will not be misunderstood or misconstrued.
Most of all, maintain self-control when arresting labor or management
representatives.

Duty at Scene

At a strike location, the duties of officers are the same as in any
other situation requiring police attention. It is their duty to see that
persons have the right to enter and leave at will, if they so desire.
It is also their duty to see that strikers have the right to picket the
plant in a legal manner. The only purpose for which officers are
detailed to a strike scene is to maintain the peace. The issues of the
strike are of no concern to the officers.

Although the police do not have legal authority to establish a strike
zone, they should enlist the aid of the union in restricting the operations of the picket in order not to block sidewalks unduly. Picketing
strikers should be kept on the move. They should not be permitted to
collect in standing crowds or remain loitering on the sidewalks, streets,

or any other public place and should not be permitted to picket in a manner that would block any entrance being used, hindering or impeding passage of pedestrians or vehicles.

Many cases of strike violence have been initiated by nonstrikers. Therefore, the fewer persons present at the strike scene, the less chance of group action. Keeping the general public away from the strike scene prevents trouble and allows working room for the police when and if violence should break out.

Giving Commands

When giving commands to the disputants, follow the chain of command, i.e., place responsibility by issuing commands to either the picket line captain or the ranking company official. Union pickets and management representatives expect their orders to come from those in immediate charge of them, and are not as resentful in receiving orders from those sources as they would be from a policeman.

MASS PICKETING PROBLEMS

When a strike develops, the union encourages a full turnout of striking personnel to be present at the strike location. This then becomes a crowd control problem for law enforcement. In some cases, the union might encourage mass picketing in front of personnel gates in order to keep these gates closed to those persons desiring to use them. It is the responsibility of the police commander to have his personnel deployed prior to this buildup. The officers detailed must keep the gates from becoming jammed and must keep an open passageway for those persons desiring to move in or out of the plant.

Officers must also observe closely the strategy in the picket line. Orders are passed through the line in whispers, and the picket line may move slowly and surreptitiously closer to the gate. Officers must keep pickets moving. Under no condition, must they allow the gate to become closed. Officers must move the pickets back before the passageway becomes jammed. It is difficult to disperse the crowd once a gate is closed, and an attempt to reopen the entrance may lead to a clash between the pickets and officers.

Another problem of mass picketing is the traffic hazard caused by a crowd overflowing into the street. The officers must keep these people as close to the curbing as possible so a traffic hazard will not be created, and pickets will not be injured by passing vehicles.

HANDLING MOVEMENT THROUGH PICKET LINE

One of the principal causes of trouble at a strike scene is the movement of pedestrians and motor vehicles. For this reason, at the very offset of the dispute, the parties must be informed of their rights and the legal limitations on their action. The pickets must realize that all persons and vehicles have the right to enter and leave at will. It is the duty of officers to see that persons have the opportunity to enter and leave the plant, and to keep the peace when this is done.

The suggested method is to allow a person—the union official or his delegate—to talk to the vehicle driver. This talk should occur in the presence of an officer. Pickets should have the right to present their case to the truck driver—that they are on strike and have established a picket line. They should be allowed a reasonable time to present their case so the driver may make his decision. If advice is requested from the officer at the location, he must be careful to notify the driver that he may stay out, or enter the plant. Preferably, this should be done in the presence of the picket captain. Under no circumstances should the officer advise the driver to enter the plant. The driver must make his own decision whether or not to enter the plant. If the driver has decided to enter the plant, it should be made clear that upon his leaving the premises, a convoy will not be provided for him. In order to avoid creating a traffic hazard, care should be taken that vehicles are not stopped in the street. Arrangements should be made for the vehicle to park so the normal flow of traffic will not be interrupted.

If the driver decides to enter, the picket captain should be asked to clear his pickets from the path so that the vehicle may enter. The pickets should be allowed adequate time to disburse. If the persons still refuse to move, labor leaders and possibly the Central Labor Council should be contacted and told of the problems and asked to alleviate it so that police action is not necessary. If the picket captain fails to comply with the request, or the pickets do not respond to his orders, the officers should open the line without hesitation and allow the movement of persons or vehicles. The line should be broken only temporarily. When broken, sufficient clearance should be made to allow for safe passage.

When picket lines are opened by officers, the officers should face the pickets rather than the persons or vehicles entering the gate. This action affords the officers the opportunity to observe the actions of the pickets and prevents the possibility of assault being committed, or damage being done to vehicles entering the plants. This affords an opportunity also for the officers to identify any pickets who might commit a crime.

If the picket line is small, the officer's caution to the group to "watch the cars" will, in most cases, suffice. The use of hand signals by the officer, normal procedure in working traffic, is always interpreted as directing the vehicle to enter struck premises. This should be avoided in most instances.

Trains Entering a Strike Location

One of the most serious problems which faces law enforcement at a strike location is that of trains entering the location. It should be made clear here that railroads are involved in interstate commerce. Therefore, deliveries of materials will be made to a plant and finished products will be removed. In many cases this creates misunderstandings with representatives of labor, as they feel enforcement is being partial to both management and the railroad. In the past, a procedure was developed by the railroad to accomplish this movement of trains.

The railroad representative always notifies the station or commander in advance, and establishes the time the shift will be made. Special agents of the railroad are detailed to the location to assist with the railroad movement. Inasmuch as railway personnel are unionized, they disembark at the location and a supervisory train crew takes over in order to move the cars into the plant.

The commander at this time notifies the picket captain that the train will be moved in, and requests his cooperation in removing the pickets from the railroad tracks. If the pickets refuse to move, the railroad special agent will require the strike commander to remove the pickets. Arrangements should be made beforehand with the special agent to allow the picket captain and pickets time to discuss the entire situation before the special agent requests the officers to remove the strikers. This precludes charges of the union that labor did not have an opportunity to present its case, and that officers are siding with management and the railroads.

In the event it is necessary to remove pickets, officers should be certain that they are removed from the truck only so the train can be moved in. Pickets should not be removed from adjoining railroad property, as this is a problem for the railway special agents.

SPECIAL PROBLEMS

Police officers assigned to a labor-management dispute should be alert and observe unusual acts requiring police action such as the following:

1. Putting sugar in gas tanks.
2. Cutting ignition wires, etc.
3. Breaking into railroad cars.
4. Cutting tires.
5. Threats.
6. One side following members of the other side to their homes and threatening them or members of their family.
7. "Palming" or concealing in the sleeve sharp objects such as can openers which are scraped along the sides of vehicles passing a bunched picket group. Sometimes flat rocks or metal plates are used in the same way to fracture glass windows or headlights.
8. Scattering tacks or sharpened devices on the road or in entrances to provide flat tires. Children's play jacks have been used in this way after the points were filed. Nails have been similarly used after "pretzel folding" in a vise. Often the items will be allowed to slip through a deliberately made trouser pocket hole.
9. Lock-step picketing which presents a continuous barrier and does not permit passage through the line.
10. Falling or lying in front of vehicles or in entrance ways. This is often combined with feigned injuries from an alleged accident.
11. Inciting to riot or encouraging a breach of the peace through specific, inflammatory words, or actions (including placards).

12. Abandoning a motor vehicle or deliberately blocking a thorough-
fare. Frequently a car is driven to or through a gate and then
deliberately stalled. Other vehicles follow and the area is
effectively sealed. A well-prepared enterprise will have equipment on hand at entry gates to move such vehicles. Police
should also consider including a wrecker or similar vehicles in
their "on-site" supplies.
13. Hurling missiles or explosives at the struck premises or non-
striking personnel, or even police.
14. Making, carrying or using unlawful implements such as slingshots, billy clubs, switchblade knives, etc.
15. Assault on nonstriker or police officer from the crowd when the
assaulted person's attention is directed elsewhere.
16. Employment of bullies and thugs.
17. Activities of professional agitators.

Incidents

REPORTING. It is the duty of officers assigned to a strike situation
to keep their supervisors and the command post informed of all incidents and changes in the local situation. The method of reporting
incidents on the strike line is the same as in any other situation. Every
incident that occurs must be reported to the command post and
cleared on the strike log. The same reporting procedure for normal
operation is in effect at this time. Minor disturbances and incidents
reported can be cleared by the usual log entry, such as "kept the
peace," "separated involved parties," etc. The more serious crimes
that occur such as assault and battery, malicious mischief, etc., require
a report. If it is necessary to make an arrest, the usual report will be
submitted.

HANDLING. If an incident arises, or it is apparent that a dangerous
situation may arise, the matter should be discussed with the union
representative, and he should be encouraged to handle the problem.
In many cases this will eliminate the need for the intervention of law
enforcement.

Drinking at a Strike Scene

Drinking and intoxication are common problems at the scene of a strike, particularly the first day or two. Without exception, drinking always leads to trouble when carried on during labor-management disputes. Drinking is usually not condoned by either side at the scene of a labor-management dispute, as drunkenness tends to hamper negotiations and gives the general public an adverse impression of those involved in the dispute. Officers must be observant, not only of those persons on the picket line, but also parking lots and other places where strikers assemble. Cafes and bars in the vicinity of a strike area also present a problem. The strike commander should request the union to police these locations insofar as their own striking personnel are concerned. However, roving patrols should keep these bars and locations under surveillance at all times. Any observations of drinking being done by strikers should be reported to the strike commander immediately.

When an officer observes a person who is drunk, he must take immediate steps for his removal from the area. First, this fact should be referred to the person(s) in charge (labor representative, management representative).

The officials will usually be cooperative and willing to remove a drinking person. When a person is removed from the scene in this manner, it gives emphasis to the fact that the police are not at the scene to harass either side. This practice, if used advantageously, will often tend to reduce emotional situations. If it is apparent that drinking is being condoned by the labor or management representatives, regular arrest procedures should be followed.

ARRESTS

Arrests as a result of incidents on the picket line should be kept to an absolute minimum and should be made only as a last resort. This is true for many reasons. First, because of the emotional setting, the making of an arrest might create an explosive situation. Second, most violations at a strike scene are of an emotional nature, done in a moment of anger and quickly forgotten.

Most alleged misdemeanor offenses that occur at the scene of a labor-management dispute are colored by feelings and emotions, and are all too often exaggerated. Experience has taught that 95 per cent of the misdemeanors that do occur at a strike cannot be successfully prosecuted due to the failure of the complaining party to appear.

Satisfaction seems to have been had when a physical arrest was made. Third, although feelings run high between labor and management during a dispute, as soon as the dispute is settled, both usually end up friends. There then is no longer any desire on the part of the complainant to pursue prosecution. Indeed, the arrest is embarrassing to that friendship, therefore the police become the scapegoat for ill feelings. Because of the nature of the violations and the relationship of the people involved, it often is more practical to handle these incidents by a citation hearing or by the warrant process, rather than by an outright arrest.

This certainly does not mean that no arrests are to be made. If a serious crime has been committed, or an injury has resulted from a battery, an arrest at the scene should be made. If an apprehension is clearly indicated, the speed and certainty with which it is accomplished will do much to deter other persons from disorderly or criminal acts.

Naturally, when possible, the officer should call for assistance before making the arrest in order to protect the officer, and also display a show of force. This cannot always be done because many incidents occur spontaneously, and it is necessary for the officer to make an immediate arrest. However, when possible, the call for assistance should be made prior to the officer's attempting to take the offending person into custody.

Once an arrest is accomplished, it is important that the person or persons arrested be removed from the area immediately. Any delay after an arrest is made may lead to an attempted rescue of the prisoner from the custody of the officer.

Citizens Arrest

Citizens arrests should be discouraged at the scene of a labor-management dispute. However, when an arrest must be made, have the complaining citizen effect the arrest whenever possible. Inform him as to his responsibilities. Make him identify the perpetrator and his or her action.

SUMMARY OF THE DO'S AND DON'TS

Do's

1. Be absolutely impartial and neutral.

2. Limit your conversation primarily to the picket line captain and ranking company official.

    a. Get to know the other disputants and converse with them when you believe it is advantageous.

    b. However, keep conversation to a minimum.

3. Keep the general public away from the dispute, thereby lessening tension.

4. Place responsibility by issuing instructions to either the picket line captain or the ranking company official.

5. Be aware of professional agitators. They will often put the police in a position where they appear to be taking sides.

6. Whenever possible, use the intelligence section to obtain information pertaining to the dispute.

7. Forward all information to the commands primarily concerned with labor disputes.

8. Give verbal instructions when asked directions by a disputant.

9. In handling trucks and automobiles, break the line only temporarily. Make sure of sufficient clearance to allow the auto to pass. Beware of the use of regular hand signals as they give the impression you are directing cars to enter. The best policy is to have the union representative direct his men to clear the entrance. Let the union official, in police presence, talk to the drivers of all trucks. The driver makes his own decision to enter or leave.

10. Union officials should be notified of and given an opportunity to take proper action in the case of the drinking of alcoholic beverages by the pickets.

11. All bars in area should be given special attention.

12. Arrange for periodic relief of police on line.

Don'ts

1. Do not give an impression, by an overt act such as waving, smirks or any gesture, that would make others believe you are biased.

2. Do not become provoked by name-calling or derogatory remarks directed at you.

3. Do not at any time go to the scene of a dispute in numbers

to obtain information, thereby creating restlessness among the disputants and the onlookers.

4. Do not drive on the property of management.
5. Do not under any circumstances talk over the merits of the dispute with anybody.
6. Do not give any advice pertaining to injunctions.
7. Do not discuss an injunction with anyone involved in the dispute. This procedure is civil in nature and should be treated as such. Advise them to contact an attorney for advice.
8. Do not physically assist or escort a disputant where it would give the impression you are taking sides in the dispute.
9. Do not lead a person or vehicle with a police vehicle when asked for directions.
10. Do not drink coffee or eat in establishments that are frequented by the disputants.
11. Do not perform a police task immediately after conversing with a disputant. This gives the impression you are taking orders from him.
12. Do not go on company property unless such action is necessary to enforce the law.
13. Arrange toilet facilities away from company property.
14. Do not accept gifts—donuts and coffee. This gives the impression of partiality.
15. Do not let plant guards assist police on public property.
16. Do not, by outward indications of sympathy such as smirks, gestures or wearing a campaign button on your uniform, cause resentment.

Chapter 29

GENERAL PRINCIPLE OF RIOT CONTROL

INTRODUCTION

Violent and illegal actions which jeopardize lives and property cannot be justified or condoned, whatever may be the objectives or provocations of those engaging in them. Moreover, uncontrolled violence does not solve problems; it only increases bitterness and sows seeds of future disorders. When a riot erupts, the police must be prepared and ready to regain control and maintain law and order.

One of the most succinct but most definitive declarations of strategy is found in the orders issued by General St. Arnaud to his troops during the riots in Paris in 1851:

> Concentrate the troops in masses, care for them, feed them well, keep them from contact with the people, withdraw the too feeble posts, dispense with patrols, allow barricades to be constructed; then, the moment for action being carefully chosen, attack unexpectedly with compact force and crush all resistance.

ERRORS TO AVOID

Before discussing the strategy and tactics of law enforcement, it is well to pause for a moment and consider some of the errors which have been made in the past:

1. Committing an inadequate force to action.
2. Improper placement of police.
3. Improper formation used to meet the particular situation.
4. Failure to maintain reserves.
5. Failure to protect the police flanks with lateral support.
6. Dispersing of forces in response to false diversionary action.
7. Being "suckered" into breaking up formation by mob action.
8. Prematurely disbanding after the mob appears to disperse, only to find that it has reorganized.

PRINCIPLES

In general, the same principles of war which govern the movements and disposition of large armies in the field may be applied in controlling rioting mobs. Each principle is a vital consideration in itself but is related to the other principles. Indeed, depending on the circumstances, they may tend to reinforce one another or to be in conflict. Consequently, the degree of application of any specific principle will vary with the situation.

Principle of the Objective

Every police operation must be directed toward a clearly defined, decisive and attainable objective. The basic objectives of riot control operations are the protection of life and property, the destruction of the mob's organization and the breaking of its will to resist and the restoration of law and order. Police operations must move toward these objectives by the most rapid and direct means. Each intermediate objective must be such that its attainment will most directly, quickly, and economically contribute to the purpose of the operation. The selection of an intermediate objective is based upon consideration of the means available, the enemy and the area of operations.

Principle of the Offensive

Offensive action is necessary to achieve decisive results and to maintain freedom of action. It permits the police commander to exercise initiative and impose his will upon the mob; to set the pace and determine the course of operation; to exploit the mob's weaknesses; to take advantage of rapidly changing situations; and to meet unexpected developments. The defensive may be forced on the police commander, but it should be adopted only as a temporary status for the purpose of economizing forces in an area in which a decisive action has not been concluded or used as a delaying tactic until the offensive can again be regained. Even on the defensive, the commander seeks every opportunity to seize the initiative and achieve decisive results by offensive action.

Principle of Mass

Superior combat power must be concentrated at the critical time and place for a decisive purpose. Superior power results from the effective combining of police strength and equipment so as to be able to apply the maximum measure of force. Correct application of the principle of mass, in conjunction with the other principles of riot control, may permit numerically inferior police forces to achieve desired results.

Principle of Economy of Force

This principle is the corollary of the principle of mass. It does not imply husbanding but rather the measured allocation of available combat power to the primary task as well as secondary tasks such as limited attacks, the defense, deception or even retrograde action in order to insure sufficient combat power at the point of decision.

Principle of Maneuver

Maneuver is an essential ingredient of force. The object of maneuver is to dispose of police force in such a manner as to place the mob at a relative disadvantage and thus achieve results which would otherwise be more costly in men and material. Successful maneuver requires organizational flexibility, administrative support, command and control.

Principle of Unity of Command

The decisive application of necessary force requires unity of command. Unity of command obtains unity of effort by the coordinated action of all police forces toward a common goal. While coordination may be attained by cooperation, it is best achieved by vesting a single commander with the requisite authority.

Principle of Security

Security is essential.

Security is achieved by measures taken to prevent surprise, preserve freedom of action, and deny the mob information of the police force. Since risk is inherent in riots, application of the principle of security does not imply undue caution and the avoidance of calculated risk. Security frequently is enhanced by bold seizure and retention of the initiative which denies to mob the opportunity to interfere.

Principle of Surprise

Surprise can decisively shift the balance of power. By surprise, success out of proportion to the effort expended may be obtained. Surprise is achieved by striking a mob at a time, place, and in a manner for which it is not prepared to react effectively. Factors contributing to gaining surprise include speed, deception, application of unexpected force, effective intelligence, and counterintelligence, to include communication and electronic security, and variations in tactics and methods of operation.

Principle of Simplicity

Simplicity contributes to successful operations. Direct, simple plans and clear, concise orders minimize misunderstanding and confusion. The simplest workable plan is best.

PSYCHOLOGICAL STRATEGY

Law enforcement must tailor its plans to conform to the psychological nature of the situation. It should take into account the various psychological factors which influence the behavior of the rioters. Effective action applied at psychologically propitious places and times is likely to be more effective than indiscriminate application of brute force. In fact, injudicious use of force will more than likely aggravate matters and result in rapid deterioration of law enforcement control.

Indeed the police will encounter circumstances or conditions that require the formulation and use of special measures wholly psychological in nature and intent. For example, countering rumors with facts may become a vital necessity.

Facts can be prepared to dissemination through skillful combinations of words and symbols, valuable tools in communicating ideas. Care must be exercised to see to it that unsubstantial rumors are not spread through the mass news media. Many people who might be willing to believe almost anything will become firmly convinced of the truth of even the wildest rumors if they learn of them through these media of public communication.

Police agencies having staff psychologists or access to psychologists should solicit their aid in preparing such materials. Means of dissemination can include dropping leaflets from aircraft, posting signs, placards and posters in public places or conveyances, radio or public address system announcements, and any other available method. Timing is of particular importance.

Exposure

When it is discovered that professional agitators are attempting to incite a riot, the most effective countermeasure is to expose them. Advance notice should be provided to the public that a "spontaneous" eruption is planned. Then the citizenry will realize that they are dupes of opportunists if they succumb to such intrigue.

As we have seen, many people are suggestible under the influence of the excitement of a mob. They are willing to follow uncritically the lead of a demagogue or even some rabid mob member. Through a program of public education properly conducted in advance, it is possible to plant in the minds of many people suggestions for proper social conduct which will act as deterrents to the suggestions of the mob leader. Also, during the disturbance itself, the law enforcement executive can plant countersuggestions through a public address system and through selected officers stationed among the crowd. These countersuggestions, even if not fully accepted by the mob members, will have the effect of creating wavering and uncertainty.

Psychology likewise plays an important part during the riot. Indeed, the basic tactics which have evolved over the years have a psychological basis.

Consider the spiral of emotional stimulation. In a mob, A stimulates B, B stimulates C, C stimulates D, and so on throughout the mob. In turn, C stimulates B and A, D stimulates C, B and A, etc., in a kind of circular reverberation, thus heightening the overall potential for emotional excitement.

The wise course for law enforcement officers to follow to defeat this process is to break up the mob into ever smaller groups. The shattering of a group limits the degree of reinforcement of the comman excitement. Another reason for splitting the mob into ever smaller groups is that this practice destroys the protective anonymity which the crowd affords. The individual who is thus isolated or shunted off into a very small group is exposed to identification and experiences a hesitancy about engaging in violence, a hesitancy which the cover of the crowd might eliminate.

The show of force is effective for it strikes terror into the hearts of the mob. Terror has no unifying force. Terror scatters; pluck unites. Hence the crowd-sung prestige of bravery, and the crowd-condemned disgrace of fear. Courage is the highest crowd-virtue, because it makes for the crowd's success. Fear is the worst of crowd vices, because it makes for crowd-disintegration. For this reason, any victory of police authority undermines the leadership of the mob and once the leadership has been lost, the leaders are usually unsuccessful in regaining it.

Every organized crowd is jealous of its dignity and honor and is bent upon keeping up appearances. Nothing is more fatal to it than a successful assault upon its prestige. Every crowd, even the casual street mob, clothes the egoistic desires of its members or participants in terms of the loftiest moral motive. No crowd can afford to be laughed at. Crowd men have little sense of humor, certainly none concerning themselves and their crowd-ideas. Any laughter they indulge in is more likely to be directed at those who do not believe with them. On the other hand, the mob, psychologically a coward, will show little respect for an inadequate adversary.

Any victory by the mob makes doubly difficult any subsequent attempts to bring the mob under control. This is why the police must never try to bluff a mob or threaten to do things that they cannot do or enforce. A threat is always antagonizing and may be accepted as a dare. Should the bluff be successfully called, the mob will be encouraged by this obvious display of police weakness to prolong the violence, indeed to become more lawless, more dangerous. For the same reason, the police must not attempt to do more than they can reasonably expect to accomplish with the force available.

The leader of the police must maintain the psychological advantage throughout the operations by firm decisive action as required by the situation. He must never harangue, dare, threaten, or bluff. He must never display hesitancy or weakness. He must pursue each action vigorously and aggressively.

A psychological tactic which has met with considerable success is to set up loud speaker systems on the outskirts of the crowd and direct it from its outermost edges to break up and go home. The blare of the loud speaker and the authoritative tones of command attracts the attention of the members of the mob, turns their attention away from the agitating influence and breaks up the influence of the mob's leaders.

This tactic has proven to be unquestionably helpful in breaking up crowds in an early stage and has been used to penetrate the consciousness of groups that were already well organized. The police should use any device by which they can attract the attention of the individual members of a mob and turn that attention away from the original incident. When the crowd's attention has been focused upon the police and the commands they give, much progress has been made toward the breaking up of a riot.

This method can also be useful to distract the mob's attention and thus divert them. To do this effectively the police should broadcast prepared scripts or music. This not only distracts the mob but helps to jam the mob's internal communication.

Another psychological weapon to use against the crowd is the camera. Cameras which are being used to film the disturbance should be conspicuously displayed. This will bring home to many the realization that they have lost the anonymity that is so important to sustain participation in the mob. For the same reason it is often most effective to direct the action against individuals rather than the entire crowd. One who is singled out for attention is made painfully aware of the fact that he is an individual.

POLICE RESPONSIBILITY

Police responsibility at any disaster is as follows:
1. Preserve the peace-control of the scene.
2. Protection of life and property.
3. Aid and assistance to the citizens and strangers.
4. Prevention and detection of crime.
5. The arrest of violators.

To meet this responsibility the police must do the following:
1. Always have a specific plan of action.
2. Rapidly execute the plan.
3. Be firm in executing the plan.

The police must not experiment with half-way measures. They must not experiment with inadequate facilities. If they do and fail, the mob will be encouraged by the failure of the police and its own success to engage in more violent action. The police must make and execute decisions promptly. Their action must be decisive and must be pursued vigorously and aggressively. Under no circumstances should the police display hesitancy or weakness. Likewise, the police must show discipline, self-control and coordinated action. All of these characteristics are usually absent in mobs. But they are highly respected and their demonstration is impressive to mob members. Naturally, whenever possible the police should capitalize on surprise.

FORCE

Priority of Force

In times of riots the power employed to restore peaceful conditions should have the potential force to quell the disturbance, but the actual force used should leave few scars. The objective of the law enforcement agency whose responsibility it is to bring a civil disturbance under control is to do so by the use of the least stringent means possible. Unnecessary damage and bloodshed must be avoided. If persuasion fails to dissolve a riotous assemblage, then progressively more stringent actions must be taken. In the implementation of this principle, the concept of priority of force has been expanded until it now includes six elements:

1. The presence of specially trained men in a show of force.
2. Ultimatum to crowd to disperse, leave the area and resume normal pursuits, or face arrest.
3. Tactical use of riot formations.
4. Use of chemical agents.
5. Use of selected fire power to render the mob's leadership ineffective.
6. Use of full fire power. Fire power is to be used only where the condition is critical and no alternative is left.

The above priority is normally followed. In a rapidly developing or extremely violent situation, however, one or more of the elements of force may have to be bypassed. The commander at the scene has the authority to determine such action if, in his judgment, it is necessary to the accomplishment of his mission.

Amount of Force

The amount of force that is used to control any particular disorder will have an important bearing on the amount of force that may have to be employed to quell future disorders. We must constantly remember the following:

1. Use only so much force as may be necessary.
2. The unit must not attempt to punish.
3. Private property must be respected.
4. Public property must be protected.
5. Every endeavor must be made to induce rioters to disperse before using special weapons.

The degree of force will be dictated by the stage of development of the mob. It is thus important to distinguish those various stages and the action that should be initiated, for it is vitally important that proper police action be taken in the first few minutes of a disorder.

Initial Stage

This stage is either the initial incident or the time when the individuals are still in the milling process. The crowd is potentially disorderly. The first thing officers should do when arriving at the scene of a police incident is to gain control of the scene, because until this is done, they cannot effectively protect life and property. They will quickly determine the facts and report the following to their commanders:

1. Location of the riot (include full area).
2. Nature of the riot (vandalism, looting, fighting, etc.).
3. Extent of the damage or looting.
4. Cause or origin of the riot.
5. Number of persons participating in the riot.
6. Identification of any groups or individuals participating in the riot.
7. An evaluation of the potential magnitude of the riot.
8. Number of policemen present at the scene.
9. Number of vehicles present at the scene.
10. Manpower needs to suppress the riot.

11. Equipment needs.

12. Possible access routes to the riot cenetr.

They will continue to observe and report, and take immediate action to resolve and isolate the incident and to discourage curiosity seekers.

Remember, these people may have real or fancied troubles, or may be victims of circumstances which are frustrating to them. Although there are incidents of impending violence, it must be remembered that there are others in the crowd who do not condone these things and they, in the absence of provocations by belligerent acts of the police, will often tend to restrain the more excited members of the crowd. Generally, the difference between having a pacified crowd and having a riot is on the slender thread of which side has the greatest patience and forbearance, the police or the crowd.

The commander, on receipt of the warning, should act as follows:

1. Report to area.
2. Inspect. Establish a command post.
3. Order out personnel required.
4. Deploy personnel. Place staging area out of sight. Be organized in view.
5. Set up traffic posts.
6. Order required equipment.
7. Call for leaders of the group to talk to the crowd. Urge peaceful efforts.
8. Call for agitators and activists in crowd to come up front to be seen and heard. Putting them in the spotlight and making them responsible.
9. Use crowd control personnel to single these people out and help them forward.
10. Use cameras to preserve the scene.
11. Isolate the critical area, permitting components to leave and allowing no new joiners. Traffic is one way out of critical area.

Second Stage

This is the stage where the crowd has milled itself into a mob verging on riot. The agitators and activists are inciting action. Voices will be raised in the crowd shouting for action. "Let's get 'em."

"Come on." and similar action comments. At this stage the crowd is losing individual identity and the spirit of universality is obvious.

The police must interfere with the milling and rumor process; the crowd must be dispersed. If dispersal is not accomplished, the crowd stands on the brink of action, needing only a leader who will initiate unlawful action and so demonstrate the general readiness to take such action, the police may still save the situation by spotting potential leaders and picking them off for arrest. The police should take the following action:

1. Make an adequate show of force.
2. Mobilize reserves.
3. Establish a cordon of police around the affected area to keep it isolated.
4. Use loudspeakers and police details to encourage the crowd to break up and leave the area.
5. When persons known to the police are in the crowd, the officer should call on them by name to help control it. This also destroys the feeling of the anonymity in the crowd, and the members feel that they are already identified or identifiable and will be more likely to cooperate. If the members of the crowd are unknown, nominate or point out somebody as a leader to help police. Call on women, people in uniform. Be specific, as a general call for volunteers will not usually work. By this and other procedures the feeling of anonymity can be broken up. It is a fact that when some crowd members are willing to be cooperative, others will follow.
6. Separate spectators on the fringes of the mob from the actual mob members; thus the mob will be kept to a minimum number by making it physically difficult for spectators to get caught up in its emotional vortex.
7. Agitators and activists should be identified. If law enforcement agencies act promptly against these individuals and keep the crowd under control, the collective hesitancy of the group will keep it from developing into a mob. But, let these acts be unopposed, they will so affect the crowd that a state of aggressive tension bordering on mob violence is created. The police should either make the agitator keep quiet or go away,

or deflate him in the eyes of the crowd. He should not be permitted to continue with his inflammatory acts. If he has to be removed, this should be done as quickly as possible before he has had time to rally and unify the crowd behind him.

8. Backed by sufficient force, the officer in charge will direct the mob to disperse.

9. Use appropriate force to disperse the crowd. The core squad will provide sufficient frontal attack to move the crowd back. Use only sufficient force to move the crowd and overcome resistance. Move it, don't fight it.

These people are actually citizens under control of forces beyond them, and when sanity returns they will be unable to explain why they did what they were doing.

Third Stage, Riot

The third stage arrives when the mob is fully formed and has moved into action. The first officers to arrive at the scene must not try to disperse a mob without sufficient help. Their primary duty at this time will be to relay to their commander the following so he can have available information in order to evaluate properly the situation and take the necessary action:

1. Area involved.
2. Background of the area population.
3. Knowledge of events leading up to the disturbance.
4. Ringleaders if possible.
5. Strength and equipment available in the disturbed area. Consider equipment, etc. available to members of the mob as well as to the department.
6. Objective of rioters.

The commander must take immediate action to limit the area of the riot and bring it under control by immediately using all necessary force and tactics.

BASIC TACTICS

The basic tactics to be employed in controlling a mob are the following.

RAPIDLY DISPERSE. If there are no crowds, there will be no mobs and thus no rioting. Mob violence has a tendency to grow, and gather momentum due to its very nature. If the mob is allowed to grow and is not checked at the outset, its strength will increase automatically and it will draw many type of non-affiliated elements to itself.

Dangerous persons and those who are criminally inclined will travel long distances to join a mob. Vengeful teenagers, looking for a fight, perhaps basically even wanting to get into trouble, come on the run. "Professional hate-mongers" grasp the opportunity to have some means finally of expressing their hostility in action. These persons are not likely to be at the initial situation in any numbers; if they were, it would be a matter of chance. They are not likely to know about the situation until it becomes a matter of general public knowledge. This takes a certain amount of time.

The mob, if permitted to operate over a long period of time and to commit acts of violence, becomes bolder, more dangerous and more uncontrollable. To prevent all of this, law enforcement personnel must disperse the rioting at its inception and prior to its organization. The speed with which the gathering can be dispersed is important as it gives the agitators less time in which to organize and infuriate the mob. The less time given the agitators, the easier the problem of control.

PREVENT REGROUPING. When the tactical principle of dispersal has been successfully accomplished, the professional agitators and leaders will attempt to reorganize the mob. It is important, therefore, to prevent further gatherings, thereby eliminating additional policing problems. When the rioters are not permitted to gather, reorganization is impossible.

ARREST OF LEADERS. A mob requires leadership to remain active. It is a known fact that a mob without a leader is seldom a major problem, therefore, agitators should be identified, sought out, isolated and arrested or removed from the scene of the disturbance as soon as possible, preventing such persons from inciting the mob or committing overt acts of violence. The professional agitator normally operates well back in the crowd in a safe place. This agitator uses the indigenous leader to do his "dirty work," remaining comparatively safe himself. These agitators and leaders are normally recognized by their activities within the crowds. This is why it is important to obtain information in reference to the professional agitators who might be difficult to recognize.

Chapter 30

DEFENSIVE TACTICS

BLOCKADE

A MOB WILL AT TIMES have a specific target, such as a public building, a key utility, or a business district. Initial police action in quelling such a riot will consist of blocking the mob at a point short of its objective. Blocking is accomplished through the rapid positioning of personnel and barricades. In this way the mob will be forced to attack to accomplish its destructive purpose. Further, the frustration of the mob's movement toward a goal itself aids in the dispersal and eventual disintegration of the mob. Such a maneuver has the following advantages:

1. Impedes the continous forward movement of the mob.
2. Limits mob potential.
3. Direct confrontation with mob leaders which will normally handicap mob leadership.
4. Does not require any complex operational procedures. It is a simple tactic to place in operation.
5. Has a positive effect upon the mob, indicates police readiness.

At the same time the following disadvantages must be considered:

1. It is sometimes difficult to identify and locate the forward movement of the mob.
2. It is also dependent upon the speed of the advancing mob, a factor which is difficult to ascertain at times.

Previous experience indicates that the business streets in densely populated areas are most susceptible to riots. Because of the nature of such a street, it is highly vulnerable to looting and vandalism. Accordingly, police efforts must be focused on this street to effectively control and contain the mob. However, it must also be remembered that riotous activity may occur in residential and recreational areas. It is for this reason that in the accompanying illustrations a business street is designated as the primary street and is used as the focal point

[395]

in the illustrations. Certain definitions are in order to fully explain the tactics and illustrations. They are as follows:

PRIMARY STREET is that street where the riot is occurring. This street will normally be the street where business establishments are concentrated. In addition where more than one street is involved, the primary street will be that street which is most vulnerable to vandalism and looting and consequently the street in which police activity shall be focused.

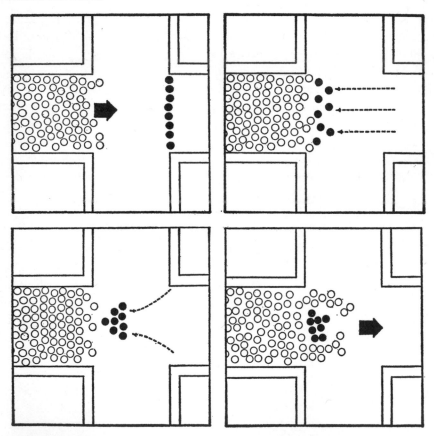

The above charts depict a frontal assault upon police units which are attempting to block a mob. The basic mistake in this example is the advance of the police from their relatively secure position in A into the intersection when their strength is inadequate to control a numerically superior mob. Once in the open the mob will engage each officer while others swarm around the police and render them useless to prevent the movement on to the mob's objective.

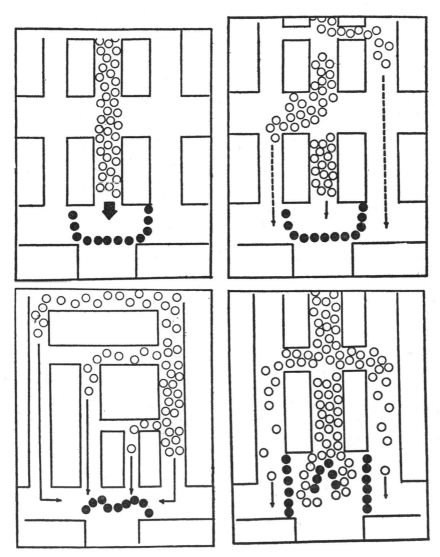

The above illustrations depict the tactics utilized by a mob to outflank a police blockade by breaking up into various groups which converge on the police on a broad front in order to force the police to spread their units too thin and allow the mob to encircle and bypass the police blockade.

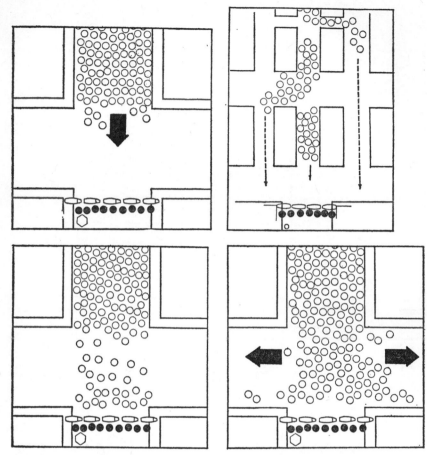

The above illustrations depict suggested tactics to be employed by the police when the mob attempts a direct frontal assault. Rather than advancing into the intersection or engaging in offensive action at a time when they lack sufficient manpower to repulse the mob, the police establish a defensive line. Vehicles are placed in barricade fashion behind the building line. The police take their position behind the vehicles. The mob will then be dissipated along the intersecting street, because of the pressure from its rear.

SECONDARY STREET is the street, other than the primary street, in which rioting occurs. This street may be an intersecting street, or in the case of multiple streets (such as center city) may be parallel to the primary street.

The basic tactic involves establishing a "blockade" at a given point in front of an advancing mob by utilizing patrol vehicles parked in barricade fashion behind the intersection at that given point. By establishing this blockage, mob movement is stifled and potential mob damage is limited. This direct confrontation with the blockade precludes the rioters from gaining momentum as they advance. The obvious show of police strength and organization will have a positive effect upon rioters. When coupled with a police formation pursuing from behind, this tactic should facilitate dispersal along intersecting streets. When a mob, moving in a given direction, meets a real obstacle, confusion results. If egress is available to the confused mob, many participants will disperse. The police formation advancing from behind will "mousetrap" the mob and effect dispersal.

The effectiveness of the blockade tactic is dependent upon the rapidity with which it can be activated and the choice of the locations where it is established. The location chosen as the blockade point must be made by the ranking supervisor at the scene. The intersecting street at the blockade point, used for dispersal purposes, should not be of a business nature which will further increase riotous activity.

Stages

The blockade operation can be divided into the following five stages of operation: initial incident; assembly and formation; confrontation; dispersal; and area security.

INITIAL INCIDENT. In the first stage, the initial incident, the ranking supervisor at the scene should do the following:

1. Notify the radio room of the nature of the incident. In particular, attention must be given to the size and speed of the mob and direction in which it is advancing.
2. Establish and maintain communication (both radio and telephone) at the scene.
3. Ascertain location where a blockade formation shall be assembled. This location shall be sufficiently in advance of the mob to permit police vehicles to assemble in adequate strength to meet mob activity. Caution must be exercised in order that the location selected is not where two business streets intersect, which would only increase mob activity.
4. Ascertain location where the riot control formation shall be

assembled. Normally the riot control formation shall be assembled on the primary street behind the advancing mob.

5. Supervise police activity at the riot center.

ASSEMBLY AND FORMATION. Upon being notified by the ranking supervisor at the scene, police radio should do the following:

1. Deploy vehicles to proceed to the blockade location. Radio should designate access routes to arrive at that location. Vehicles should proceed on streets parallel to the primary streets rather than on intersecting streets which may impede mob dispersal.

2. Designate a supervisor to proceed to the blockade location who shall arrange the blockade.

3. Deploy vehicles and other equipment to the location where the riot control formation will be assembled.

The supervisor at the blockade formation should do the following:

1. Arrange vehicles in formation in back of the building line behind the selected intersection. The vehicles should be placed in a line across the width of the primary street. To strengthen the blockade formation, additional vehicles shall be placed at both ends and the center of the formation.

2. Establish and maintain a communication post.

3. All police personnel should be placed in back of the vehicles.

4. Assemble vehicles and personnel to protect the rear of the blockade formation.

The supervisor at the location of the riot control formation should do the following:

1. Muster personnel and equipment.

2. Form the riot control formation.

3. Establish and maintain communications.

CONFRONTATION. Ranking supervisor at blockade location should do the following:

1. When vehicles have been placed across the primary street, behind the building lines of the intersecting street, ensure that all police personnel are deployed behind the blockade.

2. Except if sufficient force has been assembled to handle the mob, take no offensive action at this stage; engage in tactics of a defensive nature when confronting the mob.

3. Ensure that the rear of the blockade formation is protected.

The ranking supervisor of riot control formation should do the following:

1. When sufficient strength has been assembled, lead riot control formation toward mob and continue pursuit until the mob has dispersed.
2. Secure street areas and intersections as they are cleared.

DISPERSAL. At this stage, the blockade formation will impede the riotous mob from advancing on the primary street. The riot control formation actively engages in pursuing the mob. The mob will be forced to disperse along the intersecting streets. The ranking officers must ensure that each area is secured as it is cleared. Sufficient patrol coverage must be deployed to ensure that law and order are maintained in the area.

When dispersing mob, caution must be exercised that the mob does not encircle the blockade point. Accordingly, patrol vehicles must be assigned to intersections parallel to the blockade point to prevent the mob from entering the parallel street.

AREA SECURITY. The ranking supervisor at the scene must establish area security when the mob has been dispersed. The blockade formation may be removed when it is evident that the mob has dispersed and the area is under effective control. Patrol car assignments, both fixed and mobile, should be established along the perimeter of the riot zone as conditions warrant.

ISOLATION OF THE RIOT AREA

Once a crowd has become a mob, the police should act to confine the disorder by setting up road blocks around a large perimeter diverting all unauthorized traffic from the area. The immediate area of the disturbance should then be blocked off permitting no vehicles and only authorized personnel to enter. Persons wishing to leave should be allowed to do so. Public transit authorities should be promptly notified of detours. It may be necessary to request the radio and TV stations to broadcast warnings to the public to avoid the area. Residents within the area should be ordered to stay in their homes. The isolating measure is critical in preventing further growth of the disorder and the possible development of tumultuous conditions beyond the control of the police. People not yet involved in the disorder must be prevented access to the affected area.

Containment must never materialize as the sole effort to deal with a riot. It is purely defensive and must be recognized as a temporary measure. Nor is this maneuver to be given priority over the move to suppress the riot or disorder itself. Action should be taken in conjunction with the advance with force into the affected area. The important thing for the police commander is not to overlook or downgrade this action. It prevents reinforcements from reaching the rioters, and prevents the rioters from escaping into another area of possible operations.

As efforts to contain or disperse a mob by encircling it with widely dispersed forces may invite attack and may result in a loss of control, troops should be deployed in compact units of sufficient strength to insure the completion of their mission.

Perimeters

For the most effective isolation, two lines should be established. They are the following:

INNER PERIMETER is the police line that surrounds and isolates the critical area, which includes:

1. *Riot center,* that is, the focal point of the riot; that point where the riot originated or where the riotous activity is centered.
2. *Riot zone,* that is the immediate are around the riot center where the likelihood or potentiality of riotous activity or disorder is high.

This inner police cordon should isolate or "freeze" the critical area. By means of a police cordon, individuals are permitted to escape from the crowd. When people are allowed to leave, they are freed from the excitement of the mob.

It should be stressed, however, that when persons are permitted to leave the scene of a mob action, they should be required to do so as individuals and not as groups. If large groups are permitted to leave the scene together, the nucleus of disorder in other areas is provided.

No vehicles and only authorized personnel are permitted within this zone. The strategy here is to prevent the curious from joining the disorderly and thereby contain the existing situation. Keeping them out of the area means that the mob spirit will not be able to possess them.

OUTER PERIMETER. The outer blockade or perimeter may be defined as being that blockade which encircles the inner blockade at a safe distance from the disaster. Enclosed within it is the riot control area, the larger geographical area surrounding the riot zone which is susceptible to riotous activity or civil disorder.

The special zone between the inner and outer blockade is the isolation zone and should be considerably larger than the critical area as its purpose is to provide a place where responding personnel and equipment may assemble and maneuver in preparation for whatever tactical movement or assaults may be required. Also it is the area within which the various operational units will be established, such as temporary headquarters, temporary morgue, press center, parking areas, etc. The perimeter line should be set up at corners of streets from building line to building line as this minimizes the need for barriers and, in addition, persons and vehicles may be dispersed in several directions.

Insofar as possible, only one well-policed entrance or check point should be allowed in the line where the connecting route intersects the line. If necessary, a second entrance through the line may be maintained on the opposite side of the perimeter to facilitate the entry of emergency personnel and equipment. Personnel and equipment arriving at the entrance check point will be directed to the parking area, staging area, or other special location.

Members maintaining police lines will exclude unauthorized persons, and will direct authorized personnel and equipment to the entrance check point. However, emergency personnel and equipment shall not be delayed or rerouted. Emergency personnel and equipment shall be allowed through the lines at any point and directed to the scene. The superior officer assigned to that portion of the lines through which the emergency vehicles pass shall notify the temporary headquarters of the number of personnel and amount and type of equipment that passed through.

Prior to any disaster, a list of those who will be allowed to pass should be established and circulated to the members of the force. The requirements of the situation coupled with the availability of personnel, space and equipment will serve as limiting or modifying factors in the preparation of any plan.

To facilitate ready identification of individuals and to control their circulation in and out of an affected area, a pass system should be established. If restrictions are continued for an extended period of

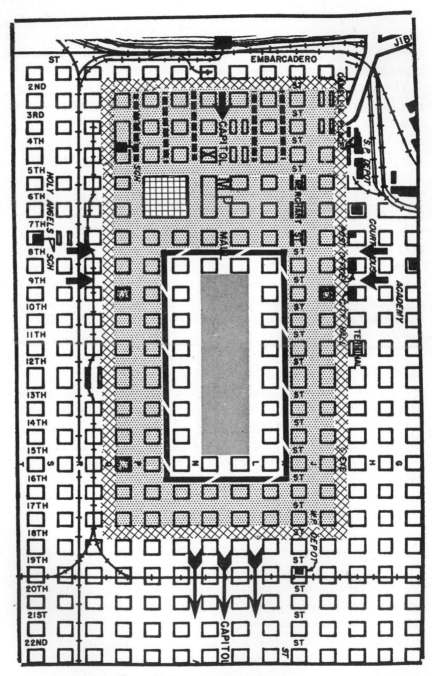

Perimeters and riot zones.

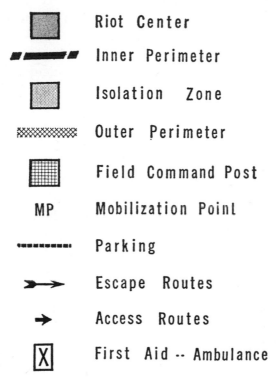

Riot Center

Inner Perimeter

Isolation Zone

Outer Perimeter

Field Command Post

MP   Mobilization Point

Parking

Escape Routes

Access Routes

First Aid -- Ambulance

time, police officials can anticipate the use of counterfeit passes by unauthorized personnel. To counter this possibility, the color of passes can be changed frequently at irregular intervals. The police must check all outbound traffic to halt the transportation of loot and inbound traffic to control the flow of spectators, sympathizers, and arms.

The measures employed to deny ingress to the affected area will vary based on the type of area, terrain, size of the disorder, attitude of the rioters, attitude of individuals in the adjacent areas, and the possibility of other "anti" or "pro" groups attempting to enter the affected area. Good police intelligence, planning and operations will readily provide the police commander with this necessary information. The following steps should be taken to isolate the disaster area:

1. Establish police lines immediately.
2. Remove all unauthorized persons from the area.
3. Allow only authorized personnel to enter the area.
4. Restrict entry into the area to one or two points through police lines.

5. Assign a superior officer at these points to check identity of persons desiring to enter the area.

6. A police coordinator shall keep the superior officer assigned to the check point informed as to the locations of the various phases of the operation so that he may direct authorized persons intelligently to the various locations and prevent their wandering in the area.

7. If there are any locations within the lines where a large number of persons are gathered, i.e., schools, theatres, etc., but where there is no immediate danger, dismissals shall be delayed until arrangements can be made for orderly evacuation.

8. If bars and taverns in the neighborhood are being used as rallying points by crowd members, they should be ordered closed. Stores in the vicinity selling articles that can be thrown or used as weapons should also be requested to close.

9. If it can be anticipated where a mob action will take place, close all businesses in the area and order people to stay inside the buildings. Be sure that liquor stores, bars, gun stores, and hardware stores are closed and protected.

CURFEW

The enactment of an ordinance or law imposing curfew upon the population assists police materially in isolating the affected area. Indeed, recent riots proved that curfew is a must, not only to discourage rioters but to discourage curiosity seekers. Law-abiding citizens of the society not affected by the disorder will normally comply with curfew regulations. Violators of curfew restrictions can be easily apprehended and prosecuted. A show of force in order to enforce a curfew is good, but the use of force is necessary. Once rioting begins, the news of it spreads. This is a signal for unlawful elements and hoodlums to participate. Recently this has meant that by the second night the destruction and looting will be carried on in four or five locations of the city at one time.

The ordinance or law imposing curfew regulations should be specific, and include provisions for the curtailment of the sale of intoxicating beverages, firearms and ammunition, and other sensitive items that could add to the further agitation of the civil disorder. If the disorder extends for a period of time, a pass system may be initiated to identify persons and to control their movements in and out of the affected area.

CONTROL OF SENSITIVE ITEMS

It is desirable to enact laws and ordinances to permit the control of sensitive items during the civil disorder. Sensitive items can be defined as those things that could add to the further agitation of the civil disorder. Examples of sensitive items might include intoxicating beverages and firearms.

BARRIER AND DENIAL OPERATIONS

A barrier is a coordinated series of obstacles designed to canalize or delay movement of an opposing force. Barricades enable setting up of boundaries and clear zones which better enable the police to keep their distance from the mob body and to control movements of the crowd.

The concept of the defense requires fewer personnel to accomplish than the concept of the offense. The execution of the defense through the use of roadblocks and barricades assists the commander in isolating the affected area and preventing further complication of the problem. Roadblocks and barricades help channelize movements of people, block routes, prevent assembly of hostile or agitated crowds, and isolate affected areas.

Police use of manned barricades is only advisable if sufficient forces are on hand or can be quickly called to protect them. Roadblocks and barricades should be manned by trained police observers and the positions must be defensible. Such positions must not be located so as to permit them to be easily surrounded or cut off.

Along a blockade line, the points of greatest stress are the center and at each end. Because these are the weakest points, additional vehicles or barricades should be provided, if possible, at these points. In addition, a point along the barricade line should be provided to permit ingress or egress of police because it may be necessary to move police in or out.

During riots, critical barricades can be manned with special terms or squads that can include radio communication, gas weapons, and fire power capabilities. At these points it is advisable to utilize the double barricade. The double barricade acts as a sifting device since usually only the violent fringe demonstrator will elect to cross it. The first barricade can consist of merely a rope and a sign warning that anyone who passes will be shot. The second barricade is constructed of concertina. At these latter points mounted police and dog teams can be used effectively to prevent penetration.

Construction

Barricades should be strongly constructed and so designed that they are difficult to tip over. They should be of sufficient size to present a real obstacle to persons trying to go over, under, or around. If the barricade does not meet these general requirements, it will have to be backed up by manpower.

Roadblocks and barricades may be constructed from such available materials as trolley cars, buses, trucks, other vehicles, sandbags, earthworks, trees, timbers, wire, or various combinations of such materials. Materials tending to chip, shatter, or splinter can be covered with canvas, to minimize casualties caused by flying fragments.

Road Blocks for Personnel

Concertina wire is considered the best material for the rapid construction of temporary road blocks for personnel. These road blocks should be prepared in advance and carried in a truck or one-ton trailer to the location where they will be employed. Each road block should extend approximately forty to fifty feet; two or more are required for a wide street. A single strand of wire should be stretched across the street seventy-five to one hundred feet in front of the road block. To the wire should be attached a sign warning the people not to approach closer to the road block. At night the sign should be lighted by a lantern or flare.

Police officers defending the position should be protected by sand bag implacements if small arms fire is anticipated. Provisions for lighting approaches to the position during the hours of darkness should be made; however, care should be used to avoid silhouetting the position or officers manning it.

Road Blocks for Trains

Railroads may be blocked by wrapping a heavy chain around one rail with each wrap on top of the others and padlocking the ends of the chain. The chain should be placed sufficiently far from the road block to prevent the train from crashing into the road block when it is derailed. A sign and a sufficient number of warning lights to warn the engineer should be placed in advance of the chain. This method is used when it is undesirable to destroy the roadbed. Obviously if that is of no concern, that method can be utilized.

Motor Vehicles

Road blocks at vehicular approaches must be designed to deny passage to large or high speed vehicles. An effective method is to park several heavy vehicles perpendicular to the curbing at opposite sides of the street at intervals of twenty-five to fifty feet. The "weaving" traverse of this obstacle would accommodate slow moving vehicles, but would prohibit high speed access through it. In addition, the vehicles would provide some measure of protection for the personnel manning the road block.

Realignment of Barriers

Persons crowding against barriers constitute an additional problem. A large crowd may become unruly when its movement is restricted and the area becomes too congested. The member of the force in charge at an area where large crowds are beginning to form must realize the necessity of either dispersing or dividing the crowd into smaller groups before the congestion becomes unmanageable. Barriers may be realigned or an additional police line may be formed far enough away to correct the condition.

If it becomes necessary, because of conditions at the scene, to move the police lines further to the rear, a new line of barriers should be set up in the rear prior to moving crowds back. When the new line is established, the crowds will be directed behind it. The original line of barriers shall not be moved until the crowd has been relocated behind the new line.

PATROLS

Patrolling of the boundaries and points of ingress and egress into the affected area reduces the opportunity for unauthorized individuals to circulate in the area adjacent to the disorder, can prevent assembly of individuals by dispersing individuals who begin to congregate, and can provide the commander with timely information of possible problem areas and movement of the rioters or other groups.

A constant patrol by radio cars and foot patrols on streets adjacent to affected areas is essential. Special "contact" points should be patrolled with constant vigilance, such as main streetcar routes and transfer points.

Persons carrying bundles or packages must be suspect and should be checked out thoroughly. Those carrying sticks, clubs, stones or dangerous articles should be placed under arrest.

Patrol Duties

1. Primary responsibility is the protection of life and property, and the preservation of order.
2. Contain, isolate and disperse.
3. Stand guard at critical points.
4. Prevent entry into critical areas of unauthorized persons.
5. Apprehend violators of every type.
6. Conduct preliminary criminal investigations.
7. Set up anti-looting units.
8. Perform traffic and regulatory duties.
9. Other special services to the public.

Objectives

Patrolling of the boundaries and points of entry into the affected area accomplishes several important objectives. (1) Patrolling reduces the opportunity for unauthorized persons to circulate between the secure area and the affected area. Patrols can normally cope with individuals and small groups composed of two or three persons. (2) Patrols prevent the assembly of people by dispersal of individuals who begin to congregate. (3) Patrols can provide the commander with timely information of possible problem areas, movement of the rioters, and conditions within the respective patrol areas.

Types of Patrols

As the situation dictates, patrols such as motor patrols, foot patrols, water patrols and air patrols may be employed either separately or in combination. When specifically authorized, dog patrols may be utilized to augment appropriate patrols.

Motor Patrols

Motor patrols are valuable because of their ability to cover distance rapidly. Through radio communications, contact with the controlling headquarters can be maintained. Motor patrols can maintain contact with stationary posts that may lack dependable communications. Because of their speed and mobility, motor patrols are able to provide the commander with timely ground reconnaisance. Irregular or frequently changed schedules and routes are important considerations for an effective motor patrol.

In critical areas more than one car should be used in a patrol to increase the security of the patrol. Further, no car should be so used unless it contains at least four men. In this way if the convoy system is used, the cars can be parked and a security guard posted to protect them while the other officers in the convoy form a force of police which can be used to restore order or to apprehend malefactors.

Foot Patrols

Roving foot patrols can be employed effectively in some areas for detailed reconnaissance and where population movement is heavy. Roving foot patrols may be used to cope with possible outbreaks on the flanks and rear of the main operating force. Foot patrols are considered effective in narrow areas where vehicles might be blocked. Patrols of this type are limited in the effective range of operations. When foot patrols are used to seal a disturbed area, adequate communications, equipment, and personnel should be provided. Foot patrols can be coordinated through the use of motor patrols. Such patrols must be capable of defending themselves and coping with limited numbers of disorderly individuals.

Air Patrols

Air patrols perform visual reconnaissance, liaison, photoreconnaissance, riot control agent attacks, escort duties, or resupply operations. In making visual reconnaissance, air patrols report to the commander information concerning mob elements, the condition of roads and bridges, the presence of natural or artificial obstacles, and the location and movement of friendly forces. Air patrols may help in directing troop movements, controlling traffic, and locating mob reassembly sites.

Water Patrols

If riot control operations are conducted near dock, lake, or river areas, the commander may establish water patrols to reduce the threat of attack on his position by waterborne forces. Water patrols may be employed to protect vital ships or waterfront installations, and as a base to launch riot control agents on the rioters.

SECURITY MEASURES AND DEFENSIVE TACTICS

Introduction

POLICE SECURITY MEASURES. In most cases the rioters will outnumber the police. The rear and flanks of the police units will be subject to surprise attack. Police assembly areas will be vulnerable, as will the various supply points, field command headquarters and temporary detention facilities, aid stations and the vital installations. To prevent surprise attack and insure a secure operational and administrative base of operations, these critical areas must be provided with security. Although the security forces will be relatively small, they must be capable of self defense and be equipped with adequate communications.

POLICE UNIT DEFENSE. In many instances, riotous mobs will advance toward police formations according to a preconceived plan that will attempt to render the police ineffective so that the rioters may achieve their goals. These mob plans will vary according to the formation and location of the police formation that the mob encounters. In general, there are several principles involved in meeting mob activity. These include the following points.

1. Never engage in aggressive offensive action against a mob un-

less sufficient police strength is available to achieve the desired goal. When greatly outnumbered, police should engage in defensive or holding tactics until sufficient manpower can be assembled. To accomplish this they must make a stand in a strong defensive position where the best use can be made of their limited forces, taking advantage of terrain, narrow streets and buildings.

2. Always be mindful of protecting the rear and flanks of the police formation. One of the most dangerous aspects when engaging a numerically superior mob is that of being encircled and isolated.

3. Remember the principle of the strategic retreat. When engaging an apparently numerically superior force, a strategic retreat and regrouping at a more advantageous position should be considered rather than taking an obviously futile stand and attempting to contain the mob at a given point.

4. When meeting a mob, the location of the confrontation is important. Engaging the mob in an intersection is more hazardous than at other locations because the larger street area and exposed sides facilitate encirclement by the mob.

The police should engage the mob in the single street layout, either by advancing in front of, or behind, the intersection. Advancing behind the intersection and holding at that location is advantageous because the intersecting street can be used for dispersing the rioters. Intersecting streets should be used for dispersal; attempting to drive the mob back through the same route in which they advanced is extremely difficult.

5. Use vehicles or barricades to block the street from an advancing mob and limit their movement. Policemen should be stationed behind rather than in front of the barricades or vehicles. By establishing such a barricade line, the advancing mob, unless highly disciplined, will dissipate somewhat along the intersecting street because of the pressure from the rear of the mob.

When aggressive mob action can be anticipated, target areas can be made temporarily untenable by dusting the ground or floor area with a thin film of micro-pulverized CN (tear gas) particles from a dust projector. Bulk CN micro-pulverized material can also be used.

Persons entering the contaminated area will by means of movement of feet stir up the talc-fine micro CN particles into the air and make the area untenable to themselves. The area can be easily decontaminated, after being vacated, by washing down with a fire hose.

Chemical foam used in fire fighting can also be used as an effective barricade. Commercial stench compounds such as tertiary butyl mercaptan and dimethylsulfide can also be used with great success with the same technique; but decontamination problems are more difficult, and therefore the suppliers should first be consulted on this aspect.

Planning

Development of the best overall defense plan requires consideration of the following:

1. The mission.
2. The nature of the terrain and the degree to which specific terrain must be held.
3. Relative mobility.
4. The depth of the defensive area.
5. The relative combat power of opposing forces.
6. Reserves available.

Mobile Defense

The mobile defense is the method of defense in which minimum forces are deployed forward to warn of impending attack, canalize the attacking forces into less favorable terrain, and impede, harass, and disorganize them. The bulk of the defending force is employed in vigorous offensive action to destroy the enemy at a decisive time and place. In general, the forward forces employ the principles of the delaying action, while the remainder of the force utilizes the principles of offensive combat. The mobile defense offers an opportunity to destroy or immobilize the attacking force and regain the initiative. Set patterns of action are avoided. The defendant commander must retain freedom of action to choose the decisive time and place to launch his counterblow. This form of defense requires that the defending force have mobility comparable, or superior, to that of the enemy.

Area Defense

This is a defense based on retention of specific terrain. When retention of specific terrain is mandatory, the commander places primary reliance on the ability of fires and forces deployed in position to stop and repulse the attacker. In retaining specific terrain, the commander must use sufficient forces in the forward area to create the necessary combat power on or to dominate the terrain to be defended. The forward area normally has a higher priority for forces than does the reserve. The reserve is employed to block and destroy the enemy, to eliminate penetrations if they occur, or to reinforce threatened areas.

Defense of Critical Installations

During a period of civil disorder, careful consideration must be given to the protection of vital community installations. The destruction of public facilities by a mob can create longlasting adverse effects on the economic and physical well-being of the population and seriously hamper the continuing operation of the community government.

There will seldom be sufficient police forces to furnish individual protection to all affected plants. It may be necessary to divide the disturbed area into sectors and assign part of the forces to each of these sectors. In such a situation the sector commander should place his reserves at a central location, depending on the road net. He should determine the vital points that require continuous protection and detail a detachment at each. The number of such detachments must be kept to a minimum. The success of such a plan will depend on many factors including:

1. The organization at the reserve station of a mobile column. It must be prepared to move to any critical area on a few minutes' notice.
2. The availability of suitable radio, weapons and chemical munitions to give the troops a decided superiority over the rioters.
3. Adequate motor transportation.
4. The organization of a competent intelligence service, which must be able to furnish the military commander with the plans of the rioters in time for the military to take effective countermeasures.
5. A knowledge of the road net of the area, to assure prompt reinforcement of outlying detachments.

When defensive action is necessary, troops organize positions for an all-around defense. No building should be defended from within itself until all its outlying defenses have been forced. The first defense should be outside of and at a considerable distance from the building. The building should be regarded solely as the citadel of the defense, the last refuge of the defenders.

Given the defense of an important building, the defenders should erect and occupy barricades on all possible avenues of approach to the building, and at such distances that neither dynamite nor fire could be used against the building by the rioters; these barricades may be designated the outer line of defense. Defensive points are occupied by skeleton forces, while strong reserves are held mobile within easy supporting distance of such forces. All surrounding buildings that command the fronts and entrances to the building should be simultaneously occupied as a second or interior line of defense. In anticipation of the possibility of both the outer and inner lines of defense being carried, a reserve should be posted within the building with instructions to prepare it for resisting assault and to protect the retreat of the outlying troops if they should be forced to seek refuge in it.

The buildings should be organized as the final position, with the reserve, consisting of the bulk of the troops, placed at the upper windows and on the roof; the lower windows and doors barricaded; and an abundant supply of gas grenades ready to be dropped on the mob from the upper windows.

In preparing a building to resist assault, as many entrances as possible should be closed, and all the outer doors and windows of the basement and first story carefully barricaded with furniture, rolls of carpet, mattresses, piles of books, or any available material. Loopholes should invariably be made so high that the assailants cannot use them from the outside, boxes and chairs being provided to enable the defenders to use them from the inside. Supplies of food, water, means of lighting, and facilities for extinguishing fire should be provided. If the building is accessible from adjoining buildings, the roof should be occupied, and partition walls on each story loopholed. If the situation seems to demand extreme precautions for defense, the stairways should be demolished and ladders substituted, all interior doors and partitions loopholed, and long halls or passageways barricaded.

Relieve Pressure

Where the pressure of the mob threatens to break through the fence or gates, water or riot control agents may be employed on the rioters to relieve the pressure. Other means of denying an area to rioters are the following:

1. Flood it with water.
2. Subject it to a concentration of riot control agents.
3. Block all its entrances.
4. Occupy it with troops.

Get Police into the Installation

If all gates to an installation are besieged by rioters, troops on the outside may have to be passed over the top of the fence to reach the inside. Another method is to cut a passageway through the wire.

The police can also use gas and smoke in quantity from flanks and rear to confuse and panic the mob and drive it off.

In a situation where an installation is besieged by rioters, and it is necessary for troops to enter it but the use of riot control agents is not desirable, the rioters may be forced away from a gate by troops in wedge formation in mass, with lateral support and a strong reserve in

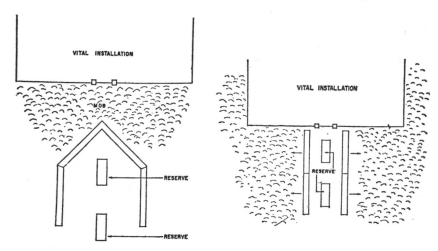

The above illustrations demonstrate how a wedge formation can be used to force a mob away from the gate of a vital installation to allow reserves to gain entrance to strengthen the defending forces.

the center of the wedge. A fire hose disseminating water under high pressure from the point of the wedge may be used to aid in forcing rioters back. When the gate is reached by the point of the wedge, the two echelons of the wedge face right and left, respectively, and move outward in a line to clear the rioters from the gate. Then troops may enter the installation through the opened passageway.

DEFENSE OF A SECTION OF THE CITY

In recent riots the target of the hit and run guerrilla bands has been retail stores. The protection of this area by a strong defensive deployment of police would deny them their target and thus frustrate the purpose of the riot. To accomplish this a strong mobile force should be rushed into the area. Rather than detrucking at one end of the business area and slowly deploying through it on foot, the convoy should smash down the center of it, detrucking holding forces at regular intervals. These units should spread out over the area assigned to them. They must secure the tops of buildings and post guards on them to protect the exposed units in the streets below. Any individuals apprehended should be placed in the vehicles which brought the police, for shipment to the detention area. Once the area is secured, guard posts should be established and the bulk of the men concentrated in centrally located reserve units which would be drawn on in the event of an attack at any point.

RETREAT

There are times when retreat is mandatory. This is one of the most difficult of all maneuvers, for it is well known among the military that the withdrawal of troops in the face of enemy action must be carefully controlled because it carries with it the danger of group panic. The police must be carefully informed about why they are being withdrawn and how and where the new line of resistance will be established. Unexplained, unexpected rearward movements of even a few men can cause a rout, even among good troops.

RIOTS – OFFENSIVE TACTICS

INTRODUCTION

ALL OF THE PREVIOUS phases of containment and defense are developed on the premise that counteraction will be necessary, that an offensive will be launched. In performing this action, the police must never forget that theirs is the responsibility to apprehend—not to punish—for violations of the law. The method of enforcement used in counteraction must instill in the rioters a belief in the following:

1. The soundness, justness and reasonableness of laws.
2. The fact that no area of our state or nation exists as a vacuum of police authority.
3. The certainty of police action.
4. The fact that courts will respond to violence with prompt and adequate penalties for the guilty.

Counteraction is the method used to disperse the mob systematically and focus attention on individuals within the mob. The emphasis is to deprive members of the mob their anonymity. This is done by identification and arrest for violations of the law. Once the process has begun and is shown to be effective, the natural tendency of rioters is to disconnect themselves from the melee. There are rabid exceptions, of course.

FIELD FORCES

The field force can be divided into segments based upon the function assigned to each. The strike force will be that unit used in the show of force and, if necessary, moved against the mob to disperse it. The strike force units will be backed up by reserve, perimeter and housekeeping units. It should be protected by flank and rear guard units.

The perimeter units are charged with maintaining the outer and inner blockade, patrolling those areas and maintaining the routes of escape and defending vital points.

The housekeeping units accompany the strike force into the action. Their responsibility is to handle prisoners, take wounded to the rear, assume patrol actions and form road blocks on the flanks and "by-passed" areas, and perform other housekeeping and cleanup details that are necessary in the wake of a moving mob action.

A reserve should be maintained at all times. It should be organized into a "flying column" and must be on constant alert with plans to depart to any critical spot on a few minutes notice. Communication between strike force and reserve must be established and maintained. Sufficient motor transportation must always be available. When the reserve is committed to action, it should be replaced as soon as possible.

In a riot control operation against a mob which greatly outnumber the troops, an unexpected attack against the rear or flanks of a police unit can have serious effects and may render the unit ineffective. This consideration applies during any phase of riot control regardless of whether police forces are engaged in motor movement, foot marches, or tactical riot control formations.

To give warning and prevent surprise, the flanks and rear of the troops should be patrolled by radio equipped, motorized patrols or airborne observers. The area covered should be sufficiently distant from the scene of operations to insure timely warnings to the commander. These security forces should be capable of self-defense and of fighting a delaying action.

TYPES OF MOB

Riots or mob disorder will generally follow one of two patterns, the "conventional" or the "insurgency." The conventional riot envisions a large group of individuals, under the stimulus of intense excitement or agitation, congregated in a relatively limited, easily defined area. Leadership is present, and motion rules in a kind of collective hypnosis. At the proper time this mob moves as one to vent its rage on some object chosen for violence.

The insurgency riot, although initiated by an assemblage of a group of individuals, does not move as one body to a specific object; it reverts to guerrilla or hit-and-run tactics to accomplish its mission.

Leadership and organization are much more refined in this type tactic, and planning by the insurgent leadership is more detailed and scientific. In this situation the initial mob action may be only a "smoke screen" for the looting, plundering, or planned destruction that is to be initiated by designated individuals and/or small groups.

The basic principles of riot control are valid in both circumstances. In the conventional riot situation, the initial action normally consists of blocking a mob along a selected line short of its objective and emplacing necessary roadblocks, presenting a display of police strength, issuing an order of proclamation directing the people to disperse within a prescribed time and retire peaceably to their homes, and insuring an avenue of escape for their use. As the mob retires, police follow at the speed of retirement, continually breaking the mob into smaller and yet smaller groups.

In the case of an insurgency mob, upon the initial show of force by the police, the mob may immediately and rapidly disperse in all directions, and immediately commence burning, looting and other destructive acts. On the other hand, it may retain all indications common to the conventional mob, moving hesitatingly as the police begin moving the people down preplanned avenues of escape. The purpose of the mob is to force the police to commit as much of the police manpower to the mob movement as possible, thus allowing individuals and small groups to burn, loot and destroy in other areas. This is the smoke screen tactic that the police commander must be alert to detect as early as possible.

SHOW OF FORCE

No matter which tactic the mob employs, the best recourse available to the police commander initially is the rapid and impressive display of police power. This is the show of force. As the words imply, this is merely a show of the strength available for use against the rioters. The purpose of this tactic is to convince the mob of the ability of the police to maintain law and order and to disperse the mob with physical force if necessary.

The show of force must be made by a force large enough to demonstrate to the mob that the police are serious and are able and prepared to use all necessary force to disburse the mob. This requires the presence of a sufficient number of uniformed men to awe the crowd so that it becomes unnecessary to use actual forces in dispersing the mob.

To stage a show of strength which is deficient is to parade weakness in the face of opposition and thereby invite added resistance. Thus recently, the ordering of extra men into an area in two-men mobile patrols proved to be a show of weakness as they were unable to respond to attacks on their cars, for when they alighted to apprehend the attacker he would flee. If they gave chase their car was attacked by others. To be effective the crew of mobile units must be large enough to apprehend attackers, but still protect the autos.

Preliminary Procedure

To use the show of force to the greatest advantage against mobs, units should make a surprise, formidable appearance. To insure this, the following procedures should be used:

When arriving by car or truck, the police should dismount and assemble at some point beyond the sight of the mob. This point should be as near the mob as is practicable to save time and to conserve energy, and yet far enough from the scene of the disturbance to insure security.

When using helicopters as a method of transporting men to the scene of the riot, the psychological impact on the mob should not be overlooked. When feasible, police should dismount from the helicopter in sight of the mob but far enough away to preclude damage to the aircraft by thrown objects. Normally the first echelon to dismount from the aircraft acts as a security element for the landing area.

In column formation, the unit marches to a reasonably safe distance from the mob and within plain view of the mob. The shock effect can be enhanced if the police are wearing gas masks, particularly if rioting groups are made up of illiterate elements. Likewise, the display of firearms in such a way as to impress upon the mob their availability and police determination to use them will add to the respect for the police strength.

It must again be stressed that the first minutes of visual contact are the most important. The first impressions endure, and they influence most subsequent actions. It is imperative, then, that the first impression to be made by the police in these disturbances be one of ability to cope with the situation by being prepared, fully equipped, and in sufficient numbers. To appear uncertain or hesitant will frequently be construed as a sign of weakness and fear and will have exactly the opposite effect from that intended by the show of force.

The show of force should not be made until the commander has decided on the alternative action that will follow it, for officers cannot be exposed to prolonged physical violence at the hands of a mob, while a course of action is being decided on. A show of force should be made as follows:

1. Place units of riot-equipped police in disciplined formation in full view of the people at the nearest point of contact.
2. Advance against mob in direction in which they are to be dispersed.
3. March in column formation down center of the street.
4. Deploy into desired riot control formation in full view of rioters. The best policy is to use plenty of police at the beginning of the situation and to make withdrawals from time to time as conditions become more normal.

If successful, the show of force will so mentally overwhelm the mob that the individual mind will be shocked back to normalcy, at which time the mob will dissolve with no further force being required other than to patrol the effected area.

If a mob is known to be well-armed and intelligence reports indicate that the rioters intend to open fire as soon as police appear, the commander should not expose his men in a senseless show of force. Rather his units should utilize the techniques of attack explained elsewhere in this book.

PERSONAL APPEALS

One of the most successful ways of dissolving mobs peacefully is to bring in some leading citizen, some individual known to have the self-interest of the mob members at heart or known to have sufficient authority, determination and integrity to carry out punishment for mob members who break the law. Get attention fixed on the presence of such an individual, have him talk to the mob, win their sympathy, and urge dispersal.

ORDER TO DISPERSE

If personal appeals and the show of force fail to break up the mob, the next step is to order it to disperse. The order should not be given until the force is sufficient to back up the command, is in position, and is ready to execute that order.

Selection of Areas and Routes for Mob Dispersal

Before any move is made to disperse the mob, the police must select the area or areas into which it will be dispersed and the routes to be used in moving the mob to those areas. The police commander should never exert pressure against a mob unless it has available to it an open route of withdrawal. Never trap a mob. Leave at least one avenue by which to disperse. The object is to disperse a mob, not destroy it. If trapped, the mob's resistance will be desperate. In selecting the area, the following are desirable features to look for.

1. The area should be where the majority of the rioters live or similar type residential areas or an open area. It is obvious that one who is part of a mob that is rushing into his neighborhood will be prone to seek the safety and seclusion of his own home. Likewise, history shows a reluctance to injure or destroy residential property of those of similar social and economic status.

2. It should be an area of little tactical value and should avoid industrial and commercial areas, public service facilities and vital installations.

3. Areas should be large enough to permit complete dispersion.

4. Areas should be as close as possible to scene of mob activity so as not to overextend and commit police strength.

5. If possible, the area should be down hill as it will be easier to move the mob down rather than up hill.

Routes

Provision should always be made in advance for permitting the rioters more than one avenue of dispersal. The more avenues of dispersal a crowd is given, the more easily it is broken up. In selecting the routes the shortest and most direct route to the dispersal area is to be preferred. Further, it should not take the mob near business districts or vital facilities, or police equipment or property as there would be danger of destruction by mob violence.

Once the selections have been made all units should be advised. They should immediately seal off undesirable escape routes and open dispersal routes prior to any advance against the crowd.

The route along which a mob is to be moved will normally contain several side street intersections which must be crossed by the mob prior to reaching the selected dispersal area. Police commanders must seal these side streets in order to channel the movement of the mob along the desired route. Under certain circumstances, it is possible for the police commander to displace the sealing force from intersection to intersection, in leapfrog fashion, thereby adhering to the principle of economy of force.

Rear of Crowd

Special attention should be given the rear of a crowd, which is generally a troublesome area. Persons in the front ranks will be unable to comply with an order to disperse if their movement to the rear is restricted. Persons in the comparative safety of the rear may continue to launch stones and other missiles after the front has been brought under control. If possible, formations should be placed in the rear of the crowd to relieve pressure, spot leaders and agitators, and disarm members of the mob who display weapons or who pick up rocks or other missiles and take any further action necessary to open the escape route. Officers in formation covering the rear of the crowd remain alert, but inactive, so long as the crowd is peaceable. If the rear of the mob prevents its retreat, pressure on the front should be withheld until the mob's rear section is broken up and an avenue of retreat assured.

Announcement

Once all is in readiness, the order to disperse is made. Orders to disperse should be given, using loudspeakers or amplifying devices to insure that all members of the crowd can hear clearly. Undercover police should be located at the rear of the mob to verify that the order was audible and heard by the entire mob. The order will be most effective if the police display the powerful organized force they are prepared to utilize.

When the mob is composed of people who do not speak English, interpreters should be employed. He interprets the proclamation and instructions when directed by the commander. He also listens to instructions issued by mob leaders to the mob and relays them to the commander.

The order should be in positive terms, spoken clearly, distinctively, slowly and in a commanding tone of voice. The proclamation should be delivered or repeated in a foreign language when appropriate . The force of the words used in the proclamation should be gauged to the composition and temperament of the crowd. In such an order, the prevailing law should be enunciated, a firm order to disperse issued, the avenues of exit from the area designated, and an unequivocal time limit for dispersal should be set. No particular form of proclamation is required, only that there be something in the nature of a general command to disperse and that it purport to be in the name of the people of the state. The order should be repeated three times, and officers should be stationed at the rear of the assembly to verify that all persons present can hear.

Never give an unreasonable order or one that cannot be easily understood or carried out. Once an order is given insist on prompt obedience. Failure to insist on obedience may be interpreted by the crowd as evidence of indecision or weakness. If the order is obeyed again the police have only a security patrol duty. If it is not you must be prepared to do what you say you will do. The police commander must never bluff, threaten to do things he is unable to do nor attempt to accomplish an objective without sufficient force.

USE OF FORCE IN DISPERSING A MOB

Force should be used to disperse a mob only when all else fails or when the situation is such that resort to the other methods is obviously inadequate. Generally, the basic military tactics of concentration of force, mass penetration and exploitation are applicable.

Preliminary Security Measures

The police should be alert for persons carrying or attempting to conceal rocks or other dangerous objects on their persons and take them into custody. These tactics will function best when plainclothes officers are assigned to infiltrate the crowd and point out such persons. Plainclothes officers may also be able to gain other valuable intelligence concerning the actions and intentions of the crowd.

When possible, bricks, trash baskets and other objects that may be used as weapons or throwing objects by the crowd should be removed from the scene. Police should secure control of rooftops before attempting to use force against a mob. Both sides of the street must be secured. Where rooftops vary in height, selected marksmen should be positioned on the tallest building in order to be able to cover adjoining lower rooftops to prevent objects from being thrown onto the riot control force. Rooftops also provide excellent positions from which riot control agents can be delivered against the mob.

Act as a Unit

The police must move and act as a unit. As crowds and mobs will

LEGEND

⬡	COMMUNICATION CAR
◁	PATROL CAR
▭	EMERGENCY PATROL
○	POLICE
▪	POLICE ON ORIGINAL CALL
▭○	SUPPLY TRUCK
◀━	POLICE MOVEMENT
┝━━┥	BARRICADES
◀━	RIOTER MOVEMENT
◎	RIOT AREA
▭	BUS

usually be greatly superior in numbers, one member must not be allowed to struggle with one rioter. It must be remembered that the unit will work as a team, not as individuals. Should any rioter lay hands on an individual member, other members of the unit must instantly converge on the adversary and completely overwhelm him.

Officers should not break ranks and congregate around other officers

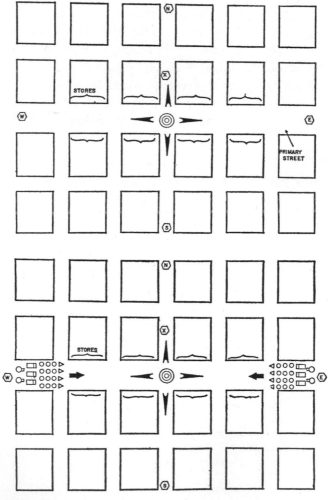

Single street incident. Illustrations depict the rapid deployment of police approaching from both ends of a primary street. These units occupy the riot torn street, disperse the rioters and establish security. ➡➡→

struggling with a rioter. Only enough officers to handle the situation should be diverted, no more. Other officers in the line should continue to face the crowd, hold their positions and be on the alert for other attacks. The best method of handling such attacks is to station several support squads behind the front line of police to handle rioters breaking through the lines and to bolster weak spots or fill gaps in the line.

Never allow a crowd to surround a group of officers. If this becomes

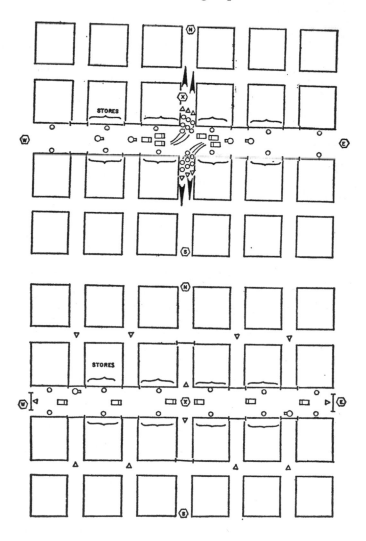

imminent, the officers should move out and get clear. The retreat should always be made in formation, and slowly, in order not to give any indication of panic. The police should face the mob while withdrawing.

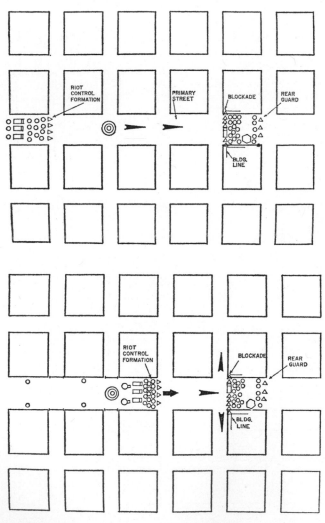

Single street incident. As in the preceding illustrations, the police quickly sweep a primary street. The difference here is that only one police unit moves while the other maintains a defensive holding position. ⟶

The prestige of the uniform must be maintained at all costs. An offense against an individual member of the unit is an offense against all members of the unit. Each rioter must be made to feel that if he attacks an individual member he will have to cope with the entire unit.

Do not split the police force into a number of small detachments to try to quell minor diversionary disorders at scattered points. Concentrate on the main body of the mob. Do not send small units into areas

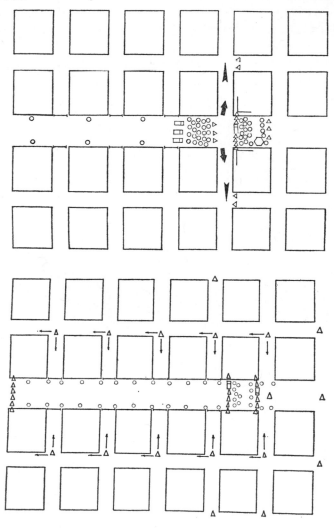

where they can be surrounded. Protect your flanks and rear. Do not let the mob envelope your unit.

Remove Leaders and Agitators

Before moving to break up the mob, the location and identity of

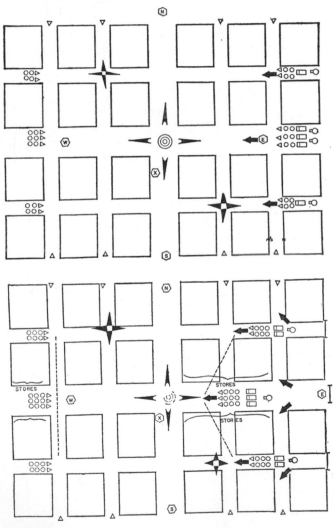

Multi-street incident. Illustrations depict the method of movement against riotous mobs that have spread over a wide area. As in the case of a single street incident, the police move in, disperse the mobs, and secure the area. ⇉→

the leaders should be discovered by observation and infiltration of the mob with plainclothes men. To remove the leaders is to strike at the heart of the disorder. A leaderless group is a bewildered and confused group which does not function effectively. The leaders, who would ordinarily supply the initiative, the rallying symbols, and the sustaining force of the emotional enthusiasm, should be taken in hand

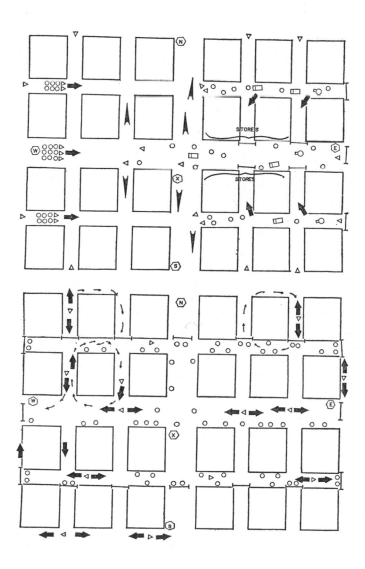

and restrained. When, and how, to remove the leaders is an important and crucial decision that the police commander must make. Improper action and excessive force to consummate such an arrest could precipitate the riot. The leaders could be hoping for the police action to remove them, just for this very reason. Depending on the situation,

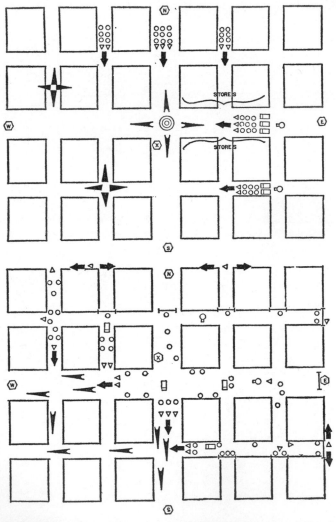

Multi-street incident. The attack on the mobs here, rather than being launched from both sides, is a simultaneous movement on two fronts from one corner of the affected area. Again the object is to disperse and secure.

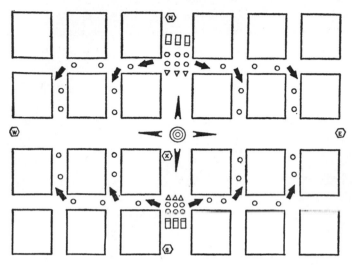

Operation encirclement. There will be instances when the objective of the police is not to disperse the mob but rather to capture as many of the participants as possible. In such instances the simultaneous movement of encircling units is the best approach.

it may be advisable at the time only to identify and photograph the leaders, hotheads, demogogues, psychopaths and others, the arrests being made at a later time, out of sight of the public view. This identification and photographing should be as detailed and complete as available equipment will permit, to include tape recording their speeches if at all possible. Such a tactic should not be considered as an indication of police weakness; it is a display of discretion and sound judgment on the part of the police commander. Trained leaders will be quick to recognize the impact of this police tactic, and knowledge of what will ensue may be sufficient to cause them to depart the scene rather than face imminent court action. Without violence, the police will have accomplished their mission—removing the leaders.

Cut Mob's Communication

If intelligence information indicates the existence of lines of communication being used by a mob they should be located and cut. By tracing such lines to their sources it may be possible to capture key mob leaders and important documents or equipment.

Use standard formation to accomplish the breakup of the mob. The advance on the crowd or mob should be made in deployed formations. If the mob is in an open place such as a field, etc., the formations may be loose or extended, making sure the flanks are protected. If in a confined area such as streets or buildings, the formations should be tight. No changes in formations and movement should be made quickly, but movement in counteraction must be slow and deliberate.

The attack on the mob should be swift and sure, but never permit the men to rush into contact. Panic is the inevitable consequence of police rushing a group of demonstrators. Men on the line must remember that there is a physical advantage in keeping the point platoon in physical contact with the crowd. It restricts the activity of "throwers." However, the formation must guard against burying itself in the crowd and becoming encircled. If sufficient manpower is available, a mob should be attacked from two sides simultaneously. To start the crowd dispersing, use part of the force to hit the flank or rear where the least violent and courageous members will be. A large percentage may be spectators. When they discover police attacking on the flank and rear, some will begin to disperse. If a small part of the mob takes flight, the remainder will be thrown into panic and confusion. The sight of members fleeing will demoralize the spirit of resistence of the more determined.

When dispersing a mob, it is a good method to put its members on the run in different directions; for where their unity of front is broken, the officers may, if the rioters return, meet them in smaller groups.

During the retreat no more force should be applied than is necessary. When the mob retreats, diminishing force should be applied in proportion to the speed of retreat or the degree of disintegration. The offensive is to be maintained constantly once an action has begun.

Search

Clearing mobs out of a built-up area includes searching houses or buildings to prevent sizable groups from secreting themselves until the troops pass.

SPECIAL SITUATIONS—TACTICS

The tactical plan is based on the following:

1. The organization or formation of the dissident elements, which may comprise
   a. A large compact mob with great density.
   b. A large, widely dispersed, rapidly moving mob.
   c. A small, compact group.
   d. Many small, widely dispersed groups.
2. The nature of the area of operations which may comprise
   a. Large open areas, such as open fields.
   b. Smaller, open areas, such as courtyards or public squares.
   c. Confined areas, such as city streets.
   d. Interiors of buildings or similar structures.

Here are possible situations and suggested procedures to control them.

Mob Occupying Large Population Section of a City

Isolate the affected areas; split the area, using the most natural dividing line available, usually the center of riotous activity. Next, clean up the area by patrols; work from the center outward.

Large Compact Mob in Open Area

The action here is to disperse the mob and split it in segments, separate the segments, and then disperse each segment. Only the number of officers necessary to accomplish this action should be used.

Large Compact Mob on Unenclosed Square

A large compact mob is massed on an unenclosed public square. Utilize a striking wedge to drive through the point of least expected resistance to arrest the leader. In a coordinated movement, segment the mob; then separate and disperse the segments.

Large Compact Mob Massed on a City Street

Using whichever riot control formation is deemed most appropriate, move the mob in the direction desired. As the rioters are dispersed into the various streets, seal the streets off to prevent reformation of the mob. Use patrols to prevent regrouping of the rioters.

Loose Crowds

Loose crowds are successfully handled by sweeping them in a body.

Mob Moving Along a Street

Meet it at an intersection and split it so that its parts are sent down side streets in opposite directions. Reserves should be stationed at the right and left of the point of contact to prevent the mob from returning and regrouping.

Street Crowd

Such a crowd is usually long and narrow and is best broken up by attacking its flanks.

Small Compact Mob on Street Corner

Use the wedge, diagonal, or line as the situation demands. Strike the mob on its flanks simultaneously. If the group is located tight against a building, the diagonal may be employed. This formation is also good for clearing streets and alleys.

Mob Massed in a Court Yard

The mob must first be driven from the court yard and then dispersed using the same tactics as above. The control group should enter the court yard in a column, form a diagonal, and force the mob away from the enclosed area and into the open. It is important to remember, "Never trap a crowd or mob."

Mob in Building

The routes of escape from buildings are normally the windows and doors of the ground floor. Where possible, the building should be cleared from the top downward. In some instances, however, it will be difficult or impossible to reach the top of the building in order to drive the rioters downward. It may be necessary to start clearing a building on the lower floor. If so, clear that floor, then proceed upward, floor by floor, until the building is cleared. Basements and underground passageways must not be overlooked. When clearing a building from the lower floor to the top, routes of escape normally will not exist, and it may be necessary for individuals or small groups to be escorted to the exits on the ground floor.

Mob in Large Room or Hall

One unit of police should enter the door and move their formation along the walls, ejecting a small part of the crowd at a time. Another unit should remain at the entrance to handle the rioters as they are ejected and to prevent others from entering the room. These formations furnish mutual support while entering and prevent the rioters from crowding in rear of the troops.

PURSUIT OPERATIONS

When the mob line has been broken and rioters withdraw, police forces should continue to pursue. It is an advantage to make them move at least three blocks from the scene of disorder for they then are less likely to return. Pursuit of a mob is normally begun by police marching rapidly on foot. When the mob breaks and runs, contact is maintained by special pursuit vehicles which pass through police riot control formations to continue the dispersal of the rioters.

At times, a predesignated line is determined on the basis of the situation and terrain in conformance with the operation order. When the police reach the predesignated line, they should halt and motorized patrols should continue the pursuit and patrol the area to prevent reassembly. Police commanders who fail in the pursuit phase may encounter a rapidly reformed mob.

POST-DISPERSAL OPERATIONS

Once a mob is dispersed, police must prevent it from reforming. The main objective of the attack upon the mob is to scatter it. Once the crowd has been put on the move, it must be kept on the move and fragmented. It should be driven away from its objective and, when possible, forced back into its own section of the city. In scattering, the mob loses its aggressiveness and cohesion. To accomplish this the following methods are utilized:

1. Mobile units patrolling area.
2. Develop a system of guards on fixed posts.

3. Roving foot patrol.

4. System of communications to keep on tops of the situation.

The effect of these measures is to place the law enforcement personnel in a constant view of the public. They also provide liaison through communications systems which enables reserve and support groups to be called up immediately if necessary.

GUERRILLA-TYPE RIOT

When rioters employ hit-and-run or guerrilla tactics and persist in returning to the area once cleared, a system of "street sweeps" should be initated. Once cleared, the street is secured by positioning a force at the street corners and, if necessary, patrols roving within the block. In conjunction with street sweeps, buildings that might contain rioters should be cleared systematically from the top floor down to the ground level. This method permits use of a minimum number of police and allows the rioter an avenue of escape from the building. During street sweep operations, vehicles should be used in conjunction with the foot forces to provide protection against rioters using vehicles to break police formations.

Where sniper action is prevalent, police response must be positive and instantaneous. If the sniper is positioned in a building and firing from a window, a gas projectile may suffice in silencing him. If not, the countersniper marksman should be employed to dislodge him from the building or the rooftop.

Looting and other destruction may occur in other areas of the community, especially near the periphery of the riot area. Those criminals will use the riot activity as a smoke screen for their operations. "Flying teams," consisting of a squad of properly equipped police officers can be effectively employed to counteract this activity. They should be equipped with shotguns and chemical munitions. Within the riot area, similar teams may be employed, either on foot or with vehicles. If foot teams are employed, they must be provided with communications and an adequate logistical back-up.

HOLD POLICE IN THE FIELD

The field commander should be careful to keep his tactical unit, with its reserve, intact for some time after initial dispersal has been achieved. For patrolling he should use other available units and men even if they are not especially trained in riot formations. Violent riots of great size may flare up again if patrolling is not immediately initiated and maintained.

For this reason, a community which has experienced a civil disorder should not be released from restrictions imposed by police until public unrest has disappeared. The decision to release restrictions should be based on sound intelligence information obtained through both overt and covert collection techniques.

The restoration of order is attained when all disturbances are ended and there is no indication of further threat to peace and order. Police should turn back to ordinary control any activities for which they have had to assume responsibility during the turmoil (public utilities, transportation, distribution facilities). This should be accomplished in an orderly, phased procedure. All regulations and restrictive measures imposed during the emergency should be clearly rescinded by the commander at the scene. All barricades, entanglements, posters, debris and other evidence of extraordinary circumstances should be removed. For a favorable psychological effect, the police, upon leaving, may be paraded through the area, giving the definite impression that their task is completed.

Unfortunately the exercise of violence during a riot does not result in a purification of the atmosphere, leading to peace. It is not a situation in which excess energy is worked off, leaving the decks cleared for cooperation. Deep scars are left on both sides through this failure of law enforcement to control the people. The rioters, especially the more active ones, are not remorseful. Rather they feel (1) pride of accomplishment on the part of participants of both racial groups regardless of the outcome; (2) an absence of guilt feelings, justified by the fact that so many were associated with them in the riots and that they had such "excellent" and "moral" reasons for their actions, and (3) a stimulation of organization to prepare for the "next time," based upon the *esprit de corps* created by common experience and alleged threats to the welfare of the social group or race represented. Far from eliminating the differences which caused the violence in the first place, they are consolidated, reinforced and deepened.

In short, the riot pattern cannot be eliminated by suppression alone.

On the contrary, suppression may merely sweep surface symptoms "under the carpet" and force the riot-prone to organize more thoroughly for their next outbreak. What is needed is an intelligent diagnosis of this social disease and then an adequate court of treatment. In other words, we must have a program for riot prevention that will attack the causes of riots in a broad and adequate fashion.

To counter this, the police and the courts must see to it that all those who were guilty of serious offenses are prosecuted. Further, every effort must be made to prevent further incitement of public passion, ensuring that an atmosphere has been established in which law and order clearly prevail maintained by the police.

To achieve this, factors causing the disorder should be carefully analyzed and corrective action initiated. All groups concerned should meet on neutral ground to discuss the incident. Press coverage should be encouraged. Affirmative action should be taken to rectify the conditions which precipitated the riot. To this end, all interested groups should be contacted and appropriate action taken.

Chapter 32

CITY BATTLE TACTICS

POSSIBLE REVOLUTION OR REBELLION

IN TODAY'S WORLD it is possible for organized riots to take place in a dozen locations as part of a timed program. Decoy riots may be directed while the real targets receive undiverted attention of combat rioters. The key assault would be directed at prime targets such as public structures, utilities, fuel depots, sources of weapons, terminals and other areas whose loss would cripple organization of the community. A whole city or a section of it might be engulfed in riot and seized by the mob.

This possibility cannot be rejected as ridiculous conjecture. It has happened! The possibility must therefore be considered in planning.

All the methods used in quelling an uncoordinated riot depend upon the fact that the mob is unorganized. None of these methods will be very effective when they are directed against a coordinated mob. In a small and less efficient way, a coordinated mob is comparable to an army and can usually defend itself against formations, batons or tear gas. Consequently, breaking up a coordinated riot usually forces the utilization of the tactics of warfare.

HOLDING AND COUNTERACTING

In all large cities the strategic points in the city should be determined and studied beforehand. In case of a general uprising, the troops should be concentrated at these points as rapidly as they can be assembled. Strategic points are those by which, or from which, the various districts of the city can be completely isolated from each other. These points having been thus occupied, a simultaneous movement, with each part supporting the others, and an overwhelming attack on the most important stronghold of the rioters would probably crush the uprising completely or make further operations simply similar to the pursuit and breaking up of a defeated and demoralized army.

In determining the selection of strategic points and the movements of troops in a general uprising, a city should be regarded as a broken or mountainous country, with innumerable defiles which make parallel, flanking and rear movements possible and easy. In occupying the strategic points selected, it is well to keep the mass of the troops concealed as much as practicable until the time for action arrives, so that their sudden appearance may be an overwhelming surprise.

RECAPTURE OPERATIONS

During widespread disorders it may become necessary to occupy or retake entire sections of a city which are held by rioters who have abandoned the streets and set up defense points in buildings. In such instances, the police and military will proceed to attack as though those sections were held by enemy military personnel. The only real difference will consist in the amount of fire power brought to bear.

Prior to the attack, aircraft should be employed on reconnaissance and photographic missions to search out critical areas held by the rioters. Continuous employment of liaison planes will afford commanders and their staff officers firsthand information about the areas occupied by the rioters and any changes in their dispositions.

One basic plan for recovering a city or section of the city designates certain buildings or localities well inside the city or area as first objectives. At first, small and then large parties of troops will force their way to these objectives to form strong points from which the core of the town may be eaten out and any perimeter defenses attacked from the rear. The objectives will be selected in order to be cooperative, i.e., success in obtaining objective A will aid those troops who are trying to gain objective B.

Another approach is to deploy the police and military across one side of the most important area. A unit is assigned to each street. At the designated time they begin a coordinated sweep block by block through the city. If the rioters are concentrated in one section of the city it will usually be advisable to converge on that section with two or three columns, depending on the number of police available.

Whichever plan is used, it must be simple. Each unit must be given a clear limited objective, and complicated maneuvers such as a change of direction should generally be avoided.

CORDONS

The object of cordoning is to prevent enemy movement, whether for reinforcement, counter-attack, or escape.

When the object of an attack is to clear an area of enemy, the procedure should be to cordon a sub-area, clear it, and keep it cordoned from the uncleared area. When the object of an attack is to penetrate to an area, it frequently may be advisable to cordon the line of advance. A cordon may be placed around a building containing rioters in order to capture emerging rioters, and to prevent rioters receiving reinforcements during an attack.

STRIKE UNITS

The strike units should be divided into four sections: (1) street; (2) roof; (3) search, and (4) security. The street unit is the main strike force which moves against the enemy on the street level. Whenever possible it should be supported by armored units. In close support will be the search unit.

As the troops advance through the areas held by the rioters, a careful search of all buildings should be made, especially for leaders, arms and ammunition. When there is determined resistance, all buildings must be completely searched, and all occupants arrested as the troops advance.

All searching units should have gas grenades, crowbars and other equipment to break down doors and force entrances into buildings. The roof unit secures the roofs in the area. It should be lightly armed and equipped and provided with scaling ladders and ropes to permit rapid progress in moving along the roofs.

The security unit should secure all arrested persons promptly and thus relieve other units of the responsibility of guarding them. Motor transportation must be provided to transport the prisoners to the nearest jail or temporary prisoners' cage.

MINES AND BOMBS

The use of mines, booby-trap devices and explosive charges to prevent police from performing their function in mob control can be expected, especially in a large, well-planned and directed action. A general knowledge of such tactics is advisable. If possible, designated elements in the riot control unit should receive some training in this field. These same men can also be trained in using explosives to clear mob-installed blockades. The increasing use by communists of guerrilla warfare, and their training in the use and improvisation of such explosive devices, make this an important consideration. Good prior intelligence will generally determine if use of explosives will be a mob tactic.

BARRICADES

The police may be confronted with one or many individuals who have assumed a purely defensive attitude, and entrench themselves by means of barricades. The purpose of barricades constructed by rioters is to impede the advance of the police by opposing them from a strong defensive position.

Direct attack on such barricades should never be attempted until all other methods of capturing them have been tried and failed, or are evidently useless to attempt. In some cases the position might be such that, if the number of troops were sufficient to warrant it, the whole entrenched position could be cut off and isolated while the work of suppressing the riot in other portions of the city proceeded. The use of riot control agents is normally an effective means of neutralizing the position. If large groups are assembled behind the barricades, they may be driven away by riot control gases and then dealt with separately.

If the barricade must be attacked, the attack should be made from above and on the flanks or rear. An enterprising commander, with a very small force of courageous men, may surprise and capture a barricade in the night by watching the opportunities offered through want of discipline and proper guard duty on the part of its defenders, as they might generally be caught in a condition of drunken stupor.

Barricades may be removed by bulldozers, or dragged out of the way by heavy trucks if these vehicles can be protected during the process. It is also possible to break them down, by the use of grapples or other means, prior to capture. Barricades in the open, constructed of combustible material, may be destroyed by fire; in this case, precautions must be taken to prevent the fire from spreading to nearby buildings. If available, armed vehicles can be used to overrun the barricade. When barricades have been carried, they should immediately be removed or destroyed.

COVER

Cover should be afforded all movements. To afford cover from the rear, units must be high enough to fire over the heads of those advancing until the last possible moment. Likewise, fire from a position higher than the enemy will search his position best and will cause the most damage. Positions should be established on the roofs of the highest buildings in the area to cover all rooftops as far as possible. It is very hard for troops in streets to deal with attackers above them as rooftops are relatively safe from below.

There is usually a house whose windows dominate a whole street. It may be placed at the end of the street or on rising ground farther away. If there is such a house, make preparations to pacify it before attacking the street.

METHOD OF MOVEMENT

The first officers to break cover comprise the point section, consisting of the following.

Scouts

The duty of the scouts is to find out where the enemy is. They move, one or two on each side of the street, by short bounds, stopping under the cover of doorways, buttresses, gateposts, alleyways, etc., to observe the opposite side of the street. When moving, they should keep as close to the side wall as possible, and must go at the highest possible speed. If fired on, the scouts should take cover and try to work into position to give covering fire to the assault party.

Observers

Behind the scouts move the observers. Their duty is to observe and report on any enemy movements. The normal number is two

for each side of the street. This is a minimum, for should there be
anything to report, one must go back, leaving one to observe. Like
the scouts, they should move rapidly, and close to the side walls.
They should be so far up that they can see what is happening to the
scouts; and so far back that they are not exposed to the same fire
as the scouts, and can get back to report. If they are pinned to
cover by enemy fire, they can usually shout back a message.

In the case the enemy opens fire, the message should contain the
following:

1. Strength and armament of enemy.
2. Exact position, side of street, number or description of house,
   first or second floor, right or left window.
3. Whether a scout is in position to give covering fire.
4. What possible covered approach there is to the house.

Remainder of Section

The remainder of the point section works along behind the scouts
and observers, helping to search out the enemy or protect the section.

The two rear sections should advance, one on each side of the
street, searching the houses. Men working in pairs, pass rapidly from
house to house. The search need not be thorough, for a single enemy
concealed in a cupboard will be cut off from his friends and in no
mood for a stout resistance.

STRONG POINTS

When a strong point is contacted, a decision must be made whether
to avoid, to isolate, or to attack it. An attack is the least desirable
of the alternatives and should not be made unless necessary. The
determination of which approach to follow will in the last analysis
be dependent upon many factors.

The houses may have been occupied by the rioters without fore-
thought or plan, simply on the impulse of the moment, as a vantage
ground from which to impede or annoy the passage of troops through
a street when the rioters are not in sufficient force to resist their passage in the open street. If it can be bypassed without threat to the
police, it should be. If, however, houses so occupied would remain
as a menace in the rear of the advancing police, or as an obstacle

to their retreat in case of disaster, it would be better to isolate or blockade the block in which the houses are located, so that the occupants would be held in a trap from which escape would be impossible, and in which they might be held and dealt with at the proper time.

If houses have been occupied as a place of refuge and defense by rioters who have been defeated in the open streets, or under the directions of competent leaders for flank defenses of barricaded positions or vantage grounds for fighting; or if, for any reason, it becomes necessary to dislodge the rioters, the attack on such houses must be made systematically and with thorough preparation of all the appliances needed to make the attack successful.

If the houses occupied by the rioters are part of a block of houses, the troops should take possession of the first house in the block not so occupied. If the roofs are flat, the troops should attack the first occupied house by way of the roof, gaining access through the scuttles or by cutting holes in the roof. If the roofs are steep, access should be gained by breaking through the walls in the top story. It is infinitely better to fight downwards in a house than to fight upwards, and the latter should not be attempted if there is any possible way of avoiding it. Hand grenades or light dynamite bombs dropped down the roof scuttles or chimneys are good preliminaries to the descent of the troops. After getting into a house no pause should be allowed in the attack; the defenders should be followed closely from room to room and floor to floor until resistance ceases or they are driven from the lower floor into the hands of the troops in the streets. The first house in the block having been cleared, the next adjoining should be attacked in the same manner, and so on until the whole block is cleared.

If all of the houses in a block are occupied by the rioters, and it becomes necessary to make a direct attack on one of them in order to obtain a foothold from which to attack the others in the method described, the mode of attack must be determined by circumstances.

If the houses on both sides of the street are occupied by rioters, it may be found best to make the attack on the rear of the house, as it is less likely to be well guarded and protected. In such a case, if the houses on the parallel street are not occupied by the rioters, sharpshooters should be stationed in their rear windows to cover the attacking party while they are forcing entrance into the opposite house.

In the same way if the rioters only occupy the houses on one side of a street, and it becomes necessary to make the attack on the front of a house, the attackers may be covered by sharpshooters from the windows of the houses on the opposite side of the street.

LINES OF ASSAULT

There are many lines of assault. An assault may be made up main streets, up side streets, through back gardens, over rooftops, through neighboring houses, through a house opposite and across a road, possibly even through sewers or contiguous cellars. In deciding upon a line or lines of assault the following points should be borne in mind.

Before attacking the enemy, it should be as nearly encircled as possible. Occupy the house on either side or behind it. Gain the houses on one side of a street before you enter the street.

Fields of fire must be set up that will cover all possible exits. First, attack the enemy most threatened by your own position. Attacks from several points, although difficult to synchronize, are most effective, as are those that can be covered by fire from your own forces. Any attack that has as its objective the entry of a building should be initiated and covered by heavily concentrated fire on windows, doors, roof, or other points from which enemy fire is being received.

If men, who are in position or who are advancing while firing, are likely to be subject to crossfire from their flanks, they must be protected by placing additional men and weapons to provide covering fire on these danger areas. Adequate cover should be selected for all firing points.

The Assault

The whole assault must be carried through at the highest possible speed by the shortest exposed route, with the heaviest possible covering fire until the last possible moment.

Gas should first be used to dislodge the occupants of a house. It may be introduced into the house by dropping gas grenades down chimneys, skylight, or firing a projectal or throwing a grenade into the house.

The attack by troops should be indirect whenever possible.

If the building is separated from other buildings, smoke is used to screen the approach of troops. If the structure is one of a row of buildings of approximately the same height, it may be attacked from an adjoining roof. A direct attack on a house that has been barricaded for defense should never be made unless it is demonstrated that all other methods would be useless, and when made should be preceded by artillery fire that will destroy the interior defenses.

A running advance, from cover to cover or toward the defended building, should be made in a zig-zag manner, with the body in a crouched position. Such an advance should be made in short runs, or bounds, so that the time of exposure to gunfire is short. To delay in the open is suicide. Many buildings have blind sides—with few, if any, doors and windows—so that they can be approached safely. Once the blind side of a building is reached, the party can follow around the outside walls and enter at a previously chosen section. If accurate covering fire supports the men who are gaining entry in this manner, it is difficult for the defenders to reach them by fire without unduly exposing themselves.

Preparations must be made to force an entrance to the house with the shortest delay outside. The best method is for a single man to run forward under covering fire, place an explosive against the house and dodge under cover. He should avoid doors and windows in placing his explosive; possibly a point in the side wall is best. When storming the objective building, employ all available means to climb to the upper stories. These include fire escapes, downspouts, lightning rods, ropes, rope ladders, etc.

If explosives are not obtainable, second-best are a heavy axe and a crowbar. Their employment means delay in the open and should be avoided whenever possible. Then men who are using them should always be accompanied by a man watching for bombs and grenades thrown from windows or a roof, ready to seize and throw them over a wall or down the street.

If explosives are used to force an entrance, the remainder of the assault party must be under cover well up, ready to dash in before the enemy has recovered from the shock of the explosion. Whatever the method employed of forcing an entrance, the assault party must attempt all methods of getting in. They need not necessarily confine themselves to going in through the gap they have made; the enemy will be concentrating their attention on it, and a man going in over the roof of a lean-to shed, up a drainpipe or down the skylight may escape notice.

Clearing the House

Having made an entrance, the assault party still has half its task before it. Inside the building, the initial objective is to seize stairwells, entrances and exits to seal off the defenders in small groups and to destroy them one after the other. Before leaving cover to assault the house, the officer in charge must allot tasks to each member of his party to ensure that there is no hanging about inside the house and that no room, cellar or attic is unsearched.

After securing an entrance, troops advance from room to room and from floor to floor until the building is cleared. Every room must be searched. Members of the searching party must tender each other continuous support. Two men should search a room while two other men stand in the doorway prepared to give whatever support is necessary. Troops outside the building should arrest all persons trying to leave.

Before entering each room a gas grenade thrown into the room will lessen resistance. In some cases rioters may remain in locked rooms. If necessary, holes should be punched through the walls and gas grenades thrown into the rooms.

It may be necessary to shoot through the walls or floors to dislodge armed and determined rioters. After the attack is begun there should be no pause in progress from room to room until the last of the rioters has been subdued.

MOPPING UP OPERATIONS

Upon overcoming armed resistance in an area, the commander takes immediate measures to eliminate further opposition. If the lawless elements are organized, for example, the commander may continue to expect simultaneous and sporadic attacks.

To cope with possible outbreaks, roving foot and vehicle patrols are employed within the area, usually on irregular or frequently changed schedules and routes. All the patrols should operate under one commander, who should have adequate reserves available at all times. Motor patrols may be used to patrol in isolation zones but they should carry crew sufficient in number to respond to any attack. Airplanes may be employed for reconnaissance and for directing motor patrols by means of radio or other signals.

In mopping up operations, it may be necessary to make house-to-house searches for arms or to apprehend individuals. Mopping up and searching parties may be sent through the houses on each side of a street. Where the houses are not connected, searching parties, protected by necessary fire, may approach their objectives simultaneously from several directions.

To conduct a house-to-house search of a large portion of a city, the area should be divided into sections. Each section should be thoroughly searched, then sealed off to prevent unauthorized persons from entering. Then the next adjoining area should be searched. Meanwhile patrols within and around the perimeter prevent the escape of suspected persons. No unauthorized person should be permitted to enter or leave a section being searched. If sufficient troops and police are available, two or more sections may be searched simultaneously.

Chapter 33

RIOTS – ARREST PROCEDURE

ARRESTS

CERTAIN GENERAL PRINCIPLES are applicable to the making of arrests during a riot. Make the arrest legally, quickly, with no unnecessary force or commentary by the police. Don't debate the issue with person arrested. Stick to the violation involved. Always consider your safety, that of your fellow officers and other citizens.

When a decision to arrest is made, officers who intend to make the arrests should approach the assembly in squads of not less than six men. This number assures mutual defense from assault, guarantees progress in the crowd and offers less chance of the rescue of arrested persons. These officers could be equipped with small tear gas bombs which may be dropped in a crowd as they progress through it.

If a leader in the mob is to be arrested, a penetration of the mob will be required. The squad wedge provides an excellent maneuvering unit for capturing individual leaders from near the edge of a crowd or mob. But if the formation must plunge deeply into the mob, a circular or a diamond formation formation should be used. In the center of the diamond will be the special arrest officers, who have been specially trained for this type of arrest.

When the formation reaches the individual to be apprehended, a gap is opened and the arrest team captures the culprit and brings the individual inside the formation. The gap is closed. The squad leader will at once command (1) To the rear, (2) Move. Still at the double, the squad should emerge with the captured rioter inside the wedge. All arrested persons must be removed as soon as possible from the scene to eliminate a focal point of sympathy and frustrate possible rescue attempts by the crowd.

In executing this arrest maneuver, the arrest squad should be utilized. These squads will consist of men carrying out special requirements of the arrest process. The arrest squad will consist of the following: (1) the commander; (2) a photographer; (3) identification officer; (4) two arresting, and (5) four transporting officers. Variations may be necessary under different circumstances, but the arrest squad complement described is believed to be most adequate.

The arrest process will usually begin when the company formation has made contact with the mob and is marching "in place" at the point of contact. The company commander directs, by prearranged signal, the squad leader to begin taking persons into custody. This is when the arrest squad begins to operate.

ARREST SQUAD OPERATION

The squad leader directs two men in the line to open, thus permitting the arrest officers to enter the line and seize the person selected by the squad leader for arrest. The line officers do not take part in the arrest unless forced to by circumstances. The line officers close the gap in the line as soon as the rioter is drawn into the formation. The seized rioter is immediately moved toward the rear of the formation and searched. Items taken from the subject will be marked and tagged as evidence.

The identification officer will be located at a safe, practical location to the rear of the formation. He will have facilities to enable him to complete the identification cards and obtain the right index fingerprint of prisoners. A photo officer will photograph the arresting officer with the person arrested, and any stolen property or weapons in his possession at the time of his arrest. The completed identification card on the arrest will be held before the accused when he is photographed.

All acts of resistance to arrest or defiance should be photographed. Blood from scratches should be wiped off before photographing. Some subjects scratch themselves or use large fake bandages to create the illusion of injury.

The transporting officers will remove the prisoner to the detention site. Handcuffs should be used when necessary. The short identification card furnished by the identification officer will be given to the detention supervisors by the transporting officers. If temporary detention is used, advance planning must determine the further transportation and processing of prisoners to fixed detention sites. Full fingerprints will be obtained at the detention sites. Officers involved in the arrest process will strive to insure accuracy and continuity in their operations.

TRANSPORTATION TEAM

Just as an arrest team backs up the strike force, it is in turn backed up by the transportation unit. Experience has taught that if a member of the strike force is required to arrest and transport his prisoner, he is taken from the strike force which is then weakened. It is obvious that if such a system were tolerated, the strike force would soon be depleted. This is the reason for the arrest team. Even more important is the transportation team. It should follow as close behind the strike force as is safe with mobile holding units such as paddy wagons and prison buses. In this way, the minimum time is lost by the arrest team in turning prisoners over to the holding force, and consequently less manpower is lost. Plans should be made so that as soon as a transporting unit is full, it will be replaced with another to avoid any extended delay in the operation.

EVIDENCE

Gathering evidence during a riot for later presentation in court is important. Evidence should be gathered of intent, identity of leaders and their lieutenants, their plan, how it was executed, and time and place of execution. Plainclothes men are useful for this purpose. It is important to remember that in times of high excitement and rapidly developing events officers will find it difficult later to remember incidents in all their details or in proper sequence or to identify the participants accurately. Evidence is also necessary to counteract accusations against the police.

CAMERAS

One of the best methods of obtaining and preserving an accurate record of the events is by the use of cameras. The use of motion pictures, particularly cameras with telescopic zoom lenses, has been found to be extremely valuable. They later bring to light clear evidence of the conduct of the police and of riot leaders. Photographs should be taken of the following: all principals associated with the riot; the general area and the mob, as well as any ensuing action; any person appearing intoxicated or acting unusual; all vehicles used by rioter.

At times it is psychologically beneficial to display the motion picture equipment conspicuously. When people feel they are being photographed by the police, they are restrained from engaging in illegal action. Thus the mere presence of such cameras has proven effective in preventing conflicts. When such equipment is so displayed, strong measures should be employed to protect it and the camera crew, for if an attack is made upon the police, it is certain that the cameras will be a prime target.

Sound recording equipment is desirable to record statements of agitators and the noise of the mob. This together with the motion pictures will recreate the event for the jury. Radio monitoring equipment and recording equipment should be used in those instances where rioters use radio to give orders.

Each police department should have a special detail at all scenes of disorder to gather evidence and to qualify themselves to testify. Better yet, those so employed should be appointed from outside the police department, i.e., committees composed of prominent and reputable citizens willing to go immediately to any scene of riot when the alarm is given. If possible, concentrate at least two police officers on each person to be arrested, thus enabling them to testify about specific illegal acts by that agitator.

Chapter 34

FIRE DEPARTMENT – RIOT TACTICS

INTRODUCTION

Recent riots have seen the rioters deliberately set fire to commercial establishments and automobiles throughout the riot area. When the fire units responded, the mob delayed and prevented access to the fires and hampered fire ground operations by harassing and physically assaulting the firemen. The means encompassed the entire gamut of force, from verbal taunts to attacks with rocks, cans, bottles, Molitov cocktails and rifle fire. To meet the challenge of such wide scale holocaust under such adverse conditions requires advance planning, leadership and courage.

POLICE GUARDS

The police shall notify a designated fire department representative of the nature and location of the incident. That representative will in turn notify the police of the location of all fire houses which service the affected area.

As soon as practicable, two patrol vehicles will be dispatched to each fire house to act as escorts in case of runs. Escort personnel will protect equipment while firemen work. Sufficient personnel should be assigned to escorts to permit a guard on vacated fire houses.

FIRE FIGHTING COMMANDER

An overall fire fighting commander should be designated and charged with the responsibility of coordinating and commanding all fire units utilized in the riot area. He should be designated in advance of any riot and his staff selected and instructed regarding its duties and procedure.

As soon as the field command post is established, the designated fire fighting commander should be notified. He should immediately alert and assemble his staff and proceed to the field command post.

He should establish his headquarters at the field command post where he can maintain close contact with the police commander and be in the best position to keep abreast of the situation.

DISPATCH CENTER AND STAFF

The fire commander should establish a dispatch center at the command post. It will be responsible for maintaining a record of all fires and the location of all fire fighting equipment. To achieve this requires the establishment of a reconnaisance and reporting network. Helicopters are ideal for this task.

The fire fighting commander should have on his staff officers designated to handle personnel including its call-up and assignment; supplies, their procurement and disbursement; and equipment, its procurement, dispatch and repair.

FIRE ALARM PROCEDURE

All box and local alarms in the riot area should be transmitted over to fire communication command post center at the field. Police patrol vehicles will be dispatched to the location of the alarm to determine an actual need for fire equipment, or, if available, a helicopter will conduct this reconnaisance.

The patrol vehicle will report conditions to the field command post. When a patrol vehicle checks an alarm location and finds fire equipment necessary, the best access route should be transmitted to the police. All decisions relative to the use of fire equipment will be made by the fire fighting commander.

THE PROBLEM AND BASIC TACTICS

Flammable liquids, either in hastily manufactured fire bombs or in a variety of portable containers, are widely used by the incendiarists to fire structures. There is usually no orderly progression from a state of minor incipiency through stages of gradual enlargement to a condition of total involvement. The fiery impetus produced by the volatile fluids flood building interiors with flames the instant ignition occurs. As a result, fire units only rarely are able to arrive at structural fires while involvement of the building is minor. A series of huge, roaring holocausts which pours flames from building openings, threatening adjacent structures, confronts the fire fighters.

To combat such conditions most effectively, the fire department is obliged to embark upon a strategy incorporating a wide use of large stream appliances and a high degree of fire-fighting unit mobility. The overriding principle involved is the necessity to limit the spread of all fires, as nearly as possible, to their areas of origin. Otherwise, the underlying possibility of a widespread, sweeping conflagration might burst into devastating reality.

The moment that a fire is overcome, the units must quickly break off operations and proceed to another raging inferno. Extensive overhauling operations must be abandoned during the disorder. If units expended hours digging and hauling in gutted buildings to extinguish every hidden remaining spark, there would soon be no units available to combat the newly-ignited fires. Salvage work must also be suspended for the duration of the riot.

TASK FORCE

To cope effectively with the problems, and to give the maximum protection to the fire fighting personnel, task forces should be employed. The task force consists of two or more engine companies, a ladder truck and a chief officer. It responds to fires as a complete and unified fire-fighting body. Police and/or military personnel should be permanently assigned as part of this force for escort and defensive duty. The police may either ride on the fire equipment or in their own vehicles. When possible, maintenance service personnel of the various public utilities should also be a part of this task force, for in such wide scale fires poles, wires, switches and transformers carrying high voltages become involved in the fires. Firemen cannot attempt to control high voltages beyond certain limits. Consequently, the fire-fighters will be exposed to the additional hazard of working under burning poles and falling live high voltage wires.

Each task force should move as a unit in convoy for maximum protection. At the scene of the fire it should remain in a closely-knit group while working on emergencies and leave in a body when operations are completed.

The police or military escort should establish a defense ring about the unit and protect it from attacking mobs and snipers. Where mobs are present, companies are discouraged from proceeding down narrow alleyways in the rear of buildings. Caution must be exercised to prevent engineers from becoming isolated at remote hydrants.

Advantages

Security of personnel and apparatus is improved by the presence of a relatively large number of men at a location. Smaller groups of rioters are discouraged from attacking a task force where they might not hesitate to assault a lone engine company. This added security, tenuous as it actually is, supplies an important degree of confidence and morale to beleaguered firemen. The commanding officer knows from the moment of dispatch what units are in the force and may begin deployment of the entire group immediately upon arrival at a fire. Unity of command is simplified because all members can identify and be responsible to the task force commander. The amount of radio traffic is reduced because only the officer in charge is required to transmit to the signal office. The danger of intersection accidents with apparatus is minimized because units are not responding over a number of separate, unfamiliar routes to an emergency. Dispatching procedures at the command post are much simpler. The assignment of individual companies to respond is not necessary. It is only required that the commander of a particular task force be notified of a dispatch and all of the involved units are aware of their inclusion on the response.

Disadvantages

There are a few disadvantages inherent in the task force method of operation. It tends to delay initial response. Distances to an emergency are sometimes considerably greater than they would be under normal response patterns. Also, companies are frequently held together at small fires and are not individually available for other alarms. Under the circumstances prevailing during a riot, the disadvantages are hardly worth consideration.

MOLOTOV COCKTAILS

For protection against fire bombs (Molotov cocktails) personnel should note the following:

1. Dry chemical extinguishers are most effective.
2. Personnel protection depends much on clothing and facial protection.
3. Short sleeve shirts should be avoided. Blouse coats and gloves provide the most protection.
4. Until proper equipment is available, strategic retreat is in order.

Chapter 35

COUNTER-INSURGENCY OPERATIONS

IMPORTANCE OF THE POLICE

Society is dependent on effective law enforcement machinery, for the smooth functioning of its highly evolved and complicated social and economic existence. In all the greater existing independent communities of modern times, the responsibility for controlling the menace to internal order resides in the police. So long as the police are effective, government authority, laws, courts and the entire social and economic organization of the community will function with a degree of smoothness which assures their continuity.

Unfortunately there appears to be less awareness that the police have an important role within the arena of present day international politics. Within the realm of sub-limited warfare, it is possible for the police of a nation to insure the preservation of internal order. It is even possible to prevent an insurgency through the proper use of a professionally trained and loyal police force. This is because the police are the eye and the arm of the government in all matters pertaining to internal order.

In the early stages of development of the insurrection the police are of particular importance. In the beginning the success of the insurgency is dependent upon secrecy. The government police force must not be aroused, but lulled into a false sense of security until the insurgency is sufficiently perfected and other preparations well on the way.

It is realized in the international arena that civil disobedience can easily lead to revolution. Insurgency can, unfortunately, progress to a dangerous state through nonviolent means. It is the police who are primarily utilized to control such disobediences. Military force is only resorted to when the disorder becomes of such magnitude as to pose a serious threat to the government in power.

The police are, therefore, obviously a key factor in the early stages

[463]

of an insurgency; they are the first counterinsurgent organization. It is an insurgent's vital interest to negate the power and effectiveness of the police in the early stages of an insurgency. To do this, he must infiltrate, neutralize, discredit, or destroy. The earlier in the insurgency stage this can be accomplished, the more significant the gains will be. Once the police are rendered incapable of dealing with mob violence and civil disorder, the insurgency movement is able to move rapidly. Without such a force to act as a deterrent, internal order and harmony break down and lead to complete disintegration of the cohesive force which binds single individuals together in a civilized society. Briefly put, it is recognized that a successful guerrilla action requires a weak government and an ineffective police force.

INSURGENCY MOVEMENT

Definitions

A *resistance movement* is an organized effort by some portion of the civil population of a country to resist the legally established government or an occupying power. Initially, such resistance may consist of subversive political activities, and other actions, designed to agitate and propagandize the populace into distrust of and loss of confidence in the legally established government or occupying power. If not suppressed, such resistance can result in insurgency by irregular forces.

Insurgency movement is the broad category of opposition to an existing government including political, social, economic and military actions. Within this broad category of opposition, the terms revolution, rebellion and insurrection can be used interchangeably.

The Cause

The first basic need for a resistance or insurgency movement which aims at more than simply making trouble is an attractive cause, particularly in view of the risks involved and in view of the fact that the early supporters and the active supporters—not necessarily the same persons—have to be recruited by persuasion. For the insurgent, the best cause is one that all the population, or most of it, would support. A cause must be lasting, if not for the duration of the revolutionary war, at least until the insurgent movement is well on its feet.

Rationally, whatever the cause, it must be both plausible and compelling. It must invoke a vision of life after the struggle that can sustain the lonely guerrilla's morale. It must overcome his fears when he undertakes a hazardous mission alone and against odds.

It must also possess a high moral appeal that justifies violations of traditional norms of behavior when the guerrilla is sent out to assassinate in cold blood a rival, an enemy, or an innocent bystander. A cause inspired by lust for power, by a clique, or simply for loot will enlist only the mercenary, the outlaw and the criminal. For the less bold noncombatant supporter on whom the fighters rely for food, supplies and vital information, it must also justify the risk of enemy reprisal to himself and his family if the adversary discovers his treachery. The cause must appear to be unachievable by less violent means, for only if the political or legal system seems to deny redress will the risks of violence be acceptable.

In addition to inciting to violence, a cause must be capable of disrupting traditional or historic loyalties. In civilized countries these loyalties may be to a nation, a system or government, or even to a single political party. Whereas the cause of a genuine, indigenous movement and that of a communist-led "liberation war" have much in common, they also have fundamental differences. For the first, the cause is the ultimate aim. For the communist the cause is a means to an end—the establishment of a communist regime. The cause is usually centered around one of the following:

1. National independence.
2. Relief from actual or alleged oppression.
3. Elimination of foreign occupation or exploitation.
4. Economic and social improvement.
5. Elimination of corruption.
6. Religious expression.

Finally, no matter how right the cause may seem, unless it has some hope of fulfillment and unless its champion has some chance of survival, no one but the fool, the suicidal maniac or the fanatic will risk his life for it.

Development of the Movement

Insurgency movements begin to form when dissatisfaction occurs among motivated individuals who cannot further their cause by peace-

ful and legal means. Under appropriate conditions, the attitudes and
beliefs of these individuals, who are willing to risk their lives for their
beliefs, spread to family groups and neighbors. The population of
entire areas may soon evidence widespread discontent. When legal
recourse is denied, discontent grows into dissatisfaction and members
of the population participate in irregular activities.

Small dissident groups living and working within the established
order gradually organize into underground elements that conduct
covert irregular activities. As members of underground organizations
are identified and as the spirit of resistance grows, overt guerrilla
bands form in secure areas and become the military arm of the
irregular force. Characteristically, the scope of irregular activities
progress in this order: passive objection; individual expression of
opposition; minor sabotage; major sabotage; individual violent action,
and organized group violent action. Once individuals have participated in irregular activities, should there be any change of heart,
they are usually forced to continue, either by pressure from their
comrades or by being designated criminals by local authority.

Motivation

The sociological climate produces many motivating factors which
have a profound effect upon the movement. Strong individual motivation is essential to the formation of a insurrectionist force. Although
some individual motives are not ideal and, if openly expressed, may do
harm to the guerrilla effort, the following are examples of what some
of the true motives may be.

IDEOLOGY. In guerrilla units some individuals have developed strong
ideological motives for taking up arms. These ideologies take root in
two broad areas—politics and religion. The individual tends to subordinate his own personality to these ideologies and works constantly
and solely for the "cause."

ECONOMIC. Many individuals join insurrectionist movements to
keep from starving or to keep from losing their livelihood. An organized guerrilla force can exert economic influence on individuals who
fail to support their movement.

PERSONAL GAIN. Personal gain is the motivating force of some
volunteers. An individual, so motivated, may change sides if he
believes he can gain more by fighting for the opposing force.

HATE. People who have lost loved ones due to enemy actions may fight against that enemy as a result of engendered hatred. Uncontrolled hatred can pose problems for the sponsor because it is difficult to curb the fanaticism of such individuals and direct their efforts properly.

SECURITY. If the insurrection movement is strong or gives the impression of being powerful, many individuals join out of a feeling of personal safety. Usually, this situation occurs only after the movement is well organized and the enemy has been weakened by other actions. Others join in order to escape recruitment into the service of the enemy.

FEAR. Some individuals become a part of the movement through no personal desire of their own. They join the movement out of fear of reprisals against themselves or their families.

Stages of Operation

The first and often the most decisive phase of all is the precombat, organizational or conspiratorial phase. During this preparatory stage, the guerrilla leader organizes his immediate staff and recruits and trains the nucleus of his fighting force. At the same time he tries to enlist the sympathy of the population in order to be sure of its support when combat operations start. He caches arms and supplies, prepares hideouts and builds up a secret communications network whereby he can transmit orders and receive secret intelligence about the enemy when he later takes the field.

In the second phase, the guerrillas are still too weak to attack the enemy and must constantly retreat before him. But as they retreat they gather strength, while the enemy, extending his lines and penetrating deep into country already politically disaffected by the guerrillas, overextends and weakens himself.

Phase three begins when the guerrillas begin to worry the enemy, attacking his communications, harrying him when he pauses, ambushing his supply columns and capturing the weapons they need to form new guerrilla units. Finally comes the fourth phase when the enemy is too extended and weakened, and the guerrillas, reenforced and better trained, move into the offensive, driving the enemy back and eventually defeating him. In this, the final phase, the guerrillas no longer operate in small bands but in large division size units.

The trick is, however, to recognize the moment at which to switch from one phase to another. If it is done too soon by an impatient commander, his units will be defeated in open battle against better equipped, seasoned enemy troops. If it is postponed too long, one's own troops begin to get discouraged and the magic moment slips by forever.

IRREGULAR FORCES

Irregular forces refer in a broad sense to all types of insurgents including, for example, partisans, subversionists, terrorists, revolutionaries and guerrillas.

Organization

The organization of irregular forces varies according to purpose, terrain, character and density of population, availability of food, medical supplies, arms and equipment, quality of leadership, amount and nature of external support and direction, and the countermeasures used against them. Units or elements may vary in size from a few saboteurs to organized paramilitary units of division size or larger with extensive support organizations.

A large irregular force normally consists of two organized elements: a guerrilla element which operates overtly, and an underground element which operates covertly. Members of large guerrilla units are usually severed from their normal civilian pursuits while members of small guerrilla bands may alternately be either guerrillas or apparently peaceful citizens. Members of the underground usually maintain their civilian pursuits. Both elements are usually supported by individuals and small groups who may or may not be formal members of either element but who furnish aid in intelligence, evasion and escape, and supplies.

The underground elements of an irregular force must conduct the majority of their activities in a covert manner because of the countermeasures used against them. Successful organizations are compartmented by cells for security reasons. The cellular organization prevents one member, upon capture, from compromising the entire organization.

Activities

An irregular force presents an elusive target, since it will usually disperse before superior opposition, and then reform to strike again. However, as the guerrilla elements of an irregular force grow and approach parity with regular units in organization, equipment, training and leadership, their capabilities and tactics likewise change and become similar to those of a regular unit.

Overt irregular activities include acts of destruction against public and private property, transportation and communications systems; raids and ambushes against military and police headquarters, garrisons, conveys, patrols and depots; terrorism by assassination, bombing, armed robbery, torture, mutilation and kidnaping; provocation of incidents, reprisals and holding of hostages; and denial activities, such as arson, flooding, demolition, use of chemical or biological agents, or other acts designed to prevent use of an installation, area, product, or facility.

Covert irregular activities include espionage, sabotage, dissemination of propaganda and rumors, delaying or misdirecting orders, issuing false or misleading orders or reports, assassination, extortion, blackmail, theft, counterfeiting and identifying individuals for terroristic attack.

Tactics

Irregular force tactics vary; however, the following tactics are common to all irregular forces.

GUERRILLA TACTICS. The tactics used by the guerrilla are designed to weaken his enemy and to gain support of the population. Guerrilla tactics follow well-known precepts. If the enemy attacks, *disappear;* if he defends, *harass;* and if he withdraws or at any time he is vulnerable, *attack.*

Guerrilla tactics are primarily small-unit, infantry-type tactics which make full use of accurate intelligence, detailed planning and rehearsal, simple techniques of maneuver, speed, surprise, infiltration, specialization in night operations, and the undermining of enemy morale. Surprise is gained by the combined elements of speed, secrecy, selection of unsuspected objectives and deliberate deception. Infiltration is a basic tactic of successful guerrilla units and they quickly develop great skill in infiltrating areas occupied by military units. Enemy morale is undermined by constant harassment, exhibition of a violent combative spirit, fanaticism, self-sacrifice, and extensive use of propaganda, threats, blackmail and bribery.

UNDERGROUND ELEMENT TACTICS. The tactics employed by underground elements are designed to gain the same results as guerrilla tactics. Underground organizations attempt, through nonviolent persuasion, to indoctrinate and gain the participation of groups of the population who are easily deceived by promises and, through coercion by terror tactics, to force others to participate. Espionage and sabotage are common to all underground groups. Terroristic attack such as assassination and bombings are used to establish tension and reduce police or military control. Propaganda is disseminated by implanting rumors, distributing leaflets and placards, and when possible, by operating clandestine radio stations for broadcasting purposes. Agitation tactics include fostering of black markets, and promoting demonstrations, riots, strikes and work slowdown.

URBAN GUERRILLA WARFARE

Contrary to the views of many specialists in unconventional warfare, recent history has proven that unconventional urban warfare operations are possible. A great city provides hidden paths through alleys and cellars, attics and rooftops, just as inaccessible to strangers as a hidden jungle trail. The labryinth sewer system may not smell as sweet as a forest path, but provides a highly effective system of communications.

Every fugitive knows the safety in numbers, and few who seek to escape notice seek refuge in the wilderness. Instead they lose themselves in crowds in populated areas. They must seek concealment in their ability to merge with the masses—being a peaceful electrician by day and a skilled saboteur by night.

In cities, guerrillas can get the cooperation of the local population in a way that is impossible in the country. In rural areas, guerrillas depend largely on people acting individually to aid them, or they count on protection and aid from a number of individuals in a small village. In such cases the majority of these people have been tipped off in advance just what they are supposed to do to help. But in cities the guerrilla can get mass aid from thousands of people, who will do the right thing at the right moment even though not more than one or two out of a thousand people have been "in on" the plans.

City guerrillas can be even more invisible than any others. They can work through so many thousands of people that it is well-nigh impossible to trace the origin of any "spot of trouble." In this way the enemy is made to feel the guerrilla is an impalpable presence, until every ordinary pedestrian seems likely to be a guerrilla in disguise.

Conventional guerrillas operating in the jungle or in the desert are vitally dependent on supplies from elsewhere. The urban guerrilla, on the other hand, operates in the very heart of the supply system. Not only food markets, but pharmacies with their medicines, and workshops for the repair of arms and manufacture of bombs and other weapons are readily available.

Nevertheless, the urban guerrilla operates under many disadvantages unknown to the rural guerrilla, which limit the kinds of operations he can undertake. The assembly of large numbers of men and their dispersal after a strike in force is well-nigh impossible under the eyes of a vigilant police. The risk of recognition, even in a crowd, by informers requires a much more sophisticated security system than in the case of rural guerrillas.

Hence, until they undertake an all-out uprising, urban guerrillas must confine themselves to operations which can be carried out in small numbers and avoid all risks of open street fights in which the rebels can be identified. Yet even in this respect they enjoy some advantages over rural guerrillas. Because they are in the heart of a communications center, which ordinarily houses the headquarters of large enemy forces, their opportunities for intelligence gathering are greatly increased. Furthermore, the communications center itself is more vulnerable to damage than the individual rail or telegraph lines stretching through a rural area. The sabotage of a marshaling yard, for example, can damage the enemy more severely than the blowing up of a culvert on a single line. The destruction of a telephone or telegraph center can cripple the enemy far more than cutting an individual wire. While the urban guerrilla can seldom ambush and annihilate enemy patrols, he has far better opportunities in a headquarters town to liquidate key enemy personnel as they travel through its confined streets.

Finally, guerrillas operating in densely populated areas, where the level of education is normally much higher than in remote villages, have a greater opportunity to carry on their propaganda and recruiting. From the scrawling of antienemy slogans on walls, to the distribution of pamphlets and posters and the holding of secret meetings, they are in a much better position to instill their ideas in the masses than the guerrilla operating among semiliterate or illiterate peasants.

TERROR

Terror is an induced state of fear or anxiety within an individual or group of individuals. Terror has also been defined as the attempt to govern or to violence for political ends, or as a symbolic act designed to influence political behavior by extranormal means, entailing the use or threat of violence. These definitions are broad. They cover both agitational terror designed to disrupt the existing order and achieve power, as well as enforcement terror, activity by an encumbent who wishes to suppress the challenge to its authority. They include activities far beyond the stereotype view of terror, the dynamiting of buildings or the mass execution of a village's council or notables. As used here, terror involved (1) terror acts which are part of military of paramilitary assaults either offensively against installations or units, or defensively in the field against military operations; (2) terror acts which are part of the ambush, which may be directed at military units, or at civilians traveling along roads; (3) harassing citizens for coercive or intimidation purposes with or without the taking of life; (4) sabotage and subversive acts which involve direct use of violence; (5) acts directed against specific individuals, such as kidnappings, assassinations and executions. The violence may range from burning crosses on political opponents' front lawns to sabotage, the burning of villages, kidnapping, assassination and mutilation.

The objectives of a terrorist campaign are the following:

1. To build the morale of the terrorist group. A successful terrorist act does much to create the aura of invulnerability within a guerrilla band and helps bolster spirits throughout the insurgent organization.

2. To advertise the insurrectionist movement. Undoubtedly there is no cheaper or easier way for an insurgent band or dissident group to single itself out from other opposition than by use of terror.

3. To disorientate and psychologically isolate the individual in the society. This is done by destroying the structure of authority previously a source of security. Thus in Vietman, the particular target is the Vietnamese villager. The response which the Viet Cong seek through use of terror is fright, anxiety and despair. Terror removes the underpinnings of the orderly system in which the villager lives out his life. It disorients the villager by demonstrating to him that his government cannot give him the safety and order he normally expects from it. The usual protections of his life suddenly vanish and disorientation results. This Viet Cong demonstration, however, it but one aspect of the disorientation process. On a much deeper level, the Viet Cong seek to isolate the villager in his social context. Terror isolates. A villager can no longer draw strength from customary social supports. He can rely only on himself. He may be physically undisturbed, but he is terribly alone in his anguish. Villagers then become impotent and of no threat to the Viet Cong. A terrorized villager is in a condition associated with anxiety neurosis. He seeks only one thing—means of fixing his own security.

4. To eliminate the opposing forces, either physically or by neutralizing their effectiveness. Again Vietnam gives us the classic example. By means of terror the Viet Cong have sought to eliminate an entire class of Vietnamese villagers, the local officials and governmental representatives as well as the natural leaders of the village. A leaderless village is further disorientated.

5. To provoke the government into acts of retaliation which will alienate the people. There were, in the early years of Viet Cong, terror acts committed with the express purpose of provoking reprisals, but the practice was not as widespread as in other insurgencies. Any government faced with terror acts finds it necessary to attempt to suppress the terrorists. Ideally that suppression is by regular and orthodox use of law enforcement. But if the terrorist is effective and if the government sees itself in a crisis, it will almost inevitably use extraordinary repressive measures.

Terrorists quite obviously must be strongly dedicated and highly

militant. Most of them have been young, for the young are more
easily influenced in their thinking, are more willing to take risks,
physically are more capable of the tasks assigned them, are less prone
to question orders, and less likely to be or to become double agents.

Terror can be used against the enemy to destroy his will to resist.
However, against a resolute enemy, terror seldom succeeds, and by its
very horror it often increases the will to resist. However, in conjunction with other circumstances, it can succeed as it did against the
British in Palestine, in 1947, and again in the Suez Canal zone, in
1954, when the cost of suppression began to exceed the value of the
objective in dispute.

In non-Communist areas terror is more frequently used against the
native population, or elements of it which refuse to support the guerrillas and either remain passive or collaborate with the enemy. In
such cases the purpose of terror is in part to punish "traitors" but
more important to discourage others from aiding the enemy and to
encourage contributions to the guerrilla force.

Ordinarily, guerrillas resort to violence of this nature only when
other forms or irregular warfare are denied them by lack of followers
or lack of suitable weapons. Terror is the weapon of the weak.

In this regard an analysis of the Viet Cong doctrinal approach to
terror is quite revealing. Viet Cong cadres consider the proper use
of terror demands that terror be applied judiciously, selectively and
sparingly. They have found that terror, turned on and off, para-
doxically produces both pro and antiguerrilla feelings among villagers.
On the one hand, of course, it engenders fear and hatred, with the
first usually predominating over the second. But when relaxed after
an area-wide terror campaign, an exaggerated sense of relief spreads
through the villages and villagers tend to regard the guerrillas as being not nearly as inhumane as they are capable of being. Terror, in
the Viet Cong hold, is virtually useless against a dedicated opponent.
In general, Viet Cong theoreticians consider terror to be the weapon
of the weak and hold that as guerrilla control increases, it should be
quickly diminishing returns. They believe that terror methods are
successful only when the objectives of the terrorist have popular support. And to judge from their terror acts, they believe that terror works
better on friends than on enemies. It is also true, whether or not the

Viet Cong recognize it, that terror is most effective when the general population is sympathetic to the cause and least effective when the population actively is committed against the terrorist.

It is obvious that a terrorist killer enjoys many advantages in crowded city streets. An effective counter to the ruthless killer is not easy to find. To fill the streets with police and armed soldiery is exorbitantly expensive in manpower and can only be maintained for short periods. Snap searches of male passersby in the hope of catching the terrorist with a weapon on his person may have some deterrent effect. So also may the arming of civilians, the use of decoys, and other methods of deception. But it will only be a matter of time before a patient killer will find a safe opportunity to shoot.

Reprisal

The counterpart of terror is reprisal. Its purpose is, of course, to discourage further acts of rebellion. Reprisal can be as mild as collective fines imposed on a community where a terrorist act has been committed. It can involve the shooting of hundreds of innocent enemy civilians in retribution for every counterinsurgent killed. As we have seen, the Germans successfully persuaded Mikhailovitch's force to desist from acts of sabotage against the occupation because of fear of reprisal against either their families at home in Belgrade or against the villagers who supported the Chetniks in the provinces. In the case of the Partisans, however, reprisal was singularly ineffective. In their case it merely stimulated recruitment and increased the determination of the individual Partisan to destroy the Nazis. Similarly, German reprisals failed completely to deter the Soviet Partisans in Russia in World War II.

Terror and its counterpart, reprisal, are dangerous double-edged weapons. Though they may enforce obedience through fear, they seldom enlist sympathetic support. Inevitably, terror when countered by reprisal, provokes more brutal terror which in turn brings down more ferocious reprisals.

The pressure to meet terror with counterterror will at times seem irresistible, but to do so is to play the guerrilla's game without his particular advantages. Brutality, fear and the resultant social disorganization can work only for the guerrillas, no matter who initiates them.

By forcing the legitimate power to adopt their own methods, the guerrillas gain a vital point. All government is based on the discriminating application of power; its indiscriminate use over extended periods implies a surrender both of policy and of ethics, and releases the kind of internal conflict that frequently destroys the capacity of a political and social organism to defend itself.

COUNTER-INSURGENCY

The term *counter-insurgency operations* refers to those operations conducted against insurgent forces. Those operations include police, social, political and military measures designed to combat and eliminate insurgent elements within an area. An essential ingredient is the execution of a positive action program which seeks to eliminate the causes which lead to political and social unrest within an area. Generally speaking, the more public support the police have in a nation, the less likelihood of its domination by a subversive group.

It is of importance to realize that the willing observance of public rules is the keystone of community existence. In the history of communities, absence or weakness of effective law enforcement machinery can be seen to be, very frequently, the true cause of failure in battle.

The insurgent has no responsibility for maintaining order within the target country. The counterinsurgent, however, has a paramount responsibility to maintain public order within the legal framework of its governmental national goals. Insurgency has much to gain and nothing to lose if its incipient forces can infiltrate or immobilize the police entities of a nation. Thus, mob violence can work only to the detriment of free world society.

The government must be able to meet the insurgent with military force, present a logical plan of action to the people and assure the people that the government has their best interests at heart.

BASIC COUNTER-INSURGENCY THEORIES

Various methods have been devised and are advocated for handling insurrections. One regards the insurrectionists as a legitimate aggressive force, fighting for a cause which they believe, and who should be accorded Geneva Convention treatment.

Another school of thought believes in fighting the guerrilla on his own terms. It utilizes the tactics and techniques of the guerrilla him-self—terrorism, a powerful secret police, arbitrary military tribunals, public executions and intimidation. It relies on brute force without regard to constitutional or other legal or ethical restraints, justifying its brutalities under the slogan of fighting fire with fire. This is the method employed by the Russians in Berlin in 1953 and again in Budapest in 1956. Basically it is the approach Chiang Kai-shek used against the communists in the 1930's and which the French employed against the Vietminh and again against the Algerian rebels.

The pattern is familiar. When a popular uprising or guerrilla move-ment develops to the combat phase, the entire police and military force is directed not only against the guerrilla combatants but against all elements which can be suspected of supporting or even sympathizing with the movement. Using reprisal and terror indiscriminantely with-out judicial restraints it can, if it strikes early and vigorously enough, halt the movement.

The method has two drawbacks. To be in a position to strike a timely blow it must depend on an efficient, powerful political police and intelligence system. Such a system is costly both in manpower and in the limitations it imposes on popular civil liberties. It cannot tolerate any laxness or complacency that might allow a guerrilla conspiracy to organize cadres, caches of arms or hideouts. Thus far, the Soviet sys-tem alone has been able to afford this luxury to the extent that a successful uprising of the discontented satellites is virtually impossible.

The second pitfall of this approach is that instead of mitigating grievances to the point of toleration, it tends to aggravate them. Those who might have spurned resorting to force, despite their frustrations, tend to become more frustrated so that the potential civilian support for a mass movement and the potential recruits for guerrilla bands grow.

A third method emphasizes the establishing of law and order through a strong police force and an effective civil administration, rather than on waging warfare. Here the fundamental premise is that insurrec-tions represent an illegal armed civil disobedience movement, there-fore prisoners are to be treated as common criminals and tried and punished in civilian courts for violation of the law. Under this theory, negotiations with the insurrectionists are impossible, since the obvious position of the government must be that a legally constituted government does not bargain with gangsters.

This theory believes that communism does not primarily feed on peasant grievances or rely on armed strength but rather comes to power by exploiting "internal contradictions of bourgeois society," by fomenting internal divisions, playing on personal ambitions and using intimidation. The distinguishing feature of this method is to defeat the insurgent without sacrificing the normal restraints of popular government.

Still another theory relies upon the premise that grievances are the main cause for the growth of insurrectionist movements, and thus the accent must be placed upon the remedy of such grievances. The prime theory of this school of thought is to oppose an idea with a better idea and to launch a social revolution led by a worthy and dynamic leader, which concentrates upon improving the condition of the poor.

Still another theory combines military force with demonstration of superior civilization, accenting the equality of man, rule of law, and social and technical engineering skills.

Communistic Counter-insurgency Tactics

Probably the most effective system of suppressing insurrection is to be found in the communist countries. They demonstrated their methods when they advanced to "liberate" the nations of eastern Europe from the Germans. The Soviet political police were hard on the heels of the combat troops. While communist propagandists endeavored to enlist the active support of the formerly discontented elements of the population, these police assiduously rounded up those who they knew would never support them.

Since the proportion of the population favorable to them was usually small, it was occasionally necessary to establish a transitional government in which other parties were represented in order to obtain even a minimum of popular support. However, in each of these governments, Soviet commissars made sure that the minister of interior and the police chiefs of the principle towns were either avowed or secret Party members. Their immediate function was to harass, render impotent and, if necessary, liquidate politicians and patriots whose loyalty they could not hope to win over by less drastic forms of persuasion. Thus from the very beginning the communist leaders in the satellites made sure that any potential opposition would never have that first noncombatant phase of conspiratorial preparation essential to a successiveful guerrilla operation.

It is common practice for the communists to undertake provocative activities designed to test the loyalty of each individual in the regime. A person may at any time be contacted by someone purporting to represent a clandestine organization. Even though the sympathies of the person approached may be strongly anticommunist and his fondest hopes that the communists be overthrown, he must assume that this is not a genuine resistance movement but rather one conducted under the control of, and at the direction of, the secret police. To prove his loyalty he must not only refuse to join the purported clandestine organization, but must also inform the police. If he does not, he will have failed to demonstrate his positive loyalty to the regime and will be subject to reprisals and imprisonment. Thus a clandestinely organized resistance within a consolidated communist regime is not likely to get very far before someone has, out of fear, reported its existence to the police.

A second device used by the communists is to form a clandestine anticommunist organization under their own secret control, to encourage its growth by recruiting unwitting members, and to permit them to conduct actual operations against the regime until finally, having attracted a large number of the most aggressive anticommunists, its entire membership is arrested.

TASKS OF THE COUNTER-INSURRECTIONIST

The ultimate objective of operations against an irregular force is to eliminate the irregular force and prevent its resurgence. To attain this objective certain tasks must be accomplished. Generally, these must be pursued simultaneously since success in one area depends on progress in the others. In a very real sense, it is only for purposes of analysis that they can be discussed separately. The tasks are the following ones:

ISOLATE. No effective guerrilla movement can exist without, as a minimum, the passive sympathy of the local population; therefore, a basic objective of counterguerrilla operations is to separate guerrilla forces from all forms and sources of support by separation of the guerrilla force from the local civilian population and supporting states. Physically, this may be done by military means; psychologically it can be done, among other ways, by identifying and ostracizing the core group who may subsequently be exploited as scapegoats for guerrilla failures.

DESTROY. This means not only the military defeat of the guerrilla forces, but also destruction implies the physical and psychological operation designed to cause disaffection, to convert elements of the guerrilla force, and to eliminate hard core elements. The main objectives are the leaders and chiefs of the insurgents.

RECONSTRUCT. Reconstruction is that phase of counter-insurgency operations, when units previously concerned with the conduct of armed operations are diverted either in whole or in part to the implementation of previously determined national objectives embodied in a positive program.

ISOLATION

Means

The means to solve the first task of the problem, i.e., isolation of the insurgents, are the following:

1. Use of propaganda.
2. The discovery and internment of the underground leaders of pro-guerrilla organizations, as well as the "go-betweens and suppliers."
3. The organization and arming of the antiguerrilla forces.
4. Development of plans to close the guerrilla supply routes, the borders and coasts, and the denial of airdrops for supplies.

Although the methods suggested may seem very simple, their implementation is extremely difficult where the population is friendly to the guerrillas.

Control of the Population

The government cannot afford to lose control of the population. There are many techniques of control which may be employed by the authorities. They may be in the form of verbal or written communication, propaganda, group meetings, and by utilization of the following methods:

1. Confiscate weapons to reduce their availability to guerrilla seizure and set up an accountability system for those weapons retained by civilians.
2. Register all civilians and set up an identity card system.
3. Established a curfew with due consideration for civilian needs.
4. Set up circulation controls.
5. Suspend such personal rights as may be necessary to allow searches and arrest on suspicion.
6. Evacuate designated areas.
7. Provide security for friendly civilians and their families.
8. Establish a reporting system covering treatment of wounds and administration of designated medical aid.
9. Furnish relief supplies to insurrectionists' victims and other indigent persons.
10. Conduct educational forums to counter insurrectionist propaganda and outline positive programs.
11. Secure reports on absentee employees.
12. Maintain control and accountability over foodstuffs, medicine, livestock, raw material, or other matter which may be of assistance to guerrillas.
13. Establish price control and rationing systems for critical items.
14. Confiscate property of adjudged collaborators.
15. Censor media of public communication.
16. License all forms of transportation.
17. Establish an information program with the support of psychological warfare personnel to publicize measures taken, reasons therefore, and punishments for noncompliance.
18. Reward civilians who contribute actively to counter-insurrection programs.
19. Restore normal community processes of public health, safety, education, communications, transportation, waste disposal, water supply, legal processes and other expressions of civil government and administration.
20. Introduce necessary governmental and legal reforms.

21. Stimulate production of agricultural products and other essential goods.
22. Increase development and utilization of local resources.
23. Improve community relations activities.
24. Encourage civic action programs.

Since the police are already known to the public, their use in enforcing these restrictive measures can, if accomplished without brutality or terrorism, rally the population to support the counter-insurgency rather than the insurgency.

Win the Support of the People

As we have pointed out time and time again, the most important fact is that guerrillas depend on the active support of the local inhabitants for food, medical supplies, shelter, intelligence and personnel. Thus, the true objective of guerrilla warfare is control of the people; this is one type of war in which friend-or-foe thinking is inapplicable.

It is essential to induce the local population to support the counter-insurrection operations and to establish good will between the population and the military force. Appropriate consideration is given to the use of rewards for friendly assistance, imposition of punishment for collaboration with guerrillas, utilization of propaganda followed by the implementation of promises, and the utilization of necessary restrictive measures.

When the local population collaborates with hostile guerrilla forces, rigid controls and restrictions are imposed. Such controls and restrictions may be relaxed subsequently according to the requirements of the situation. Punishment for violation of regulations and restrictions must be just and deserved to prevent exploitation by guerrillas. Maximum publicity is given to those offenses for which punishment is imposed. In order to reduce collaboration with guerrillas, it may be desirable to impose strict rationing controls on the production, distribution, and consumption of food, clothing and medical supplies.

Since a large proportion of any population is usually politically inert, it will throw its support and favor to that side in a guerrilla war which provides it the greatest personal security and allows it to continue its normal routines with the least interference or interruption. In short, the side which can promise friends the greatest protection—and its enemies the greatest harassment—will gain the largest share of support from the otherwise neutral mass. It is therefore essential to create an image of goodwill and superiority of force to induce them to support the legal authorities. Further, because the people will not support civic actions and furnish information if they fear they will come to harm in doing so, eliminating their fear is, therefore, one of the first objectives. This can only be done if the police are able to protect the local population from guerrilla coercion and exploitation.

Thus, we come back to our original proposition that the cause which attracts the greatest following is likely to be the winner. But to accomplish this, it must be effectively propagated among the otherwise neutral mass, for a cause, no matter how forceful in other respects, can only attract by becoming known. This is the task of the propagandist.

Propaganda

Propaganda is planned and employed in the campaign to achieve the following immediate goals:
1. Divide, disorganize and induce defection of irregular force members.
2. Reduce or eliminate civilian support of guerrilla elements.
3. Dissuade civilians from participating in covert activities on the side of the irregular force.
4. Win the active support of noncommitted civilians.
5. Preserve and strengthen the support of friendly civilians.
6. Win popular approval of the local presence of friendly military forces.
7. Obtain national unity or disunity as desired.

Propaganda activities aimed at achieving the immediate goals cited above must, as a minimum, be in consonance with each of the desired long-range goals, and should, where possible, contribute to their attainment.

For purposes of planning and directing the propaganda program, the population is divided into five target audiences. These are the following:
1. Guerrilla units.
2. Underground elements.

3. Those civilians who provide information, supplies, refuge and other assistance to the guerrillas and the underground.
4. The noncommitted civil population.
5. Friendly elements of the civil population.

Propaganda themes are based on the recognizable aspects of friendly economic and political programs and on potentially divisive characteristics of hostile target audiences. Thus the propaganda will do the following:

1. Advertise the existence and accomplishments of the nation's positive program.
2. Persuade the local people, including guerrilla auxiliaries and underground elements, that their objectives can be obtained through specific, peaceful negotiation rather than through guerrilla warfare activities.
3. Illustrate the futility and terrible cost of guerrilla warfare and its total effect upon the future of the nation.
4. Show that the guerrilla movement has come under the control of a third power which is using the conflict to further its own ends in the area.
5. Emphasize the fact that certain insurgent leaders are, in reality, bandit types who seek the continuance of the war for their own personal gain.
6. Bring the weight of international public opinion to bear upon third party nations actively supporting the guerrilla force in its attempts to overthrow the legitimate government.
7. Explain the necessity for population control and guerrilla movement control operations; and
8. Expose the fallacies of the insurgent ideology.

Objective

Under appropriate circumstances, these themes, and others dictated by the local environment, can be utilized in a counterinsurgent operation to create a favorable image of the legitimate government, and to destroy the emotional attachment of the local people to the insurgent cause. Only when the real causes of the resistance movement are uncovered and eliminated, and the minds of the indigenous population conditioned to support government programs and policies, will the total defeat of the insurgent force be assured. Psychologically, the objective sought is the cohesion of all elements of the population in support of the legal government and its programs. The initial step should divide the major elements of the population from dissident elements seeking violent and terroristic change.

Propaganda Media and Techniques

While all propaganda media may be employed, some emphasis should be placed upon face-to-face communication and the employment and exploitation of psychological actions. The counterinsurgent military forces can contribute to the isolation of the guerrilla by emphasizing their role as protectors, the guardians of peace. Rallies, mass demonstrations, personal contact between police and civilian, participating in civilian sports and social gatherings, emphasizing law and order, all contribute to building faith in the legal government and destroying support of the insurgent/guerrilla. A small number of well-behaved troops have a greater positive psychological effect by their words and deeds upon the populace and are more valuable to the counterinsurgency program than a large number of soldiers indifferent to civilians.

Civic Action

Civic action can be a major contributing factor to the development of favorable public opinion and in accomplishing the defeat of the irregular force. Civic action is any action performed by the military force utilizing military manpower and material resources in cooperation with civil authorities, agencies, or groups, which is designed to secure the economic or social betterment of the civilian community. Civic action can include assistance to the local population as construction or rehabilitation of transportation and communication means, schools, hospitals and churches; assisting in agricultural improvement programs, crop planting, harvesting, or processing; and furnishing emergency food, clothing and medical aid as in periods of natural disaster.

Civic action programs are often designed to employ the maximum number of civilians until a suitable economy is established. The energies of civilians should be directed into constructive channels and toward ends which support the purpose of the campaign. Unemployed and discontented masses of people, lacking the bare necessities of life, are a constant hindrance and may preclude successful accomplishment of the mission.

DESTRUCTION

Isolation of guerrilla insurgent elements is not enough for the counterinsurgency operations to be completely effective. The guerrilla must be physically and psychologically destroyed as an effective agent of disruption and disturbance. Unless this is done, the guerrilla force may become inactive and may disband and its members melt into the surrounding population, with the threat remaining to reappear as the time is right.

To deal with the second part of the problem, i.e., the destruction of the insurrectionist, a means must be found to do the following:

1. Establish a proper intelligence and counterespionage organization.
2. Mobilize a sufficient fighting force.
3. Use the proper fighting tactics.

Mistakes of the Past

In the past, the counterinsurgents have tended to underrate their adversary, pursuing at leisure and according to the rules of the book. Loath to take the irregulars seriously at first, the counterinsurgent authorities likewise almost invariably assigned inadequate forces and material to their liquidation. As if intentionally making things more difficult for themselves, they tended to treat the civilian population which has harbored the guerrillas as traitors and alienate themselves even more from this source of support. Only when the counterinsurgent found himself unable to run down the insurgents by orthodox methods did he begin to take his task seriously. But by then it was often too late.

The worst military mistake in fighting guerrillas has been to treat them as if they were conventional opponents. There are crucial differences between tactical operations against a conventional opponent and those against guerrillas. Against the latter, physical destruction of the enemy becomes relatively more important, control of key terrain less.

Conduct of Police Forces

The conduct of troops and police in the field can easily undo governmental propaganda or policy, however wise in conception these may be. The police must never forget that fair dealing with the population is as much a part of effective dealing with the population is as much a part of effective military action as aggressive patrolling. Correct treatment of civilians who seem to have done nothing to merit it is perhaps no more unnatural than combat itself, and it needs to be incorporated into the framework of military thought. Results in the field may not be apparent immediately, but without such behavior, there is little hope of success.

Rarely can guerrillas be isolated from the people without the use of unusually harsh coercive measures. Nevertheless, counterguerrillas must comprehend that their mission is essentially conservative, while that of the guerrillas is destructive. Unless harsh measures are employed rationally and with the clear understanding by all that they are emergency measures, to be stopped as soon as possible, they may actually break down the sense of security that governments must induce if they are to succeed.

If peaceful contact already exists, it should be fostered by all appropriate means. Of first importance is a constantly correct behavior which is to be continued even in case of treacherous conduct by the adversary.

Intelligence

The anti-guerrilla forces must maintain accurate and current information on guerrilla activity. This is necessary for two reasons. First, they must have this information to protect their own property and troops. Secondly, they must have it to plan effective counter measures against the guerrilla groups. Underlying any psychological operations destruction effort is the need for adequate intelligence. Before any appeals can be made to special groups, or leaders, the police must know what the groups are, who the leaders are, what they think, want, and what will appeal to them. The intelligence collection effort, then, must be complete to provide the required data. A detailed study of the local conditions, history of the guerrilla movement, reasons for the movement, guerrilla vulnerabilities and weaknesses must be made. Complete information on each unit, to include each member of these units, is desired. Detailed dossiers should be made on all of the leaders. Personality files should include all local connections such as relatives, girl friends and auxiliary supporters.

An efficient police force is invaluable in this connection, and in countries where the latter does not exist, building one up may have to be the first step in the campaign. The static nature of police deployment enables the police to build up the intelligence picture in one area over a long period. Unquestionably the best source of information in such a campaign is a loyal citizenry.

Lacking the intelligence that the civilian population might have provided, the defending forces must employ to the fullest all other means, such as informants, defecting guerrillas, spies, scouts, reconnaissance patrols. In addition, the following methods may be used:

1. Monitoring radio communication between guerrilla groups.
2. Intercepting written, signaled, or telephoned messages.
3. Patrols may penetrate territory dominated by the guerrillas. When they withdraw they may leave a single member behind, carefully camouflaged with two or three weeks supply of food. He will be in a position to scan large areas with binoculars and report any movement he sees by radio.

One of the most effective means of gathering information about guerrilla groups is by aerial photography. One plane can photograph hundreds of square miles in a single day. Later each small picture is blown up as big as a table and gone over inch by inch with a magnifying glass. It is amazing what such photographs can show.

Intelligence Collection Plan

Prior to moving into any area of operations, an intelligence collection plan must be drafted and implemented to develop maximum information on the area and its people and on source material and agencies essential for the collection of the data. For planning and operational purposes, the information will include, but not be limited to, the following:

1. Topography, hydrography, climate, weather and terrain including land forms, drainage, vegetation and soils.
2. Census, location, ethnic composition and health factors.
3. Attitude of the population including ideological, religious, and cultural aspects.
4. Governmental structure including forms, personalities, laws in being and political heritage.
5. Educational standards and facilities and important cultural activities and repositories.
6. Communication, transportation, utility, power and natural resources.
7. Labor potential including availability by type and skill, practices, and organization.
8. Economic, development including principal industries, scientific and technical capabilities, commercial processes, banking structure, monetary system, price and commodity controls, extent and nature of agricultural production and accustomed population dietary habits.
9. Cores of resistance movements.
10. Organization and operation of guerrilla forces in rear areas and the extent and degree of volition involved in local support.
11. Hostile activities including espionage, sabotage and other factors of subversion and disaffection.

Psychological Destruction

The following conditions make guerrilla forces particularly susceptible to propaganda efforts, thus opening ways for their psychological destruction:

1. Political, social, economic and ideological differences among elements of the irregular force.
2. Rivalries between irregular force leaders.
3. Danger of betrayal.
4. Harsh living conditions of guerrilla elements.
5. Scarcity of arms and supplies.

6. Selfish motivation of opportunities and apparent supporters of the resistance movement.

The requirement for any organized group action is morale; one of the strengths of most revolutionary movements has been high internal morale. Yet, herein is their weakness as well, for in spite of their manifest unity of purpose, revolutionaries represent a wide range of motives, many of them incompatible. The goal for psychological operations is to exploit the incompatibilities so that individual motives override the commonality. To do this, the resistance movement must be analyzed and potential differences identified.

Principles of Operation

Certain general principles of operation are important. They are the following:

1. Direction of the military and civil effort at each level is vested in a single authority, either military or civil.
2. Military actions are conducted in consonance with specified civil rights, liberties and objectives.
3. Operations are planned to be predominantly offensive operations.
4. Police, combat and civic action operations are conducted simultaneously.
5. Task forces employed against guerrilla elements are organized to have a higher degree of aggressiveness and mobility than the guerrilla elements.

The operational area, military forces, civil forces and the population must be organized to provide the following:

1. Military or civil area administration.
2. Static security posts and combat bases.
3. Security detachments for protecting critical military and civil installations, essential routes of communication, and key communities.
4. Task forces for conducting police operations against underground elements.
5. Task forces for conducting combat operations against guerrilla elements.
6. Civil self-defense units for protecting individual villages and small towns.

The operational area is subdivided into geographic sectors, or sectors coinciding with internal political subdivisions. Specific sector responsibility for administration and local operations should be arranged for delegaton to a single authority—either military or civil.

Static security posts should be established to protect installations, routes of communication and communities; maintain control in rural areas; and as bases for local reaction operations. No attempt should be made to cordon or cover an area with strong points as this immobilizes forces, surrenders the initiative to the irregular force, and invites defeat in detail. Static security posts are organized to be as self-sufficient as possible, reducing dependence on vulnerable land routes of communication.

Combat bases should be established as needed to facilitate administration and support combat units. Combat bases should be located within or are immediately adjacent to the units' area of operations and placed within established static security posts when practicable. A combat base must be moved as often as is necessary to remain within effective striking range of guerrilla elements. Air and ground vehicles are employed extensively for deployment and support of troops to reduce the number of required combat bases.

A mobile force is based at each static security post and combat base which is capable of rapidly engaging reported hostile elements or reinforcing other friendly forces. This force is capable of rapid movement by foot, truck, or aircraft. The extensive use of patrols is required to assist in local security of installations and to locate and keep the irregular force on the defensive. To minimize the requirement for military units, maximum assistance must be sought from, and use made of, civil police, paramilitary units and local individuals who are sympathetic to the friendly cause.

When policy and the situation permit, local individuals of both sexes who have had experience or training as soldiers, police, or guerrillas, should be organized into auxiliary police, and village self-defense units. Those without such experience may be employed individually as laborers, informants, propaganda agents, guards, guides and trackers, interpreters and translators.

The local defense of communities against guerrilla raids for supplies and terroristic attack may be accomplished in whole, or in part, by organizing, equipping and training self-defense units. Self-defense units are formed from the local inhabitants and organization is based on villages, counties and provinces. A self-defense unit must be capable of repelling guerrilla attack or immediate reinforcement must be available to preclude loss of supplies and equipment to guerrillas.

Friendly guerrilla units that have operated in the same area as the hostile guerrilla units are usually willing to assist in the counterguerrilla effort. Such units may be effectively employed in extended combat patrol harassing missions. In addition, members of friendly guerrilla units can serve as trackers, guides, interpreters, translators and espionage agents, and can man observation posts and warning stations.

Troops should never be introduced "cold" to such operations. A carefully coordinated training program, preferably carried out in a comparatively safe area within the country in which they are going to fight, enables them to learn their trade in the right locale and at the same time become thoroughly acclimatized. In this kind of warfare, a unit's initial showing has a profound effect, for good or bad, on the enemy's morale. The better the preparation, the more chance there is of getting the team away to a flying start. Furthermore, an early success can have a sharp effect on a wavering local population. It may well coax information from a loyal but hitherto frightened civilian, and information is the lifeblood of the antiguerrilla system, for it leads to that most profitable form of operation—the ambush.

Strategy

The basic principle of counterguerrilla military operations is to maintain the offensive and thereby deny the guerrillas the initiative. The guerrilla strategy, in turn, will be to attempt to seize and hold the initiative by mounting a variety of attacks against fixed installations in order to force the government to take a defensive position. Defensive measures alone result in an ever-increasing commitment and dissipation of forces and give the guerrillas an opportunity to unify, train and develop communications and logistical support. A defensive attitude also permits the guerrillas to concentrate superior forces, inflict severe casualties, and lower morale. However, the deliberate use of a defensive attitude in a local area as a deceptive measure may prove effective.

Utmost importance must be attributed to the principles of the offensive, surprise and security in counterguerrilla operations. A counterguerrilla offensive, then, will have these objectives:

1. To keep guerrilla units off balance at all times by maintaining constant pressure against them by vigorous combat patrolling, continuing attack and restless pursuit. Once contact is made with a guerrilla unit, it is maintained until that guerrilla unit is destroyed. This keeps the guerrillas on the move, disrupts their security and organization, separates them from their sources of support, weakens them physically, destroys their morale, and denies them the opportunity to mount attacks on vital communication lines and military installations or to lay ambushes.

2. By maintaining the initiative, to force guerrilla units to overrun their intelligence screens, and thereby to deny them the protective cover they need to survive against superior military forces.

3. To prevent guerrilla forces from grouping for strong attacks against isolated points.

4. To tire them out, and keep them tired out, through constant offensive action against them; to force them into more isolated hinterlands where food supplies are less and less available; to force them through constant offensive action to expend their limited ammunition.

The population soon puts its trust in the government's capability to protect them because it has established an aura of omnipresence. The people then become more cooperative and willing to furnish information and services.

Guerrillas must be fought with guerrilla methods by specially trained units. The core of the counterguerrilla troops must be a highly mobile attacking force. Normally it need not be substantially larger than the guerrilla elements opposed to it. It should be able to meet and defeat guerrilla forces essentially on their own terms; that is, with small mobile units capable of moving in patrols over extended periods in enemy territory. As soon as one patrol is withdrawn for rest, another should take its place.

The mobile striking forces require the very best regulars, organized and trained to fight in an unorthodox manner, but exploiting the benefits of modern administration and technology. Modern communications, helicopters and weapons should not be downgraded when unconventional tactics are adopted. The mobile striking forces should not be bands of progovernment civilians, hastily recruited and trained by special military advisers. On the contrary, they should be tough, disciplined and thoroughly professional. Mobile counterguerrilla units should operate without fixed plans, and with the ability to modify their operations quickly, in order to take advantage of unforseen targets and to concentrate superior forces against guerrilla units that have been located and brought to combat.

In contrast, the government force that relies on "setpiece" offensives, based on plans drawn up days in advance, will always be at a disadvantage. Even before the operation is launched, such plans may find their way into the hands of the guerrillas, who will have moved meanwhile to another area. Periodic offensives of limited duration have the further disadvantage of permitting the guerrillas to hold the initiative between offensives. A strategy of constant offensive can effectively deprive the guerrillas of the opportunity to conduct the war on terms favorable to themselves.

Surprise is sought in all operations, but against well-organized guerrillas it is difficult to achieve. Surprise may be gained by attacking at night, or in bad weather, or in difficult terrain; by employing small units; by varying operations in important particulars; and by unorthodox or unusual operations. Counterintelligence measures must be exercised throughout planning, preparation and execution of operations to prevent the guerrillas from learning the nature and scope of plans in advance. Lower echelons, upon receiving orders, are careful not to alter their dispositions and daily habits too suddenly. Tactical cover and deception plans are exposed to guerrilla intelligence to deceive the guerrillas as to the purpose of necessary preparations and movements.

Reaction Operations

Reaction operations are those operations conducted by mobile combat units, operating from static security posts and combat bases, for the purpose of reacting to local guerrilla activities. When a guerrilla unit is located, the reaction force deploys rapidly to engage the guerrilla unit, disrupt its cohesion, and destroy it by capturing or killing its members. If the guerrilla force cannot be contained and destroyed, contact is maintained, reinforcements are dispatched if needed, and the guerrillas are pursued. Flank elements seek to envelop and cut off the retreating guerrillas. The guerrillas should be prevented from reaching populated areas where they can lose their identity among the people, and from disbanding and disappearing by hiding and infiltration. When escape routes have been effectively blocked, the attack is continued to destroy the guerrilla force.

Harassing Operations

Harassing operations prevent guerrillas from resting and regrouping, inflict casualties, and gain detailed knowledge of the terrain. They are executed by extended combat patrols and larger combat units. Specific harassing missions include: reconnaissance to locate guerrilla units and camps; raids against guerrilla camps, supply installations, patrols, and outposts; ambushes; assisting major combat forces sent to destroy guerrilla groups; and mining guerrilla routes of communication.

Denial Operations

Operations to deny guerrilla elements contact with, and support by, an external sponsoring power are initiated simultaneously with other measures. Denial operations require effective measures to secure extensive border or seacoast areas and to preclude communications and supply operations between a sponsoring power and guerrilla units.

The method of contact and delivery of personnel, supplies, and equipment whether by air, water, or land must be determined at the earliest possible time. Border areas are secured by employing border control static security posts, reaction forces, ground and aerial observers, listening posts equipped with electronic devices, and patrols. When time and resources permit, wire and other obstacles, minefields, cleared areas, illumination and extensive informant nets are established throughout the border area.

Elimination Operations

Elimination operations are designed to destroy definitely located guerrilla forces. A force much larger than the guerrilla force is usually required. The subarea commander is normally designated as overall commander for the operation. The plan for the operation is carefully prepared, and the troops are thoroughly briefed and rehearsed. Approaches to the guerrilla area are carefully reconnoitered. Deception operations are conducted to prevent premature disclosure of the operation.

The encirclement of guerrilla forces is usually the most effective way to fix them in position to permit their complete destruction. If terrain or inadequate forces preclude the effective encirclement of the entire guerrilla-held area, then the most important part of the area is encircled. The encirclement is made in depth with adequate reserves and supporting elements to meet possible guerrilla attack in force and to block all avenues of escape.

The planning, preparation and execution of the operation are aimed at sudden, complete encirclement that will totally surprise the guerrillas. The move into position and the encirclement is normally accomplished at night to permit maximum security and surprise. The encirclement should be completed by daybreak to permit good visibility for the remainder of the operation.

Support and reserve units are committed as required to insure sufficient density and depth of troops and to establish and maintain contact between units. Speed is emphasized throughout the early phases of the advance to the line of encirclement. Upon arriving on the line of encirclement, units occupy defensive positions. The most critical period in the operation is the occupation of the line of encirclement, especially if the operation is at night. Large guerrilla formations may be expected to react violently upon discovering that they have been encircled. The guerrillas will probe for gaps and attack weak points to force a gap. Escape routes may be deliberately established as ambushes.

Units organizing the line of encirclement deploy strong patrols to their front. Air reconnaissance is used to supplement ground reconnaissance. Reserves are committed if guerrilla forces succeed in breaking through or infiltrating the line of encirclement.

Once the encirclement is firmly established, the elimination of the guerrilla force is conducted methodically and thoroughly. A carefully controlled contraction of the perimeter is begun, which may be conducted in any one of three ways:

1. By a simultaneous, controlled contraction of the encirclement.
2. By driving a wedge through the guerrilla force to divide the area, followed by the destruction of the guerrillas in each subarea.
3. By establishing a holding force on one or more sides of the perimeter and tightening the others against them.

During any of the foregoing maneuvers the units that advance from the initial line of encirclement must be impressed with the necessity of thoroughly combing every possible hiding place for guerrilla personnel and equipment. Successive echelons comb all the terrain again. Areas that appear totally inaccessible, such as swamps or marshes, must be thoroughly searched. Guerrilla ruses discovered during the operation are reported promptly to all participating units and agencies. All local individuals, including men, women and children, found in the area are held in custody and are released only after identification and on orders from appropriate authority.

Lack of time, inadequate forces, or difficult terrain may prevent encirclement operations. Surprise attacks followed by aggressive pursuit may prove successful in these cases. The position, probable escape routes and the strength of the guerrilla forces must be ascertained before launching the operation. Ambushes should be established early on possible escape routes. Patrolling should be conducted in a manner designed to confuse the guerrillas about specific plans or intentions.

After a successful attack on a guerrilla formation, the area is combed for concealed guerrilla personnel and equipment. Documents and records are collected for intelligence analysis. Ambushes are retained along trails in the area for extended periods to kill or capture escapees and stragglers from the guerrilla force.

Once an area is pacified, the government consolidates its control and moves its forces on to the next section of land to be cleared. The main ingredients then are constant patrols, good communication facilities, rapid mobility and a capacity for rapid concentration.

One further point should be made. The operations must cause minimum harm to the people, lest they become antagonistic to the government. The troops must be highly disciplined to respect civilian

rights and property. Cargo planes should carry in supplies so that
the forces do not have to live off the countryside. The onus for anti-
civilian behavior should be diverted squarely to the guerrillas themselves. They are the ones who are compelled to take to repressive
measures, seizing rice or conscripting men in their desperation. As
they lose popular support, they will have nothing to fall back on
when they suffer military defeats.

Apprehended Irregular Force Members

Operations against irregular forces may generate sizable groups of
prisoners which can create serious problems for both the military force
and civil administration. Large numbers of confined personnel can
generate further political, social and economic difficulties. Therefore,
the evaluation and disposition of prisoners must contribute to the
ultimate objective.

When irregular force members defect or surrender voluntarily, they
have indicated that their attitudes and beliefs have changed, at least
in part, and that they will no longer participate in irregular activities.
The following action should be considered:

1. Confinement should be temporary, only for screening and
   processing, and be separate from prisoners who have not
   exhibited a change in attitude.
2. Promises made to induce defection or surrender must be met.
3. Postrelease supervision is essential but need not be stringent.
4. Relocation may be required to prevent reprisal from former
   comrades.

When irregular force members are captured, they can be expected
to retain the attitude which prompted their participation in irregular
activities. The following action should be taken:

1. Confinement is required and may continue for an extended
   period.
2. Prisoners against whom specific crimes can be charged should
   be brought to justice immediately. Charges of crimes against
   persons, such as murder, should be made, if possible, rather
   than charges of crimes directly affiliated with the resistance
   movement which may result in martyrdom and serve as a
   rallying point for increased irregular activity.

3. Prisoners charged only with being a member of the irregular force will require intensive reeducation and reorientation while confined. In time, consistent with security, those who have demonstrated a willingness to cooperate may be considered for release under parole. Relocation away from previous comrads may be necessary and provision of a means for earning a living must be considered.

4. Families of prisoners may have no means of support and a program should be initiated to care for them, educate them in the advantages of law and order, and enlist their aid in reshaping the attitudes and beliefs of their confined family members.

POLICE OPERATIONS

As has been stated repeatedly, the support of the population is vital to the insurgent and the counterinsurgent alike. Generally, such support is won by political persuasion and maintained by military success, for a population will generally support the power which is capable of protecting it. The police, therefore, acting in their capacity as defenders of law and order and that of a paramilitary unit, have a crucial role to play. This is particularly true as the most sensitive sections of a country are its areas of highest population density, the areas where the police are the most numerous and effectively organized.

Since guerrillas thrive on confusion and the disorganization of government, police operations must be so conducted that they will engender stable conditions unfavorable to guerrilla activities through the relief of local destitution, restoration of law and order, resumption of agricultural production, reestablishment of local government, and measures to enlist the active support and sympathy of the local population. The routine police functions all have significance for maintaining public order, controlling and protecting populations, and offering a solid governmental front. It must be stressed that the measures herein suggested are not normal procedures; quite the contrary, they are emergency tactics utilized in the emergency situation generated by an insurrection.

The activities and movements of the civil population are restricted and controlled, as necessary, to maintain law and order and to prevent a guerrilla force from mingling with and receiving support from the civil population. Restrictive measures are limited to those which are absolutely essential and can be enforced. Every effort is made to gain the willing cooperation of the local population in complying with controls and restrictions. However, established measures are enforced firmly and justly. Free movement of civilians is normally confined to their local communities. Exceptions should be made to permit securing food, attendance at public worship, and necessary travel in the event of illness.

Punishment of civilians, when authorized, must be used with realistic discretion. If the people become frustrated and alienated as a result of unjust punishment, the purpose is defeated. Care is taken to punish the true offender, since subversive acts are often committed to provoke unjust retaliation against individuals or communities cooperating with friendly forces.

Police operations employ roadblocks and patrol, search and seizure, surveillance, and apprehension techniques. The following list is representative of the police-type controls and restrictions which may be necessary.

1. Prevention of illegal political meetings or rallies.
2. Registration and documentation of all civilians.
3. Inspection of individual identification documents, permits, and passes.
4. Restrictions on public and private transportation and communication means.
5. Curfew.
6. Censorship.
7. Controls on the production, storage and distribution of foodstuffs and protection of food-producing areas.
8. Controlled possession of arms, ammunition, demolitions, drugs, medicines and money.

Roadblocks

Roadblocks are employed to control illegal possession and movement of goods, to check the adequacy of other controls, and to apprehend members of the irregular force. Since roadblocks cause considerable inconveniences and even fear, it is important that the civilian population understand that they are entirely a preventive and not a punitive measure. Broadly speaking, there are two types of roadblocks: deliberate and hasty.

DELIBERATE. This type of roadblock is positioned in a town or in the open country, often on a main road. It will act as a useful deterrent to unlawful movement. This type of roadblock may not achieve spectacular results.

HASTY. This type of roadblock is quickly positioned in a town or in the open country, and the actual location is often related to some item of intelligence. The hasty roadblock initially may achieve a quick success, but it eventually becomes a deliberate roadblock.

Concealment of a roadblock is desirable, but often impossible. The location should make it difficult for a person to turn back or reverse a vehicle without being noticed. Culverts, bridges, or deep cuts may be suitable locations. Positions beyond sharp curves have the advantage that drivers do not see the roadblock in sufficient time to avoid inspection. Safety disadvantages may outweigh the advantages in such positions. A scarcity of good roads will increase the effect of a well-placed roadblock.

A roadblock must have adequate troops to prevent ambush and surprise. An element of the roadblock unit should be positioned and concealed an appropriate distance (one hundred to several hundred yards) from the approach side of the roadblock to prevent the escape of any vehicle or person attempting to turn around and flee upon sighting the block. An element should search the vehicle and its passengers and drivers. If the roadblock is manned for any length of time, part of the troops are allowed to rest. The rest area is located near the search area so that the troops can be turned out quickly.

For the roadblock to achieve maximum results, special equipment is required. Portable signs should be available. Signs denoting the vehicle search area, vehicle parking area, male and female search area, and dismount point speed movement. Adequate lighting is needed for the search area if the roadblock is to function efficiently at night. Communication equipment between the various police and troop units must be supplied. Barbed wire obstacles across the road and around the search area should be provided. Police must have adequate firepower to withstand an attack or to repulse a vehicle attempting to flee or crash through a roadblock. If possible, there should be a place in the search area where large vehicles can be examined without delaying the flow of other traffic which can be dealt with quickly. Accommodations are required for searching women suspects and holding persons for further interrogation. When a vehicle is searched, all occupants are made to get out and stand clear of the vehicle. The owner or driver should be made to watch the search of his vehicle. The searcher is always covered by another officer. Depending on the type and cargo of vehicles, a careful search of likely hidden places may require a probe. The occupants of the vehicle can be searched simultaneously if sufficient searchers are available. . .

The inspection of documents and the search of persons and vehicles must be rapid and thorough. The attitude of personnel performing these duties must be impersonal and correct because many of the people searched will be friendly or neutral.

Search and Seizure Operations

Search and seizure operations are conducted to screen a built-up area, apprehend irregular force members, and uncover and seize illegal arms, communication means, medicines, and supplies. Search and seizure operations may be conducted at any hour of night or day.

A search and seizure operation is intended to be a controlled inconvenience to the population concerned. The persons whose property is searched and whose goods are seized should be irritated and frightened to such an extent that they will neither harbor irregular force members nor support them in the future. Conversely, the action must not be so harsh as to drive them to collaboration with the irregular force because of resentment.

The large scale search of a village or built-up area is normally a combined police and military operation. It is preplanned in detail and rehearsed. Secrecy is maintained in order to achieve surprise. For success, the search plan is simple and is executed swiftly. Methods and techniques can be varied.

As villages and built-up areas vary, a force is task organized for each search. An organization consisting of troops and police is designed to accomplish the following:

1. To surround the area to prevent escape.
2. To establish roadblocks.
3. To prevent an attack or interference by forces outside the area.
4. To search houses and individuals as necessary and to identify a suspect.
5. To escort wanted persons to the place designated.

Normally, a search involving a battalion or more is best controlled by the military commander with the police in support. For a smaller search, it is often best for the police to be in control with the military in support. Regardless of the controlling agency, the actual search is best performed by the police, when feasible.

Method

The area to be searched should first be divided into sections. As each section is searched, it must be sealed off. The adjoining section may then be searched. No unauthorized personnel are allowed to enter or depart a sealed area until the search has been terminated.

An area is approached and surrounded before the inhabitants realize what is happening. Sometimes it is best to drive into the area; on other occasions it is best to disembark at a distance. The decision depends on the available approaches and exits, and the local situation.

During darkness, troops should approach by as many different routes and as silently as possible. When close to their positions, they should double-time. After daylight, the area can be covered by a chain of observation posts with gaps covered by patrols. Normally, it is impossible to surround an area completely for any length of time, due to the large number of troops required. If necessary, troops should dig in, take advantage of natural cover, and use barbed wire to help maintain their line.

If there is a chance that hostile elements from the outside could interfere, reserves are employed to prevent them from joining the inhabitants of an area under search. An air observer can assist by detecting and giving early warning of any large scale movement outside the isolated area.

The officer in command of the operation makes known that the area is to be searched, a house curfew is in force, and all inhabitants are to remain indoors or gather at a central point for searching. Each search party should consist of at least one native policeman, protective escort and a woman searcher. When the search is in a building that has people in it, the first action required is to get everyone into one room. The police may give the necessary orders and do the actual searching. The object of this search is to screen for suspected persons. Buildings are best searched from bottom to top. Mine detectors are used to search for arms and ammunition. Every effort is made to avoid unnecessary damage.

After a house is searched, it is marked. Persons awaiting search are not allowed to move into a searched building. In the case of a vacant house, or in cases of resistance, it may be necessary to force entry. After searching a house that contains property but whose occupants are away, the search party can nail it up and place a sentry outside to prevent looting. Before troops depart, arrangements are made in the community to protect empty houses until the occupants return.

When it is decided to search inhabitants in one central area, the head of the house remains behind so that he can be present when the house itself is searched. If this is not done, the head of the house is in a position to deny knowledge of anything incriminating that is found.

Block Control

Block control is the constant surveillance and reporting of personnel movements within a block or other small populated area by a resident of that block or area who has been appointed and is supervised by an appropriate authority.

Block control is established by dividing each block or like area into zones, each of which includes all the buildings on one side of a street within a block. A resident zone leader is appointed for each zone, and a separate resident block leader is appointed for each block. Heads of households and businesses in each zone are required to report all movements of people to the zone leader; to include arrivals and departures of their own families or employees, neighbors, and strangers. Zone leaders report all movements in their zone to the block leader. The block leader reports daily, to an appointed authority, on normal movements; the presence of strangers and other unusual circumstances are reported immediately.

Informants are established separately within each block to submit reports as a check against the appointed block and zone leaders. An informant net system is established using key informants for the covert control of a number of block informants.

Installation and Community Security

Critical military and civil installations and key communities must be secured against sabotage and guerrilla attack. Special attention must be given to the security of food supplies, arms, ammunition and other equipment of value to the irregular force. Maximum use is made of natural and manmade obstacles, alarms, illumination, electronic surveillance devices and restricted areas. Fields of fire are cleared and field fortifications are constructed for guards and other local security forces. The local security system is supplemented by vigorous patrolling using varying schedules and routes. Patrolling distance from the installation or community is at least that of light mortar range. Specially trained dogs may be used with guards and patrols. As a defense against espionage and sabotage within installations, rigid security measures must be enforced on labor, to include screening, identification and supervision. The routine means of securing an installation are altered frequently to prevent irregular forces from obtaining detailed accurate information about the composition and habits of the defense.

Security of Surface Lines of Communication

Surface lines of communication which have proved particularly vulnerable to guerrilla attack and sabotage should be abandoned, at least temporarily, if at all possible. Long surface lines of communication cannot be completely protected against a determined irregular force without committing an excessive number of troops. When a railroad, canal, pipeline, or highway must be utilized, the following measures may be required.

Regular defensive measures are taken to protect control and maintenance installations, repair and maintenance crews, and traffic. Vulnerable features such as major cuts in mountain passes, underpasses, tunnels, bridges, locks, pumping stations, water towers, power stations and roundhouses require permanent guards or continuous surveillance of approaches. If necessary, the right-of-way of high-

ways, railroads, canals and pipelines are declared and posted as a
restricted zone. Civilian inhabitants are evacuated from the zone;
underbrush is cleared and wooded areas are thinned to permit good
visibility.

Frequent air and ground patrols are made at varying times, night
and day, along the right-of-way and to the flanks, to discourage
trespassing and to detect mines, sabotage, and hostile movements.
Armored vehicles, aircraft and armored railroad cars are used by
patrols when appropriate. Lone vehicles, trains and convoys which
cannot provide their own security are grouped if practicable and
are escorted through danger areas by armed security detachments.
All traffic is controlled and reported from station to station.

REESTABLISHMENT OF GOVERNMENT

The final task of counterguerrilla action is the reestablishment of
government authority and social order. The obvious initial step is
a reform program to allay the grievances that originally permitted
the outbreak of violence. But, reform is not as easy as it may seem.
By itself, economic aid is not enough. Reform must have at least
two aspects if it is to be effective. First, the administration of reform
must be reasonably honest; not only must it not be compromised by
corruption, but it must not seem to be simply responding to the
program of the guerrillas. Economic and social problems must be
attacked on their own merits, and not as if the government were itself a political party.

Second, and even more difficult, is the fostering of political activity,
including political groups critical of government policy. Despite certain obvious disadvantages, legal political activity provides a third
choice for discontented persons otherwise forced to choose between
supporting the government or the guerrillas. It also keeps the government in touch with the sources of discontent.

Positive Building Program

No tactical counterinsurgency program can be effective without concurrent major building programs. The causes for unrest must be
eliminated to assure the successful counterinsurgency operation. This
implies extensive political, economic and social reform. But to build

support for legal, nontotalitarian government, the government itself must be worthy of that support. Thus, counterinsurgency operations cannot be considered as separate from political aspects and considerations.

The Role of Psychological Operations in Reconstruction

Reconstruction is that phase of counterinsurgency operations when the military units, previously concerned with the conduct of armed operations, are directed either in whole or in part to the implementation of previously determined national objectives embodied in a positive program. Reconstruction then is both an objective and a phase of the positive action program conducted during counterinsurgency operations. Psychological operations play an important and integral role during the reconstruction period.

A reconstruction program is designed to develop faith and confidence in the legally constituted government of the country where counterinsurgency operations are taking place. This program must stimulate cooperation and support among appropriate segments of the civil population. The degree of cooperation and support will depend upon the extent of the civil population's support of insurgent groups and upon the depth of popular grievance against the government. Reconstruction as an aspect of counterinsurgency operations, should involve programs of constructive action designed to restore to the civil community a condition of normalcy and a manner of daily living which will eradicate, or at least diminish, the causes for disaffection and insurgency.

At the national level, the programs are prepared and are designed primarily to nullify the basic causes of disaffection by segments of the civil population. These programs will normally include the initiation of political, economic, social, military and psychological programs in an operational area. Provision is also made for a continuing review of these plans and a constant evaluation of programs in each area. These programs take a variety of forms. They may include governmental and legal reform, community relations activities to stimulate exchange of ideas, civic action, development of local resources, improvement of agricultural and manufacturing techniques, improving health conditions, expansion of educational facilities, troop information to instill a social conscience, etc. In all of these programs military personnel can be utilized to assist in their development.

Consolidation psychological operations and psychological operations in the counterinsurgency reconstruction phase are quite similar. Many of the techniques and media employed in consolidation are applicable to reconstruction psychological operations, for the objectives of each are similar.

Psychological operations assist in reconstruction in a variety of ways. Briefly, among these are the following:

1. The dissemination of information concerning the proposed plans for economic, political and social reconstruction.
2. The reeducation of the civil population through the use of its media, as well as rendering a community service by publishing and broadcasting news and directives.
3. In exposing the causes of disaffection which are many-factured and fallacious; in short, counterpropaganda. (Insurgent groups may have conducted such an active propaganda campaign that the people can no longer recognize and distinguish between real and imagined needs.)
4. In the building and reinforcing of morale of the local national military as well as the civilian population.
5. Pointing out to the civil sector the efforts of the military in assisting them in the building of needed schools, community projects and the like. (This action underscores the cooperation of the military and civilians in working toward common goals.)

Psychological operations can provide the vehicle through which national and community goals and their interrelationships are explained. Without an extensive program in psychological operations, necessary cooperation for the counterinsurgency reconstruction program cannot be obtained.

In conducting reconstruction psychological operations, all basic principles of propaganda and its dissemination apply. All media, radio, loudspeakers, leaflets, face-to-face communication, are employed as they are feasible. In reconstruction, particular emphasis can be placed on psychological actions (or planned actions) designed to carry a propaganda appeal. (The positive program itself is in a sense a psychological appeal.) Good works may best conduct a message to a community by illustrating the validity of the positive program as opposed to what insurgent groups may offer. Objectives and policies governing the psychological operations program must be followed closely as in any other situation.

INDEX